ICONS OF MODERN CULTURE

Series Editor: David Ellis

That Man Shakespeare

Mr. WILLIAM
SHAKESPEARES
COMEDIES,
HISTORIES, &
TRAGEDIES.

Published according to the True Originall Copies.

LONDON
Printed by Iſaac Iaggard, and Ed. Blount. 1623.

1. 'This Figure, that thou here see'st put / It was for gentle Shakespeare cut', (Ben Jonson). Engraving by Martin Droeshout from the First Folio, 1623.

That Man Shakespeare: Icon of Modern Culture

David Ellis

HELM INFORMATION LTD

© David Ellis 2005

ISBN 1-903206-18-9

A CIP catalogue record for this book is available from the
British Library.

Published in Great Britain in 2005 by
Helm Information Ltd,
The Banks, Mountfield,
near Robertsbridge,
East Sussex TN32 5JY
U.K.

Jacket illustration: *Shakespeare's Portrait* by John Hagan, oil
on canvas, 2003. Portrait of Shakespeare combining an
anatomical drawing of his skull, the Chandos portrait and the
Droeshout engraving.

Printed on acid-free paper and bound by
Antony Rowe Ltd, Chippenham, Wiltshire

Contents

List of Illustrations

Acknowledgements

A good deal of the work for this book was completed at the Institute for Advanced Study of La Trobe University in Australia. I am very grateful to the Director of the Institute, Professor Gilah Leder, and to its secretary, Julia Anderson, for making me so welcome there. While I was at La Trobe, I received valuable help and advice from many present or past members of the university and would like particularly to thank John Wiltshire, Iain Topliss, Derick Marsh, Ann Blake and Alec Hyslop.

Back at the University of Kent I find myself constantly indebted to Angela Faunch and her associates in the Document Delivery department of the Templeman Library. They could not be more helpful. The same is true of Sue Crabtree and Lindsay McInally in Special Collections; Spencer Scott in the Photographic Unit; Nicholas Hiley and Jane Newton in the Centre for Cartoons and Caricature; and Derek Whittaker in the slide library. I am grateful to various colleagues at Kent whose specialist knowledge is much greater than mine and who have been generous with their time and assistance. In particular I would like to thank Marion O'Connor, Andrew Butcher, Jan Montefiore, Graham Anderson, Ken Fincham and Peter Roberts and record my gratitude to two ex-colleagues, Molly Mahood and Reg Foakes, for encouraging my attempts to think about Shakespeare. My friends Frank Cioffi and Edward Greenwood have helped me to think about biography, as they have about so many other things; and I owe a special debt to my cousin Eldon Pethybridge for valuable information about Shakespeare's will. Osman Durrani was responsible for finding the illustration which appears on the cover of this book and, throughout both its writing and production, I have been sustained by the calm, good humour and fortitude of my publisher Amanda Helm. Finally, I would like to thank my wife, Geneviève, for all kinds of assistance, and Hezekiah for lightening my mood during the gloomier periods of composition.

All possible care has been taken to trace ownership of copyright material and to make full acknowledgement. Listed below are details received at the time of going to press. In some cases it has not been possible to locate, or even identify, the owner of copyright and Helm Information would be pleased to hear from any copyright holder not acknowledged so that appropriate arrangements can be made.

We would like to thank the following for permission to reproduce this material:

Artellus Ltd on behalf of the Estate of Anthony Burgess for permission to reproduce pages 33-6 and 135-8 from 'Nothing like the Sun' © The Estate of Anthony Burgess;

The Revd Brooke Kingsmill-Lunn for permission to reprint pages from Hugh Kingsmill, *The Return of William Shakespeare*, (London: Duckworth, 1929);

Ned Sherrin for permission to reprint pages from Caryl Brahms and S. J. Simon, *No Bed for Bacon*, (Penguin Books, 1948);

Casarotto Ramsay & Associates Ltd for permission to reprint from *Bingo*, in *Bond Plays 3*, (Methuen Publishing Ltd, 1974), BINGO © 1974 Edward Bond;

PFD for material reproduced from *Will Shakespeare (An Entertainment)* by John Mortimer (Copyright © Advanpress Ltd 1977) by permission of PFD on behalf of Advanpress Ltd for the services of John Mortimer;

Sheil Land Associates for permission to reprint pages from Robert Nye, *The Late Mr Shakespeare*, (London: Chatto and Windus, 1998);

Curtis Brown Group Ltd for permission to reprint pages from Robert Nye, *Mrs Shakespeare: the complete works* (London: Sinclair-Stevenson, 1993) reproduced with permission of Curtis Brown Group Ltd, London on behalf of Robert Nye © 1993;

Cambridge University Press for permission to reprint from Caroline F. E. Spurgeon, *Shakespeare's Imagery and What it Tells Us*, 1935, pp. 200-207 © Cambridge University Press, reproduced with permission;

Random House, Inc. for permission to reprint 'pete the parrot and shakespeare' from *Archy and Mehitabel* by Don Marquis, © 1927 by Doubleday, a division of Random House, Inc. Used by permission of Doubleday, a division of Random House, Inc.

We would like to thank the following for these images:

John Hagan for allowing us to use his painting, *Shakespeare's Portrait*, (oil on canvas, 2003) on the jacket of the book;

The Folger Shakespeare Library (and Bettina Smith) for supplying three images: 'Shakespeare before the court of Elizabeth reading *Macbeth*' (no. 9); 'Shakespeare composing' (no. 22) and 'Shakespeare with his family at Stratford' (no. 31);

Malcolm Crowthers for the photograph (no. 10) of Peter Scheemaker's statue of Shakespeare in Westminster Abbey, originally published in John Field, *Kingdom, Power and Glory: an Historical Guide to Westminster Abbey*, (London: James and James, 1996);

The Shakespeare Birthplace Trust Records Office (with especial gratitude to Cathy Millwood) for supplying four images: *Garrick reciting his Jublilee Ode* (no. 13); *Sir Walter Scott before the Shakespeare monument* (no 18); Poster for the sale of the Henley Street House in 1847 (no. 28); and State of the Birthplace in 1972 (no. 30); and the nineteenth-century beer bottle label from the Flower Brewery (no. 36);

The Art Archive on behalf of The Garrick Club for the image of Louis François Roubiliac's bust of William Shakespeare c. 1758 (no. 14);

His Grace the Duke of Buccleuch and Queensbury, K.T. for the portrait, *Southampton in the Tower* attributed to John de Critz the Elder, 1603, (no. 25);

Wally Faulkes and George Melly for allowing us to use three of their Flook cartoon strips: 'The First Plague Victims' (no. 33); 'Queen Elizabeth's opinion of Shakespeare' and ' Mrs Cordite-Smith is disappointed' (no. 34);

Miramax Film Corp for the photograph of Joseph Fiennes from the film *Shakespeare in Love* (1998) used under licence from Miramax Film Corp. All rights reserved;

Berlin Associates for two cartoons by Max Beerbohm, 'Had Shakespeare asked me ... Frank Harris wondering what might have been' (no. 27) and 'William Shakespeare: His Method of Work', from *Poet's Corner*, 1904, (no. 31) © the Estate of Max Beerbohm reprinted by permission of Berlin Associates;

Miramax Films for permission to use the still of Joseph Fiennes as Shakespeare in their film, *Shakespeare in Love* (no. 35);

High Street Trading Company as the owner of both the liqueur and images of it for the photograph of William Shakespeare's Whisky Liqueur (no. 37). Please contact Hebridean Liqueurs, www.hebridean-liqueurs.co.uk for further information.

Shakespeare's Portrait by John Hagan, oil on canvas, 2003

The basis of the portrait is a phrenological drawing (1807) of what was supposed to be Shakespeare's skull, attributed to the French natural scientist Georges Cuvier, when he was an admirer of the Viennese physician and phrenologist Franz-Joseph Gall. Rumour has it that this skull was taken from its original resting place by an infamous 'resurrection man' (later transported to New Holland) who was acting on behalf of the businessman and amateur natural scientist, James Deville, and that Deville then carried or sent the skull to Paris. There it came into the possession of another admirer of Gall, Johan Kaspar Spurzheim, who later took it to America on one of his many lecture tours in that country. It has not been seen since.

John Hagan has overlaid the original anatomical drawings with the Chandos portrait and the Droeshout engraving to arrive at a new composite portrait of what Shakespeare might have looked like. For a fuller account of John Hagan's work, visit the websites: www.geocities.com/jlhagan and www.linknet.com.au/johnhaga/

Shakespeare's tombstone (see pp. 23–4) reads

> Good friend for Jesus sake forbear
> To dig the dust enclosed here!
> Blest be the man that spares these stones,
> And curst be he that moves my bones.

Series Editor's Preface

EVERY CULTURE HAS ITS ICONS, figures who populate the collective consciousness and provide it with essential points of reference. Any two members of the culture in question might well have different ideas as to what particular figures represent but both will recognise them as items in a common currency. It is in part through the different and sometimes competing meanings we give to the prevailing icons that we organise our knowledge and evince our views of the world.

In some instances the birth of an icon is an historical event, one which took place around 1412 in the case of Joan of Arc, for example, but more certainly in 1855 as far as Ned Kelly is concerned. Falstaff's first appearance in the world is also a matter of historical record but in a very different sense while that of Faust or Robin Hood is far less determinate. As these examples illustrate our icons are a varied band. They come in all shapes and sizes, quite what shape or size depending partly of course on the social or cultural position from which they are viewed, as well as the tastes and temperament of the viewer. Their essential heterogeneity and their vulnerability to private, idiosyncratic appropriation make them difficult to talk about in general, but if they have one characteristic in common it is that they have left their real, literary or mythical origins well behind. They have transcended those origins in order to represent for us qualities we admire or detest, facets of human failure or achievement which it would be uncomfortable to discuss in the abstract. It is through these figures that we often prefer to do our thinking. Close study of history is for the majority of a population esoteric, and however much 'celebrities' may temporarily engage public attention everyone is aware that they are fleeting phenomena, that they come and go. Icons on the other hand are deeply embedded. They provide a link with the generations which went before and characterise what we are quite as much as our clothes, our food or our anthems.

1

Each volume in this series describes and above all illustrates the process whereby a certain figure became iconic. It aims to show the different ways that figure has functioned for different interest groups and what role it plays in our culture now. Much of the illustration is literary but attention is also paid to music, painting, photography and film (how people visualise their icons can be as significant as how they write or read about them). A few recent essays of an analytic nature may also be included and the authors of individual volumes will offer their comments on some of the controversial aspects of their subject, but the chief intention is to provide a descriptive context for the *display* of material. In that way readers can watch the sometimes chequered history of an icon develop and see for themselves how the figure concerned came to play such an important role in our common awareness.

DAVID ELLIS

Introduction

Y
ET ANOTHER WORK on Shakespeare will always require justification but I
need to make clear first of all what this book is *not*. My interest is in the
afterlife of Shakespeare and, in using that name I refer to the individual
who wrote the plays and not, as is so often the habit, to those plays (or poems)
themselves. The history of 'Shakespeare' in this latter sense would require
several volumes, each one fatter than this, yet 'the man Shakespeare', to employ
the phrase which the title of Frank Harris's 1909 biography popularised, is still
a large subject. To make it manageable I have limited my enquires chiefly to
the United Kingdom although books on the same pattern as this, and of similar
bulk, could no doubt be written on the way Shakespeare was conceived and
imagined in Europe and in the United States.

This book tells how the British constructed an image and built an icon out
of the little that was initially known, or eventually came to be known, about
Shakespeare. To make that process more comprehensible I begin in Chapter 1
with a review of the available biographical data, reproducing or referring to
everything which I believe is directly relevant to any biographical enquiry into
the circumstances of his life. Because my main aim has been both to make the
extracts easier to read and to convey their substance as directly as possible, I
have often modernised their spelling and sometimes added punctuation as I
have done also in Chapter 2, where I describe (and often reproduce) the myths
and legends which were mostly recorded for the first time long after Shakespeare's death and which compensated for the absence of reliable information.
As I explain in this chapter, calling these stories myths or legends does not
mean that I think them inevitably without foundation, only that, if you were
on trial for your life, you might not want them used in evidence against you.

In the third chapter I describe but mostly illustrate the growth of
Shakespeare's image in the late seventeenth century and then throughout the
eighteenth. Selection of material is not the kind of problem here which it
becomes in Chapter 4 since that deals with the Romantics and early Victorians

amongst whom representations of Shakespeare proliferate in both fictional and non-fictional writings. That this proliferation only increases in the nineteenth and then in the twentieth centuries means that this book has the form of an inverted pyramid with very little that is contentious about whatever clusters close to the apex but with a base whose composition must to some extent be arbitrary.

In Chapter 5 I desert temporarily my rough chronology to take up the special case of Shakespeare's sonnets. Considering the significance of these poems for the development of Shakespeare's image, I illustrate their emergence from obscurity and then track efforts to take up their disconcerting challenge into the early twentieth century. After a brief retrospective look at the growth of Stratford-upon-Avon as a tourist centre, I pick up in Chapter 6 the story of the Shakespeare legend where I had left it in Chapter 4, the mid-nineteenth century, and carry it forward to the first World War and beyond.

My general practice has been to consider together representations of Shakespeare in both fictional and non-fictional texts, but in Chapter 7 I concentrate on those which can be found in twentieth- or twenty-first-century novels, plays and films. When in Chapter 8 I come to deal with the stream of biographies which have appeared in that period, and still do appear now, I abandon the anthology mode which characterises this book (as well as the series in which it features) and, exchanging description for analysis, try to show what kind of methods have to be used by those who, with no new information available, feel constrained to produce new biographies. The intended method of presentation in the bulk of this work is objective. That is to say that I have not thought it useful to make too much comment on the literary or intellectual merits of extracts whose chief interest is, in the majority of cases, historical. But, in the first place, true objectivity is impossible and, in the second, the purposes the extracts I reproduce were designed to serve becomes a more urgent matter for examination the nearer we are to our own time. Although I have no doubt that I have shown my hand on several occasions in the first seven chapters, I make no bones about doing so in Chapter 8 and in the Conclusion.

Because the authors of the extracts in this book are all concerned with Shakespeare's life, invaluable aid in preparing it was furnished by the two volumes of *William Shakespeare: A Study of Facts and Problems* published in 1930 by the indispensable E. K. Chambers. Equally useful has been S. Schoenbaum's *Shakespeare's Lives* (1991). This remarkable book – deeply scholarly, shrewd and witty – offers a comprehensive review of all Shakespeare's biographers from the earliest times until the 1980s; but it works by descriptive account rather than illustration and is not concerned with fiction. That its one weakness is an occasional descent into sarcasm only testifies to the exemplary patience Schoenbaum showed in ploughing conscientiously through so many dull tomes. Three books from an earlier period which have been very useful are Ivor Brown and George Fearon's *The Shakespeare Industry* (1939), F. E. Halliday's *The Cult of Shakespeare* (1957) and Christian Deelman's excellent study of *The Great Shakespeare Jubilee* (1964). Although he is mostly concerned with the afterlife of Shakespeare's plays I have found interesting suggestions in the much more recent book by Michael Dobson, *The Making of the National Poet. Shakespeare, Adaptation, and Authorship, 1660-1769* (1992). The chief focus of Douglas Lanier's *Shakespeare and Modern Popular Culture* (2002) is on the United States, and only one of his chapters deals with Shakespeare in the biographical sense, but he has interesting things to say. I take issue with several of Lanier's assertions in my concluding chapters, but I admire the work which he has done.

All these books I cite, and several others which might also have been mentioned here, describe rather than illustrate the development of Shakespeare as an icon of the national culture. The only work close in design to mine is therefore *Shakespeare's Other Lives: An Anthology of Fictional Depictions of the Bard*, edited by Maurice J. O'Sullivan, Jr. and published by McFarland and Co. in 1997. Yet the subtitle of this book already makes for a major difference and two others are that the book is just over 200 pages long and limited to texts which can be found in the Shakespeare Centre Library at Stratford-upon-Avon. O'Sullivan describes himself as the editor of his book because he eschews narrative and restricts himself to writing short biographical accounts of the authors of the extracts he selects while the overlap between those extracts and my own choices is minimal. The justification I offer for another book on Shakespeare, therefore, is that what is done here has not been done before. Whether or not it was worth doing is a question which only the reader can decide.

Note

Stephen Greenblatt's long-awaited biography of Shakespeare, *Will in the World. How Shakespeare became Shakespeare,* was published just as this book was going to press. Its American provenance makes it not strictly relevant to my concerns but Greenblatt is such an important and influential figure that I have included an occasional reference to his work in my endnotes. A full review of how I believe his efforts to imagine Shakespeare's life are related to the methods I describe in Chapter 8 can be found in the July 2005 number of *Essays in Criticism.*

2. 'A self-satisfied pork-butcher' (J. Dover Wilson)? The memorial bust by Gheerart Janssen, 1623, in the Church of Holy Trinity, Stratford-upon-Avon

Chapter One

Bare Facts

A CCORDING TO THE RECORDS of his parish church at Stratford-upon-Avon, Shakespeare was baptised on 26 April 1564. The date of his birth is not known. 23 April, which happens to be St George's Day, has long been celebrated as his birthday: it has seemed fitting to honour England's patron saint and her most famous writer at the same time. Given what is known of the relation between births and christenings in the 1560s, the 23rd is a reasonable guess.

Although he may have engaged in other trades from time to time, Shakespeare's father was predominantly a glover, that is to say that he prepared the leather suitable for making gloves and then both manufactured and sold them. His mother, Mary Arden, was the daughter of a local farmer who may have had connections with gentry elsewhere in the county. William was the eldest of their children to survive into adulthood. He had a younger sister called Joan who outlived him and then three younger brothers, Gilbert, Richard and Edmund, all of whom died before he did. Edmund became an actor and died in London in 1607 but his other three surviving siblings appear to have spent most of their lives in Stratford.

Nothing certain is known of Shakespeare's boyhood. It is assumed that he must have been educated at the local grammar school although there are no surviving records to prove that he was. Strongly in favour of the assumption are the lack of reasonable alternatives and the many references in the plays to texts which exhaustive research has shown were part of the standard grammar school curriculum in his time. If very few doubt that Shakespeare had a grammar school education, there is considerable disagreement as to how long it lasted. All the documents show is that by the age of eighteen he was married. His wedding to Anne Hathaway was facilitated by the issue of a special licence, presumably because the bride, another local farmer's daughter, was pregnant and there was therefore a need to short-circuit the more traditional preliminaries. The ceremony appears to have taken place at the end of November 1582 and the couple's first child, Susanna, was christened on 26

May 1583. Their only other children were twins, christened Hamnet and Judith on 2 February 1585. There is a record of Hamnet's burial on 11 August 1596 but the two girls long outlived their father. Much is made of Anne Hathaway having been eight years older than her husband. She probably was but there is no record of her christening. When she died in August 1623 the inscription on her tombstone described her as being sixty-seven but tombstone inscriptions are not always reliable.

The first direct public recognition of Shakespeare's existence, apart from the church records, comes in 1592. That was the year of Robert Greene's *Groats-worth of wit,* towards the end of which there is an open letter by Greene 'To those Gentlemen his Quondam acquaintance, that spend their wits in making plays'. One famous extract from this letter reads:

> Base minded men all three of you, if by my misery ye be not warned: for unto none of you (like me) sought those burrs to cleave: those Puppets (I mean) that speak from our mouths, those Antics garnished in our colours. Is it not strange that I, to whom they all have been beholding: is it not like that you, to whom they all have been beholding, shall (were ye in that case that I am now) be both at once of them forsaken? Yes trust them not: for there is an upstart Crow, beautified with our feathers, that with his *Tigers heart wrapped in a Players hide,* supposes he is as well able to bombast out a blank verse as the best of you: and being an absolute *Johannes fac totum,* is in his own conceit the only Shake-scene in a country. O that I might entreat your rare wits to be employed in more profitable courses: & let those Apes imitate your past excellence, and never more acquaint them with your admired inventions. I know the best husband of you all will never prove an Usurer, and the kindest of them all will never prove a kind nurse: yet whilst you may, seek you better Masters; for it is pity men of such rare wits, should be subject to the pleasures of such rude grooms.[1]

The three 'quondam' acquaintances Greene is assumed to be addressing here are Marlowe, Nashe and Peele all of whom were, like Greene himself, university-educated playwrights. The reference to Shakespeare is made certain by the combination of the play on his name ('Shake-scene') with an adapted quotation from the third part of *Henry VI,* 'O tiger's heart wrapp'd in a woman's hide', York complains to Queen Margaret in 1.4. It is sometimes maintained that 'beautified with our feathers' is an accusation of plagiarism, but the general context suggests rather that Greene is reminding his reader that Shakespeare began his career as an actor, one of those 'rude grooms' on whom the rare wits of the gentlemen authors have had the misfortune to be dependent.

Greene's attack indicates that by 1592 Shakespeare must have been a highly successful actor/playwright on the London scene. (Nashe claimed that 'ten thousand spectators at least, (at several times)' wept over the death of Talbot in the first part of *Henry VI*[2]). How he reached that position is not clear. No-one knows what occupation he took up on leaving school, when he decided to leave Stratford (although it is unlikely to have been before the birth, or at least the conception, of his twins), and which acting company he first joined. The prominence Greene implicitly accords him is confirmed by Henry Chettle in his address 'To the Gentlemen Readers' of his *Kind-Harts Dreame*, also published in 1592. Chettle was known to have prepared the *Groats-worth of wit* for the press after Greene's death and was therefore suspected of having himself written parts of it.

> About three months since died M. Robert Greene, leaving many papers in sundry Book sellers hands, among other his *Groats-worth of wit*, in which a letter written to divers play-makers, is offensively by one or two of them taken, and because on the dead they cannot be avenged, they wilfully forge in their conceits a living Author: and after tossing it to and fro, no remedy, but it must light on me. How I have all the time in my conversing in printing hindered the bitter inveighing against scholars, it hath been very well known; and how in that I dealt I can sufficiently prove. With neither of them that take offence was I acquainted, and with one of them I care not if I never be: The other, whom at that time I did not so much spare, as since I wish I had, for that as I have moderated the heat of living writers, and might have used my own discretion (especially in such a case) the Author being dead, that I did not, I am as sorry, as if the original fault had been my fault, because myself have seen his demeanour no less civil than he excellent in the quality he professes: Besides, divers of worship have reported, his uprightness of dealing, which argues his honesty, and his facetious grace in writing, that approves his Art.[3]

The only two contemporary writers Greene speaks ill of in his letter are Marlowe (whom he accuses of atheism) and Shakespeare. If Marlowe, who in late 1592 may already have been under surveillance for heretical opinions, is the man with whom Chettle would not care to be acquainted then Shakespeare is the one whose civil demeanour Chettle himself has observed and whom he has heard praised by 'divers of worship'. What this suggests is that by 1592 Shakespeare had sufficient power and influence for his resentment of a public insult to mean something. Apart from arrogance and cruelty, Greene had accused him of being a social upstart, a mere actor. In 1596 an application for a coat of arms which Shakespeare's father had originally begun to make some time after 1568 and then not pursued was reactivated, probably at the instigation of his now prosperous son. Its success meant that, although Shakespeare would never be able to write M. A. after his name like Greene, he could nevertheless distinguish himself from 'rude grooms' by writing 'Gent.'

The first documentary proof of Shakespeare's association with a specific acting company is dated 15 March 1595. This is a record in the accounts of the treasurer of the Queen's chamber of payments to Shakespeare and two other members of the Lord Chamberlain's Men (Richard Burbage and William Kemp) for performances at Greenwich Palace the previous December. The Lord Chamberlain's Men had been formed in 1594 after a period during which the theatres had been often been closed, chiefly because of plague. It may have been precisely because they were closed that in 1593 Shakespeare sought an alternative source of income by dedicating his narrative poem *Venus and Adonis* to the nineteen-year old Earl of Southampton.

> To the Right Honourable
> Henry Wriothesley,
> Earl of Southampton, and Baron of Titchfield
>
> Right Honourable,
>   I know not how I shall offend in dedicating my unpolished lines to your Lordship, nor how the world will censure me for choosing so strong a prop to support so weak a burden; only, if your Honour seem but pleased, I account myself highly praised, and vow to take advantage of all idle hours, till I have honoured you with some graver labour. But if the first heir of my invention prove deformed, I shall be sorry it had so noble a godfather, and never after ear [plough] so barren a land, for fear it yield me still so bad a harvest. I leave it to your honourable survey, and your Honour to your heart's content; which I wish may always answer your own wish and the world's hopeful expectation.
> Your Honour's in all duty,
> William Shakespeare.[4]

Shakespeare presumably calls *Venus and Adonis* the first heir of his invention because it was his first published poem or the first publication of any kind to bear his name. His tone is tentative and very different from the dedication to Southampton which preceded his second narrative poem, *The Rape of Lucrece*, published in the summer of 1594.

> To the Right Honourable
> Henry Wriothesley,
> Earl of Southampton, and Baron of Titchfield
> The love I dedicate to your Lordship is without end; whereof this pamphlet without beginning is but a superfluous moiety. The warrant I have of your honourable disposition, not the worth of my untutored lines, makes it assured of acceptance. What I have done is yours; what I have to do is yours; being part in all I have, devoted yours. Were my worth greater, my duty would show greater; meantime, as it is, it is bound to your Lordship, to whom I wish long life still lengthened with happiness.
> Your Lordship's in all duty,
> William Shakespeare.[5]

The striking difference between these two dedications is usually taken as firm evidence that Shakespeare had succeeded in acquiring Southampton as a patron, but there is no absolute proof that he did so, and nothing to tell us what form - if he had been successful - the patronage took. We do not know, for example, whether he ever became a member of Southampton's household and therefore spent time in the Earl's country house at Titchfield in Hampshire (where some have conjectured that *Love's Labour's Lost* was composed for private performance). It is possible, even likely, that Southampton gave Shakespeare money but no-one knows how much or whether it was enough, as others have speculated, to allow Shakespeare to buy his 'share' in the Lord Chamberlain's Men.

The Earl of Southampton was a prominent and often controversial figure. His father, a staunch Catholic, died when he was very young so that he was brought up as a ward of Lord Burghley. In 1595 he made pregnant one of Elizabeth I's maids of honour, Elizabeth Vernon, and then married her much to the disgust of the Queen who imprisoned the newly-weds for a while. In spite of his family background, he allied himself at Court with the aggressively Protestant Essex faction and took part in Essex's abortive uprising in 1601. As a result he was sentenced to death. This sentence was commuted to imprisonment and he remained in the Tower until James I's accession in 1603. During his lifetime he attracted a good deal of attention but none of that attention, nor the care with which his affairs have been examined since, reveals any reliable indication of a connection between him and Shakespeare other than that which is provided by the two dedications. Investigation is therefore thrown back on items such as an enigmatic poem published in 1594 and entitled *Willobie his Avisa* (a real Henry Willobie being the presumed author). Through a series of verse dialogues the virtuous Avisa of the title repels in this work a number of would-be seducers the last of whom is H. W. who is described as follows in the argument which introduces the final part of the poem:

Henrico Willobego. Italo-Hispalensis
H. W. being suddenly infected with the contagion of a fantastical fit, at the first sight of A, pineth a while in secret grief, at length not able any longer to endure the burning heat of so fervent a humour, bewrayeth the secrecy of his disease unto his familiar friend W. S. who not long before had tried the courtesy of the like passion, and was now newly recovered of the like infection; yet finding his friend let blood in the same vein, he took pleasure for a time to see him bleed, & instead of stopping the issue, he enlargeth the wound, with the sharp razor of a willing conceit, persuading him that he thought it a matter very easy to be compassed, & no doubt with pain, diligence & some cost in time to be obtained. Thus this miserable comforter comforting his friend with an impossibility, either for that he now would secretly laugh at his friend's folly, that had given occasion not long before unto others to laugh at his own, or because he would see whether another could play his part better than himself, & in viewing a far off the course of this loving Comedy, he determined to see whether it would sort to a happier end for this new actor, than it did for the old player. But at length this Comedy was like to have grown to a Tragedy, by the weak and feeble estate that H. W. was brought unto, by a desperate view of an impossibility of obtaining his purpose, till Time & Necessity, being his best Physicians brought him a plaster, if not to heal, yet in part to ease his malady. In all which discourse is lively represented the unruly rage of unbridled fancy, having the reins to rove at liberty, with the divers & sundry changes of affections & temptations, which Will, set loose from Reason, can devise. &c[6]

Willobie his Avisa went through five editions before 1610 and in a government ordinance of 1599 was included in the category of books to be burned. One reasonable explanation of this puzzle is that Avisa is meant to be Elizabeth and that the poem is thus an allusion to the highly controversial issues surrounding the question of whether (or whom) the Queen should marry. But some commentators point out that H. W. could stand for Henry Wriothesley and in that case W. S. could be Shakespeare, 'the old player'. The 'argument' above bears some slight similarity to certain episodes implied in Shakespeare's sonnets although, even if the allusions were indeed to Shakespeare and Southampton, they still would not tell us very much about them.

Whatever success *Venus and Adonis* eventually brought Shakespeare in the patronage stakes, the poem itself seems to have very popular (there were sixteen editions before 1640) and to have earned him a reputation additional to the one he already had, or was developing, as a leading playwright. One indication of this is the 'comparative discourse of our English Poets with the Greek, Latin, and Italian poets' which appeared in Francis Meres's 1598 *Paladis Tamia*, conveniently translated in its subtitle as *Wit's Treasury*.

> [...] the English tongue is mightily enriched, and gorgeously invested in rare ornaments and resplendent habiliments by Sir Philip Sidney, Spencer, Daniel, Drayton, Warner, Shakespeare, Marlowe and Chapman. [...]
>
> As the soul of Euphorbus was thought to live in Pythagoras: so the sweet witty soul of Ovid lives in mellifluous & honey-tongued Shakespeare, witness his *Venus and Adonis*, his *Lucrece*, his sugared Sonnets among his private friends, &c.
>
> As Plautus and Seneca are accounted the best for Comedy and Tragedy among the Latins: so Shakespeare among the English is the most excellent in both kinds for the stage; for Comedy, witness his *Gentlemen of Verona*, his *Errors*, his *Love's Labour's Lost*, his *Love's Labour's Won*, his *Midsummer Night's Dream*, and his *Merchant of Venice*: for Tragedy his *Richard II*, *Richard III*, *Henry IV*, *King John*, *Titus Andronicus* and his *Romeo and Juliet*.
>
> As Epius Stolo said, that the Muses would speak with Plautus's tongue, if they would speak Latin: so I say that the Muses would speak with Shakespeare's fine filed phrase, if they would speak English. [...]
>
> [...] these are our best for Tragedy, the Lord Buckhurst, Dr Legge of Cambridge, Dr Edes of Oxford, Master Edward Ferris, the author of the *Mirror for Magistrates*, Marlowe, Peele, Watson, Kyd, Shakespeare, Drayton, Chapman, Decker, and Benjamin Jonson. [...]
>
> The best for Comedy amongst us be, Edward Earl of Oxford, Dr. Gager of Oxford, Master Rowley once a rare scholar of learned Pembroke Hall in Cambridge, Master Edwards one of her Majesty's Chapel, eloquent and witty John Lilly, Lodge, Gascoigne, Greene, Shakespeare, Thomas Nashe, Thomas Heywood, Anthony Munday our best plotter, Chapman, Porter, Wilson, Hathway, and Henry Chettle. [...]

[...] these are the most passionate among us to bewail and bemoan the perplexities of Love, Henry Howard Earl of Surrey, Sir Thomas Wyatt the elder, Sir Francis Brian, Sir Philip Sidney, Sir Walter Raleigh, Sir Edward Dyer, Spencer, Daniel, Drayton, Shakespeare, Whetstone, Gascoigne, Samuel Page sometimes fellow of Corpus Christi College in Oxford, Churchyard, Bretton.[7]

This gives every appearance of being an idiot's guide to contemporary English literature by someone who was himself not very intelligent, and certainly not very discriminating. Meres's lists have nevertheless proved invaluable for establishing what Shakespeare had written by 1598 even if, since all the other items check out, they have left scholars with the puzzle of *Love's Labour's Won* (usually presumed to have been lost). What they show is that if in 1592, when Greene attacked him, Shakespeare's star was rising, by the time Meres was writing it had very definitely risen.

Should the extracts from Greene, Chettle and Meres be felt insufficient to establish the 'bare fact' that in the final decade of the sixteenth century Shakespeare had become well known in London as a poet, playwright and actor, further (and far more entertaining) confirmation can be found in what are known as the 'Parnassus plays', three satirical vehicles written by and for Cambridge students and performed in St John's College on various occasions between 1598 and 1603. At one moment during the second of these – the first part of *The Return from Parnassus* – Ingenioso, who is usually thought to be a portrait of Nashe, is discussing with his foolish and boastful patron, Gullio, the latter's mistress (most of Ingenioso's remarks take the form of asides to the audience).

INGENIOSO: But you have digressed from your mistress, for whose sake you and I began this parley.

GULLIO: Marry, well remembered! I'll repeat unto you an enthusiastical oration wherewith my new Mistress's ears were very lately made happy. The carriage of my body, by the report of my mistress, was excellent: I stood stroking up my hair, which became me very admirably, gave a low congey at the beginning of each period, made every sentence end sweetly with an oath. It is the part of an Orator to persuade, and I know not how better than to conclude with such earnest protestations. Suppose also that thou wert my Mistress, as sometime wooden statues represent the goddesses; thus I would look amorously, thus I would pace, thus I would salute thee.

INGENIOSO: (It will be my luck to die no other death than by hearing of his follies; I fear this speech that's a coming will breed a deadly disease in my ears.)

GULLIO: Pardon, fair lady, though sick-thoughted Gullio makes amain unto thee, & like a bold-faced suitor 'gins to woo thee.

INGENIOSO: (We shall have nothing but pure Shakespeare, and shreds of poetry that he hath gathered at the theatres!)

GULLIO: Pardon me moy mistressa, as I am a gentleman, the moon in

13

	comparison of thy bright hue a mere slut, Anthony's Cleopatra a black browed milkmaid, Helen a dowdy.
INGENIOSO:	(Mark *Romeo and Juliet!* O monstrous theft! I think he will run through a whole book of Samuel Daniel's.)
GULLIO:	*Thrice fairer than myself* (thus I began),

The gods fair riches, sweet above compare,
Stain to all Nymphs, more lovely than a man,
More white and red than doves and roses are:
Nature that made thee, with herself at strife,
Saith that the world hath ending with thy life.

| INGENIOSO: | Sweet Mr Shakespeare! |
| GULLIO: | As I am a scholar, *these arms of mine are long and strong withall,* |

Thus elms by vines are compassed ere they fall.

INGENIOSO:	Faith, gentleman! your reading is wonderful in our English poets!
GULLIO:	Sweet mistress, I vouchsafe to take some of their words, and apply them to mine own matters by a scholastical invitation.
	Report thou, upon thy credit; is not my vein in courting gallant and honourable?
INGENIOSO:	Admirable, *sans* compare, never was so mellifluous a wit joined to so pure a phrase, such comely gesture, such gentleman-like behaviour.
GULLIO:	But stay! it's very true good wits have bad memories. I had almost forgotten the chief point. I called thee out for new year's day approacheth, and whereas other gallants bestow jewels upon their mistresses (as I have done whilom), I now count it base to do as the common people do; I will bestow upon them the precious stones of my wit, a diamond of invention, that shall be above all value and esteem; therefore, sithens I am employed in some weighty affair of the court, I will have thee, Ingenioso, to make them, and when thou hast done, I will peruse, polish, and correct them.
INGENIOSO:	My pen is your bounded vassal to command. But what vein would it please you to have them in?
GULLIO:	Not in a vain vein (pretty y'faith!): make me them in two or three divers veins, in Chaucer's, Gower's and Spencer's, and Mr Shakespeare's. Marry, I think I shall entertain those verses which run like these:

Even as the sun with purple coloured face
Had ta'en his last leave on the weeping morn etc.

	O sweet Mr Shakespeare! I'll have his picture in my study at the court.
INGENIOSO:	(Take heed my masters, he'll kill you with tediousness ere I can rid him of the stage!)
GULLIO:	Come, let us in! I'll eat a bit of pheasant, and drink a cup of wine in my cellar, and straight to the court I'll go. A countess and two lords expect me today at dinner, they are my very honourable friends; I must not disappoint them.[8] (3.i)

Although Gullio quotes from *The Spanish Tragedy* on one occasion here ('*These arms of mine ...*'), much of what he says is taken directly from either *Venus and Adonis* or *Romeo and Juliet*. He is a Shakespeare enthusiast. When later on in this lively play Ingenioso produces samples of verse which are either directly borrowed from or in the manner of Chaucer, Spenser and Shakespeare, Gullio dismisses the first two out of hand but accepts the third:

> Ey, marry, Sir, these have some life in them! Let this duncified world esteem of Spenser and Chaucer, I'll worship sweet Mr Shakespeare, and to honour him will lay his *Venus and Adonis* under my pillow, as we read of one (I do not well remember his name, but I'm sure he was a king) slept with Homer under his bed's head.[9] (4.i)

In manuscripts jottings on contemporary literature, probably written some time between 1598 and 1601, the Cambridge don Gabriel Harvey noted that 'the younger sort takes much delight in Shakespeare's *Venus and Adonis*; but his *Lucrece*, & his tragedy of *Hamlet, Prince of Denmark*, have it in them to please the wiser sort.'[10] The vogue for Shakespeare's love poetry, bolstered as it must have been by *Romeo and Juliet*, appears to have been one of the satirical targets of whoever wrote the first part of *The Return to Parnassus* and is associated on three occasions there with the adjective 'sweet'. This word is the equivalent of Francis Meres's 'honey-tongued', a term also used by John Weever in his sonnet, 'Ad Gulielmum Shakespeare', published in 1599, while the year before Richard Barnfield had alluded to the presence in Shakespeare's poems of his 'honey-flowing Vein'.[11] There is a cluster of similar references here which makes it unlikely that Ben Jonson was thinking of his dead friend's temperament when, in the commemorative poem he wrote for the First Folio, he called Shakespeare the 'Sweet Swan of Avon'.

References like those of whoever was responsible for the Parnassus plays may indicate that Shakespeare's work was well-known but they hardly tell us much about the man – it was his poetry not he himself that some people thought sweet. From a biographical point of view, therefore, they are chiefly significant as a lion in the path of those who have wanted to argue that William Shakespeare of Stratford was not the author of the work which has been attributed to him (the 'anti-Stratfordians' as they are known). Very many of Shakespeare's contemporaries obviously thought that he was, so that, to deny him authorship, it is necessary to imagine that some of those contemporaries were merely deceived and that the ones who could not have been (his close associates in the Lord Chamberlain's Men, for example) formed part of what would have to have been a very large conspiracy. It is strange to want to contemplate that possibility when the evidence for believing that Shakespeare did not write Shakespeare usually amounts to little more than the fact that his father was a tradesman, and his formal education appears not to have gone beyond the grammar school.

What would help silence the doubters are a few eye-witness reports of the man himself but very few of these have survived. In the second volume of his

William Shakespeare: A Study of Facts and Problems, Chambers lists fifty-eight people who made what he calls 'contemporary allusions' to Shakespeare (several of them more than once). But although Chambers says in his introductory note that he has limited himself to passages which make 'some personal reference',[12] most of the allusions are not merely exceedingly brief but refer, in fact, to Shakespeare's *work.* Between Greene and Chettle, and the tributes paid to Shakespeare after his death, the only person who has anything of even remote biographical significance to say is a minor writer known as John Davies of Hereford. In one of his poems Davies refers to both Burbage and Shakespeare as men in regard to whom 'fell Fortune cannot be excus'd / That hath for better uses you refus'd.' What he means is made clear in a couplet which comes a few lines later:

> *And though the stage doth stain pure gentle blood,*
> *Yet generous ye are in mind and mood.*[13]

In another poem he complains that Shakespeare and Burbage have not been rewarded (by Fortune) 'to their desserts'. Both these references are complicated by not being to Shakespeare alone, and by the fact that we would not know who their subjects were if the initials RB and WS had not been added to the margins of the poems; but in his *Scourge of Folly,* published around 1610, Davies devoted what was then known as an epigram solely 'To Our English Terence, Mr Will. Shakes-peare':

> *Some say good Will (which I, in sport, do sing)*
> *Had'st thou not plaid some Kingly parts in sport,*
> *Thou had'st been a companion for a King;*
> *And, been a King among the meaner sort.*
> *Some others rail; but, rail, as they think fit,*
> *Thou had'st no railing, but, a reigning Wit;*
> *And honesty thou sow'st, which they do reap;*
> *So, to increase their Stock which they do keep.*[14]

It says something about contemporary allusions, not to Shakespeare's work but to the man himself, that, apart from the exceptions I have mentioned, this is the most specific.

Contemporary references to Shakespeare tell us less about the conditions of his life than do the surviving records of his financial transactions. As an investor in the Lord Chamberlain's Men and then in the theatres where they played – the Globe from 1599 and Blackfriars, an indoor theatre for winter performances, from 1609 – Shakespeare was entitled to share with a number of his colleagues all the profits from his Company's activities. Although the London theatres were periodically forced to close, for political reasons or because of the plague, and the Company would therefore have to rely on whatever it could make from performances at Court and provincial tours, the deal appears to have been an excellent one. One possible sign of this is the reactivation of John Shakespeare's application for a coat of arms. A more certain one is William's purchase in 1597 of New Place, the second largest house in Stratford. In 1602 he paid £320 for about one hundred and twenty acres of farming land near Stratford. Five months later he acquired a cottage adjacent to New Place and in 1605 he bought a half interest in a lease of tithes which a number of local farmers had to pay. The lease had thirty-one years to run, the yield on the tithes was in the region of £50 a year, and the investment cost Shakespeare £440. It is impossible to calculate precise modern equivalents of all these sums but in 1999 Anthony Holden cited a professor of economics who offered 'multiply by 500' as a useful rule of thumb.[15]

What we know for certain from transactions like these is that Shakespeare became distinctly prosperous. A number of other documents are harder to interpret. No letters written by Shakespeare survive but there is a single one to him (although its discovery among its writer's papers may suggest that it was never in fact sent).

> Loving Countryman, I am bold of you as of a friend, craving your help with £30 upon Mr Bushell's and my security, or Mr Mytton's with me. Mr Roswell is not come to London as yet & I have especial cause. You shall friend me much in helping me out of all the debts I owe in London, I thank God, and much quiet my mind, which would not be indebted. I am now towards the Court in hope of answer for the dispatch of my business. You shall neither lose credit nor money by me, the Lord willing. And now but persuade yourself so as I hope, and you shall not need to fear, but with all hearty thankfulness I will hold my time and content your friend, and if we bargain further you shall be the paymaster yourself. My time bids me hasten to an end, and so I commit this to your care and hope of your help. I fear I shall not be back this night from the Court. Haste. The Lord be with you and with us all, Amen.[16]

This letter is dated 25 October 1598, addressed to 'my loving good friend and countryman Mr Wm. Shakespeare', and was written by Richard Quiney, the son and partner of a prominent Stratford businessman, Adrian Quiney, who had been bailiff or mayor of Stratford on three occasions. Richard had himself been bailiff in 1592 as he would be again in 1601; and in 1616 his son Thomas would marry Shakespeare's younger daughter Judith. He had come to London as the representative of the Stratford corporation to petition the Privy Council for a reduction in the town's taxes. On the same day that he wrote his letter to Shakespeare he must also have written to Abraham Sturley, another Stratford associate, since on the 4th November Sturley replied,

Your letter of the 25 of October came to my hands the last of the same at night [...] which imported [...] that our countryman Mr Wm. Shakespeare would procure us money, which I will like of as I shall hear when, and where, and how; and I pray let not go that occasion if it may sort to any indifferent conditions.[17]

This may refer to the private loan which Quiney had requested, even though his letter may never have been sent, but it may also concern (and the way Sturley's letter goes on could suggest this) an investment which Shakespeare was thinking of making and which is mentioned in other letters to Quiney. The circumstances remain obscure. There is enough in Quiney's letter to indicate that by 1598 Shakespeare was known to be sufficiently wealthy to supply at short notice the large sum of £30, but not enough to suggest that, as some biographers have claimed, he was in the money-lending business.

This last conclusion is for some confirmed by the survival of records which show that in 1604 Shakespeare sued Philip Rogers, a Stratford apothecary, for an outstanding debt of 35 shillings and in 1608-9 (the action dragged on through several stages) a certain John Addenbrooke for the recovery of £6. The Rogers case is the more interesting because he had contracted the debt by buying from Shakespeare twenty bushels of malt. In 1598, after several bad harvests and government anxiety over grain shortages, Shakespeare was cited in an official survey as storing in New Place the equivalent of eighty bushels of malt (only about a dozen men in the town held more). Eighty bushels seems a lot for domestic brewing purposes but whether Shakespeare ought therefore to be regarded as a 'hoarder' - one of those people the government was worried about because in hard times they held back supply from the market in order to inflate the price - is not at all clear. A major difficulty of interpretation is that no-one knows who ran Shakespeare's affairs in Stratford, whether (that is) he managed to keep control even though, as the Quiney letter suggests, he was mostly in London, or whether he delegated authority (the authority for example for buying in malt), to his wife, his brothers or some other person or persons.

Where Shakespeare lived while he was in London is another major puzzle of his biography. The appearance of his name in a number of lists of those who had failed to pay government taxes suggests that before 1596 he lodged in St Helen's parish, Bishopsgate, in the north of the city but that by 1598 he had crossed the river and lived in Southwark. No precise address in either locality has ever been recovered nor any record of anyone with whom he might have lodged. It is this ignorance which gives such high value to documents which were discovered as late as 1909 and which, as far as Shakespeare is concerned, have come to be regarded as the greatest documentary discovery of the twentieth century. They are the record of a case brought against Christopher Mountjoy,

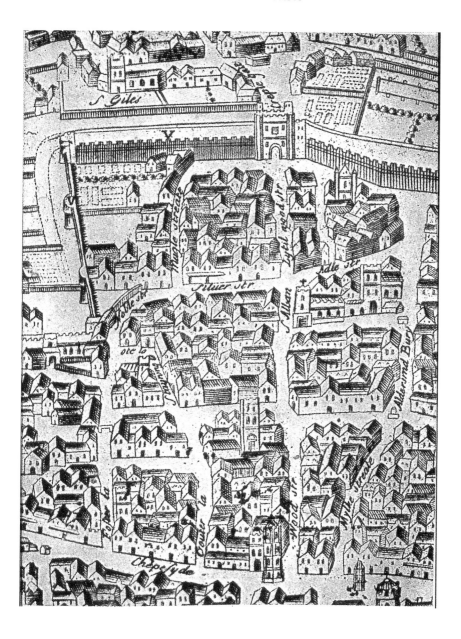

3. *The Agas map of c. 1558 showing the house at the right-hand corner of Mugle and Silver Streets, London, where Shakespeare lodged with the Mountjoys prior to 1604*

a maker of wigs and ornamental headgear for women, by Stephen Belott who had once been Mountjoy's apprentice but was also his son-in-law. Belott claimed that when he married Mountjoy's daughter in 1604 he had been made promises as to future financial advantages which, by the time he brought the case in 1612, had not been, and never looked like being, kept. As was usual in these matters, the Court drew up a series of questions or 'interrogatories' which it then proposed to put to the witnesses.

1. *Imprimis*: whether do you know the parties plaintiff and defendant, and how long have you known them and either of them.

2. *Item*: whether did you know the Complainant when he was servant with the said defendant, how and in what sort did he behave himself in the service of the said defendant, and whether did not the said defendant Confess that he had got great profit and Commodity by the service of the said Complainant.

3. *Item*: whether did not the said defendant seem to bear great good will and affection towards the said Complainant during the time of his said service and what report did he then give of the said Complainant touching his said service and whether did not the said defendant make a motion unto the said Complainant of marriage with the said Mary in the Bill mentioned, being the said defendant's sole Child and daughter, and willingly offer to perform the same if the said Complainant should seem to be content and well like therof, and whether did not he likewise send any person or no to persuade the said Complainant to the same, declare the truth of your knowledge herein.

4. *Item*: what sum or sums of money did the said defendant promise to give the said Complainant for a portion in marriage with the said Mary his daughter, whether the sum of threescore pounds or what other sum as you know or have heard and when was the same to be paid, whether at the day of Marriage of the said Complainant and the said Mary or what other time, and what further portion did the said defendant promise to give unto the said Complainant with the said Mary at the time of his decease, whether the sum two hundred pounds or what other sums, and whether upon the said persuasions and promises of the said defendant did not the said Complainant shortly after marry with her, the said Mary, declare the truth herein as you know, verily believe or have credibly heard.

5. *Item*: what parcels of goods or household stuff did the defendant promise to give unto the Complainant in Marriage with his said wife, And what parcels of goods did he give him in Marriage with his said wife. Did he not give him these parcels viz. One old featherbed, one old feather bolster, A flock bolster, a thin green Rug, two ordinary blankets woven, two pair sheets, A dozen of napkins of Coarse Dyper, two short table Clothes, six short Towels & one long one, an old drawing table, two old joint stools, one wainscot cupboard, one twisting wheel of wood, two pair of little Scissors, one old Trunk and a like old Trunk, One Bobbin box: And what do you think in your Conscience all these said parcels might be worth at the time when they were delivered by the defendant's appointment, unto the plaintiffs, declare the truth herein at large.[18]

Through the dust thrown up by the barbarous legal jargon it is possible to see with reasonable clarity here the grounds and nature of the dispute. Belott had married Mountjoy's daughter in the expectation of considerable financial reward which had not materialised and there had followed acrimonious and unseemly disputes as to what precisely the financial arrangements had been, whether Belott had not been an excellent apprentice who had brought his master considerable profit, and precisely what items of furniture (down to the last bobbin box) he and his wife had been given. It was an American couple called Wallace who, after labouring for years in the Public Record Office, discovered that Shakespeare had not only been a witness in this case but could also be identified as the person referred to in item 3 who helped negotiate Mary Mountjoy's marriage. This was his signed statement:

William Shakespeare of Stratford upon Avon in the County of Warwick gentleman of the age of xlviii years or thereabouts swore and examined the day and year abovesaid deposeth and sayeth:

1   To the first Interrogatory this deponent sayeth he Knoweth the parties plaintiff and defendant and hath known them both as he now remembereth for the space of ten years or thereabouts.

2   To the second Interrogatory this deponent sayeth he did know the complainant when he was a servant with the defendant, and that during the time of his the complainant's service with the said defendant he the said Complainant to this deponents knowledge did well and honestly behave himself, but to this deponents remembrance he hath not heard the defendant confess that he had got any great profit and commodity by the service of the said complainant, but this deponent sayeth he verily thinketh that the said complainant was a very good and industrious servant in the said service and more he cannot depose to the said Interrogatory.

3   To the third Interrogatory this deponent sayeth that it did evidently appear that the said defendant did all the time of the said complainants service with him bear and show great good will and affection towards the said complainant, and that he hath heard the defendant and his wife divers and sundry times say and report that the said complainant was a very honest fellow: And this deponent sayeth that the said defendant did make a motion unto the complainant of marriage with the said Mary in the bill mentioned, being the said defendants sole child and daughter, and willingly offered to perform the same if the said Complainant should seem to be content and well like thereof: And further this deponent sayeth that the said defendants wife did solicit and entreat this deponent to move and persuade the said Complainant to effect the said Marriage and accordingly this deponent did move and persuade the Complainant thereunto: And more to this Interrogatory he cannot depose.

4   To the fourth Interrogatory this deponent sayeth that the defendant promised to give the said Complainant a portion in Marriage with Mary his daughter: but what certain portion he Remembereth not nor when to be paid, nor knoweth that the defendant promised the plaintiff two hundred pounds with his daughter Mary at the time of his decease. But sayeth that the plaintiff was dwelling with the defendant in his house And they had Amongst themselves many Conferences about their Marriage which afterwards was Consummated and solemnised. And more he cannot depose.

5   To the fifth Interrogatory this deponent sayeth he can say nothing touching any part or point of the same Interrogatory for he knoweth not what

Implements and necessaries of household stuff the defendant gave the plaintiff in Marriage with this daughter Mary.[19]

From the other witnesses who gave evidence in this case it is clear that Shakespeare had been a lodger in the Mountjoys' house for at least the period which led up to their daughter's marriage. If his statement that he had known them for ten years were to be taken literally, it might suggest that he had been with them since 1602 but if what he said in response to the third Interrogatory is taken to imply that he had always been on hand to observe Bellott's apprenticeship, then his period of residence could be stretched back to 1598. Yet the time during which he knew the Mountjoys and could watch closely their relationship with their apprentice is not necessarily co-extensive with being a lodger in their house. Immediately prior to the marriage, however, Shakespeare was certainly living with them and he himself confirms in his statement what others also testify: that he helped to bring about that marriage by acting as a go-between. Because it is possible to establish that the Mountjoys lived in Cripplegate ward, at the intersection of what were then Mugle and Silver Streets and in a house still identifiable on at least one sixteenth century street map, here at last is not only a precise London address for Shakespeare, but also his apparent association with a distinct *milieu*. The Mountjoys were Huguenot refugees who may have supplied headgear to the theatre as well as the aristocracy. One of their acquaintances was George Wilkins since he is recorded as responding to the fifth interrogatory by saying that he would not have valued the 'implements and necessaries of house-hold stuff' which Mountjoy gave his daughter at more than £5. Wilkins had an unpleasant reputation as a brothel-keeper and beater-up of women but he was also a playwright who may well have collaborated with Shakespeare on *Pericles*.

The documents in the Mountjoy/Bellott case are highly informative but the question they leave open concerns the exact nature of Shakespeare's relation to their world. Was he a close friend of the family or did the appeal to act as a go-between come rather because he happened to be their lodger (for someone who may have been a friend he has a very poor memory of the details of the transaction)? One might have expected his deposition to point in the general direction of an answer to these questions but, in the first place, his words are filtered through whoever recorded them and, in the second, they are largely determined by those in the interrogatories. Even the high moment of Mountjoy's wife soliciting and entreating Shakespeare to move and persuade Belott to marry her daughter may not indicate his memory of any special fervour on her part but a Jacobean official's fondness for doubling. Only if there were other surviving depositions by Shakespeare could the fact that his answers are so unhelpful on the principal questions which troubled the court be taken as the sign of a man who was reluctant to commit himself, always likely to keep his head down.

Shakespeare was listed to give evidence a second time in the Belott/Mountjoy dispute but failed to do so. This may have been because he was too far away in Stratford, although when he retired there permanently, or if he ever did so, is not known. The last play of what is commonly assumed to have been his London career is *All is True* which was called *Henry VIII* in the First Folio and almost certainly written in collaboration with John Fletcher. In June 1613, at one of the first performances of this play at the Globe, small canons which were being used for special effects set fire to the theatre's thatched roof and it was completely destroyed. The absence of Shakespeare's name from the syndicate which was then formed to have the Globe rebuilt has been taken to suggest that he might have chosen this moment to call it a day.

In 1613 Shakespeare bought a house in London (the Blackfriars Gatehouse) in a highly complicated legal arrangement which involved an initial down-payment of £80. It is usually assumed that this was not a house he ever meant to live in but rather an investment. The following year he may well have been made anxious by proposals to enclose some of the land in Stratford from which he drew his tithe income. Since the effect of enclosure might have been to reduce that income, he signed an agreement with one of its supporters which indemnified him against any financial loss should their proposals be successful. A prominent opponent of the scheme was Thomas Greene who identities himself as a cousin of Shakespeare's but who was also the Stratford corporation's town clerk. His surviving diary suggests that he wanted to enrol Shakespeare in the anti-enclosure campaign but it is not clear whether he was successful or what Shakespeare's attitude to the whole affair was. At the centre of the puzzle is an entry inserted retrospectively in the diary which reads: 'Sept. W Shakespeare telling J Greene that J was not able to bear the enclosing of Welcombe.' 'J Greene' is usually taken as a reference to Thomas's brother John while the second 'J' has – Jacobean handwriting being what it is – sometimes been read as 'I' (Thomas) or 'he' (Shakespeare). It was in part the impenetrable ambiguity of these words which prompted Chambers to say, after a careful review of all the evidence, 'Once more, Shakespeare's sentiments elude us'.[20]

One entry which is reasonably clear in Greene's diary is his report that, whatever Shakespeare's attitude to the enclosure proposal might have been, he did not believe it would succeed. After several years of often bitter and sometimes violent wrangling that proved to be the case although Shakespeare did not live long enough to see his prediction come true. His death occurred in 1616, probably on the same day in April as his supposed birthday. There is a record of his burial on the 25th April in Holy Trinity church where visitors can still see a tombstone in the chancel which bears the strange words:

Good friend for Jesus sake forbear,
To dig the dust enclosed here!
Blest be the man that spares these stones,
And curst be he that moves my bones.

It was towards the end of the seventeenth century that this injunction was attributed to Shakespeare himself, the general assumption then being that he was apprehensive of finishing up in the charnel house which adjoined the church. But the stone on which it was written does not bear his or any other name and is, according to the great Victorian scholar, J. O. Halliwell-Phillipps, not the original tombstone but a replacement.[21]

Shakespeare left a will which has become so much a part of the legend of his life, and is still so much the subject of controversy, that I need to reproduce it here in full. Because it is such a complicated document I have in transcribing it tried to produce a more easily readable version by not only modernising the spelling and adding punctuation but also filling out some of the words abbreviated in the original, giving each of the will's provisions a new paragraph, and changing many capital letters to lower case.

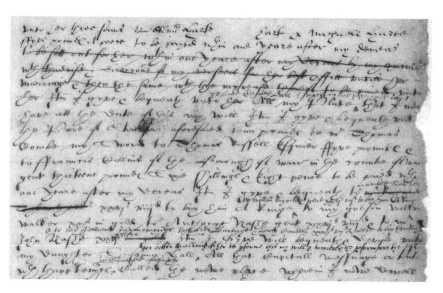

4. *Details from the top of the second sheet of Shakespeare's will which indicate that it was revised and a new first sheet added to the original document.*

In the name of god Amen I William Shakespeare of Stratford upon Avon in the county of Warwick, gentleman in perfect health & memory, god be praised, do make & ordain this my last will & testament in manner & form following. That is to say first I commend my Soul into the hands of god my creator hoping &

24

assuredly believing through the only merits of Jesus Christ my Saviour to be made partaker of life everlasting, and my body to the earth whereof it is made.

Item: I give & bequeath unto my daughter Judith one hundred & fifty pounds of lawful English money to be paid unto her in manner & form following: That is to say one hundred pounds in discharge of her marriage portion within one year after my decease, with consideration after the rate of two shillings in the pound for so long time as the same shall be unpaid unto her after my decease, & the fifty pounds residue thereof upon her surrendering of, or giving of such sufficient security as the overseers of this my will shall like of, to surrender or grant all her estate & right that shall descend or come unto her after my decease or that she now hath of in or to one copyhold tenement[†] with the appurtenances lying & being in Stratford upon Avon aforesaid in the said county of Warwick being parcel or holden of the manor of Rowington, unto my daughter Susanna Hall & her heirs forever.

Item: I give & bequeath unto my said daughter Judith one hundred & fifty pounds more if she or any issue of her body be living at the end of three years next ensuing the day of the date of this my will, during which time my executors to pay her consideration from my decease according to the rate aforesaid. And if she die within the said terms without issue of her body then my will is & I do give and bequeath one hundred pounds thereof to my niece Elizabeth Hall & the fifty pounds to be set forth by my executors during the life of my sister Joan Hart & the use and profit thereof coming shall be paid to my said sister Joan, & after her decease the said £50 shall remain amongst the children of my said sister equally to be divided amongst them. But if my said daughter Judith be living at the end of the said three years or any issue of her body, then my will is & so I devise & bequeath the said hundred & fifty pounds to be set out by my executors and overseers for the best benefit of her & her issue & the stock not to be paid unto her so long as she shall be married & covert barren,[‡] but my will is that she shall have the consideration yearly paid unto her during her life & after her decease the said stock and consideration to be paid to her children if she have any &, if not, to her executors or assigns she living the said term after my decease. Provided that if such husband as she shall at the end of the said three years be married unto or attain after do sufficiently assure unto her & the issue of her body, lands answerable to the portion by this my will given unto her & to be adjudged so by my executors & overseers then my will is that the said £150 shall be paid to such husband as shall make such assurance to his own use.

Item: I give and bequeath unto my said sister Joan £20 & all my wearing apparel to be paid and delivered within one year after my decease, and I do will & devise unto her the house with the appurtenances in Stratford wherein she dwelleth for her natural life under the yearly rent of twelve pence.

Item: I give and bequeath unto her three sons William Hart, [——][*] Hart & Michael Hart five pounds a piece to be paid within one year after my decease.

Item: I give and bequeath unto the said Elizabeth Hall all my plate (except my broad silver and gilt bowl) that I now have at the date of this my will.

[†] This is the cottage Shakespeare had bought in 1602. There is some mystery as to why it needed special legal 'clearance'.
[‡] A legal term meaning 'under the protection of her husband'.
[*] For some reason the Christian name of the second son is missing.

Item: I give and bequeath unto the poor of Stratford aforesaid ten pounds, to Mr Thomas Combe my Sword, to Thomas Russell Esq five pounds, & to Francis Collins of the borough of Warwick in the county of Warwick, gentleman, thirteen pounds six shillings & eight pence to be paid within one year after my decease.

Item: I give and bequeath to Hamlett Sadler 26 shillings 8 pence to buy him a ring, to William Reynolds gentleman 26 shillings 8 pence to buy him a ring, to my godson William Walker 20 shillings in gold, to Anthony Nashe gent 26 shillings 8 pence, & to Mr John Nashe 26 shillings 8 pence, & to my fellows John Heminge, Richard Burbage & Henry Condell 26 shillings 8 pence a piece to buy them rings.

Item: I give, will, bequeath & devise unto my daughter Susanna Hall for better enabling of her to perform this my will & towards the performance thereof, all that capital messuage or tenament with the appurtenances in Stratford aforesaid called the New Place wherein I now dwell & two messuages or tenements with the appurtenances situate lying & being in Henley street within the borough of Stratford aforesaid, and all my barns, stables, Orchards, gardens, lands, tenements & hereditaments whatsoever situate lying & being or to be had, received, perceived or taken within the towns Hamlets, villages, fields & grounds of Stratford upon Avon, Oldstratford, Bushopton & Welcombe or in any of them in the said county of Warwick, and also all that messuage or tenements with the appurtenances wherein one John Robinson dwelleth, situate lying & being in the Blackfriars in London near the Wardrobe, & all other my lands, tenements and hereditaments whatsoever; to have & to hold all & singular the said premises with their appurtenances unto the said Susanna Hall for & during the term of her natural life, & after her decease to the first son of her body lawfully issuing & to the heirs males of the body of the said first son lawfully issuing, & for default of such issue to the second son of her body lawfully issuing & to the heirs males of the body of the said second son lawfully issuing, & for default of such heirs to the third son of the body of the said Susanna lawfully issuing and of the heirs males of the body of the said third son lawfully issuing, and for default of such issue the same so to be & remain to the fourth, fifth, sixth & seventh sons of her body lawfully issuing one after another & to the heirs males of the bodies of the said fourth fifth sixth & seventh sons lawfully issuing in such manner as it is before limited to be & remain to the first second and third sons of her body & to their heirs males; and for default of such issue the said premises to be & remain to my said niece Hall & the heirs males of her body lawfully issuing, and for default of issue to my daughter Judith & the heirs males of her body lawfully issuing, and for default of such issue to the right heirs of me the said William Shakespeare for ever.

Item: I give unto my wife my second best bed with the furniture.

Item: I give & bequeath to my said daughter Judith my broad silver gilt bowl. All the rest of my goods, chattels, leases, plate, jewels & household stuff whatsoever, after my debts and legacies paid & my funeral expenses discharged, I give devise and bequeath to my son-in-law John Hall gent & my daughter Susanna his wife whom I ordain and make executors of this my last will and testament. And I do entreat and appoint the said Thomas Russell Esquire and Francis Collins gent to be overseers hereof. And do revoke all former wills & publish this to be my last will and testament. In witness whereof I have hereunto put my hand the day & year first above written.[22]

26

5. *Detail from the final sheet of Shakespeare's will showing the interpolated bequest of the second best bed to his wife.*

The 'day and year first above written' were 25 March 1616 but only the first of the three sheets of paper on which the will is written belong to that date. The other two were retained from a version which had been prepared earlier, probably in January. The reason for the re-drafting is commonly held to be the marriage of Shakespeare's younger daughter Judith to Thomas Quiney on 10 February 1616, an event which is assumed to have altered Shakespeare's notions of how he ought to provide for her. Some commentators believe that the provisions he did make are only what might have been expected, but most have associated them with the fact that, on 26 March, Thomas Quiney was convicted in the local ecclesiastical court of having enjoyed carnal copulation with a certain Margaret Wheeler who had died in childbirth a fortnight earlier (condemned to perform open penance in a white sheet at three successive Sunday services, Quiney's sentence was then commuted to a fine of five shillings). It is thought by some that Shakespeare's elaborate arrangements for the second payment of £150 to Judith show that he was doing all he could to prevent Quiney getting his hands on the money.

Whether or not this is the case there is no doubt that Shakespeare's will provides a good deal of information about his life. It indicates roughly how much he was worth at his death and provides minor details such as the name of the man to whom he had rented the Blackfriars gatehouse. It gives a check list of his Stratford friends or acquaintances (Francis Collins was his lawyer so that the bequest of £13 6s. 8d to him may have been partly in payment for drawing up the will), and suggests which of his former colleagues in the Lord Chamberlain's Men (Burbage, Heminge, Condell) he most valued in the final months of his life. But there is, nonetheless, disagreement on the question of how much it can reveal about what *kind* of man Shakespeare was.

Typical of his class and time is one answer suggested by the will's chief feature. By leaving the overwhelming bulk of his property to his elder daughter, now married to a highly respected local doctor called Hall, Shakespeare clearly indicated an intention to prevent its dispersal and maintain in the future the gentlemanly status his family had so recently achieved. The provisions of the will show a conventional desire to found a line. This had been made difficult by the early death of Shakespeare's only son: since his brothers had all died childless there could be no future prospect of maintaining the family name. Giving most of his property to Susanna and then insisting that it should always percolate down the centuries through the most nearly related male (one of those 'entails' which Jane Austen's heroines so often suffer from) seems to have been the next best thing to handing on the responsibility for ensuring family survival to an eldest son. Shakespeare may have hoped that Susanna would eventually have a boy; but the Elizabeth who is confusingly referred to the will as his 'niece', and who was eight years old at the time, remained the Halls' only child. Although she married twice, Elizabeth herself died childless and although Judith had three boys, they all died young and before they had time to reproduce. Descendants of his sister Joan, whose husband Thomas Hart died only a week before Shakespeare, continued to flourish, but the direct Shakespeare 'line' was extinct before the end of the seventeenth century.

The unequal division of property between Shakespeare's two daughters has usually been regarded as too characteristic of the period to be revealing of character and attention has therefore focused on less central aspects of the will. The opening declaration of religious commitment is taken almost word for word from a contemporary handbook on how to draft wills[23] and its relevance to the issue of Shakespeare's supposed Catholicism has therefore been discounted; but it has been suggested that his failure to leave any money to his local parish church is significant and there are disputes as to whether the £10 he left for the poor was, for a man with his assets, mean or generous. But what has chiefly exercised minds since the will was first unearthed in the eighteenth century is, of course, Shakespeare's bequest to his wife of that 'second best bed' (an interlinear addition to the last sheet or page). What if anything can this tell us about his marital relations? For the great eighteenth-century scholar Edward Malone the bequest indicated how little Shakespeare esteemed his wife – he had 'cut her off, not indeed with a shilling, but with an old bed.' Many since have endorsed his interpretation but others have pointed out that beds were highly valuable items in Jacobean England and the second best one could have been the bed the Shakespeares slept in (the best bed being reserved for guests). The absence of any other reference to Anne in the will has been explained by the fact that in Elizabethan common law a wife had an automatic right to the income from a third of her dead husband's estate (although how widely this right was granted has been disputed). A further consideration is that whatever was indicated in wills might well have been supplemented by private, unrecorded arrangements. Interpreting wills is very difficult but, even assuming that the various provisions of Shakespeare's can be legitimately interrogated for signs of his character, or that there is in its wording a 'tone' which can be attributed to him rather than to his lawyer's house style, what it could tell us only relates to Shakespeare's thoughts and feelings in one, perhaps not especially representative, phase of his life.

It may or may not be significant that two of the people to whom Shakespeare left a traditional 2 marks (26 shillings 8 pence) for the purchase of mourning rings, Heminge and Condell, were crucially involved in making him remembered to the extent that he now is. It was they who were chiefly responsible for the appearance in 1623 of what is known as the First Folio, an edition of thirty-six of his plays, 'Published according to the True Original Copies', half of which had never been in print before. In addition to their dedication of this volume to the Earl of Pembroke and his brother the Earl of Montgomery, and an address 'To the great Variety of Readers', Heminge and Condell prefaced Shakespeare's plays with five poems in praise of Shakespeare, two of which were by Ben Jonson. The first and much shorter of the two appeared opposite an engraving of Shakespeare by Martin Droeshout which, along with the memorial bust that had by this time already been erected in the church at Stratford,[24] is generally regarded as authentic, mainly because it must have commissioned by people who knew what he looked like. But it is the second and longer of the Jonson poems – 'To the memory of my beloved, The Author Mr William Shakespeare And what he hath left us' – which has seemed more important for those trying to form a satisfactory idea of Shakespeare the man:

> To draw no envy (Shakespeare) on thy name,
> Am I thus ample to thy Book, and Fame:
> While I confess thy writings to be such,
> As neither Man, nor Muse, can praise too much.
> 'Tis true, and all mens suffrage. But these ways
> Were not the paths I meant unto thy praise:
> For seeliest Ignorance on these may light,
> Which, when it sounds at best, but echoes right;
> Or blind Affection, which doth ne'er advance
> The truth, but gropes, and urgeth all by chance;
> Or crafty Malice, might pretend this praise,
> And think to ruin, where it seemed to raise.
> These are, as some infamous Bawd, or Whore,
> Should praise a Matron. What could hurt her more?
> But thou art proof against them, and indeed
> Above th'ill fortune of them, or the need.
> I, therefore, will begin. Soul of the Age!
> The applause! delight! the wonder of our Stage!

My Shakespeare, rise; I will not lodge thee by
Chaucer, or Spenser, or bid Beaumont lie
A little further, to make thee a room:
Thou art a Monument, without a tomb,
And art alive still, while thy Book doth live,
And we have wits to read, and praise to give.
That I not mix thee so, my brain excuses;
I mean with great, but disproportioned Muses:
For, if I thought my judgement were of years,
I should commit thee surely with thy peers,
And tell, how far thou didst our Lyly out-shine,
Or sporting Kyd, or Marlowes mighty line.
And though thou hadst small Latin, and less Greek,
From thence to honour thee, I would not seek
For names; but call forth thund'ring Aeschylus,
Euripides, and Sophocles to us,
Pacuvius, Accius, him of Cordova dead,
To life again, to hear thy Buskin tread,
And shake a Stage: Or, when thy Socks were on,
Leave thee alone, for the comparison
Of all, that insolent Greece, or haughty Rome
Sent forth, or since did from their ashes come.
Triumph, my Britain, thou hast one to show,
To whom all Scenes of Europe homage owe.
He was not of an age, but for all time!
And all the Muses still were in their prime,
When like Apollo he came forth to warm
Our ears, or like a Mercury to charm!
Nature herself was proud of his designs,
And joyed to wear the dressing of his lines!
Which were so richly spun, and woven so fit,
As, since, she will vouchsafe no other Wit.
The merry Greek, tart Aristophanes,
Neat Terence, witty Plautus, now not please;
But antiquated, and deserted lie
As they were not of Natures family.
Yet must I not give Nature all: Thy Art,
My gentle Shakespeare, must enjoy a part.
For though the Poets matter, Nature be,
His Art doth give the fashion. And, that he,
Who casts to write a living line, must sweat,
(Such as thine are), and strike the second heat
Upon the Muses anvil: turn the same,
(And himself with it) that he thinks to frame;
Or for the laurel, he may gain a scorn,
For a good poet's made, as well as born.
And such wert thou. Look how the fathers face
Lives in his issue, even so, the race
Of Shakespeares mind, and manners brightly shines
In his well turned, and true-filed lines:

> In each of which, he seems to shake a Lance,
> As brandished at the eyes of Ignorance.
> Sweet Swan of Avon! what a sight it were
> To see thee in our waters yet appear,
> And make those flights upon the banks of Thames,
> That so did take Eliza, and our James!
> But stay, I see thee in the Hemisphere
> Advanced, and made a Constellation there!
> Shine forth, thou Star of Poets, and with rage,
> Or influence, chide, or cheer the drooping Stage;
> Which, since thy flight from hence, hath mourn'd like night,
> And despairs day, but for thy Volumes light.[25]

This famous poem takes a long time to get going and contains a good deal of filler but it is nonetheless an impressive tribute. It is especially significant that it should be Jonson, with his reputation for classical learning, who elevates Shakespeare above the Greek and Latin writers although it is at the same time a pity that, in doing so, he inaugurates the tradition of using him to elevate Britain above other countries. No-one could have written this poem who did not greatly admire Shakespeare's writings but it is these writings which are its chief subject rather than their author. We learn nothing of biographical interest beyond the endlessly glossed 'small Latin, and less Greek'. 'Sweet' was (as I have said) a common way of referring to the mellifluous character of some of Shakespeare's verse and it is likely that 'gentle', if not a direct reference to his social status, is more descriptive of that verse than of any particular aspect of his nature. This at least is what can be inferred from the phrase 'gentle expressions' in a notebook entry by Jonson published three years after his death in the section of the 1640 edition of his works called *Timber, Discoveries*.

I remember, the Players have often mentioned it as an honour to Shakespeare, that in his writing, (whatsoever he penned) he never blotted out line. My answer hath been, Would he had blotted a thousand. Which they thought a malevolent speech. I had not told posterity this, but for their ignorance, who chose that circumstance to commend their friend by, wherein he most faulted. And to justify mine own candour, (for I loved the man, and do honour his memory (on this side Idolatry) as much as any.) He was (indeed) honest, and of an open, and free nature: had an excellent Phantasy; brave notions, and gentle expressions: wherein he flowed with that facility, that sometime it was necessary he should be stopped: *Sufflaminandus erat*; as Augustus said of Haterius. His wit was in his own power; would the rule of it had been so too. Many times he fell into those things, could not escape laughter: As when he said in the person of Caesar, one speaking to him: *Caesar, thou dost me wrong*. He replied: *Caesar did never wrong, but with just cause*: and such like; which were ridiculous. But he redeemed his vices, with his virtues. There was ever more in him to be praised, than to be pardoned.[26]

This is by far the most valuable, surviving account of Shakespeare's character that we have. From Jonson's contributions to the First Folio, and our knowledge that Shakespeare acted in at least two of his plays,[27] it is reasonable to assume that the two must have known each other fairly well. Of 'Timber' the editors of what is still the standard edition of Jonson's work say: 'The Folio arrangement of the text is haphazard. It is clear that Sir Kenelm Digby gathered up Jonson's loose papers and handed them over to the publisher just as he found them.'[28] What this suggests is that Jonson's comments here were not meant for immediate public consumption and not subject therefore to the inevitable distortions which occur when, for example, people are paying public tribute to the dead or encouraging the sale of their work. His tribute to Shakespeare gains added value by being only a parenthesis in what is a sharp criticism of that work. In their 'address to the great variety of readers' Heminge and Condell had said that Shakespeare's 'mind and hand went together: And what he thought, he uttered with that easiness, that we have scarce received from him a blot in his papers';[29] but Jonson in the poem which immediately followed insisted on the sweat which is involved in writing and that good poets are made as well as born. Here he accuses Shakespeare of not always having sweated enough but is anxious to separate this criticism from his liking and admiration of the man. There is no more informative remark in all the scattered allusions to Shakespeare than the insistence of Jonson – a particularly reliable witness – that he loved the man, honours his memory ('this side Idolotry') and found him both honest and of a open as well as free nature. Vague and general as they are, these words matter and if there were a dozen more like them from similarly reliable sources, and in similarly trustworthy contexts, they would begin to mean something. As it is they proved a feeble and inadequate response to the hunger which soon manifested itself to know more about the man taken to be responsible for so many memorable works.

Notes

1. Alexander B. Grosart (ed.), *Life and Complete Works [...] of Robert Greene* (1881–6), vol. 8, pp. 143–4.
2. See *Pierce Penniless: his Supplication to the Divell* in *The Bodley Head Quartos*, ed. G. B. Harrison (1924), p. 87.
3. Henry Chettle, *Kind-Hartes Dreame* (1592) in *The Bodley Head Quartos*, ed. G. B. Harrison (London, 1923), pp. 5–6.
4. Dedication to *Venus and Adonis* (1593). Southampton was twenty-one in October 1594.
5. Dedication to *The Rape of Lucrece* (1594).
6. See B. N. Luna, *The Queen declined: an Interpretation of 'Willobie his Avisa'*, (Oxford, 1970), pp. 190–1.
7. Don Cameron Allen (ed.), *Francis Meres's treatise 'Poetrie'* (University of Illinois studies in language and literature, 1933), pp. 73, 76, 78–9.
8. W. D. Macray (ed.), *Pilgrimage to Parnassus, with the two parts of the Return from Parnassus* (Oxford, 1886), pp. 56–8.
9. *Ibid.*, p. 63.

10. G. C. Moore Smith, *Gabriel Harvey's Memorabilia* (Stratford-upon-Avon: Shakespeare Head Press, 1913), p. 232.

11. See E. K. Chambers, *William Shakespeare: A Study of Facts and Problems* (Oxford, 1930), vol. 2, pp. 199 &195. Neither of these poems has anything to say about Shakespeare himself.

12. Chambers, vol. 2, p. 186.

13. Alexander B. Grosart (ed.), *Complete Works of John Davies of Hereford* (1878), vol. 1, p. 82.

14. *Ibid.*, vol. 2, p. 26.

15. Anthony Holden, *William Shakespeare: His Life and Work* (1999), p. 7.

16. E. I. Fripp. *Master Richard Quiney: Bailiff of Stratford-upon-Avon and Friend of William Shakespeare* (Oxford University Press, 1914), pp. 137-8.

17. Chambers, vol. 2, p. 103. See Shoenbaum's excellent treatment of these questions in *A Documentary Life* (Oxford, 1975), pp. 180-1.

18. C. W. Wallace, 'New Shakespeare Discoveries: Shakespeare as a Man among Men', *Harper's Monthly Magazine*, vol. 120 (March, 1910), pp. 495-6.

19. *Ibid.* pp. 498-500.

20. Chambers, vol. 2, p. 149.

21. J. O. Halliwell-Phillipps, *Outlines of the Life of Shakespeare* (1887: 7th. edition), vol. 1, pp. 269-70, and Chambers, vol. 2, pp. 181, 259. The precise date of Shakespeare's death is left blank in Fuller's text.

22. My version is based on the transcript of the will in R. Roland Lewis, *The Shakespeare Documents* (Standford University Press, 1940).

23. *The first part of the syboleography: which may be termed the art, or description, of instruments and presidents by William West* (1598).

24. There is a reference to Shakespeare's 'Stratford monument' in the poem by Leoard Digges at the beginning of the First Folio.

25. C. H. Herford and P & E. Simpson (eds), *Works of Ben Jonson* (Oxford, 1954), vol. 8, p. 390.

26. *Ibid.*, pp. 583-4. A rough paraphrase of Augustus' remark about Haterius would be 'our friend has got to be gagged'. The phrase from *Julius Caesar* which Jonson criticises does not appear in any of the extant texts.

27. Shakespeare's name appears in cast lists for the original productions of *Every Man in His Humour* and *Sejanus* in the 1616 Folio edition of Jonson's plays.

28. *Works*, vol. 8, p. 558.

29. Doug Moston (ed.), *Facsimile of the First Folio of 1623* (New York and London: Routledge, 1998), p. 7.

6. The Infant Shakespeare attended by Nature and the Passions *painted by George Romney, engraved by Benjamin Smith for John Boydell in 1799.*

Chapter Two

Myths and Legends

BIOGRAPHICAL INTEREST IN THE authors of literary works is a comparatively recent phenomenon. In Shakespeare's case it tended to follow the growing popularity of his plays after the restoration of Charles II but, by that time, too little reliable information was available to allow people to form an interesting and vivid picture of his life (many of the documents cited or referred to in the previous chapter were after all not discovered until the eighteenth and nineteenth centuries or – in the case of the Mountjoy/Belott papers – until the twentieth). The deficiency had therefore to be made up by legend or what Chambers famously called 'the Shakespeare-mythos'. As I say in my introduction, I do not, in using these two words or their derivatives, mean to imply that every episode or incident which figures in this chapter is necessarily untrue, only that there are no means of verifying any of them.

Sex, Drink and the Theatre.

We think of legends as emerging well after their subject's death and this is overwhelmingly true of Shakespeare. Yet there is one story which suggests that he must, if only in a minor way, have been a legend in his own life-time. In 1601 a young law student called John Manningham recorded the following in his diary or commonplace book:

> Upon a time when Burbage played Richard III there was a Citizen grew so far in liking with him, that before she went from the play she appointed him to come that night unto her by the name of Richard III. Shakespeare, overhearing their conclusion, went before, was entertained, and at his game ere Burbage came. Then message being brought that Richard III was at the door, Shakespeare caused return to be made that William the Conqueror was before Richard III. Shakespeare's name William. (Mr. Touse.)[1]

Manningham noted down this story along with three others (all of them more or less comic), and he indicated his source in each case. The man who told him about Shakespeare and Burbage was probably William Towse – the name has proved hard to read – who was not an actor but another member of the Middle Temple. Manningham's own distance from the action he describes is clear from that fact that he has to remind himself of Shakespeare's first name so that there can be no confusion in his own mind about the point of the joke. That what he is telling is a joke is relevant to the question of his anecdote's reliability (factual accuracy not being the most striking feature of the comic imagination), and so is a slight awkwardness or incoherence in Manningham's account. If the citizen's wife was expecting Burbage why was Shakespeare so readily entertained? This difficulty was resolved when what is recognisably the same anecdote appeared more than 150 years later in Thomas Wilkes's *General View of the Stage* (1759).

> One evening when *Richard III* was to be performed, Shakespeare observed a young woman delivering a message to Burbage in so cautious a manner as excited his curiosity to listen to. It imported, that her master was gone out of town that morning, and her mistress would be glad of his company after Play; and to know what signal he would appoint for admittance. Burbage replied, 'Three taps at the door, and "It is I, Richard III."' She immediately withdrew, and Shakespeare followed till he observed her to go into a house in the city; and enquiring in the neighbourhood, he was informed that a young lady lived there, the favourite of an old rich merchant. Near the appointed time of meeting, Shakespeare thought proper to anticipate Mr Burbage, and was introduced by the concerted signal. The lady was very much surprised at Shakespeare's presuming to act Mr Burbage's part; but as he (who had written *Romeo and Juliet*), we may be certain, did not want wit and eloquence to apologise for the intrusion, she was soon pacified, and they were mutually happy till Burbage came to the door, and repeated the same signal; but Shakespeare popping his head out of the window, bid him be gone; for that William the Conqueror had reigned before Richard III.[2]

Frank Harris once famously declared in the Café Royal that although the joys of homosexuality were a closed book to him, 'if *Shakespeare* asked me, I would have to submit'.[3] In a somewhat similar spirit, Wilkes fills the narrative gap in the Manningham anecdote by implicitly asking how any woman could refuse the author of *Romeo and Juliet*. He was almost certainly writing in ignorance of what Manningham had said, since the latter's diary was not discovered until the twentieth century, but this does not therefore mean (as is often assumed by commentators) that he *corroborates* it. What it suggests, instead, is that a certain story about Shakespeare was circulating at the beginning of the seventeenth century and different people picked up different versions of it.

Although it did not become generally available until 1759, there are two aspects of the Manningham anecdote which make it relevant to the growth of the Shakespeare legend. The first and less prominent one is that it places

Shakespeare in a theatrical milieu, an actor among actors sharing their characteristic tastes and pastimes. Many of the later dramatisations of his life, in novels or plays, show him in the company of Burbage or other members of the Lord Chamberlain's or King's Men (most of whom were conveniently listed at the beginning of the First Folio). One difficulty here is not merely a lack of information about how accomplished Shakespeare was as an actor but even about the roles he might have played. On this topic tradition or gossip was quite late in coming to the rescue. John Davies of Hereford talks of Shakespeare playing 'kingly parts' and it might be possible to infer from Jonson's remarks in *Timber* that he played Julius Caesar; but it is not until the first real attempt at a biography of Shakespeare, the one appended by Nicholas Rowe to his 1709 edition of the *Works*, that the question is squarely addressed.

> [Shakespeare's] admirable wit, and the natural turn of it to the stage, soon distinguished him, if not as an extraordinary actor, yet as an excellent writer. His name is printed, as the custom was in those times, amongst those of the other players, before some old plays, but without any particular account of what sort of parts he used to play; and though I have inquired, I could never meet with any further account of him this way, than that the top of his performance was the Ghost in his own *Hamlet*.[4]

For most of the information in his biography Rowe relied on the actor Thomas Betterton (*c.* 1635–1710) who had apparently been able to pick up no more useful green room gossip than this on the question of Shakespeare's roles. The task was not likely to become easier with the passage of time. In notes which he made for an enlarged biography of Shakespeare which he probably never completed and certainly never published,[5] William Oldys (1696–1761) has a story which begins badly because it refers to one of Shakespeare's younger brothers who 'lived to a good old age [...] even some years, as I compute, after the restoration of Charles II'. The actors would apparently ask this mythical brother what Shakespeare was like, especially 'in his dramatic character':

> But he, it seems, was so stricken in years, and possibly his memory so weakened with infirmities (which might make him the easier pass for a man of weak intellects) that he could give them but little light into their enquiries; and all that could be recollected from him of his brother Will, in that station was, the faint, general, and almost lost ideas he had of having once seen him act a part in one of his own comedies, wherein being to personate a decrepit old man, he wore a long beard, and appeared so weak and drooping and unable to walk, that he was forced to be supported and carried by another person to a table, at which he was seated among some company, who were eating, and one of them sung a song.[6]

It was left to one of Shakespeare's many eighteenth-century editors, Edward Capell, in notes he wrote for *As You Like It* in 1774, to make something more precise of this recollection.

A traditional story was current some years ago about Stratford, – that a very old man of that place, – of weak intellects, but yet related to Shakespeare, – being asked by some of his neighbours, what he remembered about him; answered, – that he saw him once brought on the stage upon another man's back; which answer was applied by the hearers, to his having seen him perform in this scene [2.6] the part of Adam: That he should have done so, is made not unlikely by another constant tradition, – that he was no extraordinary actor, and therefore took no parts upon him but such as this: for which he might also be peculiarly fitted by an accidental lameness, which, – as he himself tells us twice in his *Sonnets*, v. 37 and 89, – befell him in some part of life [...] [7]

All the more recent editors of the sonnets agree that the references to lameness in 37 and 89 are not to be taken literally so that we are left with mediocre abilities as an explanation for why Shakespeare confined himself to old men although also, if we are to believe the other witnesses, to kings and ghosts. If Hamlet's father is perhaps the part most often associated with Shakespeare it may be because, with a little leeway on the question of how old Hamlet's father actually was when he died, it could be said to combine all three.

The second relevant aspect of the Manningham anecdote is that it presents Shakespeare as someone who liked to have a good time and was not too particular about the methods he used for doing so. This image was inconsistent with the developing notion of the immortal Bard, patron saint of English letters, and did not therefore receive much attention. Yet it goes well with an anecdote which apparently circulated in Stratford in the latter half of the eighteenth century and is told in its most conveniently complete form by John Jordan, a former wheelwright who wrote poetry but then earned a living by showing visitors round the town, supplying information about Shakespeare, and dealing in the occasional forged document.

The following anecdote of Shakespeare is though a traditional Story as well authenticated as things of this nature generally are. I shall therefore not hesitate relating it as it was Verbally delivered to me. Our Poet was extremely fond of drinking hearty draughts of English Ale, and gloried in being thought a person of superior eminence in that profession if I may be allowed the phrase. In his time, but what period it is not recorded, There were two companies or fraternities of Village Yeomanry who used frequently to associate together at Bidford a town pleasantly situate on the banks of the Avon about 7 Miles below Stratford, and Who boasted themselves Superior in the Science of drinking to any set of equal number in the Kingdom; and hearing the fame of our Bard it was determined to Challenge him and his Companions to a trial of their skill which the Stratfordians accepted and accordingly repaired to Bidford which place agreeable to both parties was to be the Scene of Contention. But when Shakespeare and his Companions arrived at the destined spot, to their disagreeable disappointment they found the Topers were gone to Evesham fair and were told that if they had a mind to try their strength with the Sippers, they were there ready for the Contest. Shakespeare and his companions made a Scoff at their Opponents, but for want of better Company they agreed to the Contest and in a little time our Bard and his

Companions got so intolerable intoxicated that they was not able to Contend any longer and accordingly set out on their return to Stratford, but had not got above half a mile on the road e'er they found themselves unable to proceed any farther, and was obliged to lie down under a Crabtree which is still growing by the side of the road where they took up their repose till morning when some of the Company roused the poet and entreated him to return to Bidford and renew the Contest. He declined it saying, I have drunk with

> *Piping Pebworth, Dancing Marston,*
> *Haunted Hillborough, Hungry Grafton,*
> *Dadgeing Exhall, Papist Wicksford,*
> *Beggarly Broom, and Drunken Bidford*

meaning, by this doggerel, with the bibulous competitors who had arrived from the first-named seven villages, all of which are within a few miles of Bidford.[8]

Although he loses out in the contest, here is a Shakespeare capable of downing several pints of good old English ale just as in the Manningham anecdote he does not shy away from good old English fornication. As Schoenbaum points out, the crabtree Jordan mentions became a target for relic hunters and was eventually destroyed.

A Start in Life

There are areas of Shakespeare's life about which our ignorance could be described as partial but about his boyhood and youth it is complete. How, for example, did he first develop his taste for drama? It is known that various theatre companies visited Stratford while he was growing up (paid for by the Corporation, on some occasions when Shakespeare's father was himself the bailiff or mayor); but we can only presume his son saw them perform. What we can also only presume (as almost everyone who has offered either a fictional or non-fictional account of Shakespeare's life has) is that in 1575, when he was eleven, his father took him to various of the spectacles organised by the Earl of Leicester at nearby Kenilworth. These were in honour of a visit from Queen Elizabeth and are reasonably well documented. In an open letter to a friend, for example, Robert Laneham described how, as she was returning from the hunt and about to enter the castle, Elizabeth was greeted by an elaborate water pageant and told by a performer dressed as Triton that a cruel knight (Sir Bruce) had imprisoned the lady of the lake who could only be liberated by the Queen's own presence.

> Moving herewith from the bridge and fleeting more into the pool, chargeth [Triton] in Neptune's name: 'both Aeolus with all his winds, the waters with his springs, his fish and fowl, and all his clients in the same, that they ne be so hardy in any force to stir, but keep them calm and quiet while this Queen be present'.

At which petition her highness staying, it appeared straight how sir Bruce became unseen, his bands scaled [scattered], and the lady by and by, with her two Nymphs, floating upon her moveable islands (Triton on his mermaid skimming by,) approached towards her highness on the bridge: as well to declare that her Majesty's presence hath so graciously thus wrought her deliverance, as also to excuse her for not coming to court as she promised, and chiefly to present her Majesty (as a token of her duty and good heart) for her highness's recreation, with this gift, which was Arion, that excellent and famous Musician, in tire and appointment strange, well seeming too his person, riding aloft upon his old friend the Dolphin, (that from head to tail was a four and twenty foot long) and swimmed hard by these Islands: herewith Arion for these great benefits, after a few well couched words unto her Majesty of thanksgiving, in supplement of the same, began a delectable ditty of a song well apted to a melodious noise, compounded of six several instruments all covert, casting sound from the Dolphin's belly within; Arion, the seventh, sitting thus singing (as I say) without.[9]

It is often conjectured that Shakespeare was remembering having witnessed this intricately described pageant when, about twenty years later in *A Midsummer Night's Dream*, he has Oberon say to Puck (before he makes what might well be an oblique allusion to Queen Elizabeth):

> Thou rememb'rest
> Since once I sat upon a promontory
> And heard a mermaid on a dolphin's back
> Uttering such dulcet and harmonious breath
> That the rude sea grew civil at her song
> And certain stars shot madly from their spheres
> To hear the sea-maid's music?[10]

Apart from this possible allusion there is no way of knowing whether Shakespeare's father did in fact take him to Kenilworth in 1575.

What is being sought here is that vital structuring moment in his life when Shakespeare is first enraptured and thinks to himself, 'This is what I would like to do!' A stage-struck bard is important for the story and in the early 1680s John Aubrey provided one. The testimony of Aubrey, who appears to have derived his information from William Beeston, the son of the Christopher Beeston who was a member of the Lord Chamberlain's Men in 1598, has considerable general importance for the development of Shakespeare's image. It is Aubrey who reports that Shakespeare was a 'handsome, well shaped man: very good company, and of a very ready and pleasant smooth wit'; that he visited Stratford once a year; and (in a note which was for many years misplaced) that when he lived in Shoreditch he was not a 'company keeper' and 'would not be debauched' so that if he was invited out he would write to claim he was indisposed.[11] But what he has say about Shakespeare's early theatrical leanings is accompanied by slightly more context than these three observations.

Mr William Shakespeare was born at Stratford upon Avon in the County of Warwick. His father was a butcher, and I have been told heretofore by some of the neighbours, that when he was a boy he exercised his father's trade, but when he killed a calf he would do it in a high style, and make a speech. There was at that time another butcher's son in this town that was held not at all inferior to him for a natural wit, his acquaintance and coetanean, but died young.

This William, being inclined naturally to poetry and acting, came to London, I guess, about 18: and was an actor at one of the play-houses, and did act exceedingly well: [...][12]

Aubrey's testimony has been regularly dismissed in the past because it is known that Shakespeare's' father was a glover and not a butcher. More recently it has been pointed out that preparing leather for glove-making may have occasionally meant slaughtering animals, and one critic has asserted the relevance to Aubrey's story of an old tradition of mummers' plays which involved the ritual killing of a calf.

The calf-killing story may not be a 'patently ludicrous anecdote', but a distorted record of a Stratford mumming play acted by boys at Christmas-time, a form of mumming play like that which was performed before the young Princess Mary at Christmas 1521: 'Item, pd to a man at Wyndesore, for kylling a calfe before my ladys grace behynde a clothe.' It was something to please a child of five. The play lingered on in some villages down to this century. In his book I, Said the Sparrow (1963), Paul West, born at Eckington, Derbyshire, near Sheffield, describes how he took part in such a play in the 1920s. There the animal was a ram, and a false association was made with the famous Derby Ram. He himself was the boy who held the basin for the 'blood' as the butcher boy 'cut' the throat of the ram simulated by yet another boy under a carpet. I suggest that a calf-killing play of this type lies behind Aubrey's statement, and that the boy Shakespeare wrote, or re-wrote, the verses, and that he himself, as a butcher's son, did the 'killing' in 'high style', Shakespeare's earliest dramatic work in verse, and his first appearance as an actor. Paul West says that the only equipment needed was a basin, carpet, horns, butcher's knife, and a butcher's blue-and-white apron. The little play lasted ten minutes, and earned the actors a penny each.[13]

More killing of animals figures in the best known of the legends attached to Shakespeare's youth. Like several others associated with his life in general this story interacts with a passage from one of the plays. For some, his presence at Kenilworth in 1575 is confirmed by Oberon's words to Puck in A Midsummer Night's Dream and that he was a great drinker of local ale is attested by the presentation of Christopher Sly in the 'Induction' to The Taming of the Shrew (280 lines full of Warwickshire references). The passage which is associated with the idea that the young Shakespeare was forced to leave Stratford because he was caught poaching deer from Sir Thomas Lucy's estate at Charlecote (only a few miles from the town) comes at the very beginning of The Merry Wives of Windsor.

1.1 *Enter* JUSTICE SHALLOW, SLENDER *and* SIR HUGH EVANS.

SHALLOW: Sir Hugh, persuade me not: I will make a Star Chamber matter of it. If he were twenty Sir John Falstaffs, he shall not abuse Robert Shallow esquire.

SLENDER: In the County of Gloucester, Justice of Peace and Coram.

SHALLOW: Ay, cousin Slender, and Cust-a-lorum.

SLENDER: Ay, and Rato lorum too; and a gentleman born, master parson, who writes himself *Armigero*, in any bill, warrant, quittance, or obligation – *Armigero*.

SHALLOW: Ay, that I do, and have done any time these three hundred years.

SLENDER: All his successors – gone before him – hath done't; and all his ancestors – that come after him – may. They may give the dozen white luces in their coat.

SHALLOW: It is an old coat.

EVANS: The dozen white louses do become an old coat well. It agrees well passant. It is a familiar beast to man, and signifies love.

SHALLOW: The luce is the fresh fish – the salt fish is an old coat.[14]

Although the general topic is clearly Justice Shallow's ancestry, there are many details in these opening exchanges which are obscure (no-one is quite sure what Shallow's final remark here means). Matters are not helped for the modern reader by the humour which Shakespeare is trying to extract from Slender's misuse of both Latin and English words and the distortions attributable to Sir Hugh's Welsh accent (louse for 'luce'). Luce is a word for a pike (especially in heraldry) and there were three of them on the coat of arms of the Lucy family, or twelve in some versions of it. It has been felt significant that the reason Shallow is so angry and wants to make a 'Star Chamber matter of it' is that Falstaff has 'beaten my men, killed my deer and broke open my lodge' (1.i. 104–5).

The image of Shakespeare as a deer-poacher first surfaces in manuscript notes of the Reverend Richard Davies, some time chaplain of Corpus Christi College in Oxford. Towards the end of the seventeenth century or the beginning of the eighteenth, he suggested that Shakespeare was:

> much given to all unluckiness in stealing venison & Rabbits particularly from Sir [ ] Lucy who had him oft whipt & sometimes Imprisoned & at last made Him fly his Native Country to his great Advancement, but His revenge was so great that he is his Justice Clodpate and calls him a great man & that in allusion to his name bore three lowses rampant for his Arms.[15]

The Justice Clodpate whom Davies confuses with Justice Shallow was a character from a play by Thomas Shadwell. A more coherent account of the episode was given in 1709 by Rowe:

> [Shakespeare's] wife was the daughter of one *Hathaway*, said to have been a substantial yeoman in the neighbourhood of Stratford. In this kind of settlement

he continued for some time, till an extravagance that he was guilty of forc'd him both out of his country, and that way of living which he had taken up; and tho' it seemed at first to be a blemish upon his good manners, and a misfortune to him, yet it afterwards happily proved the occasion of exerting one of the greatest *genuises* that ever was known in dramatic poetry. He had, by a misfortune common enough to young fellows, fallen into ill company; and amongst them, some that made a frequent practice of deer-stealing, engaged him more than once in robbing a park that belonged to Sir Thomas Lucy of Charlecote, near Stratford. For this he was prosecuted by that gentleman, as he thought, somewhat too severely; and in order to revenge that ill usage, he made a ballad upon him. And though this, probably the first essay of his poetry, be lost, yet it is said to have been so very bitter, that it redoubled the prosecution against him to that degree, that he was obliged to leave his business and family in Warwickshire, for some time, and shelter himself in London.[16]

What is evidently missing here is the 'ballad' Shakespeare is described as having written, but several different versions were later to appear. One of them was provided by William Oldys whose notes on the deer-stealing episode were printed as part of the commentary on *The Merry Wives* in the 1778 edition of Shakespeare's *Works* edited by George Steevens and Samuel Johnson.

There was a very aged gentleman living in the neighbourhood of Stratford, (where he died fifty years since) who had not only heard, from several old people in that town, of Shakespeare's transgression, but could remember the first stanza of that bitter ballad, which, repeating to one of his acquaintance, he preserved it in writing; and here it is, neither better nor worse, but faithfully transcribed from the copy which his relation very curteously communicated to me.

> *A parliament member, a justice of peace,*
> *At home a poor scarecrow, at London an ass,*
> *If lousy is Lucy, as some folks miscall it,*
> *Then Lucy is lousy whatever befall it:*
> > *He thinks himself great,*
> > *Yet an ass in his state,*
> *We allow by his ears but with asses to mate.*
> > *If Lucy is lousy, as some folk miscall it,*
> > *Sing lousy Lucy, whatever befall it.*

Contemptible as this performance must now appear, at the time when it was written it might have had sufficient power to irritate a vain, weak, and vindictive magistrate; especially as it was affixed to several of his park gates, and consequently published among his neighbours.—It may be remarked likewise, that the jingle on which it turns, occurs in the first scene of *The Merry Wives of Windsor*.[17]

In 1780 Edward Capell reprinted in his notes on *The Merry Wives* this version of the ballad and also noted (in explanation of it) that the people of Stratford 'pronounce lousy like lucy'. He went on to claim that 'Sir Hugh's wit upon "luces"' in the opening of *The Merry Wives* gave to the ballad 'the appearance of genuineness'.[18] But the whole problem of the opening exchanges in *The Merry Wives* is whether they might not have been the root cause of the deer-stealing episode rather than one of its effects. As Schoenbaum neatly puts it, 'Could the legend possibly have originated, long after the dramatist's death, among Stratfordians who read *The Merry Wives of Windsor*, recollected a local jest about luces and louses, and interpreted the passage in accordance with their own resentment of a powerful local family?'[19]

Ten years later than Capell, Edmond Malone printed a version of the 'ballad' which was not only very different from that of Oldys but pre-dated it.

> In a Manuscript *History of the Stage*, full of forgeries and falsehoods of various kinds, written (I suspect by William Chetwood the prompter) some time between April 1727 and October 1730, is the following passage, to which the reader will give just as much credit as he thinks fit:
>
> 'Here we shall observe, that the learned Mr Joshua Barnes, late Greek Professor of the University of Cambridge, baiting about forty years ago at an inn in Stratford, and hearing an old woman singing part of the above-said song, such was his respect for Mr Shakespeare's genius, that he gave her a new gown for the two following stanzas in it; and, could she have said it all, he would (as he often said in company, when any discourse has casually arose about him) have given her ten guineas:
>
> > *Sir Thomas was too covetous,*
> > *To covet so much deer,*
> > *When horns enough upon his head*
> > *Most plainly did appear.*
> >
> > *Had not his worship one deer left?*
> > *What then? He had a wife*
> > *Took pains enough to find him horns*
> > *Should last him during life.'[20]*

The most strikingly new or different feature of this version is the mockery of Sir Thomas Lucy for the supposed unfaithfulness of his wife. This is absent from the eight stanzas of a ballad, more on Oldys' model, which John Jordan claimed to have discovered in a old chest of drawers and which Malone also printed, even though he had previously made clear that he thought it a forgery.

With or without the ballad, the deer-poaching episode took firm hold. It would not be dislodged by the discovery in the late eighteenth century that, at the time when Shakespeare was growing up in Stratford, there was no deer park on Sir Thomas Lucy's estate at Charlecote. That there was nonetheless there what was known as a 'free warren',[21] with rabbits and perhaps roe rather than fallow deer, meant that the story could stand with only minor adjustments as to what was poached. The episode satisfied too many needs to be discarded. It explained how it was that Shakespeare came to leave Stratford and at the same time acquitted him of any suspicion of having 'deserted' his wife and

7. 'A Fair Cop'. The young Shakespeare outside the gates of Charlecote *from Joseph Nash*, The Mansions of England in Olden Times *(1839–40)*

children (what choice did he have?). Through it one could see Shakespeare as a young man who, rather like Prince Hal, was wild in his youth (although not *too* wild) but who then sobered up; one who having been forced to leave the provinces then made good in London. Perhaps the most compelling aspect of the story was the one which showed Shakespeare in conflict with a higher social

45

class when he was later able, through his own efforts, to achieve a status comparable, or at least not too far removed, from theirs. This image of Shakespeare as a literary Dick Whittington is glimpsed again in a story about his days in London told by Robert Shiels in his *Lives of the Poets* of 1751 and then repeated by Dr Johnson in a passage which followed his reprint of Rowe's biography in his 1765 edition of Shakespeare's *Works*.

> To the foregoing accounts of Shakespeare's life, I have only one passage to add, which Mr Pope related, as communicated to him by Mr Rowe.
>
> In the time of Elizabeth, coaches being yet uncommon, and hired coaches not at all in use, those who were too proud, too tender, or too idle to walk, went on horseback to any distant business or diversion. Many came on horse-back to the play, and when Shakespeare fled to London from the terror of a criminal prosecution, his first expedient was to wait at the door of the play-house, and hold the horses of those that had no servants, that they might be ready again after the performance. In this office he became so conspicuous for his care and readiness, that in a short time every man as he alighted called for Will. Shakespeare, and scarcely any other waiter was trusted with a horse while Will. Shakespeare could be had. This was the first dawn of better fortune. Shakespeare finding more horses put into his hand than he could hold, hired boys to wait under his inspection, who, when Will. Shakespeare was summoned, were immediately to present themselves, 'I am Shakespeare's boy, Sir'. In time Shakespeare found higher employment, but as long as the practice of riding to the play-house continued, the waiters that held the horses retained the appellation of Shakespeare's Boys.[22]

It may say something about the growing public appetite for details of Shakespeare's life that an arch sceptic like Dr. Johnson should pass this story on without comment.

Jonson and the Merry Meetings.

Shakespeare and Jonson were the two greatest playwrights of their time. Since they must have known each other, it is natural to be curious about the nature of their relationship, but the only reliable clue to that is provided by Jonson's remarks on Shakespeare in the First Folio and *Timber*. The influence of those is not hard to detect in what Thomas Fuller says about Shakespeare in his *History of the Worthies of England* (1662).

> [Shakespeare] was an eminent instance of the truth of that Rule, *Poeta non fit, sed nascitur*, one is not *made*, but *born* a Poet. Indeed his Learning was very little, so that as *Cornish diamonds* are not polished by any Lapidary, but are pointed and smoothed even as they are taken out of the Earth, so *nature* itself was all the *art* which was used upon him.
>
> Many were the *wit combats* betwixt him and *Ben Jonson*, which two I behold

46

like a *Spanish great Galleon* and an *English man of War*; Master *Jonson* (like the former) was built far higher in Learning; *Solid*, but *Slow* in his performances. *Shakespeare*, with the *English-man of war*, lesser in *bulk*, but lighter in *sailing*, could turn with all tides, tack about and take advantage of all winds, by the quickness of his Wit and Invention. He died *Anno Domini 16..*, and was buried at *Stratford* upon *Avon*, the Town of his Nativity.[23]

Just as the account of the deer-poaching called out for the ballad, so Fuller's reference to 'wit combats' created a need for examples yet, by 1662, two of these were already in what was at least private circulation. Sir Nicholas L'Estrange, who died in 1655, left a manuscript collection of 'Merry Passages and Jests' one of which goes as follows (in Elizabethan English 'latten' was a brass-like alloy):

Shakespeare was Godfather to one of Ben Jonson's children, and after the christening being in a deep study, Jonson came to cheer him up, and asked why he was so Melancholy? no faith *Ben* (says he) not I, but I have been considering a great while what should be the fittest gift for me to bestow upon my God-child, and I have resolved at last; I prithee what, says he? I faith *Ben*: I'll e'en give him a dozen good Latin [Latten] Spoons, and thou shall translate them.[24]

An even less sparkling example of Shakespeare's contribution to the wit combats between him and Jonson is to be found in an anonymous manuscript dating from around 1650.

Mr Ben Jonson and Mr William Shakespeare Being Merry at a Tavern, Mr Jonson having begun this for his Epitaph

Here lies Ben Jonson that was once one

he gives it to Mr Shakespeare to make up who presently writes

Who while he lived was a slow things
and now being dead is Nothing.[25]

The problem here is similar to the one novelists have when they tell their readers that a certain character is (for example) a distinguished intellectual and are then committed to demonstrating that fact.

According to the legend merry meetings between Jonson and Shakespeare continued until the latter's death and may have even occasioned it. John Ward became vicar of Stratford in 1662 and recorded in his note books odd items of gossip about Shakespeare shortly after he arrived there. One of these is that,

Shakespeare, Drayton, and Ben Jonson, had a merry meeting and it seems drank too much, for Shakespeare died of a fever there contracted.[26]

Because Drayton was born in Warwickshire and often resident there, and because it is believed that, shortly before his death, Shakespeare was living in retirement and already not well, the location for this final drinking bout is usually taken to be the Stratford area. For all the ones before, however, the preferred meeting place is the Mermaid Tavern in London. When in the novels and plays in which Shakespeare appears as a character, he is depicted as meeting with Jonson, the scene is almost invariably set at the Mermaid. One of the people who helped Shakespeare in his purchase of the Blackfriars gatehouse, amid legal complications which have never been satisfactorily explained, has been identified as the landlord of the Mermaid,[26] and that Jonson went there is clear from a passage in a verse epistle addressed to him around 1613, the author of which is assumed to be Francis Beaumont.

> What things have we seen,
> Done at the Mermaid! heard words that have been
> So nimble, and so full of subtle flame,
> As if that everyone from whence they came
> Had meant to put his whole wit in a jest,
> And had resolved to live a fool, the rest
> Of his dull life; [...] [28]

This establishes that the author of these lines used to meet Jonson at the Mermaid but not, as William Gifford claimed in his introduction to an early nineteenth-century edition of Jonson's *Works*, that 'here, in the full flow and confidence of friendship, the lively and interesting "wit-combats" took place between Shakespeare and our author.'[29]

By the far the most important and detailed contribution to the legend of the relationship between Jonson and Shakespeare was made by Rowe in the first edition of his *Life*.

[Shakespeare's] acquaintance with Ben Jonson began with a remarkable piece of humanity and good nature; Mr Jonson, who was at that time altogether unknown to the world, had offered one of his plays to the players, in order to have it acted; and the persons into whose hands it was put, after having turned it carelessly and superciliously over, were just upon returning it to him with an ill-natured answer, that it would be of no service to their company; when Shakespeare luckily cast his eye upon it, and found something so well in it, as to engage him first to read it through, and afterwards to recommend Mr Jonson and his writings to the public. After this, they were professed friends; though I do not know whether the other ever made him an equal return of gentleness and sincerity. Ben was naturally proud and insolent, and in the days of his reputation did so far take upon him the supremacy in wit, that he could not but look with an evil eye upon any one that seemed to stand in competition with him. And if at times he has affected to commend him, it has always been with some reserve, insinuating his uncorrectness, a careless manner of writing, and want of judgement. The praise of seldom altering or blotting out what he writ, which was given him by the players, who were the first publishers of his works after his death, was what Jonson could not bear; he thought it impossible, perhaps, for another man to strike out the greatest thoughts in the finest expression, and to reach those excellencies of poetry with the ease of a first imagination, which himself with infinite labour and study could but hardly attain to.[30]

It is generally agreed that the play Rowe refers to here must have been *Every Man in His Humour* which was staged by the Lord Chamberlain's Men in 1598 with Shakespeare in one of the roles. The second part of Rowe's account is a reading of Jonson's remarks on Shakespeare in the First Folio and *Timber* which transforms the friendly competition implicit in Fuller's 'wit combats' and the associated anecdotes into frank antagonism. Of Jonson's antagonism to Shakespeare's *works* there is some evidence in his own writing. In a prologue he eventually provided for *Every Man in His Humour*, for example, he refers disparagingly to plays in which 'with three rusty swords, / And help of some few foot-and-half words' actors 'Fight over York, and Lancaster's long wars'; and in the 'Induction' to *Bartholomew Fair* there is a sarcastic reference to people who 'will swear, *Hieronimo*, or *Andronicus* are the best plays'.[31] But the only sign of *personal* disapproval or dislike has been detected in an exchange from *Every Man Out of His Humour* where Sogliardo, who is described as 'an essential clown [...] so enamoured of the name of a gentleman that he will have it though he buys it', has just acquired a coat of arms. His companions in this part of the scene are Carlo Buffone, the play's jester, and Puntarvolo, 'a vainglorious knight'.

SOGLIARDO:	By this parchment, gentlemen, I have been so toiled among the harrots [heralds] yonder, you will not believe. They do speak i' the strangest language and give a man the hardest terms for his money, that ever you knew.
CARLO:	But ha' you arms? Ha' you arms?
SOGLIARDO:	I' faith, I thank them I can write myself gentleman now. Here's my patent. It cost me thirty pounds, by this breath.
PUNTARVOLO:	A very fair coat, well charged and full of armory.
SOGLIARDO:	Nay, it has as much variety of colours in it, as you have seen a coat have. How like you the crest, sir?
PUNTARVOLO:	I understand it not well. What is 't?
SOGLIARDO:	Marry, sir, it is your boar without a head, *rampant*.
PUNTARVOLO:	A boar without a head, that's very rare!
CARLO [*To him, aside*]:	Ay, and rampant too. Troth, I commend the Heralds wit. He hath deciphered him well: a swine without a head, without brain, wit, anything, indeed, ramping to gentility. – You can blason the rest, signor? Can you not?
SOGLIARDO:	O, ay, I have it in writing here of purpose. It cost me two shillings the tricking.
CARLO:	Let's hear! Let's hear! [...]
SOGLIARDO [*reading*]:	'Gyrony of eight pieces, *azure* and *gules*; between three plates, a *chevron* engrailed checky, *or*, *vert*, and *ermines*; on a chief *argent* between two *ann'lets*, sables, a boar's head *proper*'.[...] How like you them, signor?
PUNTARVOLO:	Let the word be, *Not without mustard*. Your crest is very rare, sir.[32]

Mockery of those who aspire to more gentility than they deserve is almost as old as drama itself, as is the complaint that money buys everything. For those who understand these things the further details of Sogliardo's coat of arms were no doubt as absurd as the boar rampant, but attention has chiefly centred on the 'word' or motto Puntarvolo suggests. The primary reference appears to be to a moment in Thomas Nashe's 1592 best-seller *Pierce Penniless* when the 'young heir or cockney that is his mother's darling' vows that, if he is saved from an unpleasant situation at sea, he will never eat dried cod again. Once the danger is over, however, he adds the proviso 'Not without mustard, good Lord, not without mustard'.[33] Although nobody wants to claim that Sogliardo is in any way a portrait of Shakespeare, and everyone agrees that the coat of arms described here bears no relation to the one secured by Shakespeare's father in 1596, it has been felt that 'not without mustard' is also a mocking reference to the motto 'non sans droict' adopted by the Shakespeare family.

Any personal antagonism between Jonson and Shakespeare was firmly denied by Joseph Spence in notes he made of Pope's conversation some time between 1728 and 1730.

> It was and is a general opinion, that Ben Jonson and Shakespeare lived in enmity with each other. Betterton has assured me often that there was nothing in it, and such a supposition was founded only on the two parties, which in their lifetime listed under one, and endeavoured to lessen the character of the other mutually. – Dryden used to think that the verses Jonson made on Shakespeare's death had something of satire at the bottom; for my part, I cannot discover any thing like it in them.[34]

If it is true that Jonson is making fun of Shakespeare's pretensions to gentility in *Every Man Out of His Humour,* then there must be a chance that his uses of the word 'gentle' in the First Folio and in *Timber* are ironic; but Spence cannot have been the first person not to have been able to discover 'any thing like it in them'.

Son of Shakespeare

As Spence suggests, discussion of the drama in the later seventeenth century, and well into the eighteenth, was in part structured around an opposition between Shakespeare and Jonson, and it was often carried on in terms which had been provided by Jonson in his contributions in the First Folio. Ignoring Jonson's insistence on Shakespeare's art, critics and commentators emphasised the difference between a scholarly playwright who wrote laboriously and one who, although he had 'small Latin and less Greek', overflowed with natural talent. This distinction easily became one between the classical and native

8. *'Shakespeare humanised.' Frontispiece for* The Rape of Lucrece, 1655, *engraved by William Faithorne.*

traditions or between the foreign and the home grown. Followers of Jonson were known as his tribe or sons but there was at least one son of Shakespeare.

Although he admired Jonson, Sir William Davenant (1606-68), poet, playwright and theatrical enterpreneur, was an enthusiastic promoter of Shakespeare's work. But as Aubrey explained, in his 'brief life' of Davenant, he would also boast of a family connection.

> Sir William Davenant, knight, Poet Laureate, was born [...] in ... street in the City of Oxford at the Crown Tavern.
>
> His father was John Davenant, a vintner there, a very grave and discreet citizen; his mother was a very beautiful woman, and of a very good wit, and of conversation extremely agreeable. [...]
>
> Mr William Shakespeare was wont to go into Warwickshire once a year, and did commonly in his journey lie at this house in Oxon. where he was exceedingly respected. (I have heard parson Robert [Davenant] say that Mr W. Shakespeare has given him a hundred kisses.) Now Sir William would sometimes, when he was pleasant over a glass of wine with his most intimate friends – e.g. Sam Butler, author of *Hudibras* – etc. – say, that it seemed to him that he writ with the very spirit that did Shakespeare, and seemed contented enough to be thought his Son. He would tell them a story as above, in which way his mother had a very light report.[35]

Aubrey prepared what are known as his *Brief Lives* for the benefit of Anthony Wood who in 1692 published his *Atheniae Oxonieses*, a biographical dictionary of notable figures who had attended Oxford from 1500 up to his own time. His entry on Davenant in that work adopts the notion of Shakespeare staying at the Crown Tavern, adds the detail that Davenant's father admired Shakespeare's plays, but is silent on the paternity issue. Aubrey's notes for Wood were not published until the nineteenth century yet the idea of Davenant being Shakespeare's son was clearly not his alone. In 1709 Thomas Hearne, who worked in the Bodleian library in Oxford, recorded in his dairy:

> 'Twas reported by Tradition in Oxford that Shakespeare as he used to pass from London to Stratford upon Avon, where he lived & now lies buried, always spent some time in the Crown Tavern in Oxford, which was kept by one Davenant who had a handsome Wife, & loved witty Company, though himself a reserved and melancholy Man. He had born to him a Son who was afterwards Christened by the Name of William who proved a very Eminent Poet, and was knighted (by the name of Sir William Davenant) and the said Mr Shakespeare was his God-father & gave him his name. (In all probability he got him.) 'Tis further said that one day going from school a grave Doctor in Divinity met him, and asked him, 'Child whither art thou going in such haste?' to which the child replied, 'O Sir my God-father is come to Town, & I am going to ask his blessing'. To which the Doctor said, 'Hold Child, you must not take the name of God in vain'.[36]

Twenty years later Joseph Spence reported having heard Pope say that 'the notion of Sir William Davenant being more than a poetical child only of

Shakespeare, was common in town; & Sir William himself seemed fond of having it taken for truth'; and around 1742 he noted in his diary a version of the same example of academic wit Hearne had recorded.

> Shakespeare, in his frequent journeys between London and his native place, Stratford-upon-Avon, used to lie at Davenant's, at the Crown in Oxford. He was very well acquainted with Mrs Davenant; and her son, afterwards Sir William, was supposed to be more nearly related to him than as a godson only. One day, when Shakespeare was just arrived, and the boy sent for from school to him, a head of one of the colleges, who was pretty well acquainted with the affairs of the family, met the child running home, and asked him whither he was going in so much haste: the boy said, 'to my god-father Shakespeare'. – 'Fie, child', says the old gentleman, 'why are you so superfluous? Have you not learned yet that you should not use the name of God in vain?'[37]

Spence performs here the same useful job of clarification as does Thomas Wilkes in his re-telling of what we think of as the Manningham anecdote. The clergyman, now the 'head of one of the colleges', can say what he does because he is 'acquainted with the affairs of the family' and his reproach to young William for being 'superfluous' makes sure we do not miss the point of the joke. Contemporaries ought not to have missed it because it had been around for some time – had in fact appeared in a jest book published in 1629 with what were however quite different participants.[38] A common feature of the stories about Shakespeare and Davenant is that no-one seems entirely committed to their truth. Shakespeare did of course remember one godson in his will but his family name was neither Jonson nor Davenant but Walker, 'to my godson William Walker XX shillings in gold'.

Shakespeare and Royalty

There is no record of either Queen Elizabeth or James I visiting public theatres like the Globe but Shakespeare's company often performed for the Court (wherever it happened to be). This means that he must at least have seen both monarchs but it does not tell us whether he ever spoke to them. One story which implies that he did relates to *The Merry Wives of Windsor*. In the final scene of that play Mistress Quickly, in her guise of Queen of the Fairies, says,

> About, about!
> Search Windsor Castle, elves, within and out.
> Strew good luck, oafs, on every sacred room,
> That it may stand till perpetual doom
> In state as wholesome as in state 'tis fit,
> Worthy the owner and the owner it.
> The several chairs of Order look you scour

9. 'Shakespeare before the Court of Elizabeth reciting Macbeth' – a new light on the chronology of his compositions! Engraved in America for The Eclectic by Perine and Giles, NY, artist unknown. By permission of the Folger Shakespeare Library.

With juice of balm and every precious flower;
Each fair instalment, coat and several crest,
With loyal blazon, evermore be blest.
And nightly, meadow-fairies, look you sing,
Like to the Garter compass, in a ring.
Th'expressure that it bears, green let it be,
More fertile-fresh than all the field to see;
And *Honi soit qui mal y pense* write
In em'rald tufts, flowers purple, green and white,
Like sapphire, pearl and rich embroidery,
Buckled below fair knighthood's bending knee:
Fairies use flowers for their charactery.
Away, disperse.[39]

The unmistakable references here to the Order of the Garter suggest that *The Merry Wives* may have been written (or adapted) for the entertainment which accompanied some particular investiture. The trouble is that there is no record of an investiture at Windsor itself which is contemporary with the likely dates of its composition (although there were annual celebrations). The notion of a play especially commissioned not only for, but *by*, Elizabeth was, however, current at the beginning of the eighteenth century. In 1702, for example, John Dennis wrote in his introduction to his *Comical Gallant*, a play which was adapted from *The Merry Wives*:

> That this Comedy was not despicable, I guessed for several Reasons: First, I knew very well, that it had pleased one of the greatest Queens that ever was in the World, great not only for her Wisdom in the Arts of Government, but for her knowledge of Polite Learning, and her nice taste of the Drama, for such a taste we may be sure she had, by the relish which she had of the Ancients. This Comedy was written at her Command, and by her direction, and she was so eager to see it Acted, that she commanded it to be finished in fourteen days: and was afterwards, as Tradition tells us, very well pleased at the Representation.[40]

Seven years later Rowe added more details.

> Besides the advantages of his wit, [Shakespeare] was in himself a good natur'd man, of great sweetness in his manners, and a most agreeable companion; so that it is no wonder if, with so many good qualities, he make himself acquainted with the best conversations of those times. Queen *Elizabeth* had several of his plays acted before her, and without doubt gave him many gracious marks of her favour: it is that maiden princess plainly, whom he intends by
>
> – A fair vestal, throned by the west. (*Midsummer-Night's Dream*)
>
> And that whole passage is a compliment very properly brought in, and very handsomely applied to her. She was so well pleased with that admirable character of Falstaff, in the two parts of *Henry the Fourth*, that she commanded him to continue it for one play more, and to shew him in love. This is said to be the occasion of his writing *The Merry Wives of Windsor*. How well she was obeyed, the play itself is an admirable proof.[41]

Remarks made by Charles Gildon in a volume published a year later do not add anything new to the story but they make the link to the lines in the fifth act of *The Merry Wives of Windsor* with which it may well have begun.

> The *Fairies* in the fifth Act (of *Merry Wives of W.*) makes a Handsome Compliment to the Queen, in her Palace of *Windsor*, who had obliged him to write a Play of *Sir John Falstaff* in Love, and which I am very well assured he performed in a Fortnight; a prodigious Thing, when all is so well contrived, and carried on without the least Confusion.[42]

These are slim pickings, and it was a long time before anything substantial was added to them. In 1825 appeared *Dramatic Table Talk*, a compilation usually assumed to have been put together by a bookseller called Richard Ryan. In the second volume of this work there is a description of an encounter between Shakespeare and Queen Elizabeth not previously recorded in book form (although a version had appeared in the 1790s).

> It is well known that Queen Elizabeth was a great admirer of the immortal Shakespeare, and used frequently (as was the custom of persons of great rank in those days) to appear upon the stage before the audience, or to sit delighted behind the scenes, when the plays of our bard were being performed. One evening, when Shakespeare himself was personating the part of a King, the audience knew of her Majesty being in the house. She crossed the stage when he was performing, and, on receiving the accustomed greeting from the audience, moved politely to the poet, but he did not notice it! When behind the scenes, she caught his eye, and moved again, but still he would not throw off his character, to notice her: this made her Majesty think of some means by which she might know, whether he would depart, or not, from the dignity of his character while on stage. – Accordingly, as he was about to make his exit, she stepped before him, dropped her glove, and re-crossed the stage, which Shakespeare noticing, took up, with these words, immediately after finishing his speech, and so aptly were they delivered, that they seemed to belong to it:
>
> > And though now bent on this high embassy,
> > Yet *stoop* we to take up our *Cousin's* glove!
>
> He then walked off the stage, and presented the glove to the Queen, who was greatly pleased with his behaviour, and complimented him upon the propriety of it.[43]

When later in the nineteenth century biographers, dramatists and novelists want to bring Shakespeare and Elizabeth together, they invariably recall her supposed request to see Falstaff in love but much less often this anecdote of the glove. This may be because its exact point is not crystal clear or its tendency too democratic; but the more likely reason is that, even for those not inclined to scepticism, its improbability is too gross.

The number of stories concerning Shakespeare and Queen Elizabeth is quite out of proportion to the frequency with which the two are shown together in fictional versions of his life. She is by far his preferred companion although there is one way in which her successor might seem a more likely candidate. One of the first things James I did on his accession was to sign the documents which transformed the Lord Chamberlain's into the King's Men. This has led to the belief that he had some special interest in the drama and thus in Shakespeare himself. But although the assumption has always been that Shakespeare wrote *Macbeth* for James, there is no *story* involving him comparable to that of Elizabeth wanting to see Falstaff in love. All there is instead is the claim made in an extract from an anonymous 'Advertisement' to a 1709 edition of Shakespeare's *Poems*.

> I cannot omit inserting a Passage of Mr *Shakespeare's* Life, very much to his Honour, and very remarkable, which was either unknown, or forgotten by the Writer of it.
>
> That most learned Prince, and great Patron of Learning, King *James* the First, was pleased with his own Hand to write an amicable Letter to Mr *Shakespeare*; which Letter, tho now lost, remained long in the Hands of Sir William D'avenant, as a credible Person now living can testify.[44]

The same or a very similar claim is made by Oldys in his marginalia in a copy of Gerard Langbaine's 1691 *Account of the English Dramatic Poets*.

> I have observed in my [copy of] Fuller and repeat it here that K. James I honoured Shakespeare with an Epistolary correspondence and I think Sir W Davenant had either seen or was possessed of his Majesty's Letter to him. I have read it in Print and yet all our late Pretenders to the Exaltation of Shakespeare's Memory are quite silent of this particular. 'Tis very much if Sir William had them that he did not publish them.[45]

Oldys may be right to reproach Davenant for not having published the correspondence, but if the phrase 'I have read it in Print', refers to a letter from the king, it is a pity he omitted to tell us what it said.

Retirement and Death

As I pointed out in the previous chapter, no one knows when, or even if, Shakespeare 'retired', when or if he severed his links with London and settled permanently back in Stratford. The last play for which he was entirely responsible is *The Tempest*, usually assigned to 1611. As a result it became a tradition to take Prospero's abjuration of magic in that play as an implicit retirement speech.

> I have bedimmed
> The noontide sun, call'd forth the mutinous winds,
> And 'twixt the green sea and the azured vault
> Set roaring war: to the dread rattling thunder
> Have I given fire, and rifted Jove's stout oak
> With his own bolt; the strong-based promontory
> Have I made shake, and by the spurs pluck'd up
> The pine and cedar: graves at my command
> Have waked their sleepers, oped and let 'em forth
> By my so potent art. But this rough magic
> I here abjure; and, when I have required
> Some heavenly music (which even now I do)
> To work mine end upon their senses, that
> This airy charm is for, I'll break my staff,
> Bury it certain fadoms in the earth,
> And deeper than did ever plummet sound
> I'll drown my book.[46]

It is now clear that, after *The Tempest*, Shakespeare wrote *Henry VIII* and collaborated with John Fletcher on one or two other plays, but if he did at some point drown his books and throw away his pen there is not only little surviving documentary indication of how he spent his time up until his death in 1616 but also little in the way of myth or anecdote relating to this topic before the nineteenth century.

Apart from the story of the merry meeting with Jonson, which is supposed to have led to Shakespeare's death, the only significant contribution to the story of his last days was made by Richard Davies sometime between 1688 and 1708. Among the same notes which record a version of the deer-stealing episode, and after '[Shakespeare] died April 23 1616 probably at Stratford, for there he is buried, and hath a Monument' in the text he is annotating, Davies wrote: 'on which He lays a Heavy curse upon any one who shall remove his bones. He died a papist.' Reasons for believing this last statement is true are found in certain references in his writing or in his known or presumed association with certain contemporaries whose Catholic affiliations can be clearly established. But the main justification for the belief has been the conviction which many people have had that Shakespeare's father, John, was a fervent Catholic. The fact that in 1592 John Shakespeare was listed as not attending church as the law required is taken by some as proof that he was. His own explanation was that he stayed away from church because he was fearful of being arrested for debt there. This was accepted by those whom the government made responsible for drawing up the lists but has not been accepted by everyone since.

What convinces many that John Shakespeare was a hard-line Catholic is his supposed 'Spiritual Testament'. This is a hand-written document of several stitched-together leaves which was apparently discovered in 1757 among the rafters of the house in Henley Street, Stratford, where John Shakespeare had both lived and plied his trade. By the time these leaves were sent to Edmond Malone in the 1780s the first of them was missing but he published what remained in his 1790 edition of Shakespeare's *Plays and Poems*. His text therefore began at the end of the third of what seemed to have been fourteen numbered paragraphs. The eleven which survived intact all begin 'I John Shakespeare' and are affirmations of Christian belief in its more recognisably Catholic form. In addition to this truncated text, however, Malone also published in an 'Emendations and Corrections' section of his first volume what purported to be the missing first page of the Testament. He took this from a supposed transcript of the complete text in one of John Jordan's notebooks (the square brackets in paragraph 3 contain the words with which the truncated text began).

I

In the name of God, the father, son, and holy ghost, the most holy and blessed Virgin Mary, mother of God, the holy host of archangels, angels, patriarchs, prophets, evangelists, apostles, saints, martyrs, and all the celestial court and company of heaven, I John Shakespeare, an unworthy member of the holy Catholic religion, being at this my present writing in perfect health of body, and sound mind, memory, and understanding, but calling to mind the uncertainty of life and certainty of death, and that I may be possibly cut off in the blossom of my sins, and called to render an account of all my transgressions externally and internally, and that I may be unprepared for the dreadful trial either by sacrament, penance, fasting, or prayer, or any other purgation whatever, do in the holy presence above specified, of my own free and voluntary accord, make and ordain this my last spiritual will, testament, confession, protestation, and confession of faith, hoping hereby to receive pardon for all my sins and offences, and thereby to be made partaker of life everlasting, through the only merits of Jesus Christ my saviour and redeemer, who took upon himself the likeness of man, suffered death, and was crucified upon the cross, for the redemption of sinners.

II

Item, I John Shakespeare do by this present protest, acknowledge, and confess, that in my past life I have been a most abominable and grievous sinner, and therefore unworthy to be forgiven without a true and sincere repentance for the same. But trusting in the manifold mercies of my blessed Saviour and Redeemer, I am encouraged by relying on his sacred word, to hope for salvation and be made partaker of his heavenly kingdom, as a member of the celestial company of angels, saints and martyrs, there to reside for ever and ever in the court of my God.

III

Item, I John Shakespeare do by this present protest and declare, that as I am certain I must pass out of this transitory life into another that will last to eternity, I do hereby most humbly implore and entreat my good and guardian angel to instruct me in this my solemn preparation, protestation, and confession of faith, [at least spiritually, in will adoring and most humbly beseeching my saviour, that he will be pleased to assist me in so dangerous a voyage, to defend me from the snares and deceits of my infernal enemies, and to conduct me to the secure haven of his eternal bliss.][47]

After printing both this text and the truncated one, Malone became uneasy and said that, from documents in his possession, it was clear that the testament 'could not have been the composition of any one of the poet's family'.[48] These documents he never published, and the ones he had reprinted disappeared after he had dealt with them; but in the twentieth century another 'testament' was discovered in which John Shakespeare's name did not appear but whose final eleven paragraphs, and the end of the third, were otherwise more or less identical in form to Malone's truncated document. Since this other testament was complete, its effect was to expose the transcript of the missing first sheet in Jordan's notebook as a fabrication and to show how the first two and a half paragraphs of the truncated document should really have read. The second testament indicates at the beginning that it was written by Cardinal Borromeo, an Archbishop of Milan who died in 1585 and was canonised twenty five years later. Before the numbered paragraphs begin there is 'An Advertisement to the Devout Reader' who is urged to read through the testament often, keep it always near, carry it on journeys but also sign it at the end, 'And he that cannot write, let him make a cross (†) thus, or some such mark'. The devout reader is then instructed to kneel, stand or sit in devout manner 'before some Altar, or Oratory', as he or she recites an opening prayer and there then follows the testament's various items, the first two and a bit of which are not at all as the person responsible for Jordan's text had imagined them.

I

First, I here protest, and declare in the sight, and presence of Almighty God, Father, Son, and holy Ghost, three Persons, and one God; & of the B. V. Mary, and of all the holy Court of Heaven, that I will live and die obedient unto the Catholic, Roman, & Apostolic Church, firmly believing all the twelve Articles of the Faith taught by the holy Apostles, with the interpretation, & declaration made thereon by the same holy church, as taught defined & declared by her. And finally I protest, that I do believe all that, which a good & faithful Christian ought to believe: In which faith I purpose to live and die. And if at any time (which God forbid) I should chance by suggestion of the devil to do, say, or think contrary to this my belief, I do now for that time, in virtue of this present act, revoke, infringe, & annul the same, & will that it be held for neither spoken, or done by me.

II.

Secondly. By this my last Will I protest, that, at my death I will receive the Sacraments of Penance, & Confession; the which if by any accident I should not be able to have, or make, I do in virtue of this present, resolve from this instant, for that time, to make it from my heart, accusing myself of all my sins committed in Thought, Word, & Work, as well against God as against myself and my neighbour, whereof I do repent me with infinite sorrow, & desire time of penance, bitterly to bewail the same, for that I have offended my Sovereign Lord & God, whom I ought to love and serve above all things. The which I now firmly purpose, with his grace, to do as long as I shall live, without ever more offending him.

III

Item. I do protest, that at the end of my life, I will receive the most Blessed Sacrament for my *Viaticum* or last journey, that by means of so divine a Pledge, I may perfectly reconcile & unite myself unto my Lord. The which if through any accident, I should not then be able to perform, I do now for that time, declare, that I will receive it, [at least spiritually in will, adoring & most humbly beseeching my Saviour, that he will be pleased to assist me in so dangerous a voyage & [to] defend me from the snares, & deceits of my infernal Enemies, & to conduct me to the secure Haven of his Eternal Bliss.][49]

There is evidence to show that, in 1580, copies of Borromeo's text were brought into England by a party of Jesuit 'missionaries' led by Edmund Campion, presumably so that they could be distributed to the faithful; and also that several of these missionaries (the brother of a man who may well have taught Shakespeare at Stratford grammar school being one) had strong connections in Warwickshire.[50] It is quite possible therefore that the truncated text Malone reprinted was genuine even if its subsequent disappearance deprives us of the opportunity of investigating how (or perhaps even when) John Shakespeare's name was included in it; and also whether he signed his name at its conclusion or used instead a mark or symbol of his trade, just as he did throughout his career as a member of the Stratford Corporation (it was this use which has led people to believe he was illiterate). To accept the document would mean accepting that, in a least one phase of his life, Shakespeare's father was a sufficiently committed Catholic to risk consorting with priests who were actively pursued as enemies of the State. This would strengthen the conviction many hold that his son was brought up in an intensely Catholic household, but it would not tell us much about how his own religious beliefs subsequently developed and still less about what those beliefs were at the time of his death. Borromeo's testament is certainly authentic; that Shakespeare's father possessed a copy is possible; but that Shakespeare himself 'died a papist', even though he was granted the honour of being buried in the chancel of his local church, is part of the legend.

Notes

1. Robert Parker Sorlien (ed.), *The Diary of John Manningham of the Middle Temple. 1602–1603* (University Press of New England, 1976), p. 75.

2. Thomas Wilkes, *General View of the Stage* (1759), pp. 220-1.

3. S. Schoenbaum, *Shakespeare's Lives*, p. 481.

4. Rowe's life of Shakespeare in J. Boswell (ed.), *The Plays and Poems of William Shakespeare. With a Life of the Poet and an Enlarged History of the Stage. By the late E. Malone* (1821), vol. 1, pt. 1, p. 439.

5. Oldys is assumed to have written a short life of Shakespeare by 1750 but it has disappeared. See Chambers, vol. 2, p. 275.

6. S. Johnson and G. Steevens (eds), *Plays of William Shakespeare* (1778), vol. 1, p. 204.

7. Edward Capell, *Notes and Various Readings to Shakespeare* (1779), vol.1, p. 60.

8. J. O. Halliwell-Phillipps, *Outlines of the Life of Shakespeare*, vol. 2, p. 326.

9. F. J. Furnivall (ed.), *A Letter describing a part of the entertainment unto Queen Elizabeth at the castle of Kenilworth in 1575 by Robert Laneham* (1907), p. 34.

10. Peter Holland (ed.), *Midsummer Night's Dream* (Oxford, 1994), 2. i. 148-54.

11. See Chambers, vol. 2, pp. 252-3.

12. Andrew Clark (ed.), *'Brief Lives' chiefly of Contemporaries, set down by John Aubrey, between the Years 1669-1696* (Oxford, 1898), vol. 2, pp. 225-6.

13. Douglas Hamer, review of Schoenbaum's *Shakespeare's Lives* in the *Review of English Studies*, vol. 85 (1971), p. 484.

14. Giorgio Melchiori (ed.), *Merry Wives of Windsor* (Arden, 2000), 1. i.1-20.

15. Chambers, vol. 2, p. 257.

16. Rowe's life of Shakespeare, p. 438.

17. Notes of William Oldys in S. Johnson and G. Steevens (eds), *Plays of William Shakespeare*, vol. 1B, p. 223. The material after the stanza is the editors'.

18. Capell, *Notes and Various Readings to Shakespeare*, vol. 2, p. 75.

19. Schoenbaum, *Shakespeare's Lives*, p. 72.

20. Edmond Malone (ed.), *Plays and Poems of Shakespeare*, vol. 1, pt. 1, pp. 106-7.

21. The grant of the right of free warren to a landowner prevented members of the public from hunting in a particular area. They could kill game there only if they had started their hunt on common land. Those who hadn't risked a heavy fine but free warrens were likely to be far less severely controlled than deer parks and their more usual inhabitants were rabbits and small game birds.

22. Samuel Johnson, *Works of William Shakespeare* (1765), vol. 1, p. clii.

23. Thomas Fuller, *History of the Worthies of England: Warwickshire* (1662), p. 126.

24. Herford and Simpson (eds), *Works of Ben Jonson*, vol. 1, pp. 186-7.

25. Chambers, vol. 2, p. 246.

26. C. Severn (ed.), *The Diary of John Ward* (1839), p. 183.

27. Shakespeare bought the Blackfriars property in collaboration with three other people even though he appears to have provided all the money. For a complete account see S. Schoenbaum, *William Shakespeare: Records and Images* (1981), pp. 39-48. The notion that the legal complications of the deal were deliberately designed to block Anne Shakespeare's dower right has been taken up recently by Stephen Greenblatt who describes it as the 'only plausible explanation' of the transaction – see *Will in the World* (2004), p. 379. This suggestion was first put forward in support of the belief that Shakespeare left his wife next-to-nothing in his will. Yet a deliberate attempt to block dower right on one, relatively small, part of Shakespeare's estate would strongly imply that she held it for the rest.

28. See William Gifford (ed.), *The Works of Ben Jonson* (1816), p. lxvi.

29. *Ibid.*

30. Rowe's life of Shakespeare, pp. 441-2.

31. See Chambers, vol. 2, pp. 205-6.

32. Hereford and Simpson (eds),*Works of Ben Jonson*, vol. 3, pp. 503-5.

33. *Pierce Penniless*, pp. 25-6.

34. Edmond Malone (ed.), *Observations, Anecdotes and Characters of Books and Men by the Rev. Joseph Spence* (1820), p. 81.

35. *Brief Lives*, vol. 1, p. 204. The last sentence in this passage was crossed out, as was Aubrey's alternative version, 'whereby she was called a whore'.

36. Chambers, vol. 2, pp. 269-70.

37. *Observations, Anecdotes etc. by Joseph Spence*, pp. 82-3.

38. The first person to discover this was J. O. Halliwell-Phillips: 'This was the kind of

representative story, one which could be told of any individual at the pleasure of the narrator, and it is found in the generic form in a collection of tavern pleasantries made by Taylor, the Water Poet, in 1629.' See *Outlines of the Life of Shakespeare*, vol. 1, p. 216.

39. *Merry Wives of Windsor*, 5. v. 55-74.

40. *Epistle* to *The Comical Gallant* (1702).

41. Rowe's life of Shakespeare, p. 440.

42. Chambers, vol. 2, p. 262.

43. *Dramatic Table Talk* (1825), vol. 2, p. 156.

44. Chambers, vol. 2, p. 270.

45. Chambers, vol. 2, p,. 281

46. Virginia Mason Vaughan and Alden T. Vaughan (eds), *The Tempest* (Arden, 1999), 5. i. 41-57.

47. Edmond Malone, *Plays and Poems of William Shakespeare* (1790), vol. 1, pt.2, pp. 330-31.

48. Edmond Malone, *An Inquiry into the Authenticity of Certain Miscellaneous Papers [...] attributed to Shakespeare, Queen Elizabeth, and Henry Earl of Southampton* (1796), pp. 198-9.

49. James G. McManaway, 'John Shakespeare's Spiritual Testament' in *Studies in Shakespeare, Bibliography and Theater* (New York: Shakespeare Association of America, 1969), pp. 297-8.

50. See Schoenbaum, *A Documentary Life*, p.46.

10. *Shakespeare in Westminster Abbey. Peter Scheemaker's statue of 1740,*
designed by William Kent. The words on the scroll were added later.
Photograph by Malcolm Crowthers.

Chapter Three

Shakespeare's Growing Fame

O NCE THE THEATRES HAD reopened after 1660, a strange paradox becomes associated with the process whereby the increasingly regular performance of Shakespeare's plays fuelled an interest in the man, the individual held responsible for works which gave such intense and varied pleasure. On the one hand, that is, while the opportunities for seeing his plays steadily increased there was, on the other, always a strong chance that they would be performed in versions or adaptations that he himself would have barely recognised. Also paradoxical is the way in which playwrights were willing to complain about those who dared to alter Shakespeare's plays while cheerfully doing so themselves. In Dryden's Prologue to *Troilus and Cressida or, Truth Found Too Late*, for example, there is what may be the first fictional representation of Shakespeare (if it is true that a man's ghost can be said to represent him). The lines of the Prologue were spoken by Thomas Betterton, the great Shakespearean actor of his time and the same man who, at the very end of his long life, made the pilgrimage to Stratford in a vain effort to discover facts which would help Rowe in his composition of the first biography.

> See, my lov'd Britons, see your Shakespear rise,
> An awfull ghost confess'd to human eyes!
> Unnam'd, methinks, distinguish'd I had been
> From other shades, by this eternal green,
> About whose wreaths the vulgar Poets strive,
> And with a touch, their wither'd Bays revive.
> Untaught, unpractis'd, in a barbarous Age,
> I found not, but created first the Stage.
> And, if I drain'd no Greek or Latin store,
> 'Twas, that my own abundance gave me more.
> On foreign trade I needed not rely,
> Like fruitfull Britain, rich without supply.
> In this my rough-drawn Play, you shall behold
> Some Master-strokes, so manly and so bold,
> That he, who meant to alter, found 'em such,

He shook; and thought it Sacrilege to touch.
Now, where are the Successours to my name?
What bring they to fill out a Poets fame?
Weak, short-liv'd issues of a feeble Age;
Scarce living to be Christen'd on the Stage!
For Humour farce, for love they rhyme dispense,
That tolls the knell, for their departed sense.
Dulness might thrive in any trade but this:
'Twou'd recommend to some fat Benefice.
Dulness, that in a Playhouse meets disgrace,
Might meet with Reverence, in its proper place.
The fulsome clench† that nauseates the Town
Wou'd from a Judge or Alderman go down!
Such virtue is there in a Robe and gown!
And that insipid stuff which here you hate
Might somewhere else be call'd a grave debate:
Dulness is decent in the Church and State.
But I forget that still 'tis understood
Bad Plays are best decry'd by showing good:
Sit silent then, that my pleas'd Soul may see
A Judging Audience once, and worthy me:
My faithfull Scene from true Records shall tell
How Trojan valour did the Greek excell;
Your great forefathers shall their fame regain,
And Homers angry Ghost repine in vain.[1]

This is only one of many illustrations of the degree to which Jonson, who must have lived to regret ever having pronounced publicly on Shakespeare's competence in Latin and Greek, had set the agenda for talking about his dead friend. A home-grown genius who puts his successors to shame, the resurrected Shakespeare is here being enlisted by Dryden to fight various of his own theatrical and indeed political battles. Yet the implication that Shakespeare's work had not been much altered is quite false. So it is in the epilogue to Charles Gildon's version of *Measure for Measure* (1700) in which the Ghost of Shakespeare again appears to speak these lines:

Enough, your Cruelty Alive I knew;
And must I Dead be Persecuted too?
Injur'd so much of late upon the Stage,
My Ghost can bear no more ; but comes to Rage.
My Plays, by Scriblers, Mangl'd I have seen ;
By lifeless Actors Murder'd on the Scene.
Fat Falstaff here, with Pleasure, I beheld,
Toss off his Bottle, and his Truncheon wield:
Such as I meant him, such the Knight appear'd ;
He Bragg'd like Falstaff, and, like Falstaff, fear'd.

† a pun or play on words

But when, on yonder Stage, the Knave was shewn,
Ev'n by my Self, the Picture scarce was known.
Themselves, and not the Man I drew, they Play'd,
And Five Dull Sots, of One poor Coxcomb, made.
Hell! that on you such Tricks as these shou'd pass,
Or I be made the Burden of an Ass!
Oh! if Macbeth, or Hamlet ever pleas'd,
Or Desdemona e'r your Passions rais'd;
If Brutus, or the Bleeding Caesar e'r
Inspir'd your Pity, or provok'd your Fear,
Let me no more endure such Mighty Wrongs,
By Scriblers Folly, or by Actors Lungs.
So, late may Betterton forsake the Stage,
And long may Barry Live to Charm the Age.
May a New Otway Rise, and Learn to Move
The Men with Terror, and the Fair with Love!
Again, may Congreve, try the Comic Strain;
And Wycherly Revive his Ancient Vein:
Else may your Pleasure prove your greatest Curse;
And those who now Write dully, still Write worse.[2]

Gildon's *Measure for Measure* was performed by Betterton's company at Lincolns Inn Fields where this actor had previously triumphed as Falstaff. Shakespeare is being used in the epilogue to attack the rival company at Drury Lane ('yonder stage') and again those writers who mangle his work. Yet any impression that this is likely to be 'authentic' Shakespeare is counteracted by the play's full title: *Measure for Measure or, Beauty the Best Advocate. Written originally by Mr Shakespear: And now very much Altered; with Additions of several Entertainments of Music.* This after all is a *Measure for Measure* without (among others) Mistress Overdone, Froth, Elbow and the egregious Pompey Bum.

Presenting Shakespeare as a ghost was the preferred method for resurrecting him in the early days of his growing fame and it is one that seems especially appropriate for the stage. It was nonetheless as a ghost that he made what was probably his first appearance in British prose fiction. The *Memoirs of the Shakespear's-Head in Covent Garden: in which are introduced many entertaining adventures, and several remarkable characters* appeared in two volumes in 1755. The authorship of this otherwise anonymous work was attributed to 'the Ghost of Shakespeare' and what that meant was made clear in the introductory chapter.

A scholar of Salamanca having made his escape from some very imminent Danger over the Tops of Houses, broke through the first Sky-light that offered to view, and fell into the Laboratory of a Magician; where, breaking a Phial (on being pressed by an invisible Voice) he set at liberty the famous little Gentleman, known by the Name of the *Devil upon Crutches*: who unveiled to him the most Secret Intrigues and Combinations in that City. These are to be found faithfully set down, by Monsieur Le Sage, in his book entitled *Le Diable Boiteaux*.

I have mentioned this, because, the strange Accident which occasioned the Relations I am about to make, was something similar.

I had supped merrily, with a few select Friends, in the Tavern, known by the name of *the Shakespear's Head*, when, it growing late, my Companions departed to their several Mansions, while, for my part, I chose to remain till I had emptied my last Pipe, and drawn to the Dregs, the remains of a Bottle of *Harry Delamain's* Burgundy.

> *And now the Bat had ta'en his cloister'd flight,*
> *And to black Hecate's summons the shard-born Beetle*
> *With its drowsy Hum, had rung Night's yawning Peal.*

I nodded over my Flask; nor did I feel interruption from the Noise made in the next Room, by *Poll French, Tom Squander*, and some other Bucks and Lasses of equal Spirit: Neither was I disturbed, by the hoarse Watchman's bellowing, past one; nor the musical Voice and Art of the fair Tyrolese, who, in the Yard, *play'd over such Strains as had a dying Sound. Morpheus* had laid his Leaden Mace upon me, and closed my Eyes from care and mortal Coil.

When a hollow, but yet pleasing Voice, sounding in my Ear, at once dispelled my Slumber, and awak'd me; I rous'd, and, looking round, beheld at my Elbow, a Figure in every Part resembling that we see drawn for *Shakespear*: There ran a sacred Tremor thro' my Limbs, I rose confus'd, and bowing, own'd the Presence of the laurel'd Shade; and then address'd him, in his own Words, as *Hamlet* does his Father, 'What would thy gracious Figure?'

I would have proceeded, but he interrupted me, and thus began.

To you have I chosen to reveal my present Griefs (for tho' a Spirit I have my Griefs; which may be something abated in this Confidence) for I know you love *me*, and my Memory; besides, Nature has endowed you with a Curiosity that will lead you to listen with Patience to my Detail.

You have been informed by those who have written my Life, that in my Years of Nonage and of Folly, I was oblig'd to fly to *London*, for trespassing in a Park, not far from where I lived; and it has been lately revealed to the World, that my Distresses in *London*, consequential to my Elopement, reduc'd me to the Necessity of holding the Horses of Persons of Quality, who rode to the Play, as was then the Custom; from which Occupation my Diligence rais'd me to the Theatre; of which I have since been styled the Father.

Yet, credit me, my Friend, in this low Scene of Life, which you may be sure press'd hard upon a Fancy so luxuriant; an Imagination so warm as mine: I felt not half the heart-corroding Cares, that have gnaw'd my Soul, since fix'd the Guardian of this *Bacchanalian Temple*, a post allotted to punish me for the Errors of my youthful Conduct. Twenty Years have I here presided; nor will my Probation be completed in twenty more; however at the End of every twenty Years I am allowed a Conference with some one Person. 'Tis your Lot to be the first. Then listen attentively, until I recount such Things, as when revealed, will make my Spirits light as Air; until a train of newer scenes arise again to weigh me down.

List! be attentive! interrupt me not! except a very necessary Question offers, while I unfold to you many strange Secrets, which will surprise the World. While I strip off their gaudy Plumage, who impose with the false Lustre of a splendid Outside on the Credulity of Mankind: Observe those whom I shall show you in their native Characters; mark them as they pass; and you will find the sanctified Clergyman, an arch Hypocrite; the bluff Captain, a kick'd coward; the noble Count, a Swiss Peasant; the assuming Doctor, an ignorant Quack; and the modest Matron, a most luscious Harlot; some Harlots Women of Virtue, tho' not of Chastity; and the Woman of Chastity the most despicable Character; you will find the Gamester often a fair Dealer, and the apparently fair dealer an arrant Cheat; the Lord a Sharper; the Gentleman a Mountebank; and a Player a Gentleman; an honest Man with a bad Character; and the Villain with the Title of a Man of Honour: These, as they have passed before me, in a regular succession, for two hundred and fifty Moons past, will I raise to your View, as they appear'd to me.

'But pray', says I, 'much honour'd Shade, won't some of these heroic Folks, be for kicking me out of their Company, when they discover my Intrusion? As for you, you need not fear their Anger, or their Malice; you have your old Cloak of Air, to wrap yourself up in, which will keep you warm and safe. But consider, Sir, I have a handsome Nose, my Limbs are none of the worst, and it would be of no earthly Advantage to me to have these broke, or that flatten'd to my Face; and then, Sir, I have a mortal Aversion to *Cyclops*, I am so fond of my Eyes.'
'Hold, Sir', he cry'd,

why this unnecessary Interruption? Depend on me, and all your Fears are groundless. Take this Wand, be silent, follow me, and observe; with this thou shalt become invisible to mortal Sight; but let not a single Circumstance thou see'st, a Word, I say, escape the Volume of thy Brain. Register it safely; that when we part thou may'st set it forth, and publish it to the wide extended World for Man's Improvement.

The Improvement of Man is indeed a hackney'd Theme; 'tis a Trumpet which every Adventurer in literature now claps to his Mouth, to deceive the unwary, and make Money at their Expense; but alas! how very few are there who keep up to the letter of their Proclamation; how often do we find the supposed Advocate for Virtue the real Champion of Vice; the Treatise of Morality, a Defence of Libertinism; the Essay on Religion, a Recommendation of Atheism; and Honour and Honesty specious Names for Villainy and Deceit.

It is generally allow'd, that no Man ever understood the Vestiges of the human Heart better than myself; yet I confess to you, since I have been by cruel Fate destined to be the Genius of this House, I have been Witness to Scenes of which I had not the least Notion of; you shall share them with me, and do you apply them as I before ordain'd.'[3]

Shakespeare is here being used as a device for introducing and then organising a series of episodes in the picaresque mode. Dryden and Gildon exploit his authority as the 'Father' of the English stage but here the emphasis falls rather on the fact that 'no man ever understood the vestiges of the human heart' as Shakespeare did. How can the stories which follow not be psychologically acute, or the moral censure which often accompanies the action or the characters justified, when they both emanate from such a source? It is one of the functions of an icon to be exploited in this way but, much like Dryden and Gildon, the author of the *Memoirs of the Shakespear's-Head* makes little effort to characterise his narrator who therefore provides only minimal cover. The tales of deer-poaching and horse-holding are present, and there is a vague reference to the errors of Shakespeare's youthful conduct, but otherwise this ghost is like theirs in being true to his nature and all too easy, therefore, to see right through.

One sign of the growing enthusiasm for Shakespeare in the first half of the eighteenth century was the formation in late 1736 of the Shakespeare Ladies' Club. This was a pressure group of largely aristocratic composition (the Earl of Shaftesbury's wife was a prime mover) dedicated to promoting performances of Shakespeare at a time when it was felt by many that the British theatre was being flooded with pantomime and Italian opera.[4] In his epilogue to *Marina* (1738), which at its name suggests was an adaptation of *Pericles*, George Lillo pays tribute to its members' efforts.

> When to a future race the present days
> Shall be the theme of censure or of praise,
> When they shall blame what's wrong, what's right allow,
> Just as you treat your own fore-fathers now,
> I'm thinking what a figure you will make,
> No light concern, Sirs, where your fame's at stake.
> I hope we need not urge your country's cause,
> You'll guard her glory, and assert her laws,
> Nor force your ruin'd race, mad with their pains,
> To curse you as the authors of their chains.
> We dare not think, we wou'd not fear, you will;
> For Britons though provok'd, are Britons still.
> Yet let not this kind caution give offence:
> The surest friend to liberty is sense.
> How that declines the drooping arts declare;
> Are your diversions what your fathers were?
> At masquerades, your wisdom to display,
> You make the stupid farce for which you pay.
> Musick it self may be too dearly bought,
> Nor was it sure design'd to banish thought.
> But, Sirs, what e'er's your fate in future story,
> Well have the British Fair secured their glory.
> When worse than barbarism had sunk your taste,
> When nothing pleas'd but what laid virtue waste,
> A sacred band, determin'd, wise, and good,
> They jointly rose to stop th' exotick flood,
> And strove to wake, by Shakespear's nervous lays,
> The manly genius of Eliza's days.[5]

This is further exemplification of a tendency which Jonson could be said to have initiated in that here the 'British Fair', or the Shakespeare ladies, are congratulated for having promoted their dramatist as a manly bulwark against foreign innovation. His work is by this time regarded as so fundamentally British that to appreciate it has become a patriotic gesture.

The Shakespeare Ladies' Club deserves a mention here because it is likely to have contributed to a movement which began around this time to have a statue of Shakespeare in Westminster Abbey. Chaucer, Spenser and Jonson were all buried there already but Shakespeare's grave and monument were back in Stratford's Holy Trinity church. It was increasingly felt that the man now clearly regarded as the greatest of British dramatists ought to be represented in the country's leading mausoleum. A bust of Shakespeare had occupied one of the niches of Lord Cobham's 'Temple of British Worthies' in his country house at Stowe since 1735. This had been designed by William Kent and sculpted by Peter Scheemakers and the same two individuals were responsible for the statue which was unveiled in Westminster Abbey in 1741 and which had him leaning elegantly against a plinth. Growing curiosity about the man Shakespeare had naturally been accompanied by an anxiety to know what he looked like, or rather to have an image for the mind's eye which could correspond in some way to the impression of his abilities fostered by the plays. In this last respect admirers in the early years were not especially well served by the two portraits in circulation now most generally regarded as authentic: the engraving in the First Folio by Martin Droeshout (who may well have been only fifteen at the time of his subject's death) and the memorial bust in Holy Trinity church. As I noted in chapter 1, the argument usually deployed in favour of the authenticity of these two images is that both were commissioned by people who knew what Shakespeare had looked like; yet anyone who struggles to recognise the same person in the bust and the engraving might well wonder whether a 'good likeness' was always the chief criterion for judging Renaissance portraits but also what opportunities those who ordered an engraving or (more particularly) a bust might have for *sending it back*. Certainly Heminge and Condell ought to have sent the Droeshout engraving back since it has numerous technical flaws – as Schoenbaum notes, its subject's large head is so anatomically divorced from the puny shoulders by a wired collar that it looks as though it were being served up on a platter like the head of John the Baptist.[6] The incompetence of the engraving would make it comforting to believe that the first two lines of the Jonson poem which appears opposite –

> *This Figure, that thou here seest put,*
> *It was for gentle Shakespeare cut,* [...][7]–

were meant to convey amazed incredulity; but that seems unlikely. Although its own claims to authenticity were non-existent, the Scheemakers statue of 1741 provided a welcome alternative to the engraving and the bust, and proved so popular that it eventually became one of Shakespeare's quasi-official images.

An indication of that is that it appeared until comparatively recently on the £20 banknote.

1741 is an important date in the history of Shakespeare's growing reputation since it was in October of that year that the young David Garrick created a sensation as Richard III. For more than thirty years Garrick's performances in the major Shakespearean roles would help to confirm the public's sense of Shakespeare's pre-eminence. In the summer following this first triumph, or a little later, it is thought that Garrick visited Stratford in the company of other actors. This information was conveyed to Edmond Malone by one of the actors concerned, Charles Macklin, who in 1741 had enjoyed a triumph similar to Garrick's, but in the role of Shylock. If he was remembering correctly, then the party is likely to have been entertained by Sir Hugh Clopton, the then owner of a New Place much transformed since Shakespeare had lived there. Clopton would have shown them the mulberry tree in the garden which, according to local tradition, had been planted by Shakespeare himself. Clopton died in 1751 and New Place was eventually bought by the Reverend Thomas Gastrell who lived for most of the year in Lichfield. He is reputed to have become so impatient with people wanting to see Shakespeare's mulberry tree that he had it cut down. The wood was sold to a local craftsman, Thomas Sharp, who by beginning to make small mementoes out of it became (in Christian Deelman's words) 'the patron saint' of the literary relics industry.[8] Very soon the numbers of mulberry caskets, tobacco stoppers, or toothpick cases in circulation bore the same kind of relation to the wood Sharp had acquired as fragments of the true cross do to their putative source. Buying the wood was for Sharp a shrewd investment but it was one that Gastrell was either too rich or too principled to resent. Three years after having had the mulberry tree felled, he became so incensed at being asked to pay local taxes for which, as no more than an occasional resident, he felt he was not liable, that he had the whole of New Place pulled down and left Stratford for good. The way this episode is usually recorded makes it seem like an act of remarkable pique from someone in a position to indulge himself, but it may just be that Gastrell foresaw the way the Shakespeare industry would develop and made an unavailing, self-denying effort to halt it in its tracks. Nowadays visitors to Stratford have a choice between queuing outside the much restored house in Henley Street where Shakespeare grew up, and then paying a hefty sum to visit it, or idling away their time in the exceptionally pleasant public garden (admission free) which now occupies the site on which New Place once stood.

Stratford must have received a steady trickle of pilgrims in the years following the visit of Garrick and Macklin but it was not until 1769 that it began to develop as the mecca we know today. By that time Garrick had not only established himself as the greatest Shakespearean actor of his generation but built in the grounds of his country mansion at Hampton a temple dedicated to his idol. There he housed a fine statue of Shakespeare by Louis-François Roubillac and kept a chair designed by Hogarth but made from six blocks of mulberry wood he had bought in Stratford. Nearby flourished a mulberry tree grown from a cutting also acquired there. It was to Garrick therefore that the members of the Stratford Corporation very naturally turned when they were in a middle of building a new Town Hall and felt they needed a statue of Shakespeare for a niche in the outside wall as well as a portrait of him for its assembly room. They hoped Garrick would save them money by providing one or both and offered in return the freedom of their town. They proposed to enclose the document granting that freedom in an expensively crafted casket (made of course from Sharp's mulberry stock) and suggested that a portrait of Garrick himself might also adorn their assembly room.

In response Garrick had a casting made of the Scheemakers statue – not the one in Westminster Abbey but an improved model which the sculptor had provided for Lord Pembroke. He also commissioned from Benjamin Wilson a portrait of Shakespeare sitting in a study surrounded by books. But the cost of these two items was not much more and perhaps even less than the Gainsborough painting of himself for which he managed to make the Corporation pay. This now only exists in a copy (see p. 77) but it could be seen as offering a mildly satiric commentary on the fact that Garrick not only idolised Shakespeare but also identified with him. In the painting, the arm which he elegantly drapes round the bust of his idol seems appropriating while the glance which Shakespeare directs at the viewer appears distinctly ironic.

In May 1769 two members of Stratford Corporation came up to London to order to present Garrick with the casket which made him the first Freeman of their town. It was then that he confirmed that he would be in Stratford in September for the official opening of the Town Hall and the installation of the statue he was providing. What he proposed was to make these two events the pretext for a great celebration or jubilee in honour of Shakespeare. Since he promised to take care of most of the organisation of this Jubilee himself, the Corporation was only too happy to acquiesce in the idea that he would be its official 'Steward'.

The 1769 Stratford Jubilee excited great national and indeed international interest. It both profited from and enormously increased curiosity about the circumstances of Shakespeare's life. A correspondent in the *Gentleman's Magazine* for July of that year offers a minor indication of this interest while at the same time providing an illustration of the house in Henley Street where it is likely (although not absolutely certain) Shakespeare was born. The drawing shows the house strangely detached from its surroundings but seems otherwise reasonably accurate. With New Place already pulled down, beggars could in any case hardly be choosers.

11. *The first known illustration of the house in Henley St, Stratford-upon-Avon, in which Shakespeare was believed to have been born, from* The Gentleman's Magazine, *July 1769.*

Mr Urban, Litchfield, July 8, 1769.

There is a certain degree of pleasure, better felt than described, excited in the mind, upon visiting the birth and burial places of deceased worthies; and especially of those who have been remarkable in their time for genius or erudition. I speak this from my own feelings, having always experienced greater delight in Westminster Abby, in the purlieus of the poet's corner, than in Henry VIIth's chapel, amongst the *Reges atque Tetrarchas*. Our proximity to the remains of renowned authors raises ideas in us which the imagination loves to feed upon. Perhaps we assimulate [assimilate] the impressions and improvements we have received from their writings; and, at the same time contrasting our own existence with their departed state, feel a comparative kind of pleasure. Hence it is that a cenotaph does not give us so much delight, as the real [burial place]. Who is not better pleased to read at Stratford upon Avon, *Good Friend for Jesus Sake, &c.* than *Amor publicus posuit?* in Westminster Abby? Similar to this, is perhaps the pleasure of visiting the places of nativity of extraordinary personages deceased; and not only so, but birth places have been supposed to confer a provincial honour. Seven cities contended for the birth of Homer; and Oxfordshire and Middx still claim the credit of giving birth to Chaucer.

The most learned bishop Hacket (as we are told by Dr Plott) purposely undertook a journey to the village of Stanton, in the Moorlands of Staffordshire, to view the birth place of archbishop Sheldon; and in the room where he was born, left some pretty iambicks.

I do not know whether the apartment where the incomparable Shakespeare first drew his breath, can, at this day, be ascertained, or not; but the house of his nativity (according to undoubted tradition) is now remaining. My worthy friend Mr Greene, of this place, hath favoured me with an exact drawing of it (here inclosed) which may not possibly be an unacceptable present to such of your readers as intend to honour Stratford with their company at the approaching jubilee; and, on this account you will, peradventure, afford it a place in your next magazine.

Yours, & c. T. B.[9]

This has a characteristic eighteenth century flavour, not only in the deployment of Latin tags and the use of a Greek word for what appears above in square brackets as 'burial place', but also in the way 'T. B. ' seems caught between the pleasure literary pilgrimage brings and residual intellectual anxieties about its common sense. When the Jubilee he mentions began, the task he shirks of designating the exact room where the incomparable Shakespeare first drew breath was freely undertaken by Garrick.

From its inception the Jubilee had its critics. The great Shakespearean scholars of the day shunned it and many other people were critical because they felt that it would involve more celebration of its Steward than Shakespeare himself. Yet Garrick was sufficiently admired and sufficiently well-connected to persuade large numbers of that section of fashionable London society interested in the arts to go up to Stratford in early September armed with their tickets for the various events he had organised. Over a three-day period these included the performance of a new oratorio, a fancy-dress ball, and fireworks, although nothing by Shakespeare himself. As if to compensate for this lack, Garrick had mobilised his resources back at Drury Lane and prepared a great procession of numerous characters from Shakespeare's plays. This was to wind its way through the streets of Stratford and thereby entertain that large majority of the town's inhabitants which could not afford tickets for the special events. It was due to end up at 'The Rotunda', a huge but temporary wooden structure which had been specially erected for the occasion on the banks of the Avon. There Garrick would recite the ode he had composed as the chief part of the ceremony in which he would present his Shakespeare statue to the town. Unfortunately it rained so hard that the procession had to be cancelled but the recitation went ahead nonetheless. The ode, too long and too dull to cite in full, very clearly demonstrates how firmly Shakespeare was established by 1769 as the leading figure in the British literary pantheon ('edifice' and 'pile' are references to the new Town Hall).

> To what blest genius of the isle,
> Shall Gratitude her tribute pay,
> Decree the festive day,
> Erect the statue, and devote the pile?
> Do not your sympathetic hearts accord,
> To own the 'Bosom's Lord?'
> 'Tis he! 'tis he! – that demi-god!
> Who Avon's flow'ry margin trod,
> While sportive Fancy round him flew,
> Where Nature led him by the hand,
> Instructed him in all she knew,
> And gave him absolute command!
> 'Tis he! 'tis he!
> 'the god of our idolatry!'
> To him the song, the edifice we raise,
> He merits all our wonder, all our praise!
> Yet ere impatient joy break forth,
> In sounds that lift the soul from earth;
> And to our spell-bound minds impart
> Some faint idea of his magic art;
> Let awful silence still the air!
> From the dark cloud, the hidden light
> Bursts tenfold bright!
> Prepare! prepare! prepare!
> Now swell the choral song,
> Roll the full tide of harmony along;
> Let rapture sweep the trembling strings,
> And Fame expanding all her wings,
> With all her trumpet-tongues proclaim,
> The lov'd, rever'd, immortal name!
> Shakespeare! Shakespeare! Shakespeare!
> Let th' inchanting sound,

12. *Portrait of Garrick by Sir Thomas Gainsborough, reproduced in a print by Valentine Green in 1769. The original painting was destroyed in a fire in the Town Hall, Stratford-upon-Avon, in 1946.*

77

From Avon's shores rebound;
Thro' the air,
Let it bear,
The precious freight the envious nations round!

Chorus
Swell the choral song,
Roll the tide of harmony along,
Let rapture sweep the strings,
Fame expand her wings,
With her trumpet-tongues proclaim
The lov'd, rever'd, immortal name!
Shakespeare! Shakespeare! Shakespeare!

Air
I.
Sweetest bard that ever sung,
Nature's glory, Fancy's child;
Never sure did witching tongue,
Warble forth such wood-notes wild.

II.
Come each muse, and sister grace,
Loves and pleasures hither come;
Well you know this happy place,
Avon's banks were once your home.

III.
Bring the laurel, bring the flow'rs,
Songs of triumph to him raise;
He united all your pow'rs,
All uniting, sing his praise!
Tho' Philip's fam'd unconquer'd son,
Had ev'ry blood-stain'd laurel won;
He sigh'd – that his creative word,
(Like that which rules the skies,)
Could not bid other nations rise,
To glut his yet unsated sword:
But when our Shakespeare's matchless pen,
Like Alexander's sword, had done with men;
He heav'd no sigh, he made no moan,
Not limited to human kind,
He fir'd his wonder-teeming mind,
Rais'd other worlds, and beings of his own!

Air
When nature, smiling, hail'd his birth,
To him unbounded pow'r was given;
The whirlwind's wing to sweep the sky,
'The frenzy-rolling eye,

78

To glance from heav'n to earth,
From earth to heav'n!'
O from his muse of fire
Could but one spark be caught,
Then might these humble strains aspire,
To tell the wonders he has wrought.
To tell, – how sitting on his magic throne,
Unaided and alone,
In dreadful state,
The subject passions round him wait;
Who tho' unchain'd, and raging there,
He checks, inflames, or turns their mad career;
With that superior skill,
Which winds the fiery steed at will,
He gives the awful word –
And they all foaming, trembling, own him for their lord.
With these his slaves he can controul,
Or charm the soul;
So realiz'd are all his golden dreams,
Of terror, pity, love, and grief,
Tho' conscious that the vision only seems,
The woe-struck mind finds no relief:
Ingratitude would drop the tear,
Cold-blooded age take fire,
To see the thankless children of old Lear,
Spurn at their king, and sire!
With his our reason too grows wild!
What nature had disjoin'd,
The poet's pow'r combin'd,
Madness and age, ingratitude and child.
Ye guilty, lawless tribe,
Escap'd from punishment, by art or bribe,
At Shakespeare's bar appear!
No bribing, shuffling there –
His genius, like a rushing flood,
Cannot be withstood;
Out bursts the penitential tear!
The look appall'd, the crime reveals,
The marble-hearted monster feels,
Whose hand is stain'd with blood.

Semi-Chorus
When law is weak, and justice fails,
The poet holds the sword and scales.

Air
Though crimes from death and torture fly,
The swifter muse,
Their flight pursues,
Guilty mortals more than die!

They live indeed, but live to feel
The scourge and wheel,
'On the torture of the mind they lie:'
Should harrass'd nature sink to rest,
The poet wakes the scorpion in the breast,
Guilty mortals more than die!
When our magician, more inspir'd,
By charms, and spells, and incantations fir'd,
Exerts his most tremendous pow'r;
The thunder growls, the heavens low'r,
And to his darken'd throne repair,
The demons of the deep, and spirits of the air!
But soon these horrors pass away,
Thro' storms and night breaks forth the day:
He smiles, – they vanish into air!
The buskin'd warriors disappear!
Mute the trumpets, mute the drums,
The scene is chang'd – Thalia comes,
Leading the nymph Euphrosyne,
Goddess of joy and liberty!
She and her sisters, hand in hand,
Link'd to a num'rous frolick band,
With roses and with myrtle crown'd,
O'er the green velvet lightly bound,
Circling the monarch of th' inchanted land!

Air
I.
Wild, frantic with pleasure,
They trip it in measure,
To bring him their treasure,
The treasure of joy.

II.
How gay is the measure,
How sweet is the pleasure,
How great is the treasure,
The treasure of joy.

III.
Like roses fresh blowing,
Their dimpled cheeks glowing,
His mind is o'erflowing;
A treasure of joy!

IV.
His rapture perceiving,
They smile while they're giving,
He smiles at receiving,
A treasure of joy.

13. Mr Garrick reciting his Ode in Honour of Shakespeare at the Jubilee at Stratford. *Painting by Robert Edge Pine, 1784. The medallion Garrick is wearing was the badge of his office as official steward of the Jubilee and made from mulberry wood. By Courtesy of the Shakespeare Birthplace Trust Records Office*

With kindling cheeks, and sparkling eyes,
Surrounded thus, the bard in transport dies;
The little loves, like bees,
Clust'ring and climbing up his knees,
His brows with roses bind;
While Fancy, Wit, and Humour spread
Their wings, and hover round his head,
Impregnating his mind.
Which teeming soon, as soon brought forth,
Not a tiny spurious birth,
But out a mountain came,
A mountain of delight!
Laughter roar'd out to see the sight,
And Falstaff was his name!
With sword and shield he, puffing, strides;
The joyous revel rout
Receive him with a shout,
And modest nature holds her sides:
No single pow'r the deed had done,
But great and small,
Wit, Fancy, Humour, Whim, and Jest,
The huge, mishapen heap impress'd ;
And lo – Sir John!
A compound of 'em all,
A comic world in one. [...]

And so on in the same vein for several verses more until:

Duet
Shall the hero laurels gain,
For ravag'd fields, and thousands slain?
And shall his brows no laurels bind,
Who charms to virtue human kind?

Chorus
We will – his brows with laurel bind,
Who charms to virtue human kind:
Raise the pile, the statue raise,
Sing immortal Shakespeare's praise!
The song will cease, the stone decay,
But his name,
And undiminish'd fame,
Shall never, never pass away.[10]

It is astounding to think that visitors to the 1769 Jubilee sat patiently through all this; but even more so to learn from the admirable Christian Deelman and others that Garrick's recitation of his ode was the one unqualified success during the three days of celebration. Perhaps much of the explanation lies in the musical accompaniments and interludes which he had asked Thomas Arne to write. A novelty of Garrick's approach is the comparison between Shakespeare and Alexander the Great but otherwise the terms he employs were, or at least would become, very familiar. For the second edition of Shakespeare's works in 1632 (the 'Second Folio') Milton had written a short poem in praise of Shakespeare. This played on Jonson's conceit in his commendatory poem that someone who had written as well as Shakespeare did not need a tomb to prompt people's memory of him; but far more influential were Milton's lines in 'L'Allegro' (written around the same time): 'If Jonson's learned sock be on, / Or sweetest Shakespeare's fancy's child, / Warble his native wood-notes wild, [...].' Garrick takes up Milton's idea of Shakespeare as a child of Nature as well as making considerable play (in the verses I have omitted) with Jonson's 'Sweet swan of Avon'. Despite the tributes paid to the deployment of passion in the plays, he stresses the Bard's essentially 'gentle' nature, but the most striking feature of Garrick's ode is its ecstatic tone. Shakespeare is by this stage both (in an adaptation of lines from *Romeo and Juliet*) the god of the nation's idolatry and a 'demi-god' although the context in which this last term is used suggests an inclination to dispense with half measures.

Garrick's ode may have gone down well, but not much else did. Stratford was badly equipped for a sudden invasion of visitors who liked their comfort and there were complaints about inflated prices. The rain which led to the cancellation of the procession did not do much for the fireworks either and, since the Rotunda had been erected by the river, some of those returning from the fancy dress ball on the final evening found themselves knee-deep in water. For one complicated reason after another Garrick ended up £2,000 out of pocket once the Jubilee was over, but he recouped by incorporating a version of the procession which had been cancelled into an entertainment he staged at Drury Lane. Called simply *The Jubilee* this uses as its framework the experiences of an Irish visitor to Stratford who is first seen emerging from a coach where he has had to spend the night because no other accommodation was available. As he explains, 'I was forced to take lodgings in the first floor of a postchaise at half a crown a head. And here they have crammed a bedfellow with me into the bargain'.[11]

In addition to the procession of characters from Shakespeare's plays, Garrick incorporated into *The Jubilee* a number of songs which had been especially written for the celebrations at Stratford. Many of these had a ballad form with choruses which allowed the audience to join in. Typical was one about the famous Mulberry Tree which might have been - though it wasn't - specially commissioned by Thomas Sharp.

> Behold this fair goblet, 'twas carved from the tree
> Which, O my sweet Shakespear, was planted by thee.
> As a relic I kiss it and bow at the shrine,
> What comes from thy hand must be ever divine!

All shall yield to the Mulberry Tree,
Bend to thee,
Blest Mulberry,
Matchless was he
Who planted thee,
And thou like him immortal be!

The fame of the patron gives fame to the tree,
From him and his merits this takes its degree.
Let Phoebus and Bacchus their glories resign,
Our tree shall surpass both the Laurel and Vine.

All shall yield to the Mulberry Tree, etc.

Ye trees of the forest, so rampant and high,
Who spread round their branches, whose heads sweep
the sky,
Ye curious exotics, whom taste has brought here,
To root out the natives at prices so dear.

All shall yield to the Mulberry Tree, etc.

The oak is held royal, is Britain's great boast
Preserved once our king and will always our coast,
But of fir we make ships, we have thousands that fight;
But where is there one like our Shakespeare can write.

All shall yield to the Mulberry Tree, etc.

Let Venus delight in her gay myrtle bowers,
Pomona in fruit trees and Flora in flowers;
The Garden of Shakespeare all fancies will suit,
With the sweetest of flowers and fairest of fruit.

All shall yield to the Mulberry Tree, etc.

With learning and knowledge the well-lettered birch
Supplies Law and Physic and grace for the Church.
But Law and the Gospel in Shakespeare we find,
And he gives the best physic for body and mind.

All shall yield to the Mulberry Tree, etc. [...]

The genius of Shakespear outshines the bright day,
More rapture than wine to the heart can convey.
So the tree which he planted, by making his own,
Has Laurel, and Bays and the Vine all in one.
All shall yield to the Mulberry Tree, etc.

Then each take a relic of this hallowed tree,
From folly and fashion a charm let it be.

Fill, fill to the planter, the Cup to the brim,
To honor your country do honor to him.

All shall yield to the Mulberry Tree,
Bend to thee,
Blest Mulberry,
Matchless was he
Who planted thee,
And thou like him immortal be![12]

One might easily conclude from this that Garrick and his associates were credulous folk with no more scepticism about relics than a benighted medieval peasant in the darkest regions of Europe. That this was not the case is shown by a brief passage of comic business in *The Jubilee*. What one can only conclude from it is that Garrick and the people like him knew that the memorabilia they acquired might well be spurious, but that they liked to acquire them all the same.

Enter FELLOW *with a box of wooden ware, etc.*

FELLOW: Toothpick cases, needle cases, punch ladles, tobacco stoppers, inkstands, nutmeg graters, and all sorts of boxes made out of the famous Mulberry Tree.

FIRST GENTLEMAN: Here you, Mulberry Tree. Let me have some of the true dandy to carry back to my wife and relations in Ireland. (*Looks at the ware.*)

Enter SECOND MAN *with ware.*

SECOND MAN: Don't buy of that fellow, your honor, he never had an inch of the Mulberry Tree in his life. His goods are made out of old chairs and stools and colored to cheat gentlefolks with. It was I, your honor, bought all the true Mulberry Tree. Here's my affidavit of it.

FIRST MAN: Yes, you villain, but you sold it all two years ago, and you have purchased since more mulberry trees than would serve to hang your whole generation upon. He has got a little money, your honor, and so nobody must turn a penny or cheat gentlefolks but himself. I wonder you an't ashamed, Robin. Do, your honor, take this punch ladle.

IRISHMAN: I'll tell you what, you mulberry scoundrels you. If you don't clear the yard of yourselves this minute and let me see you out of my sight, you thieves of the world, my oak plant shall be about your trinkets and make the mulberry juice run down your rogue-pates. Get away, you spalpeens you. (*Beats 'em off.*)[13]

The songs first performed at the Jubilee, and then later incorporated into Garrick's entertainment, were published in a volume entitled *Shakespeare's Garland*. Several of them were like the following in becoming very popular.

Ye Warwickshire lads, and ye lasses,
See what at our Julibee passes,
Come revel away, rejoice and be glad,

85

For the lad of all lads was a Warwickshire lad,
Warwickshire lad,
All be glad!
For the lad of all lads, was a Warwickshire lad.

Be proud of the charms of your country,
Where nature has lavished her bounty,
Where much she has giv'n, and some to be spared,
For the Bard of all bards was a Warwickshire bard,
Warwickshire bard,
Never pair'd
For the Bard of all bards, was a Warwickshire bard. [...]

Old Ben, Thomas Otway, John Dryden,
And half a score more, we take pride in,
Of famous Will Congreve, we boast too the skill,
But the Will of all Wills, was a Warwickshire Will;
Warwickshire Will,
Matchless still,
For the Will of all Wills, was a Warwickshire Will. [...]

As ven'son is very inviting,
To steal it our bard took delight in,
To make his friends merry he never was lag,
And the wag of all wags, was a Warwickshire wag,
Warwickshire wag,
Ever brag,
For the wag of all wags, was a Warwickshire wag.

There never was seen such a creature,
Of all she was worth, he robb'd nature;
He took all her smiles, and he took all her grief,
And the thief of all thieves, was a Warwickshire thief,
Warwickshire thief
He's the chief,
For the thief of all thieves, was a Warwickshire thief.[14]

This is a song still sung in folk clubs, although perhaps not always with these identical words. No-one has to have read any Shakespeare to like it.

As I have suggested, a major effect of Garrick's Jubilee efforts was to make Shakespeare's birthplace – that is to say the Henley Street house and the town in which it stood – a prime tourist centre. They greatly stimulated the career of people like John Jordan as unofficial guides to places of Shakespearean interest in Stratford and purveyors of Shakespearean legend. It was Jordan who guided Samuel Ireland when in 1793 he visited Stratford with his seventeen-year-old

14. *Terracotta bust of Shakespeare by Louis-François Roubiliac, c. 1758, early provenance uncertain, but presented to the Garrick Club in 1855 by the Duke of Devonshire who had purchased it from Professor Owen of the Royal College of Surgeons. By courtesy of The Garrick Club and The Art Archive.*

son William Henry. Ireland was a reasonably successful and well known engraver in a period when books of engravings had become very popular. This phenomenon had a good deal to do with the efforts of the publisher John Boydell (once an engraver himself) who marketed such books very successfully and employed over 250 engravers during his long career. It was Boydell who in 1789 opened in Pall Mall an entire building dedicated to an exhibition of new paintings called 'The Shakespeare Gallery'. The paintings commissioned by him, and exhibited there during the following decade, were later engraved for the benefit of a wider public. Only a few of them dealt with Shakespeare himself rather than with episodes from his work, but all were signs of the same public enthusiasm which helped prompt Samuel Ireland's 1789 Stratford visit.[15] Some of the results of that visit were offered to the public six years later when Ireland published his *Picturesque Views on the Upper, or Warwickshire Avon*.

But professional interest was by no means the only reason Ireland went to Stratford. An antiquarian and keen collector of memorabilia, he was himself a Shakespeare enthusiast who would read the plays aloud with his family every evening. Jordan directed to him places where he could buy a mulberry toothpick and goblet and Ireland also acquired during his visit a chair from Anne Hathaway's cottage said to be the very one on which 'our bard used to sit [...] with his Ann on his knee'.[16] What he would really have liked, however, were documents of some kind. He and his son were told by Jordan to go to Clopton, a mile or so from the site of what was once New Place, but there they suffered a disappointment which is well described in the son's 1805 *Confessions*.

> The person who occupied Clopton House, and rented the lands belonging to the estate, was what is usually denominated a gentleman-farmer; rich in gold and the worldly means of accumulating wealth, but devoid of every polished refinement.
>
> On Mr Ireland's arrival he introduced himself to Mr Williams (for such was the gentleman's name); who invited us into a small gloomy parlour; where he was shortly given to understand, by Mr Ireland, that the motive of his visit was a desire to ascertain whether any old deeds or manuscripts were then existing, in any part of the mansion: and on a further statement, as to any papers of Shakspeare's being extant, the following was the reply made by Mr Williams. –
>
> 'By G–d I wish you had arrived a little sooner! Why, it isn't a fortnight since I destroyed several baskets-full of letters and papers, in order to clear a small chamber for some young partridges which I wish to bring up alive: and as to Shakspeare, why there were many bundles with his name wrote upon them. Why it was in this very fire-place I made a roaring bonfire of them.'
>
> Mr Ireland's feelings during this address, which were fully displayed in his countenance, may be more easily conceived than expressed: and it was with infinite difficulty he suffered Mr Williams to proceed thus far; when, starting from his chair, he clasped is hands together, exclaiming
>
> 'My G–d! Sir, you are not aware of the loss which the world has sustained. Would to heaven I had arrived sooner!'
>
> As my father concluded this ejaculation, Mr Williams, calling to his wife, who

was in an adjoining chamber, and who instantly came into the apartment where we were seated (being a very respectable elderly lady), he thus addressed her:

'My dear, don't you remember bringing me down those baskets of papers from the partridge-room? and that I told you there were some about Shakspeare the poet?'

The old lady immediately replied as follows, having, in all probability, heard Mr Ireland's address to her husband:

'Yes, my dear; I do remember it perfectly well! and, if you will call to mind my words, I told you not to burn the papers, as they might be of consequence.'

Mr Ireland, after expressing his regrets, requested permission to inspect the small chamber in question; which, however, contained nothing but the partridges. Having expressed a desire to go over the house, two lanterns were ordered up; when every chamber underwent the strictest scrutiny; during which research the before-mentioned furniture, chapel, &c., came under our cognisance; but as to Shaksperian manuscripts, not a line was to be found.[17]

The school career of the author of this passage had been undistinguished. Samuel Ireland seems to have had a low opinion of his son's intellectual abilities, or at least of his cultural interests, and placed him in a lawyer's office. Yet William Henry was an avid reader and a particular admirer of Thomas Chatterton, the 'marvellous boy' (as Wordsworth called him) who had temporarily deceived the world with pastiche fifteenth-century poems and then killed himself when he was only eighteen. Operating from his lawyer's office, the similarly young William Henry managed to acquire a stock of blank seventeenth-century manuscript and an ink which turned brown with apparent age when heated. He then forged a document purporting to be associated with Shakespeare (a mortgage deed), making particular efforts to ensure that the signature and the seal looked authentic. This so pleased and convinced his father that he was soon trapped into forging many more. If Samuel Ireland had been disappointed in Stratford, he was now more than compensated by the material his son fed him. To explain its regular appearance William Henry invented a mysterious acquaintance called 'Mr H.' who had special reasons to be grateful to the young man, and still others for not wanting his real name or circumstances to be known.

The documents which William Henry chose to fabricate reveal an acute sense of what his father, and the public at large, most wanted to know. There is, for example, a correspondence between Shakespeare and Southampton which on the former's side begins as follows (for obvious reasons the spelling in all the Shakespeare extracts for which William Henry was responsible ought not to be altered but I have added punctuation to make them easier to read. In the originals there is no punctuation at all).

Copye of mye Letter toe hys grace offe Southampton

Mye Lorde
   DOE notte esteeme me a sluggarde nor tardye for thus havynge delayed to

answerre or rather toe thank you for youre greate Bountye. I doe assure you my graciouse ande good Lorde that thryce I have essayed toe wryte and thryce mye efforts have benne fruitlesse. I knowe notte what toe saye, Prose, Verse, alle all is naughte, gratitude is alle I have toe utter and that is tooe greate ande tooe sublyme a feeling for poore mortalls toe expresse. O my Lord itte is a Budde which Bllossommes, Bllooms butte never dyes; itte cherishes sweete Nature ande lulls the calme Breaste toe softe softe repose. Butte mye goode Lorde forgive thys mye departure fromme mye Subjecte which was toe retturne thankes and thankes I Doe retturne. O excuse mee mye Lorde more at presente I cannotte.

Yours devotedlye and withe due respecte,
Wm Shakspeare[18]

Southampton's supposed reply to this remarkable missive was addressed 'To the Globe Theatre Forre Mastr William Shakespeare'.

Deare William

I CANNOTTE doe lesse than thanke you forre youre kynde Letterre butte Whye, dearest Freynd, talke soe muche offe gratitude; mye offerre was double the Somme butte you woulde accepte butte the halfe therefore you neede notte speake soe muche onn thatte Subjecte; as I have beene thye Freynd soe will I continue aughte thatte I canne doe forre thee; praye commande mee ande you shalle fynde mee

Yours

Julye the 4

Southampton[19]

As I have said, it could reasonably be assumed from the difference in tone between the dedications to *Venus and Adonis* and *The Rape of Lucrece* that Shakespeare had received some money from Southampton, but here was confirmation of that fact although it is a pity that William Henry did not oblige his father, and the rest of us, with some indication of the actual sum.

Another aspect of Shakespeare's life which excited great curiosity was his relations with his wife. Because Anne Hathaway's tombstone suggested that she must have been much older than Shakespeare at the time of her marriage, and the record of Susanna's baptism proved that she was already then pregnant, it was possible to feel that their courtship might have been a somewhat sordid affair. William Henry did all he could to counteract that impression by producing both a love letter and some verses from Shakespeare to Anne, accompanying both with a lock of hair which a girl had once given him and which he entwined in a length of woven silk taken from an old parchment he had been able to buy.

Dearesste Anna

AS thou haste alwaye founde mee toe mye Worde most trewe soe thou shalt see I have stryctlye kepte mye promyse. I praye you perfume thys mye poore Locke with thye balmye Eyffes forre thenne indeede shalle Kynges themmeselves bowe ande paye homage toe itte. I doe assure thee no rude hande hathe knottedde itte,

90

thye Willys alone hathe done the worke. Neytherre the gyldedde bawble thatte envyronnes the heade of Majestye, noe norre honourres moste weyghtye wulde give mee halfe the joye as didde thysse my lyttle worke forre thee. The feelinge thatte dydde neareste approache untoe itte was thatte whiche commethe nygheste untoe God, meeke ande Gentle Charytye; forre thatte Virrtue O Anna doe I love, doe I cheryshe thee inne mye hearte forre thou arte ass a talle Cedarre stretchynge forthe its branches ande succourynge smaller Plants fromme nyppynge Winneterre orr the boysterouse Wyndes. Farewelle, toe Morrowe by tymes I wille see thee. Tille thenne Adewe sweete Love,

Thyne everre,

Wm Shakspeare

Verses to Anna Haterrewaye

1

Is there inne heavenne aught more rare
Thanne thou sweete Nymphe of Avon fayre?
Is there onne Earthe a Manne more trewe
Thanne Willy Shakspeare is toe you?

2

Though fyckle fortune prove unkynde
Stille dothe she leave herre wealthe behynde,
She neere the hearte canne forme anew
Norre make thye Willys love unnetrue.

3

Though Age with witherd hand doe stryke
The forme moste fayre, the face moste bryghte,
Stille dothe she leave unnetouchedde ande trewe
Thy Willys love ande freynshyppe too.

4

Though deathe with neverre faylynge blowe
Dothe Manne ande babe alyke brynge lowe,
Yette doth he take naughte butte hys due
Ande strikes notte Willys hearte stille trewe.

5

Synce thenne norre forretune, deathe, norre Age
Canne faythfulle Willys love asswage,
Thenne doe I live ande dye forre you
Thy Willye syncere ande moste trewe.[20]

It is amazing that William Henry's forgeries were not immediately detected, if not by his father then by the world at large. But, for one thing, he took considerable pains to make everything he produced *look* old, and for another, it may be necessary to remember how avidly in the latter half of the eighteenth century, and particularly in the years following the Jubilee, knowledge of Shakespeare was sought after – Samuel Ireland was by no means the only

15. *Seventeenth-century coloured drawing which W. H. Ireland altered and then claimed was a portrait of Shakespeare in the role of Bassanio, from Samuel Ireland's* Miscellaneous Papers and Legal Instruments under the Hand and Seal of William Shakespeare, *1796.*

person whose desires put him in the same easily deceivable position of those characters in *Volpone* who are hoping to inherit a fortune. It was important also that William Henry knew how to give his public the kind of documents it most wanted. To quieten the concern which had began to circulate that Shakespeare might have been a Catholic – perhaps after the discovery of his father's real or supposed spiritual testament – William Henry wrote a spiritual testament of Shakespeare's own in an eminently Protestant style. Because everyone hoped and assumed that the Bard had been appreciated by Queen Elizabeth he confirmed that fact with a letter to Shakespeare from the Queen herself. Basing himself on a copy of the 1608 quarto of *King Lear* which his father owned, he wrote out a new version of the play in which there was no inappropriate ribaldry. But perhaps his most endearing gesture concerns the volumes from Shakespeare's library which he claimed to have obtained from 'Mr H.' These were more than a dozen books and pamphlets from the sixteenth or seventeenth centuries which he had managed to buy from booksellers and which he then equipped with a signature and marginalia in his version of Shakespeare's hand-writing. Against a passage in one of these which described in gory detail the execution of Guy Fawkes he had Shakespeare write that, 'Hee hadde beene intreatedd bye hys freynde John Hemynges to attende sayde executyonne, butte thatte he lykedde notte toe beholde syghtes of thatte kynde'.[21]

There were of course some who were suspicious, or even frankly incredulous, from the start. Working at great speed, and still very young, William Henry made mistakes. He did not know when he forged the letter from Southampton, for example, that specimens of the Earl's handwriting existed and he made Queen Elizabeth address her letter to the Globe and invite Shakespeare and his company to play for her 'bye Tuesdaye nexte asse the lorde Leicesterre wille bee withe usse',[22] even though Leicester had died in 1588 before Shakespeare was established or the Globe built. These are errors which ought to have alerted those specialists who could stomach the language and the absurd spelling of William Henry's efforts but, called to the Irelands' home to examine the documents, many declared in their favour and a fierce controversy ensued. In his 1805 *Confessions* William Henry was able to quote with pride, from one of the many pamphlets published, an extract calculated to send shivers down the spine of anyone who has ever made an attribution on stylistic grounds alone.

> One of the most strenuous and able advocates of the Shaksperian production, was Mr W*bb, who, under the assumed appellation of 'Philalethes,' gave a pamphlet to the world with the title 'Shakespeare's Manuscripts, in the Possession of Mr Ireland, examined, respecting the internal and external Evidences of their Authenticity,' &c.
>
> Speaking of the books with Shaksperian notes, Mr W*bb, in pages 20 and 21, gives the ensuing paragraph. –

He is thus surrounded with a host of witnesses: for not only every book, but almost every page of some to them, declare to whom they belonged. I therefore think I see this immortal poet rise again to life, holding these sacred relics in one hand, and hear him say, *These were mine*: at the same time pointing with the other to these important volumes, once his own, informing us, that these were his delightful companions in his leisure hours of retirement and study: by conversing with whom he derived pleasure, profit, and delight: who letting fall their sparks upon his enkindling mind, lighted up that *muse of fire*, by which inspired,

> *This Poet's eye in a fine phrensy rolling,*
> *Did glance from heav'n to earth, from earth to heav'n.*

In pages 23, 24, and 25, Mr W*bb is pleased to say that transcendent beauties of metaphor and expression frequently occur in the manuscripts, and lavishes encomiums on the style prevailing throughout. The numerous productions, he says,

> – are all brought into unity by the exalted genius and boundless imagination of him to whom they relate. They grow out of, belong to, are his appropriates: he gathers all to himself. They are sacred FASCES bound together in indissoluble union by the authoritative hand of Shakspeare himself; to which we must all, sooner or later, yield ready assent, or reluctant obedience.

In some cases, it is true, an author, as well as other men, might be imitated, both in his manner and style, as well as in the signature of his name. But that is not the case in the present instance. All great and eminent geniiuses have their characteristic peculiarities, which not only *distinguish them* from all *others*, but *make them what they are*. These none can rival, none successfully imitate. Of all men and poets, Shakspeare had the most of these. He was a particular being, he stood alone. To imitate him, so as to pass the deceit on the world, appears to me next to an impossibility. Who could soar with his sublime genius? Who rove with his boundless imagination? Who could rival his pregnant wit? Who with intuitive inspection discover the workings of the human mind, and by the natural evolutions of the passions interest us so deeply, as this matchless poet? Now these papers in question bear on them the same strong marks of his original genius, as those with which his acknowledged writings are deeply impressed. Is it then an unfair inquiry to ask, if these are not Shakspeare's, to whom do they belong? To whom else are they to be ascribed? Was ever another cast in his mould? Or can any other be paralleled with him?

For my own part, I must confess, that, if such evidences of character had appeared unsupported by any other, I should have pronounced upon them at once; and have said, that as there never was but *one* man who could have produced such works, that he, and *he only*, has produced them. The peculiarity, nature, and force of this proof, and its fair application to the case in question, is of such weight with me, that I am free to declare, that had not Shakspeare's name appeared upon these papers, I should not have hesitated to have ascribed them to him.

But these papers bear not only the signature of his hand, but also the stamp of his soul, and the traits of his genius. His *mind* is as manifest as his *hand*. The touches of the same great master every-where appear, and appear to advantage, as they have not been corrected or chastised by a bold or unskilful hand. Here they are with all their excellencies and all their imperfections on their head : and by, as well as with, these they are to be judged.

In support of the authenticity of the papers, Mr W*bb, in page 33, states the following fact :—

> I beg leave to mention one particular instance, among many others, of a learned dignified divine, whom, with two others, I introduced myself to peruse these papers; who signified his approbation and conviction in the following strong expressions: 'Dr. Farmer has proved, as nearly to mathematical demonstration as the nature of the thing will allow, that Shakspeare was not possessed of classical learning. The papers we have inspected this day come as near to the same sort of proof, respecting their authenticity, as the nature of such evidence can admit.' In which declaration he was supported by the ready assent of two other reverend and learned gentlemen, by whom we were accompanied.

> I trust I shall not be accused of inordinate fondness of self-praise for making the above extracts. So much has been said and written in reprobation of the style of my productions by *soi-disant* critics, that I hold it but an act of self-justice to give the world the opposite sentiments of at least one man of wit, learning, and sense, who wrote uninfluenced by any other consideration than regard for truth – though I am as free to confess as my contemners, that his enthusiastic regard for every thing relating to our immortal Shakspeare (which for once overcame his better judgement) has led him to pour forth praises as much above my humble deserts as his own worth is superior to any thing I could say in grateful commendation of it.[23]

The violence of the debate as to the authenticity of the documents caused Samuel Ireland to press his son very hard for the identity of 'Mr H.' Since some had accused him of orchestrating a major fraud, he felt that he could easily clear his name if their mysterious possessor would only come forward. Then all questions of provenance and ownership could be cleared up. To pacify his father, and also establish that the Irelands had a legal right to exploit the documents, William Henry was driven to extreme lengths. These included forging an account in which Shakespeare describes how he was saved from drowning by a contemporary who happened to be called William Henry Ireland and writing another will – much more obviously satisfactory in its treatment of Shakespeare's wife than the real one – in which it was hinted that Mr H was a descendant of one of the editors of the First Folio, John Heminges. But the immediate causes of his downfall had nothing to do with these ludicrous efforts.

One was that Samuel Ireland very reasonably decided that the documents should be published. Cursorily examined in a room of his house in Norfolk Street, or listened to as Ireland read them out seated in Shakespeare's courting chair, they might pass muster whereas publishing them would allow experts to examine their language and spelling minutely. The other cause was that, in

16. Malone's demonstrates that the top entry must be a forgery of Southampton's
handwriting by Ireland from his Inquiry into the Authencity of Certain
Miscellaneous Papers published by S.W. H. Ireland and attributed to
Shakespeare, Queen Elizabeth, and Henry Earl of Southampton (1796).

further pursuit of his Chattertonian ambitions, William Henry had written a whole play which was based on Holinshed's account of the fifth century English king Vortigern and which he had convinced his father was by Shakespeare. Samuel Ireland managed to persuade the management at Drury Lane to put this play on but, having signed an agreement, Sheridan and in particular the leading actor Knowles began to have cold feet. The first night had been scheduled for December 1795 but did not take place until 2 April of the following year (pressure had to be put on Knowles to stop him having it performed on April Fools' Day). Two days before its first performance Edmond Malone who, since the appearance in print of some of the documents had now had the opportunity to examine them carefully, published a book of over four hundred pages in which he demolished their claims to authenticity completely. This was not the best possible prelude to *Vortigern* which had a largely hostile reception and was withdrawn after one night. With its withdrawal the fraud was more or less over. In remarks on its final stages a satirist of the day made use of what was now the familiar device of calling up Shakespeare's ghost for appropriate comment. Or rather he imagined Samuel Ireland having done the same.

> *Ah Sammy! Sammy! Why call forth a ghost?*
> *Rather of Critics summon up an host!*
> *They – luckless wights! indite for daily bread;*
> *But you disturb the ashes of the dead!*
> *Peaceful I lay in Stratford's hallowed fane,*
> *And, but for thee, might yet enshrined remain:*
> *'Blest were the man' I said, 'who spar'd the stones;*
> *But curs'd be he, who dared to move my bones!'*
> *'Tis true, my bones lie unmolested there,*
> *Yet still my spirit's dragg'd to open air.*
> *Rich in your prize, of praise, you take your fill,*
> *But Spectres yet may speak, – and speak I will!*
>
> *Oft have I conjured, from the vasty deep,*
> *Myriads of spirits at one magic sweep!*
> *And shalt thou dare, with weak unnervate arm,*
> *To bind Will Shakespeare with a cobweb charm?*
> *His genius unconfin'd with fancy plays*
> *Where Avon's stream through fertile meadows strays;*
> *Laughs with the loves, the flitting sunbeam rides,*
> *And through the boundless paths of Nature glides.*
> *Not lock'd in trunks, – in auncient dirtie scrolls,*
> *Long shreds of parchment, deeds, and mustie rolls;*
> *Receipts for candles, bills and notes of hand,*
> *Some that you may – but more not understand.*
> *Samples of hair, love songs, and sonnets meete,*
> *Together meet by chaunce in Norfolk-street;*
> *Where, fruitful as the vine, the tiny elves*

Produce young manuscripts for Sammy's shelves.
Dramas in embrio leave their lurking holes,
And little Vortigerns start forth in shoals.
To work, ye Lawyers! Ransack all your deeds,
The bait is swallowed, and the Public bleeds.
Freely the Cash comes down, – lead boldly on,
The Book complete: – Four Guineas! – Presto! – gone!
More papers found!!! A neighbor here hard by –
An antiquarian wight, of curious eye,
Deep skill'd in pedigrees, well known to Fame –
Has found some writings in an hand the same –
The very dots, the stops, – the self-same Shak,
That soon must lay each quibbler on his back:
None shall their sanction to the truth refuse;
For, if they'll not believe, they must be Jews.

Long fam'd for finding, Sammy, art thou known,
With steady perserverance, – all thy own; [...]
When late to Stratford you incog. came down,
Peeping for relics through each lane in town,
I guess'd that something fresh was in the wind,
And thus to Davy Garrick spoke my mind:
'Since you call'd forth the wond'ring nobles round
'To see my Jubilee on Fairy ground,
'To chaunt my praises in harmonious strain,
'And strut in Pageants through a shower of rain,
'Ne'er has mine eye in Warwick's county scann'd
'So learn'd a wight as Sammy Ireland!'
The chair, the kitchen, room where I was born,
All from old Time's mysterious veil were torn;
I often thought – so steady were his pains,
And from his work, so certain were his gains –
He'd never give his deep researchers up,
Until he found my spoon and christ'ning cup:
Some curious remnants of my mother's spinning;
My little shoes, and all the child-bed linen!
 – So have I seen a Jack-daw in a yard,
With head askaunt, some chosen spot regard,
Where, deep enearthed, some dainty morsels lay, –
Wisely laid there against a rainy day:
When hunger pinches, to the ground he hies,
Now cheerful hops, and elated flies;
But not contented with his well known store,
He whets his bill, and greedy pecks for more.

But turn we now again to Norfolk-Street,
Where Authors sage and Commentators meet;
To that fam'd spot where Dramatists repair,
And Antiquarians darken all the air:
There Mister Kemble struts with solemn pace,

98

Then takes the chair; with academic grace
Pronounces all are genuine, true, and rare;
While none to contradict the Actor dare.
That wond'rous man, – the Brother, in right line,
To wond'rous Siddons, – names well-known as mine!
Who shall presume his judgement to disown,
Who makes my choicest dramas half his own?
He, Mohawk like, unfeeling cuts and lops,
That Shakespeare's Plays appear like modern Crops!
Then from the press comes forth editions true,
And John's additions meet the public view:
No faults throughout the title page we spy,
And J.P. Kemble strikes the wond'ring eye!!!
Next mount sublime, upon the critic throne,
A trusty blade, and true yclep'd Malone.
He scorns complying sentiments to sham,
And, 'spite of Kemble, states the whole a flam.
Though some declare he never saw a line,
And 'gainst his judgement all their strength combine;
Other's attempt his doubting course to steer,
And Mister Stevens, marches in the rear.
Burke Sammy aids, and Sheridan the same;
The latter, right or wrong, is not to blame;
For well he knows, 'All's grist that comes to mill!'
And Vortigern can't fail the house to fill.
Boydell looks grave, and wisely holds his peace;
For, true or false, they can't his fame decrease:
His grand edition still will stand the test,
And Ireland's Cayan gives the whole a zest.

Now Sammy, you of course, will wish to know
The Ghost's opinion, farther light to throw;
For Shakespeare's sanction must have lasting weight,
And fix for ever thy depending fate;
Give thee entire the Antiquarian rule,
Or spurn thee forth indignant from thy stool: –
Then, know, my Friend, to ease thy troubled mind,
Thy Willy's Ghost, to thee was always kind;
And, far from judging the old writings found,
Said to be mine, so long in darkness bound,
I'll not pretend thy mystic veil to draw –
Pronounce them forg'd, or pass them into law:
To speak the truth, I give it on my word;
For years long past, my Muse has felt the sword, –
Such hacking, slashing, cutting here and there,
Some parts press'd down, and others puff'd to air;
I know not what is mine, nor what is not.
If true, – thy envied fame will quickly spread,
And Britain's honours play around thy head:
If forg'd, – be prudent, vigilant, and wise;

Keep thy own counsel, and each threat despise.
But hold! – Methinks I scent the morning air;
Abrupt we part, nor can I more declare:
Lo! In the East, the glowing tints I see.
Sammy, adieu! – Farewell! – remember me![24]

The author of this splendid spoof was George Moutard ('Mustard George') Woodward, drinking companion of Thomas Rowlandson and a fine caricaturist himself, and his best joke is to have Shakespeare complain that his plays have been so mangled by people like John Kemble (brother of the famous Mrs Siddons) that he can no longer recognise what is, or is not, his own work and is not able therefore to pronounce on the Ireland documents. Several of those who like Kemble had vouched for their authenticity are named and Samuel Ireland is pilloried for wanting above all to make money out of them. It was he who was always targeted (rather than his son) but it was not long before William Henry, having left the family home, freely confessed to being the author of the forgeries. Yet his father could not be made to believe his dim-witted offspring capable of such fiendish ingenuity, so much linguistic facility, and continued to protest that the documents were authentic until his death in 1801.

The Ireland forgeries illuminate an important feature of Shakespeare's growing iconic status. The need for a satisfactory visual image of the man was rapidly being met by artists of all kinds, but that more general impression which derives from biographical writing was proving difficult to sharpen and refine because of the lack of evidence. It was precisely such evidence William Henry had offered to supply and, because he had no interest in either history or in truth, it was appropriate that he should finally have been crushed by someone deeply attached to both. By the 1790s Edmond Malone was indisputably the greatest living Shakespeare scholar, the last and best in the long line of those who, since the efforts of Rowe in 1709, had brought increasing accuracy and knowledge to the editing of Shakespeare's plays. It frustrated Malone that the progress in editorial method during the eighteenth century had not been matched by a greater understanding of the circumstances of Shakespeare's life and that Rowe's account was continually reprinted even though, in his view, it contained only eleven facts, eight of which were false and one of which was doubtful.[25] The major aim of his intellectual life became the composition of a decent biography and he collected material for this work assiduously. By the time of his death in 1812, however, it was by no means completed. What there was of it occupied just under three hundred pages in the second volume of a twenty-one volume version of his edition of Shakespeare, prepared for the press by the son of his old friend James Boswell. The introduction to this large fragment conveys the difficulty and frustration Malone felt at having to work with so little information.

Of all the accounts of literary men which have been given to the world, the history of the life of Shakspeare would be the most curious and instructive, if we were acquainted with the minute circumstances of his fortunes, the course and extent of his studies, and the means and gradations whereby he acquired that consummate knowledge of mankind, which, for two centuries, has rendered him the delight and boast of his countrymen: but many of the materials for such a biographical detail being now unattainable, we must content ourselves with such particulars as accident has preserved, or the most sedulous industry has been able to collect.

From Sir William Dugdale, who was born in 1605, and bred at the school of Coventry, but twenty miles from Stratford upon Avon, and whose *Antiquities of Warwickshire* appeared in 1656, only thirty years after the death of our poet, we might reasonably have expected some curious memorials of his illustrious countryman: but he has not given us a single particular of his private life; contenting himself with a very slight mention of him in his account of the church and tombs of Stratford upon Avon.

The next biographical printed notice that I have found, is in Fuller's *Worthies*, folio, 1662, in Warwickshire, p. 116; where there is a short quibbling account of our poet, furnishing very little information concerning him. In *Theatrum Poetarum*, which was not published till 1675 [...], Edward Phillips gives this character of our author:

William Shakspeare, the glory of the English stage, whose nativity at Stratford upon Avon is the highest honour that town can boast of, from an actor of tragedies and comedies, he became a maker; and such a maker, that though some others may perhaps pretend to a more exact decorum and economy, especially in tragedy, never any expressed a more lofty and tragick height; never any represented nature more purely to the life: and where the polishments of art are most wanting, as probably his learning was not extraordinary, he pleaseth with a certain wild and native elegance; and in all his writings hath an unvulgar style, as well in his *Venus and Adonis*, his *Rape of Lucrece*, and other various poems, as in his dramaticks.

I had long since observed, in the margin of my copy of this book, that the hand of Milton, who was the author's uncle, might be traced in the preface, and in the passage above quoted. The book was licensed for publication two months before the death of that poet. My late friend, Mr Warton, has made the same observation.

Winstanley, in his *Lives of the Poets*, 8vo. 1687, merely transcribed Dugdale and Fuller; nor did Langbaine, in 1691, Blount, in 1694, or Gildon, in 1699, add any thing to the former meagre accounts of our poet.

That Antony Wood, who was himself a native of Oxford (but thirty-six miles from Stratford), and was born but fourteen years after the death of our author, should not have collected any anecdotes of Shakspeare, has always appeared to me extraordinary. Though Shakspeare had no direct title to a place in the *Athenae Oxonienses*, that diligent antiquary could have easily found a niche for his Life, as he has done for many others, not bred at Oxford. The Life of Davenant afforded him a very fair opportunity for such an insertion.

About the year 1680, that very curious and indefatigable searcher after anecdotes relative to the eminent writers of England, Mr John Aubrey, collected some concerning Shakspeare, which I shall have occasion to mention more particularly hereafter.

But the person from whom we should probably have derived the most satisfactory intelligence concerning our poet's theatrical history, was his contemporary, and fellow comedian, Thomas Heywood, had he executed a work which he appears to have long had in contemplation. In the margin of Braithwaite's *Survey of Histories*, 4to. 1614, I find the following note : 'Homer, an excellent and heroicke poet, shadowed only, because my judicious friend, Maister Thomas Heywood, hath taken in hand, by his great industry, to make a general, though summary, description of all the poets.' Heywood himself, twenty years afterwards, mentions the same scheme, in a note to his *Hierarchy of the Blessed Angels*, folio, 1635, p. 245, in which he says, that he intends 'to commit to the publick view, The Lives of the Poets, foreign and modern, from the first before Homer, to the *novissimi* and last, of what nation or language soever;' but, unfortunately, the work was never published. Browne, the pastoral poet, who was also Shakspeare's contemporary, had a similar intention of writing the Lives of the English Poets; which, however, he never executed.

Though, between 1640 and 1670, the Lives of Hooker, Donne, Wotton, and Herbert, were given to the publick by Isaac Walton, and in 1679 some account of Spencer was prefixed to a folio edition of his works, neither the booksellers, who republished our author's plays in 1664 and 1665, employed any person to write the Life of Shakspeare; nor did Dryden, though a warm admirer of his productions, or any other poet, collect any materials for such a work, till Mr Rowe, about the year 1707, undertook an edition of his plays. Unfortunately, that was not an age of curiosity or inquiry: for Dryden might have obtained some intelligence from the old actors, who died about the time of the Restoration, when he was himself near thirty years old; and still more authentick accounts from our poet's grand-daughter, Lady Barnard, who did not die till 1670. His sister, Joan Hart, was living in 1646; his eldest daughter, Susanna Hall, in 1649; and his second daughter, Judith Queeny, in 1662.

Of those who were not thus nearly connected with our poet, a large list of persons presents itself, from whom, without doubt, much intelligence concerning him might have been obtained, between the time of the publication of the second folio edition of his works, in 1632, and of Mr Rowe's Life, in 1709.

Francis Meres, who will be more particularly mentioned hereafter, and who appears to have been well acquainted with the stage, when our author first appeared as a dramatick writer, lived till 1646.

Richard Braithwaite, a very voluminous poet, was born in 1588, and commenced a writer some years before the death of Shakspeare. Having once, as it should seem, had thoughts of compiling a history of the English poets, he probably was particularly anxious to learn all such circumstances as might be most conducive to such an undertaking. He died in 1673, at the age of eighty-five. To him may be added, 1. Dr. Jasper Mayne; 2. Penelope Lady Spencer; 3. John, the second Lord Stanhope; 4. Sir Aston Cockaine; 5. William Cavendish, Duke of Newcastle; and, 6. Frances, Countess of Dorset; who all died between the time of the Restoration and the year 1695; and Sir Robert Atkins, Sir Richard

17. *The Alto Relievo by Thomas Banks, 1789, was commissioned by John Boydell to
decorate the façade of the Shakespeare Galley in Pall Mall. It was moved in 1870 to New
Place Gardens, Stratford-upon-Avon. It shows Shakespeare between the Dramatic Muse
and the Genius of Painting. Engraved by Benjamin Smith for the Boydell Gallery and
published in 1796.*

Verney, and Sir William Bishop, whose lives were extended to the beginning of the eighteenth century. [...]

In his characteristically thorough way, Malone goes on here to give details of these people who might have provided information about Shakespeare but didn't, and also to add a few other names to that category. He then concludes:

> That almost a century should have elapsed, from the time of [Shakespeare's] death, without a single attempt having been made to discover any circumstance which could throw a light on the history of his private life, or literary career; that, when the attempt was made, it should have been so imperfectly executed by the very ingenious and elegant dramatist who undertook the task; and that for a period of eighty years afterwards, during which this 'god of our idolatry' ranked as high among us as any poet ever did in any country, all the editors of his works, and each successive English biographer, should have been contented with Mr Rowe's meagre and imperfect narrative; are circumstances which cannot be contemplated without astonishment.
>
> The information which I have been able to collect on this subject, even at this late day, however inadequate to my wishes, having far exceeded my most sanguine expectation, the perusal of the following pages, while it will ascertain the numerous errors and inaccuracies which have been so long and so patiently endured, and transmitted from book to book, will, I trust, at the same time, show, in some small degree, what may be done in biographical researches, even at a remote period, by a diligent and ardent spirit of inquiry: it must, however, necessarily be accompanied with a deep, though unavailing regret, that the same ardour did not animate those who lived nearer our author's time, whose inquiries could not fail to have been rewarded with a superior degree of success. The negligence and inattention of our English writers, after the Restoration, to the history of the celebrated men who preceded them, can never be mentioned without surprise and indignation. If Suetonius and Plutarch had been equally incurious, some of the most valuable remains of the ancient world would have been lost to posterity.[26]

No biographer ever introduced his work with a more convincing and dispiriting account of why what they were about to attempt was impossible. Malone's frustration is self-evident and does much to explain why he never finished what he came to regard as his life's work. He is in his fragment able to say little of interest about Shakespeare himself and barely gets his subject to London, breaking off before Robert Greene's 1592 attack. His 'diligent and ardent spirit of inquiry' certainly allowed him to make some valuable discoveries about Shakespeare's Stratford background which cleared up several major mis-conceptions (as to the number of his brothers and sisters, for example); and he was able to present interesting new documents including what is still the only extant letter to Shakespeare (the one from Richard Quiney asking for a £30 loan which is reproduced on p. 17 above). Yet what he mostly demonstrates is that scholarship of the most meticulous kind was not in a position to satisfy public curiosity about the private life of the man now canonised as England's greatest writer; and that the way was therefore open, if not for forgery, then at least for fiction. If there was not enough evidence to call Shakespeare's life into scholarly existence, it would have to be invented.

Notes

1. John Dryden, 'Prologue' to *Troilus and Cressida or, Truth Found Too Late* (1679) in Montague Summers (ed.), *Dryden: the Dramatic Works* (1932), vol. 2, p. 28.

2. Charles Gildon, 'Epilogue' to *Measure for Measure or, Beauty the Best Advocate* (1700).

3. *Memoirs of the Shakespear's-Head in Covent Garden* (1759), vol. 1, pp. 1-11.

4. See Emmet L. Avery, 'The Shakespeare Ladies Club', *Shakespeare Quarterly*, vol. 7 (Spring, 1958), pp. 153-8.

5. George Lillo, 'Epilogue' to *Marina* (1738), pp 59-60.

6. S. Schoenbaum, *Records and Images*, p. 169.

7. *Works of Ben Jonson*, vol. 8, p. 390.

8. Christian Deelman, *The Great Shakespeare Jubilee* (1964), p. 137. My information about Garrick's visit comes from Deelman.

9. *Gentleman's Magazine* (July, 1769), pp. 344-5.

10. David Garrick, *Ode upon dedicating a Building and erecting a Statue to Shakespeare, at Stratford-upon-Avon* (1769). Text from the *Annual Register*.

11. H. W. Pedicord and F. L. Bergmann (eds), *The Plays of David Garrick* (Southern Illinois Press, 1980), vol. 2, p. 106.

12. *Ibid.*, pp. 113-5.

13. *Ibid.*, p. 112.

14. *Shakespeare's Garland, Being a Collection of New Songs, Ballads, Roundelays, Catches, Glees, Comic-Serenatas, etc. Performed at the Jubilee at Stratford-upon-Avon* (1769), pp. 2-4.

15. For details of John Boydell and his brother Josiah see A. E. Santaniello's introduction to his selection from their *Collection of Prints from Pictures painted for the purposes of illustrating the dramatic works of Shakespeare by the artists of Great Britain* (New York, 1968), pp. 5-9.

16. *The Confessions of William-Henry Ireland – containing the particulars of his fabrication of the Shakespeare manuscripts; together with anecdotes and opinions of many distinguished persons in the literary, political, and theatrical world* (1805), p. 33.

17. *Ibid.*, pp. 30-33.

18. Samuel Ireland (ed.), *Miscellaneous Papers and Legal Instruments under the Hand and Seal of William Shakespeare* (1796). No page numbers.

19. *Ibid.*

20. *Ibid.*

21. William Henry Ireland, *Confessions*. p. 197.

22. *Miscellaneous Papers*.

23. William Henry Ireland, *Confessions*, pp. 282-6. The pamphlet from which Ireland quotes was published in 1796 and its author was Francis Webb.

24. George Moutard Woodward, *Familiar Verses from the ghost of Willy Shakespeare to Sammy Ireland* (1796), pp. 5-11.

25. See Schoenbaum, *Shakespeare's Lives*, p. 169.

26. J. Boswell (ed.), *The Plays and Poems of William Shakespeare. With a Life of the Poet and an Enlarged History of the Stage. By the late E. Malone* (1821), vol. 2, pp. 1-12.

18. *Sir Walter Scott before the Shakespeare monument in the chancel of Holy Trinity*
Church on the occasion of his visit to Stratford-upon-Avon in 1828.
Oil painting attributed to Sir Walter Allen.
By courtesy of the Shakespeare Birthplace Trust Records Office.

Chapter Four

Shakespeare in the Romantic and Early Victorian Period

R
EPEATED REPRESENTATIONS OF SHAKESPEARE as something more substantial than a ghost only came with the rise of the historical novel and all that it implied about attitudes to the past. If Walter Scott did not invent this form, it was above all through his efforts that it became so immensely popular. *Kenilworth* (1821) is the Scott novel in which Shakespeare makes a significant, if only fleeting, appearance. The action concerns the Earl of Leicester's marriage to Amy Robsart and the extent to which he, and more especially his evil henchman Richard Varney, fear that it will hamper his career as Court favourite and possible future royal consort. Shakespeare is first referred to by Queen Elizabeth when she is trying to console the hero, Edmund Tressilian, for the loss of Amy whom the Queen believes is married to Varney rather than Leicester. 'Think of what that arch-knave Shakespeare says', she tells him, and then remarks, after quoting a few lines from *Troilus and Cressida*, 'You smile, my Lord of Southampton - perchance I make your player's verse halt through my bad memory - but let it suffice'.[1] Later, Leicester is leaving a Privy Council meeting and addresses several of his suitors or followers, including Spenser:

> 'Master Edmund Spenser, touching your Irish petition, I would willingly aid you, from my love to the Muses; but thou hast nettled the Lord Treasurer.'
>
> 'My lord,' said the poet, 'were I permitted to explain' –
>
> 'Come to my lodging, Edmund,' answered the Earl - 'not tomorrow, or next day, but soon. - Ha, Will Shakespeare - wild Will! - thou hast given my nephew, Philip Sidney, love-powder - he cannot sleep without thy *Venus and Adonis* under his pillow! - we will have thee hanged for the veriest wizard in Europe. Hark thee, mad wag, I have not forgotten thy matter of the patent, and of the bears.'
>
> The Player bowed, and the Earl nodded and passed on - so that age would have told the tale - in ours, perhaps, we might say the immortal had done homage to the mortal.[2]

The supposed date of this encounter is 1575 when Shakespeare was eleven, the Southampton to whom he dedicated *Venus and Adonis* only two, and Amy Robsart long dead; but strict chronology is not a feature of the historical novel. The brevity of Shakespeare's appearance gives no indication of how often he would be represented subsequently and how detailed and prolonged those representations would be. That it was Scott who provided the template for very many of them is suggested by this extract from his version of a debate on the royal barge in which the matter of 'the patent, and of the bears', referred to above, is being discussed.

'My lords, [the Queen] said, 'having passed for a time our edict of silence upon our good Leicester, we will call you to counsel on a gamesome matter, more fitted to be now treated of, amidst mirth and music, than in the gravity of our ordinary deliberations. – Which of you, my lords,' said she, smiling, 'know aught of a petition from Orson Pinnit, the keeper, as he qualifies himself, of our royal bears? Who stands godfather to his request?'

'Marry, with your Grace's good permission, that do I,' said the Earl of Sussex. – 'Orson Pinnit was a stout soldier before he was so mangled by the skenes of the Irish clan MacDonough, and I trust your Grace will be, as you always have been, good mistress to your good and trusty servants.'

'Surely,' said the Queen, 'it is our purpose to be so, and in especial to our poor soldiers and sailors, who hazard their lives for little pay. We would give,' she said, with her eyes sparkling, 'yonder royal palace of ours to be an hospital for their use, rather than they should call their mistress ungrateful. – But this is not the question,' she said, her tone, which had been awakened by her patriotic feelings, once more subsiding into the tone of gay and easy conversation; 'for this Orson Pinnit's request goes something farther. He complains, that amidst the extreme delight with which men haunt the play-houses, and in especial their eager desire for seeing the exhibitions of one Will Shakespeare, (whom I think, my lords, we have all heard something of,) the manly amusement of bear-baiting is falling into comparative neglect; since men will rather throng to see these roguish players kill each other in jest, than to see our royal dogs and bears worry each other in bloody earnest – What say you to this, my Lord of Sussex?'

'Why, truly, gracious Madam,' said Sussex, 'you must expect little from an old soldier like me in favour of battles in sport, when they are compared with battles in earnest; and yet, by my faith, I wish Will Shakespeare no harm. He is a stout man at quarter-staff, and single falchion, as I am told, though a halting fellow; and stood, they say, a tough fight with the rangers of old Sir Thomas Lucy of Charlecot, when he broke his deer-park and kissed his keeper's daughter.'

'I cry you mercy, my Lord of Sussex,' said Queen Elizabeth, interrupting him; 'that matter was heard in council, and we will not have this fellow's offence exaggerated – there was no kissing in the matter, and the defendant hath put the denial on record. – But what say you to his present practice, my lord, on the stage? For there lies the point, and not in any ways touching his former errors, in breaking parks, or the other follies you speak of.'

'Why truly, Madam,' replied Sussex, 'as I said before, I wish the gamesome mad fellow no injury. Some of his whoreson poetry (I crave your Grace's pardon for such a phrase) has rung in mine ears as if they sounded to boot and saddle. –

But then it is all froth and folly – no substance or seriousness in it, as your Grace has already well touched. – What are half a dozen knaves, with rusty foils and tattered targets, making but a mere mockery of a stout fight, to compare to the royal game of bear-baiting, which hath been graced by your Highness's countenance, and that of your royal predecessors, in this your princely kingdom, famous for matchless mastiffs, and bold bearwards, over all Christendom? Greatly is it to be doubted that the race of both will decay, if men will rather throng to hear the lungs of an idle player belch forth nonsensical bombast, instead of bestowing their pence in encouraging the bravest image of war that can be shewn in peace, and that is the sports of the Parish-garden. There you may see the bear lying at guard with his red pinky eyes, watching the onset of the mastiff, like a wily captain, who maintains his defence that an assailant may be tempted to adventure within his danger. And then comes Sir Mastiff, like a worthy champion, in full career at the throat of his adversary – and then shall Sir Bruin teach him the reward for those who, in over-courage, neglect the policies of war, and, catching him in his arms, strain him to his breast like a lusty wrestler, until rib after rib crack like the shot of a pistolet. And then shall another mastiff, as bold, but with better aim and sounder judgment, catch Sir Bruin by the nether lip, and hang fast, while he tosses about his blood and slaver, and tries in vain to shake Sir Talbot from his hold. And then' –

'Nay, by my honour, my lord,' said the Queen laughing, 'you have described the whole so admirably, that, had we never seen a bear-baiting, as we have beheld a many, and hope, with heaven's allowance, to see many more, your words were sufficient to put the whole Bear-garden before our eyes. – But come, who speaks next in this case? – My Lord of Leicester, what say you?'

'Am I then to consider myself as unmuzzled, please your Grace?' replied Leicester.

'Surely, my lord – that is, if you feel hearty enough to take part in our game,' answered Elizabeth. 'And yet, when I think of your cognizance of the bear and ragged staff, methinks we had better hear some less partial orator.'

'Nay, on my word, gracious Princess,' said the Earl, 'though my brother Ambrose of Warwick and I do carry the ancient cognizance your Highness deigns to remember, I nevertheless desire nothing but fair play on all sides; or, as they say, "fight dog, fight bear." And in behalf of the players, I must needs say they are witty knaves whose rants and whose jests keep the minds of the commons from busying themselves with state affairs, and listening to traitorous speeches, idle rumours, and disloyal insinuations. When men are agape to see how Marlow, Shakespeare, and others, work out their fanciful plots as they call them, the mind of the spectators is withdrawn from the conduct of their rulers.'

'We would not have the mind of our subjects withdrawn from the consideration of our own conduct, my lord,' answered Elizabeth; 'because the more closely it is examined, the true motives by which we are guided will appear the more manifest.'

'I have heard, however, Madam,' said the Dean of St Asaph's, an eminent Puritan, 'that these players are wont, in their plays, not only to introduce profane and lewd expressions, tending to foster sin and harlotry, but even to bellow out such reflections on government, its origin and its object, as tend to render the subject discontented, and shake the solid foundations of civil society. And it seems to be, under your Grace's favour, far less than safe to permit these naughty foul-mouthed knaves to ridicule the godly for their decent gravity, and in blaspheming heaven, and slandering their earthly rulers, to set at defiance the laws both of God and man.'

'If we could think this were true, my lord,' said Elizabeth, 'we should give sharp correction for such offences. But it is ill arguing against the use of any thing from its abuse. And touching this Shakespeare, we think there is that in his plays that is worth twenty Bear-gardens; and that this new undertaking of his Chronicles, as he calls them, may entertain, with honest mirth, mingled with useful instruction, not only our subjects, but even the generation which may succeed to us.'

'Your Majesty's reign will need no such feeble aid to make it remembered to the latest posterity,' said Leicester. 'And yet, in his way, Shakespeare hath so touched some incidents of your Majesty's happy government, as may countervail what has been spoken by his reverence the Dean of St Asaph's. There are some lines, for example – I would my nephew, Philip Sidney, were here, they are scarce ever out of his mouth – they are in a mad tale of fairies, love-charms, and I wot not what besides; beautiful however they are, however short they may and must fall of the subject to which they bear a bold relation – and Philip murmurs them, I think, even in his dreams.'

'You tantalize us, my lord,' said the Queen – 'Master Philip Sidney is, we know, a minion of the Muses, and we are pleased it should be so. Valour never shows to more advantage than when united with taste and love of letters – but surely there are some others among our young courtiers who can recollect what your lordship has forgotten amid weightier affairs. – Master Tressilian, you are described to me as a worshipper of Minerva – remember you aught of these lines?'

Tressilian's heart was too heavy, his prospects in life too fatally blighted, to profit by the opportunity which the Queen thus offered to him of attracting her attention, but he determined to transfer the advantage to his more ambitious young friend; and, excusing himself on the score of want of recollection, he added, that he believed the beautiful verses, of which my Lord of Leicester had spoken, were in the remembrance of Master Walter Raleigh.

At the command of the Queen, that cavalier repeated, with accent and manner which even added to their exquisite delicacy of tact and beauty of description, the celebrated vision of Oberon.

> 'That very time I saw, (but thou could'st not,)
> Flying between the cold moon and the earth,
> Cupid, all arm'd: a certain aim he took
> At a fair vestal, throned by the west ;
> And loos'd his love-shaft smartly from his bow,
> As it should pierce a hundred thousand hearts:
> But I might see young Cupid's fiery shaft
> Quench'd in the chaste beams of the wat'ry moon;
> And the imperial vot'ress passed on,
> In maiden meditation, fancy free.'

The voice of Raleigh, as he repeated the last lines, became a little tremulous, as if diffident how the Sovereign to whom the homage was addressed might receive it, exquisite as it was. If this diffidence was affected, it was good policy; but if real, there was little occasion for it. The verses were not probably new to the Queen, for when was ever such elegant flattery so long in reaching the royal ear to which it was addressed? But it was not the less welcome when recited by such a speaker as Raleigh. Alike delighted with the matter, the manner, and the graceful form and animated countenance of the gallant young reciter, Elizabeth kept time to every cadence, with look and with finger. When the speaker had ceased, she murmured over the last lines as if scarce conscious that she was overheard, and as she uttered the words,

'In maiden meditation, fancy free,'

she dropt into the Thames the supplication of Orson Pinnit, keeper of the royal bears, to find more favourable acceptance at Sheerness, or wherever the tide might waft it.[3]

That bear-baiting and performances of Shakespeare's plays could take place on what was more or less the same site would be a problem for later commentators, but for Scott, who describes the cruelty of the sport so vividly, it seems to have been no more that a manifestation of what was robust and energising in the days of good Queen Bess. The Earl of Sussex has Shakespeare partake in this robustness by calling him 'a stout man at quarter-staff, and single falchion' as witnessed by the affair at Charlecote. His further reference to him as a 'halting fellow', derives from what was becoming a traditional reading of the third line in Sonnet 37: 'So I, made lame by fortune's dearest spite'. Like many future readings of lines in the Sonnets, this one depended on taking literally what was very probably metaphorical (as Katherine Duncan-Jones points out in her edition of the Sonnets, Edgar describes himself at one moment in *King Lear* as 'A most poor man, made lame by Fortune's blows'.[4]) It is interesting to have Scott's views on the attitude of the Elizabethan authorities to the drama, even if an Elizabeth who wanted her own conduct closely examined by her subjects seems wildly improbable; and to note how early it had became customary to read Oberon's vision from *A Midsummer Night's Dream* as a tribute to her. But what is significant about the extract in this context is the way relations between the characters are determined less by historical information than a shrewd estimate of which figures the reader might have heard of. The historical novel characteristically saves its readers energy by grouping together figures who, for reasons either chronological or social, might not often, or never, have been in the same spot. It also allows them to read the past according to their own scale of values. In his account of Leicester's brief meeting with Shakespeare, Scott recognises that the event has a different meaning for his age (an immortal doing homage to a mortal) than it would have had at the time. But when it comes to the discussion of Orson Pinnit's petition, Shakespeare has an importance for Elizabeth and her courtiers which is more in keeping with early nineteenth-century estimates than those of his own period.

Shakespeare bulks larger in *Kenilworth* than his lightning appearance, and the way he is discussed above, might suggest. The novel is stuffed full of what are either direct quotations from, or allusions to, his plays; and in the finale, the manner in which Varney excites in Leicester a jealousy of Tressilian that eventually leads to Amy Robsart's murder, is closely modelled on *Othello*. The actual presence of Shakespeare, however, is minor and Scott wisely avoids the challenge of having him speak: what kind of lines do you after all provide for someone whom you are presenting as the greatest writer who ever lived? Subsequent novelists, working very much in the tradition he established, would not be so inhibited.

What is probably the first novel in which Shakespeare plays a central role was published in 1824, only three years after *Kenilworth*. Its author was Nathan Drake, a Suffolk doctor, who can also claim the distinction of having written, in *Shakespeare and His Times* (1817), the first biographical study which overtly compensates for the lack of reliable information concerning its subject with masses of material about the conditions of life in Elizabethan and Jacobean England. Schoenbaum gives an excellent account of this work in his *Shakespeare's Lives* but, eagle-eyed although he usually is, he fails to mention the later novel. This may be because it appeared in such a deceptive form. Drake's 'Tale of the Days of Shakespeare' is mentioned only in the subtitle of two volumes otherwise called *Noontide Leisure; or, Sketches in Summer, Outlines from Nature and Imagination* yet the tale in question ('Montchensey') is at least a volume long and much more of a novel than anything else. A peculiarity of its presentation is that it is offered to the reader in instalments with critical essays by Drake on various poets (chiefly the Abbé de Lille) coming in between. Its plot concerns Eustace Montchensey who falls ill while travelling through Stratford with his beautiful daughter Helen in 1615 and is hospitably cared for by Shakespeare and his family. The Shakespeare of that date is thus described through the eyes of the Montchenseys, but is also not slow to describe himself, offering accounts to his guests of his childhood, the difference the Kenilworth visit made to his life, and his misspent youth, although 'I must beg to be understood as not charging myself, setting one foolish enterprise aside, with any thing more formidable than too frequently neglecting the interests of my father's business for the gratification of my youthful pleasures'.[5] The foolish enterprise referred to is not, of course, pre-marital intercourse with Anne Hathaway, a topic Drake does not broach, but the deer-stealing into which Shakespeare recalls having been led by 'several lawless and hair-brained spirits' with whom he was friendly at the time.[6] To demonstrate how far in his past this episode now is, he takes the Montchenseys on a visit to Charlecote where he exchanges pleasantries about the opening lines of *The Merry Wives* with Sir Thomas Lucy's friendly heir and grandson. When he then returns home, Ben Jonson has already arrived for a short visit.

The first part of 'Montchensey' allows Drake to display material he had collected for *Shakespeare and His Times* in a fictional context and makes him the earliest forerunner of Anthony Burgess who similarly switched easily between fictional and non-fictional forms. What other purpose he has beyond this display only becomes evident in the second part of the novel, when Shakespeare is invited to the Montchenseys' country home in wildest Derbyshire and is attacked on the way by a group of banditti, led by a mysterious gentlemanly figure who instructs his men to desist when he learns the identity of their victim (it is a surprise to realise from Schoenbaum's account of *Shakespeare and His Times* that Drake refers to Byron only once in that work). The bandit leader turns out to be identical to a young, musically-gifted neighbour of the Montchenseys to whom Helen has been attracted, but who is considered an unsuitable future partner because his parentage is unknown. Shakespeare discovers that he belongs, in fact, to a family proscribed under Elizabeth and goes to London where, with the help of his good friend the Earl of Southampton, he has the attainder on the family lifted and secures a pardon for the young man.

Shakespeare is crucial to the plot of 'Montchensey' and has a good deal to say for himself. That is also the case in a later novel, perhaps more obviously in the Scott mould, by Robert Folkestone Williams, one time professor of history at the Cavalry College in Richmond and also an editor of the *New Monthly Magazine*. Williams was the author of numerous works of historical fiction including *The Youth of Shakespeare* (1838) and, in the following year, *Shakespeare and his Friends or, 'The Golden Age' of Merry England*. In this latter novel, Williams represents his hero as even more well-known to Queen Elizabeth than he is in *Kenilworth*: in one scene he reads aloud *The Merry Wives* to her and the assembled Court in such an expert manner that he has them all in stitches. Bringing Shakespeare and Elizabeth together became a common device, as did portraying him in the company of his fellow actors. In this extract he is talking to the young protaganist, Francis.

> At that moment there entered at the door one of the players dressed as King Henry the Fourth, whom Master Shakspeare thus addressed: –
> 'Well, Lowing, and how goeth the play with her majesty?'
> 'Never went anything better,' said he, very cheerfully; 'her majesty hath shewn from the beginning an admirable interest in the story; and Green hath made her laugh till her crown tottered again'; and then he passed on. [...]
> 'There is as goodly a group yonder as you will meet with in a playhouse,' continued [Shakespeare]; 'it consisteth of young Ben Jonson, a veritable son of the muses, who promiseth to be better known than he is; my Lord Buckhurst, one who hath written a tragedy of some note, and loveth to spend his leisure upon players; Master Edmond Tilney, master of the queen's revels, a very proper gentleman, and a courteous, who hath the licensing of plays, and therefore cometh amongst us often; Dr Thomas Lodge, and Dr Thomas Legge, who have writ for our neighbour the Rose with a very fair success; and that pedantic and most conceited coxcomb Master John Lily, who hath invented many comedies, yet is like to get himself more laughed at than any of them. Ben Jonson – he that is standing up – seemeth to have the lion's share of the argument, as is his wont; for his tongue is a rattling famously; and I judge from that, the subject of dispute

concerneth the ancients, for he prideth himself mightily upon his Greek and Latin. But here cometh my excellent good friend and patron Lord Southampton.' At this he broke off, and his companion noticed a noble-looking gentleman, scarce older than himself, well attired, but not too fine in his appointments, who was advancing towards them with an easy courteousness, and a bland aspect.

'Well met, Master Shakspeare,' said he, shaking hands with the other very cordially.

'I'faith, if your lordship be in as good health as am I,' responded Master Shakspeare with a smile, 'then are we "well met," indeed.'

'Ever at it,' exclaimed the Lord Southampton laughingly. 'Surely there never was thy match at quibbles and quirks! Indeed, thou art a very juggler with words, and at the mere touch of thy wit canst give them any meaning that suits thee.'

'In truth, my good Lord,' replied the other, 'my poor words when addressed to you, however little their meaning may be, must needs have a good meaning, for they mean you well at all times; and such cannot help but *suit* me, seeing that I take abundance of care they are brought forth on a *fitting* occasion.'

'There, again!' cried my lord, laughing again very merrily. 'Sure, never was the like! But I have just left her majesty, and rarely have I seen her in a more commendable humour. She doth applaud Burbage to the very echo, and hath laughed at Green till her sides ached for it. I'll tell thee, if thou canst please the higher powers so well, hast thou no cause to fear those foolish pragmatics of the city. Let them do what they list. I have spoken on thy behalf to mine honourable and most esteemed good friend, Sir Thomas Egerton, who, for learning in the law, hath no superior; and he hath promised me to exert himself for thy advantage. Keep a good heart. Knowing that thou hast the protection of Master Attorney General, and art in such absolute favour at court, the aldermen, even if they have the power, the which have I my doubts of, shall not dare drive thee from the Blackfriars. Nay, I should take it in very monstrous hard case indeed, were a few paltry citizens allowed to interfere with the pleasures of so many worshipful lords and gentlemen as find excellent entertainment at the playhouse. Be of good cheer, Master Shakspeare – thou shalt never receive disadvantage at their hands.'

'I am infinitely beholden to you, my good Lord,' said Master Shakspeare. 'It is adding another leaf to that volume of favours your lordship's bountiful spirit hath accorded me.'

'Take not what I have done for thee as anything,' replied my Lord Southampton, putting his hand in a friendly way on t he other's shoulder. 'For, in honest truth, I am ashamed I have as yet been to thee of such exceeding poor service. Fain would I shew in more substantial fashion how honourably I regard the manifold excellencies of thy nature; and be assured I will not rest till I do something to the purpose. But I must needs be gone, for I have a party waiting, with whom is sweet Mistress Varnon; therefore, fare thee well, Master Shakspeare, till we meet again.'[7]

Shakespeare's word-play in his writing is not always of the highest quality but it seems unfortunate that he should (as Williams imagined him) have saved his worst efforts for his conversation. When immediately after Southampton's departure Thomas Green enters, fresh from playing Falstaff to Burbage's Hal, the jokes become even more painful than they had been with his lordship: 'Go to – [...] thou art Green by name and green by nature, therefore thy wit cannot be ripe – and not being ripe must needs be sour', etc. Thomas Greene was a celebrated comic actor of the early Jacobean period, and perhaps before, but he was not a member of the King's Men but of the company patronised by James's Queen (not to be confused with the 'Queen's Men' of the 1580s). Unlike 'Lowing', Greene has no known association with Shakespeare – why it came to be felt that he did, is a matter I deal with later in this chapter.[8] Here I want only to illustrate how enthusiastically, if also clumsily, the hint provided by Scott in *Kenilworth* could be taken up.

It was not only in the novel form that fictional representations of Shakespeare began to proliferate in the early nineteenth century. An idiosyncratic illustration of this is Walter Savage Landor's *Citation and Examination of William Shakespeare, Euseby Treen, Joseph Carnaby, and Silas Gough, clerk, before the worshipful Sir Thomas Lucy, Knight, on the 19th Day of September, in the Year of Grace 1582*. This work, which began as one of Landor's *Imaginary Conversations*, was published in book form in 1834 and its lengthy title gives some indication of the elaborate fancifulness with which it was conceived. To the minor characters mentioned in the title (Euseby Treen and Joseph Carnaby are witnesses who appear against Shakespeare) Landor adds others in an 'Editor's Preface'. There he reprints a letter supposedly sent in 1599 to Ephraim Barnett, the clerk responsible for having recorded Shakespeare's 'examination', by his kinsman Jacob Eldridge who had found work in London with the Earl of Essex.

> Jacob did likewise tell me in his letter, that he was sure I should be happy to hear the success of William Shakspeare, our townsman. And in truth right glad was I to hear of it, being a principal in bringing it about, as those several sheets will show which have the broken tile laid upon them to keep them down compactly.
> Jacob's words are these:

> 'Now I speak of poets, you will be in a maze at hearing that our townsman hath written a power of matter for the playhouse. Neither he nor the booksellers think it quite good enough to print: but I do assure you, on the faith of a Christian, it is not bad; and there is rare fun in the last thing of his about Venus, where a Jew, one Shiloh, is choused out of his money and his revenge. However, the best critics and the greatest lords find fault, and very justly, in the words,

> "Hath not a Jew eyes? hath not a Jew hands, organs, dimensions, senses, affections, passions? fed with the same food, hurt with the same weapons, subject to the same diseases, healed by the same means, warmed and cooled by the same winter and summer, as a Christian is?"

> Surely this is very unchristianlike. Nay, for supposition sake, suppose it to be true, was it his business to tell the people so? Was it his duty to ring

the crier's bell and cry to them, *the sorry Jews are quite as much men as you are?* The church, luckily, has let him alone for the present; and the queen winks upon it. The best defence he can make for himself is, that it comes from the mouth of a Jew, who says many other things as abominable. Master Greene may over-rate him; but Master Greene declares that if William goes on improving and taking his advice, it will be desperate hard work in another seven years to find so many as half-a-dozen chaps equal to him within the liberties.

Master Greene and myself took him with us to see the burial of Master Edmund Spenser in Westminster Abbey, on the 19th of January last. The halberdmen pushed us back as having no business there. Master Greene told them he belonged to the queen's company of players. William Shakspeare could have said the same, but did not. And I, fearing that Master Greene and he might be halberded back into the crowd, showed the badge of the Earl of Essex. Whereupon did the serjeant ground his halberd, and say unto me,

"That badge commands admittance everywhere: your folk likewise may come in."

Master Greene was red-hot angry, and told me he would bring him before the *council.*

William smiled, and Master Greene said,

"Why! Would not you, if you were in my place?"

He replied,

"I am an half inclined to do worse; to bring him before the *audience* some spare hour."

At the close of the burial-service all the poets of the age threw their pens into the grave, together with the pieces they had composed in praise or lamentation of the deceased. William Shakspeare was the only poet who abstained from throwing in either pen or poem; at which no one marvelled, he being of low estate, and the others not having yet taken him by the hand. Yet many authors recognised him, not indeed as author, but as player; and one, civiler than the rest, came up unto him triumphantly, his eyes sparkling with glee and satisfaction, and said consolatorily,

"In due time, my honest friend, you may be admitted to do as much for one of us."

"After such encouragement," replied our townsman, "I am bound in duty to give you the preference, should I indeed be worthy."

This was the only smart thing he uttered all the remainder of the day; during the whole of it he appeared to be half lost, I know not whether in melancholy or in meditation, and soon left us.'

Here endeth all that my kinsman Jacob wrote about William Shakspeare, saving and excepting his excuse for having written so much.[9]

Insofar as Landor's own mind can be detected behind or beneath the multiple ironies of his writing, there seems to have been some confusion in it between the Thomas Greene who is described at one point in the 'Editor's Preface' as 'our worthy townsman' (a real person who became clerk to the Stratford Corporation and refers to Shakespeare as his 'cousin') and the equally real Thomas Greene the actor. Yet perhaps he felt he had a poetic licence to join them together in his effort to convey how the success of Shakespeare in London might have been viewed and registered back home in Stratford. In the main body of his book he is trying to imagine how Shakespeare's extraordinary gifts would have manifested themselves in his youth. One model here is Jesus in the Temple. In most biographies of saints, great leaders or famous artists, there are episodes from early life which anticipate the achievements to come and which show the subject as dolphin-like, partly transcending the element in which he or she has been obliged by Fate to move. There are unfortunately no historical records to tell us how Shakespeare behaved in Stratford and what impression he made on his friends and acquaintances; but Landor was one of the first of very many to compensate with fiction for what is missing.

About an hour before noontide, the youth William Shakspeare, accused of deer-stealing, and apprehended for that offence, was brought into the great hall at Charlecote, where, having made his obeisance, it was most graciously permitted him to stand.

The worshipful Sir Thomas Lucy, Knight, seeing him right opposite, on the farther side of the long table, and fearing no disadvantage, did frown upon him with great dignity; then, deigning ne'er a word to the culprit, turned he his face toward his chaplain, Sir Silas Gough, who stood beside him, and said unto him most courteously, and unlike unto one who in his own right commandeth,

'Stand out of the way! What are those two varlets bringing into the room?'

'The table, sir,' replied Master Silas, 'upon the which the consumption of the venison was perpetrated.'

The youth, William Shakspeare, did thereupon pray and beseech his lordship most fervently, in this guise :

'O sir! Do not let him turn the tables against me, who am only a simple stripling, and he an old cogger.'

But Master Silas did bite his nether lip, and did cry aloud,

'Look upon those deadly spots!'

And his worship did look thereupon most staidly, and did say in the ear of Master Silas, but in such wise that it reached even unto mine,

'Good honest chandlery, methinks!'

'God grant it may turn out so!' ejaculated Master Silas.

The youth, hearing these words, said unto him,

'I fear, Master Silas, gentry like you often pray God to grant what *he* would rather not; and now and then what *you* would rather not.'

Sir Silas was wroth at this rudeness of speech about God in the face of a preacher, and said, reprovingly,

'Out upon thy foul mouth, knave! Upon which lie slaughter and venison.'

Whereupon did William Shakspeare sit mute awhile, and discomfited; then, turning toward Sir Thomas, and looking and speaking as one submiss and contrite, he thus appealed unto him :

'Worshipful sir! Were there any signs of venison on my mouth, Master Silas could not for his life cry out upon it, nor help kissing it as 'twere a wench's.'

Sir Thomas looked upon him with most lordly gravity and wisdom, and said unto him in a voice that might have come from the bench, 'Youth! Thou speakest irreverently'; and then unto master Silas, 'Silas! To the business on hand. Taste the fat upon yon boor's table, which the constable hath brought hither, good Master Silas! And declare upon oath, being sworn in my presence, first, whether said fat do proceed of venison; secondly, whether said venison be of buck or doe.'

Whereupon the reverend Sir Silas did go incontinently, and did bend forward his head, shoulders, and body, and did severally taste four white solid substances upon an oaken board; said board being about two yards long, and one yard four inches wide; found in, and brought thither from, the tenement or messuage of Andrew Haggit, who hath absconded. Of these four white solid substances, two were somewhat larger than a groat, and thicker; one about the size of King Henry the Eighth's shilling, when our late sovran lord of blessed memory was toward the lustiest; and the other, that is to say the middlemost, did resemble in some sort a mushroom, not over fresh, turned upward on its stalk.

'And what sayest thou, Master Silas?' quoth the knight.

In reply whereunto Sir Silas thus averred:

'Venison! O' my conscience!

Buck! or burn me alive!

The three splashes in the circumference are verily and indeed venison; buck, moreover, and Charlecote buck, upon my oath!'

Then carefully tasting the protuberance in the centre, he spat it out, crying,

'Pho! pho! villain! villain!' and shaking his fist at the culprit.

Whereat the said culprit smiled and winked, and said off-hand,

'Save thy spittle, Master Silas! It would supply a gaudy mess to the hungriest litter; but it would turn them from whelps into wolvets. 'Tis pity to throw the best of thee away. Nothing comes out of thy mouth that is not savory and solid, bating thy wit, thy sermons, and thy promises.'

It was my duty to write down the very words, irreverent as they are, being so commanded. More of the like, it is to be feared, would have ensued, but that Sir Thomas did check him, saying shrewdly,

'Young man! I perceive that if I do not stop thee in thy courses, thy name, being involved in thy company's, may one day or other reach across the county; and folks may handle it and turn it about, as it deserveth, from Coleshill to Nuneaton, from Bromwicham to Brownsover. And who knoweth but that, years after thy death, the very house wherein thou wert born may be pointed at, and commented on, by knots of people, gentle and simple! What a shame for an honest man's son! Thanks to me, who consider of measures to prevent it! Posterity shall laud and glorify me for plucking thee clean out of her head, and for picking up timely a ticklish skittle, that might overthrow with it a power of others just as light. I will rid the hundred of thee, with God's blessing! nay, the whole shire. We will have none such in our county: we justices are agreed upon it, and we will keep our word now and for evermore. Woe betide any that resembles thee in any part of him!'

Whereunto Sir Silas added,

'We will dog him, and worry him, and haunt him, and bedevil him; and if ever he hear a comfortable word, it shall be in a language very different from his own.'

'As different as thine is from a Christian's,' said the youth.

'Boy! Thou art slow of apprehension,' said Sir Thomas, with much gravity; and, taking up the cue, did rejoin:

'Master Silas would impress upon thy ductile and tender mind the danger of evil doing; that we, in other words, that justice, is resolved to follow him up, even beyond his country, where he shall hear nothing better than the Italian or the

Spanish, or the black language, or the language of Turk or Troubadour, or Tartar or Mongle. And forsooth, for this gentle and indirect reproof, a gentleman in priest's orders is told by a stripling that he lacketh Christianity! Who then shall give it?'

Shakespeare. Who, indeed? When the founder of the feast leaveth an invited guest so empty! Yea, sir, the guest was invited, and the board was spread. The fruits that lay upon it be there still, and fresh as ever; and the bread of life in those capacious canisters is unconsumed and unbroken.

Sir Silas (aside). The knave maketh me hungry with his mischievous similitudes.

Sir Thomas. Thou hast aggravated thy offence, Will Shakspeare! Irreverent caitiff! Is this a discourse for my chaplain and clerk? Can he or the worthy scribe Ephraim (his worship was pleased to call me worthy) write down such words as those, about litter and wolvets, for the perusal and meditation of the grand jury? If the whole corporation of Stratford had not unanimously given it against thee, still his tongue would catch thee, as the evet catcheth a gnat. Know, sirrah, the reverend Sir Silas, albeit ill appointed for riding, and not over-fond of it, goeth to every house wherein is a venison feast for thirty miles round. Not a buck's hoof on any stable-door but it awakeneth his recollections like a red letter. –

This wholesome reproof did bring the youth back again to his right senses; and then said he, with contrition, and with a wisdom beyond his years, and little to be expected from one who had spoken just before so unadvisedly and rashly,

'Well do I know it, your worship! And verily do I believe that a bone of one, being shovelled among the soil upon his coffin, would forthwith quicken him. Sooth to say, there is ne'er a buckhound in the county but he treateth him as a godchild, patting him on the head, soothing his velvety ear between thumb and fore-finger, ejecting tick from tenement, calling him *fine fellow, noble lad*, and giving him his blessing, as one dearer to him than a king's death to a debtor, or a bastard to a dad of eighty. This is the only kindness I ever heard of Master Silas toward his fellow creatures. Never hold me unjust, Sir Knight, to Master Silas. Could I learn other good of him, I would freely say it; for we do good by speaking it, and none is easier. Even bad men are not bad men while they praise the just. Their first step backward is more troublesome and wrenching to them than the first forward.'

'In God's name, where did he gather all this?' whispered his worship to the chaplain, by whose side I was sitting. 'Why, he talks like a man of forty-seven, or more!'[10]

This extract will seem long but it is short in comparison with the text as a whole and some length is necessary to convey Landor's distinctive flavour. More scholarly in manner than Williams, he clearly means to be light-hearted but as Ian Jack has said: 'The humour is laboured: it is the sort of funny book one might order with a clear conscience in the British Museum'.[11] Shakespeare emerges from it as largely a grown-up version of his own cheeky young man-servants, frustrated by the level of intelligence around him; but in the text as a whole, more interest is generated by the other characters as their creator struggles to write drama. A play is what one feels Landor would have liked the 'Examination' to be but he has too heavy a touch.

A much lighter, or at least more popular, one is demonstrated by Charles

A. Somerset in his *Shakespeare's Early Days*, first performed at the Theatre Royal in Convent Garden on 29 October 1829. This work deals with so many different aspects of the Shakespeare legend, and in certain cases does so in such a highly unusual way that, unlike the 'Examination', it is worth a close look. The first scene takes place in front of the 'House of John Shakespeare, wool-stapler, of Stratford upon Avon, in which our immortal bard was born'.[12] The notion of Shakespeare's father as a wool merchant, rather than a glover, comes from Rowe's 1709 biography, but it is not completely wrong since it has been shown in recent times that he did from time to time deal illegally in wool.[13] He is talking in this opening scene with his wife who is represented as being of much higher birth than his own: 'By marrying Mary Arden', Somerset informs any reader of the play in a note, 'Shakespeare's father obtained a grant of arms from the Herald's College'. As I have mentioned elsewhere, a coat of arms was granted to John Shakespeare in 1596. Three years later he applied to have his arms combined with those of his wife. If nothing which is now visible came of this application, it may have been because the Heralds had as much difficulty, as everyone has had since, in establishing quite how Shakespeare's maternal grandfather, an affluent yeoman rather than an obvious 'gentleman', was related to a rich and influential family of Ardens who also lived in Warwickshire, but at Castle Bromwich close to Birmingham. That his mother was well-born is, however, part of the legend and Somerset relies on it at the beginning of his play by having her state, after her husband has complained that Willy refuses to apply himself seriously to business like his brother Gilbert: 'But it liketh me well, goodman John, to see my boy herd not with boors and clodpoles, but the rather with young gentles of good degree, thereby giving proof of his noble descent. For doth he not proceed in a direct line – that is, on his mother's side, from the ancient and honourable stock of the Ardens?'[14]

In the second scene young Willy is asleep, presided over by Titania and Oberon, and has visions 'passing before him as he slumbers'. With an intended effect clearly similar to that of the pageant in Garrick's *Jubilee*, these visions consist of Falstaff, Richard III, Juliet, Hamlet (with ghost), Macbeth (with witches), and the like. He is woken up by the entrance of his family. His father believes that he is crazed and wants to have him bled, but his mother protests that 'Not a drop of his gentle blood shall my dear Willy lose – not a drop!'[15] Their dispute is cut short by the appearance of Slyboots, Sir Thomas Lucy's bailiff, who has come to arrest Willy for shooting one of Charlecote's bucks.

The third scene of Somerset's play is thus that 'examination' which Landor deals with at such length. As in Landor's version, young Shakespeare here gives Sir Thomas and those others present, which include the members of his own family, lessons in logic and eloquent expression, but what is strikingly different is the way he explains how he came to be poaching the Charlecote deer.

WIL. S.:   It was not for myself I shot the buck,
                    For I receive at home, from my dear parents,
                    Both food and raiment, better than I merit.

SIR T.:   Not for thyself, say'st thou? For whom else pray?

WIL. S.:   I'll tell your worship. In a little cottage
                    By the wood-side, there dwells an humble shepherd:
                    A man, whose life, though spent in industry,
                    Hath ever been one tissue of misfortunes;
                    Disease destroyed his flocks, and poverty
                    Hath, from a man of substance, brought him down
                    To abject wretchedness. 'Twas yester even,
                    As in my wanderings I passed his cottage,
                    I heard a moan - a second struck mine ear;
                    And, entering the poor man's humble dwelling,
                    I there beheld a scene of wretchedness
                    Too great for tongue to tell!

SIR T.   I marvel at thy speech. Proceed, young man.

WIL. S.:   His wretched wife, his helpless babes, himself,
                    On the bare earth lay stretched! - their pallid cheeks,
                    Their sunken eyes proclaimed the ruthless war,
                    Which nature then was waging 'gainst disease,
                    Hunger, and cold! Her mortal enemies!
                    'Have you no food?' quoth I.
                    'None, for the last two days,' was their reply;
                    Like one pursued by fiends, forth from the cottage
                    I madly rushed, resolved to bring them food!
                    My home I could not reach - it was too far;
                    I therefore shot the buck I chanc'd to meet,
                    And on my shoulders bore it off in triumph,
                    To the poor shepherd's dwelling; there arriv'd,
                    I lit a fire - prepared some savoury broth
                    For the poor sufferers - tended them myself
                    And when I saw their eyes beam joy again,
                    And heard them speak sweet words of gratitude,
                    And view'd the smiling infants all around me,
                    I thought them angels from the realms of light!
                    Their cottage, paradise! Myself in heaven!
                    (turning to his father)
                    Thus, my dear father, did I pass the night.

MARY S.   My boy Willy deserves to be a Parliament member, for such a speech.

JOHN S. *(crossing to William Shakspeare)*: Much more for such humanity! Thy hand, my
                    brave boy, I did thee wrong in thinking ill of thee.

GIL. S. *(half crying, going to Shakspeare)*: Let me embrace thee, brother Willy. Prithee,
                    describe unto me where about dwelleth the poor shepherd and his
                    wretched family, and I will send them, straight out of mine own
                    means, a present of fleecy hosiery.

*(He treads accidentally on Sir Thomas Lucy's toe, at which his worship is highly incensed,
and strikes at him with his cane.)*[16]

This is a splendid, pre-Victorian example of how to have your cake and eat it, conceived by someone who remembers Robin Hood but has also read Wordsworth's *Lyrical Ballads*. Shakespeare, accorded the privilege of verse while those around him have to make to do with prose, is guilty of deer-poaching, but for the best possible, humanitarian reasons. The Sir Thomas whose toe is trodden here is a comic figure, 'a second Sir John Falstaff, for corpulence',[17] as Somerset's stage directions read. He fines Shakespeare, whose parents immediately stump up the money and, in his exasperation at the manner in which he has been addressed and the way the examination has gone, he dismisses his clerk Drawl and appoints Slyboots in his stead. The problem is that Slyboots can neither read nor write so that when Sir Thomas asks him to draw up a proclamation against deer-poaching which can be pinned on the gates outside Charlecote, he has to ask Shakespeare to write it for him. The young man agrees to do so and then soliloquises about his need to leave Stratford for London.

WIL. S. *(soliloquy)*: I'm weary of this dull and rustic life,
        And for a time will quit my father's roof:
        But whither wend my steps? I do remember,
        Some few years since, a troop of merry players,
        Who came to Stratford, jovial boon companions;
        If I err not, the troop is now in London.
        What, if I join them – sure, 'twere no offence,
        For, moralizing – 'all the world's a stage,
        And all the men and women merely players; –
        They have their exits, and their entrances,
        And one man in his time plays many parts' –
        Then, why not I? Oh, for a sphere of action!
        Where the mind's vigour hath unbounded range!
        Nature and Fate both point me out the way;
        Shakspeare, it is thy duty to obey.
                (Looking off, E.)
        Father, farewell! Dear mother, do not grieve;
        Farewell, ye dear companions of my youth!
        William will ne'er forget your love and truth:
        It grieves his soul to fill your souls with sorrow,
        Yet evening storms oft bring a sunny morrow –
        In heaven's name then, Shakspeare, on to London!
                (Exit, L.[18]

Solving the problem of how to make Shakespeare talk by giving him lines taken either directly or partially from the plays would become a very common device.

Young Shakespeare has to flee to London because, of course, the 'proclamation' which he writes for Slyboots, and which is read out in front of Sir Thomas before it can be pinned on his gates, consists of the traditional lines about Lucy being an ass (without however the pun on lice or the reference to his wife's infidelity). Enraged, Sir Thomas swears to pursue Shakespeare to

London where the second Act of Somerset's play finds them both. The action begins with a dialogue between Richard Burbage and the famous Elizabethan comic actor, Tarleton, in which they discuss the prize the Queen is offering for the best poem on the comparative merits of comedy and tragedy. They lament the fact that because 'the mighty Dr Orthodox, the Master of Revels' has already put himself forward others have been discouraged; and Burbage says that the only David he knows who could defeat this Goliath of learning is his fellow Stratfordian, William Shakespeare. The legend that Shakespeare was somehow related to James Burbage comes from the fact that in 1582 his father had rented a house to a person with that same surname; but the Stratford connections of the London Burbages have never been established.[19]

It is, nonetheless, for his fellow townsman Burbage that Shakespeare is looking in Act 2 of the play. The second scene finds him outside the Globe soliloquising once again.

WIL. S. (*soliloquy*):There stands the Globe, the house of entertainment:
And yet, methinks, the players of the day
Seek more to gratify the vulgar crew
With idle foolery, than to mend the heart,
By acting Nature's self in colours true!
(*Loud cries heard without, R. S. E.*)
What cry was that? See, on the river's brink
There rides a noble knight – his foaming steed,
Refusing to be curbed by bit or rein,
Now plunges wildly : some adventurous arm
Must seize the bridle, else the rider's lost!
(*Rushes off, R. S. E. – After a momentary pause, loud shouts of acclamation are heard without.*[20]

The rider whom Shakespeare saves is 'Lord Southampton'. Refusing money for his brave act, Shakespeare says that he would have behaved just as he did had the person in danger been a poor peasant rather than a noble lord; but he is nevertheless pleased to hear Southampton say that he will be his sponsor when he competes for the Queen's imminent poetry prize. Before he does that, however, he follows Burbage's advice and pays a visit to Dr Orthodox in order to secure a licence for the play he has brought with him to London. The resulting exchanges show how firmly fixed in the public mind was the idea of Shakespeare as the poet of Nature, in every sense.

WIL. S.:   I come, most sapient sir, to crave your warrant
              For my new tragedy ; 'tis for the Globe.
DOC. (*eyeing Shakspeare suspiciously*): Thou write a tragedy! Who art thou, youngster?
              Say of what college art thou a graduate?
WIL. S.:   I cannot boast of learning; all I know
              Was taught me by a worthy schoolmistress.
DOC.:   A schoolmistress! Some old village grandam, no doubt.

WIL. S. (*with dignity*): Not so;

> Creation's boundless temple was my school –
> Mankind my study! 'Tis a royal college,
> Endowed most nobly by the King of kings!
> There in one hour nature teaches more
> Than in an age your Greek and Latin lore!

DOC.:   Profane idea! An thou art not erudite, young man, how can'st thou ever hope to be a poet?

WIL. S.:   Be my work good or ill, I crave your warrant. And wait upon your leisure.

DOC. (*contemptuously*): Where is this tragedy of yours?

WIL. S.:   You have it, sir; 'tis entitled Hamlet.

PETER (R.):   'Tis here, most sapient sir.

> (*Opening a book-case and handing the Doctor a MS.*)

DOC.:   I recollect – hem! Hamlet. (*Looking over the M.S.*) And a precious Hamlet it is, too. Here we have a ghost – a youth who feigns madness, and a young maiden truly out of her wits – then come a couple of grave-diggers, – now, really, young man, prithee tell me, art thou not often, at the full of the moon, somewhat deranged? Out of pure friendship do I counsel thee to return home, with all convenient speed, and drive a cart, hew wood, carry water, or follow the plough – but attempt not to write tragedies, for, without Greek and Latin, how canst thou possibly hope to thrive?

WIL. S. (L):   I pray you, sir, judge not too hastily.

DOC.:   Moreover, here is one Laertes, whom you, in your first act, send from Denmark to Paris, already returned again in the fourth. Marry, now, but thou must be a most unconscionable playwright! Prithee, tell me, doth thy father keep post-horses with wings, that thou requirest thy spectators to travel with this same Master Laertes no less than six hundred leagues in somewhat less than two hundred minutes? Hast thou never heard of Aristotle and his three grand unities of action, time, and place?

WIL. S.:   Never, most sapient sir.

DOC.:   So it appeareth, most assuredly. Go, youngster. And follow the plough. Six hundred leagues in two hundred minutes! Oh, monstrous violation of all rule! Oh, immortal Aristotle! What wouldst thou say to this?

WIL. S. (*with dignity*): Let Aristotle say what he thinks fit – Shakspeare replies: – What is so quick as thought?

> 'Not e'en the lightning, which doth cease to be,
> Ere we can say it lightens!'
> The glowing fancy soars aloft to heaven,
> And, in the twinkling of an eye, descends
> From thence into the fathomless abyss
> Of earth's deep centre, or the ocean's bed!
> From east to west, from pole to pole, she flies,
> Far swifter than Apollo's golden rays
> Can give the hills their early morning kiss!
> Dull souls may fail in the gigantic race,
> But nobler spirits know nor time nor space!

Doc.: Prithee, tell me, from whom didst thou learn that speech, young man?

Wil. S.: From good Dame Nature, sir, my schoolmistress.

Doc. (*with a sarcastic smile*): 'Tis evident thou art not compos mentis, youngster; and therefore –

Wil. S. (*impatiently*): The warrant, sapient sir – I crave your warrant.

Doc.: My duty compelleth me to refuse it, seeing this, thy tragedy of Hamlet, is replete with absurdity, ignorance, and profanity!

Wil. S. (*confounded, yet speedily recollecting himself*): Know you this ring, sir?

Doc. (*regarding it*): It is the signet ring of my Lord Southampton.

Wil. S.: His lordship is my patron.

Doc.: Indeed! (*Bows most obsequiously.*) Oh! that's quite another case – young gentleman, you shall have our warrant instantly. Peter! A pen here. (*Peter brings one, and a portfolio from bookcase – the Doctor signs the warrant.*) 'Tis done! (*Hands it to Shakspeare.*) Here, young gentleman, is our warrant, and most heartily do we wish you every success. Our own superior discernment leads us to discover that you have talent – much talent; and, under the high auspices of my Lord Southampton, you may, provided you study Aristotle, one day become as great a poet as the renowned Dr Orthodox, who stands before you.

Wil. S. (*pointedly*): He who is great in his own estimation,
Is like a man standing upon a mountain –
All men seem little to him, from above;
And he, heaven knows, looks little from below.
[*Exit, L.*

Doc.: Peter, follow me.
[*Exit, with a pompous air, followed by* Peter, *in humble distance, R.*[21]

In publishing his play, Somerset added a somewhat shamefaced note to his mention here of *Hamlet* which reads: 'The chronological order of Shakespeare's plays being by no means clearly established, I considered myself at liberty to select which I pleased as our bard's supposed first production'.[22] The order is certainly not clear but neither is it quite *that* unclear. Jonson's contribution to the First Folio provides the inspiration for Dr Orthodox, whose obsequiousness when Southampton's name is mentioned contrasts with Shakespeare's own sturdy independence: though his mother may be a snob he himself is an egalitarian in matters both social and intellectual and thus a figure to whom all classes in the community can respond. In the final scene which takes place in Elizabeth's palace, he of course wins the poetry prize but not before fervent expressions of patriotic loyalty from Southampton and Leicester have been interrupted by the news that the Spanish Armada has just been defeated. Somerset saves himself some trouble by having Elizabeth merely look over the two competing poems before choosing Shakespeare's but, before she can award the prize, Sir Thomas Lucy bursts in, intent on vengeance. He is then forced by the Queen to shake hands with Shakespeare who, outdoing Dick Whittington, now enjoys royal favour.

As the extracts from Scott, Drake, Williams and Somerset intermittently demonstrate, 'bardolotry' – that useful term coined by George Bernard Shaw – was in full swing in the early nineteenth century. One version of it is apparent in an essay Leigh Hunt published in *The Examiner* in 1820 on the subject of 'Shakespeare's birthday'.

> O thou divine human creature, – greater name than even divine poet or divine philosopher, – and yet thou wast all three! – a very spring and vernal abundance of all fair and noble things is to be found in thy productions! They are truly a second nature. We walk in them, with whatever society we please; either with men, or fair women, or circling spirits, or with none but the whispering airs and leaves. Thou makest worlds of green trees and gentle natures for us, in thy forests of Arden, and thy courtly retirements of Navarre. Thou bringest us among the holiday lasses on the green sward; layest us to sleep among fairies in the bowers of midsummer; wakest us with the song of the lark and the silver-sweet voices of lovers; bringest more music to our ears, both from earth and from the planets; anon settest us upon enchanted islands, where it welcomes us again, from the touching of invisible instruments; and, after all, restorest us to our still-desired haven, the arms of humanity. Whether grieving us or making us glad, thou makest us kinder and happier. The tears which thou fetchest down are like the rains of April, softening the times that come after them. Thy smiles are those of the month of love, the more blessed and universal for the tears.[23]

Since effusions in this vein were common, there must have been a secret hope in some readers that the topic of Shakespeare could be treated comically, at least from time to time. One of the writers who obliged was the playwright and journalist, Douglas Jerrold. The governing comic idea in the essay which Jerrold published in the *New Monthly Magazine* in 1837, is the popularity of Shakespeare in China and he claims to have discovered 'radiant evidence of the admission of the Great Teacher to the Sacred City'. He suggests that a theatrical company ought to be sent to Canton immediately since 'at no point of time could we spare so many actors for exportation; the pain of the sacrifice being somewhat alleviated by an indifference on the part of the town whether they ever returned again.' His irony is directed less against the actors themselves – although he does suggest that many of them play 'equally well in English or in Chinese' – than against a public taste which forces theatre managers to offer extracts from Shakespeare 'between an opera and a dance. No; we fear it is only in China that five long acts in one evening will again be placidly endured, patience being a distinguishing virtue of the Chinese'.[24] His evidence for their having discovered the delights of Shakespeare is a Chinese copy of the picture from the Boydell Gallery (see p. 128) which a friend has bought at an auction. This is the one which shows Falstaff in the buck basket, with the merry wives looking on. Inserted between the picture and the frame, Jerrold claims, was an account in Mandarin of Shakespeare's life which he has obligingly had translated.

I send, O Ting, from the barbarian ship, a picture of barbarians. Make one for your friend, like unto it; in size, in shape, and colour, even the same. But why should I waste words with Ting, whose pencil is true as the tongue of Confutzee? No; I will straightway deliver to him all my studies have made known to me of the barbarians, written on the canvas before him; for how can even Ting paint the faces of barbarians in their very truth, if he know not the history not only of themselves but of their fathers?

The he barbarian with the big belly was called Forlstoff, and in time was known as Surgeon Forlstoff; from which, there is no doubt, he was a skilful leech in the army of the barbarian king, more of whom in good season. Forlstoff's father was one Shak, or Shake, Speare or Spear; for there have been great tumults among the barbarians about the *e*. In nothing does the ignorance of the English barbarians more lamentably discover itself than in the origin they obstinately give to their Shakspeare; who, according to them, was, like the great Brahme, hatched in an egg on the bank of a river, as may be seen in a thousand idle books in which he is called the 'swan of Haveone.' And this conceit was further manifested in the building of a place called 'the Swan Theatre,' where the barbarians were wont to worship. There is little known of Shakspeare's wife, Forlstoff's mother, and that little proves her to have been an idle person, given to great sleep and sloth, as is shown by her getting nothing at the death of her husband but his 'second-best bed.'

If Forlstoff would not, at a later time of life, leave off stealing, there is little doubt that he owed the fault to his father Shakspeare, who was forced to fly to London, which is a sacred city for all thieves, for having stolen an antelope, an animal consecrated to the higher kind of barbarians, and which it is death for the poor to touch. Indeed, the flesh of the antelope is to be eaten with safety by very few of the barbarians, it having killed even many of their Eldermen immediately after dinner.

When Shakspeare came to London he was poor and without friends, and he held the horses of the rich barbarians who came to worship at a temple on the banks of the river. In time, he learned to make shoes for the horses; and in such esteem are the shoes still held by the barbarians, that they are bought at any price, and nailed at the threshold of their houses and barns; for where they are nailed, the foolish natives think no fire, no pestilence will come, and no evil thing have any strength. Such is the silly idolatry of the barbarians.

At length Shakspeare got admitted into the temple; and there he showed himself master of the greatest arts; and he wrote charms upon paper which, it is said, will make a man weep or laugh with very happiness, - will bring spirits from the sky and devils from the water, - will open the heart of a man and show what creeps within it, - will now snatch a crown from a king, and now put wings to the back of a beggar. And all this they say Shakspeare did, and studied not. No, beloved Ting, he was not like Sing, who, though but a poor cowherd, became wise by poring on his book spread between the horns of his cow, he travelling on her back.

And Shakspeare proceeded in his marvels, and he became rich; and even the queen of the barbarians was seen to smile at him, and once, with a burning look, to throw her glove at him; but Shakspeare, it is said, to the discomfiture of the queen, returned the glove, taking no further notice of the amatory invitation.

19. Falstaff in the Laundry Basket, (Act III Sc iii The Merry Wives of Windsor)
painted by the Rev. Matthew William Peters and engraved by John Peter Simon for John
Boydell's Shakespeare Gallery, 1791–1802, published 1802.

In a ripe season of his life, Shakspeare gave up conjuring, and returned to the village on the banks of the river Haveone, where, as it is ignorantly believed, he was hatched, and where he lived in the fulness of fortune. He had laid down his conjuring rod and taken off his gown, and passed for nothing more than a man, and it is said - though you, beloved Ting, who see the haughty eyes and curling noses of the lesser mandarins, can, after what I have writ of Shakspeare, hardly believe it - thought himself nothing more.

Shakspeare built himself a house and planted a tree. The house is gone, but the barbarians preserve bricks of it in their inner chambers, even - I tremble as I pen it - as we preserve the altars of our gods.

The tree was cut down by a fakir in a brain fever, but the wood is still worshipped. And this, oh Ting! I would not ask you to believe, had not your own eyes witnessed that wonderful tree, the leaves whereof falling to the ground, become mice! Hence, learn, that the leaves of Shakspeare's mulberry have become men, and on a certain day every year, with mulberry boughs about their heads, their bodies clothed in their richest garments, they chant praises to the memory of Shakspeare, and drink wine to his name.

Shakspeare - Forlstoff's father, and the father of a hundred lusty sons and daughters, such as until that time had never been born, Shakspeare - died! He was buried in a chest of cedar, set about with plates of gold. On one of these plates was writ some magic words; for thieves, breaking into the grave, were fixed and changed to stone; and are now to be seen even as they were first struck by the charm of the magician. And so much, beloved Ting, of Shakspeare, Forlstoff's father.[25]

This is hardly vintage comic writing and its readers would have been entitled to feel that Dickens, Jerrold's admirer and friend, would have developed the topic much better. But at least several prominent aspects of the Shakespeare legend are treated here without the customary awe and reverence; and both the tone and the approach are hardly less inappropriate that those which Carlyle was to adopt four years later in his comments on Shakespeare in 'The Hero as Poet'.

Curious enough how, as it were by mere accident, this man came to us. I think always, so great, quiet, complete and self-sufficing is this Shakspeare, had the Warwickshire Squire not prosecuted him for deer-stealing, we had perhaps never heard of him as a Poet! The woods and skies, the rustic Life of Man in Stratford there, had been enough for this man! But indeed that strange outbudding of our whole English Existence, which we call the Elizabethan Era, did not it too come as of its own accord? The 'Tree Igdrasil' buds and withers by its own laws, - too deep for our scanning. Yet it does bud and wither, and every bough and leaf of it is there, by fixed eternal laws; not a Sir Thomas Lucy but comes at the hour fit for him. Curious, I say, and not sufficiently considered: how everything does cooperate with all; not a leaf rotting on the highway but is indissoluble portion of solar and stellar systems; no thought, word or act of man but has sprung withal out of all men, and works sooner or later, recognisably or irrecognisably, on all men! It is all a Tree: circulation of sap and influences, mutual communication of every minutest leaf with the lowest talon of a root, with every other greatest and minutest portion of the whole. The Tree Igdrasil, that has its roots down in the Kingdoms of Hela and Death, and whose boughs overspread the highest heaven![26]

When people today talk of the interdependence of all things, they are more likely to repeat the claim that the movement of a butterfly's wings in one continent produces storms in another, rather than refer to the tree Igdrasil whose branches, according to Scandinavian mythology, extend throughout the universe and uphold it. This general notion may not, as Carlyle says, be 'sufficiently considered', but in that case neither is the fact that Sir Thomas Lucy may never have prosecuted Shakespeare for deer-poaching. A detail of this kind is however unimportant for a writer who is always happiest in generalities.

> Well: this is our poor Warwickshire Peasant, who rose to be Manager of a Playhouse, so that he could live without begging; whom the Earl of Southampton cast some kind glances on; whom Sir Thomas Lucy, many thanks to him, was for sending to the Treadmill! We did not account him a god, like Odin, while he dwelt with us; – on which point there were much to be said. But I will say rather, or repeat: In spite of the sad state Hero-worship now lies in, consider what this Shakspeare has actually become among us. Which Englishman we ever made, in this land of ours, which million of Englishmen, would we not give-up rather than the Stratford Peasant? There is no regiment of highest Dignitaries that we would sell him for. He is the grandest thing we have yet done. For our honour among foreign nations, as an ornament to our English Household, what item is there that we would not surrender rather than him? Consider now, if they asked us, Will you give-up your Indian Empire or your Shakspeare, you English; never have had any Indian Empire, or never have had any Shakspeare? Really it were a grave question. Official persons would answer doubtless in official language; but we, for our part too, should not we be forced to answer: Indian Empire, or no Indian Empire; we cannot do without Shakspeare! Indian Empire will go, at any rate, some day; but this Shakspeare does not go, he lasts for ever with us; we cannot give-up our Shakspeare![27]

As Jerrold's piece also reminds us, this was an age of continuing imperial expansion and Carlyle involves Shakespeare in the imperial debate by making him a national asset more than equivalent in importance to the Indian Empire. The choice he offers is made especially dramatic by the claim that the man whom Carlyle puts in the balance opposite India began life as a 'poor Warwickshire peasant'. Shakespeare would no doubt have been as surprised to hear himself described in this way as he would to have learned that his works were felt to be worth *any* overseas possession, however small it was.

Carlyle's reference to Shakespeare as a 'peasant' might seem to suggest that a rash of fictional portrayals had caused people to forget all Malone's hard work and put a stop to biographical enquiry. But that was far from being the case. One of the more interesting attempts at a non-fictional life is the long entry on Shakespeare which De Quincey wrote for the seventh edition of the *Encyclopaedia Britannica*, first published in 1842. There De Quincey insists on the gentility of both his subject's parents although he recognises that there must have been a time when the Shakespeare family ran into financial difficulties. Because of these, although Shakespeare's early education was probably conducted 'on as liberal a scale as the resources of Stratford would allow', De Quincey felt that it was not possible to know whether his progress thereafter lay 'through the humilities of absolute poverty, or through the chequered paths of gentry lying in the shade'.[28] But does this matter?

Yet still, it will be urged, the curiosity is not illiberal which would seek to ascertain the precise career through which Shakspeare ran. This we readily concede; and we are anxious ourselves to contribute anything in our power to the settlement of a point so obscure. What we have wished to protest against is the spirit of partisanship in which this question has too generally been discussed. For, whilst some, with a foolish affectation of plebeian sympathies, overwhelm us with the insipid commonplaces about birth and ancient descent, as honours containing nothing meritorious, and rush eagerly into an ostentatious exhibition of all the circumstances which favour the notion of a humble station and humble connexions, others, with equal forgetfulness or true dignity, plead with the intemperance and partiality of a legal advocate for the pretensions of Shakspeare to the hereditary rank of gentleman. Both parties violate the majesty of the subject. When we are seeking for the sources of the Euphrates or the St. Lawrence, we look for no proportions to the mighty volume of waters in that particular summit amongst the chain of mountains which embosoms its earliest fountains, nor are we shocked at the obscurity of these fountains. Pursuing the career of Mahommed, or of any man who has memorably impressed his own mind or agency upon the revolutions of mankind, we feel solicitude about the circumstances which might surround his cradle to be altogether unseasonable and impertinent. Whether he were born in a hovel or a palace, whether he passed his infancy in squalid poverty, or hedged around by the glittering spears of bodyguards, as mere questions of fact may be interesting, but, in the light of either accessories or counter-agencies to the native majesty of the subject, are trivial and below all philosophic valuation. So with regard to the creator of Lear and Hamlet, of Othello and Macbeth; to him from whose golden urns the nations beyond the far Atlantic, the multitude of the isles, and the generations unborn in Australian climes, even to the realms of the rising sun, must in every age draw perennial streams of intellectual life, we feel that the little accidents of birth and social condition are so unspeakably below the grandeur of the theme, are so irrelevant and disproportioned to the real interest at issue, so incommensurable with any of its relations, that a biographer of Shakspeare at once denounces himself as below his subject if he can entertain such a question as seriously affecting the glory of the poet. In some legends of saints, we find that they were born with a lambent circle or golden aureola about their heads. This angelic coronet sheds light alike upon the chambers of a cottage or a palace, upon the gloomy limits of a dungeon or the vast expansion of a cathedral; but the cottage, the palace, the dungeon, the cathedral, were all equally incapable of adding one ray of colour or one pencil of light to the supernatural halo.[29]

All this is well, if rather floridly, said; but it is a strange statement for a biographer. The usual justification for the biographies of writers is that details of their lives will illuminate their work. When these details are conceived as having no relevance to that work they become, as De Quincey implies, of antiquarian interest only. If he really believed that the brilliance of Shakespeare's writing made any enquiry into the circumstances of his life otiose, his entry in the *Encyclopaedia Britannica* would have little point.

Having spent more than a third of his text contesting the notion that Shakespeare was little known or admired during his life-time or shortly after his death, and in establishing that he was relatively well born, De Quincey finds himself with not much else to say. Yet he does tackle head-on what was often an embarrassment for bardolators in this period: the fact that when he married, Shakespeare's bride was probably very much older than he was and even more probably pregnant.

Our own reading and deciphering of the whole case is as follows. The Shakspeares were a handsome family, both father and sons. This we assume upon the following grounds: – First, on the presumption arising out of John Shakspeare's having won the favour of a young heiress higher in rank than himself; secondly, on the presumption involved in the fact of three amongst his four sons having gone upon the stage, to which the most obvious (and perhaps in those days a *sine qua non*) recommendation would be a good person and a pleasing countenance; thirdly, on the direct evidence of Aubrey, who assures us that William Shakspeare was a handsome and a well-shaped man; fourthly, on the implicit evidence of the Stratford monument, which exhibits a man of good figure and noble countenance; fifthly, on the confirmation of this evidence by the Chandos portrait, which exhibits noble features, illustrated by the utmost sweetness of expression; sixthly, on the selection of theatrical parts which it is known that Shakspeare personated, most of them being such as required some dignity of form, viz. kings, the athletic (though aged) follower of an athletic young man, and supernatural beings. On these grounds, direct or circumstantial, we believe ourselves warranted in assuming that William Shakspeare was a handsome and even noble-looking boy. Miss Anne Hathaway had herself probably some personal attractions, and, if an indigent girl, who looked for no pecuniary advantages, would probably have been early sought in marriage. But, as the daughter of 'a substantial yeoman,' who would expect some fortune in his daughter's suitors, she had, to speak coarsely, a little outlived her market. Time she had none to lose. William Shakspeare pleased her eye; and the gentleness of his nature made him an apt subject for female blandishments, possibly for female arts. Without imputing, however, to this Anne Hathaway anything so hateful as a settled plot for ensnaring him, it was easy enough for a mature woman, armed with such inevitable advantages of experience and of self-possession, to draw onward a blushing novice, and, without directly creating opportunities, to place him in the way of turning to account such as naturally offered. Young boys are generally flattered by the condescending notice of grown-up women; and perhaps Shakspeare's own lines upon a similar situation, to a young boy adorned with the same natural gifts as himself, may give us the key to the result:–

> *Gentle thou art, and therefore to be won;*
> *Beauteous thou art, therefore to be assailed*

> And, when a woman woos, what woman's son
> Will sourly leave her till she hath prevailed?

Once, indeed, entangled in such a pursuit, any person of manly feelings would be sensible that he had no retreat; *that* would be – to insult a woman, grievously to wound her sexual pride, and to insure her lasting scorn and hatred. These were consequences which the gentle-minded Shakspeare could not face; he pursued his good fortunes, half perhaps in heedlessness, half in desperation, until he was roused by the clamorous displeasure of her family upon first discovering the situation of their kinswoman. For such a situation there could be but one atonement, and that was hurried forward by both parties; whilst, out of delicacy towards the bride, the wedding was not celebrated in Stratford (where the register contains no notice of such an event); nor, as Malone imagined, in Weston-upon-Avon, that being in the diocese of Gloucester; but in some parish, as yet undiscovered, in the diocese of Worcester.[30]

Since the reasons De Quincey offers here for believing that Shakespeare was a good-looking man are relevant to the legend of his life they are worth considering in a little detail. Although Mary Arden was hardly an 'heiress' in the nineteenth-century sense, she does seem to have had better connections, or better potential connections, than her husband but of her four sons only two became actors and not all actors are good-looking. John Davies of Hereford certainly talks of Shakespeare having 'played some kingly parts in sport' but the mythos has more to say about the Ghost in *Hamlet* and Adam in *As You Like It* and neither of these roles requires outstanding physical attractiveness. Aubrey did indeed report that Shakespeare was a 'handsome well-shaped man' but opinions on the Stratford monument, which reminded Dover Wilson of a 'self-satisfied pork butcher',[31] differ wildly. As for the 'Chandos portrait' to which De Quincey refers, this painting had, with its touch of exoticism, offered Shakespeare enthusiasts an alternative to the Droeshout engraving and the Stratford bust even before the relief brought by the Scheemakers statue in 1741. The bushy-haired figure it depicts, with his loose collar and ear-ring, appears sufficiently un-English for some to have conjectured that Shakespeare must have had Italian or Jewish blood, or that the portrait shows him dressed for the part of Shylock. It was assumed that Davenant had once owned it and thought that it thereafter passed through the hands of various actors and lawyers until, in the first half of the eighteenth century, it definitely became the property of a woman who married the Duke of Chandos (and hence its name). But although it can be established that the portrait is from the right period, it is through hearsay alone that it came to be associated with Shakespeare.[32] He may very well have been as attractive as the Chandos portrait suggests he was, but at more than two hundred years after his death it would be hard to tell.

Good or ill looks are in any case not a necessary requirement for being taken advantage of by an older woman (the quotation De Quincey uses is from

20. *The Chandos portrait by Ozias Humphry drawn at Malone's request from an*
original portrait attributed to John Taylor and chosen by James Boswell as the frontispiece
for his edtion of Malone's The Plays and Poems of William Shakespeare. With a
Life of the Poet and an Enlarged History of the Stage. By the late E. Malone,
1821.

Sonnet 41). He is quite right to say that there is no record of Shakespeare's actual marriage, but the way he then goes on to insist that the marriage was unhappy is conjecture only. In his view, the young couple would have been forced to live in Henley Street at a time when Shakespeare's father was in financial difficulties and, in this condition of discomfort and dependency, the young groom would have soon come to 'appreciate the wiles by which he had been caught'. If, as he imagines, Anne Hathaway's father helped out, then she would have replied to her husband's inevitable reproaches with 'others equally stinging, on his inability to support his family, and on his obligations to his father's purse'. Thus after 'four years' conjugal discord' Shakespeare, who must have met various actors as they passed through Stratford, would have decided to take off for the metropolis and try his fortune there. 'Upon the known temperament of Shakespeare', De Quincey writes, positing what, in a Shake-speare biography, must always be in dispute, 'his genial disposition to enjoy life without disturbing his enjoyment by fretting anxieties, we build the conclusion that, had his friends furnished him with ampler funds, and had his marriage been well assorted or happy, we – the world of posterity – should have lost the whole benefit and delight which we have since reaped from his matchless faculties'.[33] This invokes the same providential scheme of things as Carlyle's, but provides a quite different antecedent for the miracle of Shakespeare's work. It means that De Quincey can reject indignantly the deer-poaching hypothesis.

We must here stop to notice, and the reader will allow us to notice with summary indignation, the slanderous and idle tale which represents Shakspeare as having fled to London in the character of a criminal from the persecutions of Sir Thomas Lucy of Charlecot. This tale has long been propagated under two separate impulses: chiefly, perhaps, under the vulgar love of pointed and glaring contrasts, – the splendour of the man was in this instance brought into a sort of epigrammatic antithesis with the humility of his fortunes; secondly, under a baser impulse, the malicious pleasure of seeing a great man degraded. Accordingly, as in the case of Milton, it has been affirmed that Shakespeare had suffered corporal chastisement, – in fact (we abhor to utter such words), that he had been judicially whipped. Now, first of all, let us mark the inconsistency of this tale: the poet was whipped, – that is, he was punished most disproportionately, – and yet he fled to avoid punishment. Next, we are informed that his offence was deer-stealing, and from the park of Sir Thomas Lucy. And it has been well ascertained that Sir Thomas had no deer, and had no park. Moreover, deer-stealing was regarded by our ancestors exactly as poaching is regarded by us. Deer ran wild in all the great forests; and no offence was looked upon as so venial, none so compatible with a noble Robin-Hood style of character, as this very trespass upon what were regarded as *ferae naturae*, and not at all as domestic property. But, had it been otherwise, a trespass was not punishable with whipping; nor had Sir Thomas Lucy the power to irritate a whole community like Stratford-upon-Avon by branding with permanent disgrace a young man so closely connected with three at least of the best families in the neighbourhood. Besides, had Shakespeare suffered any dishonour of that kind, the scandal would infallibly have pursued him at his very heels to London; and in that case Greene, who has left on record, in a posthumous work of 1592, his malicious feelings towards Shakspeare, could not have failed to notice it. [...]

This tale is fabulous, and rotten to its core; yet even this does less dishonour to Shakspeare's memory than the sequel attached to it. A sort of scurrilous rondeau, consisting of nine lines, so loathsome in its brutal stupidity and so vulgar in its expression that we shall not pollute our pages by transcribing it, has been imputed to Shakspeare ever since the days of the credulous Rowe. The total point of this idiot's drivel consists in calling Sir Thomas 'an asse'; and well it justifies the poet's own remark, – 'Let there be gall enough in thy ink, no matter though thou write with a goose pen.' Our own belief is that these lines were a production of Charles II's reign, and applied to a Sir Thomas Lucy not very far removed, if at all, from the age of him who first picked up the precious filth: the phrase 'parliament *member*'[1] we believe to be quite unknown in the colloquial use of Queen Elizabeth's reign.

But, that we may rid ourselves once and for ever of this outrageous calumny upon Shakspeare's memory, we shall pursue the story to its final stage. Even Malone has been thoughtless enough to accredit this closing chapter, which contains, in fact, such a superfetation of folly as the annals of human dulness do not exceed. Let us recapitulate the points of the story: – a baronet, who has no deer and no park, is supposed to persecute a poet for stealing these aerial deer out of this aerial park, both lying in *nephelococcygia* [cloud cuckoo land]. The poet sleeps upon this wrong for eighteen years; but at length, hearing that his persecutor is dead and buried, he conceives bloody thoughts of revenge. And this revenge he purposes to execute by picking a hole in his dead enemy's coat-of-arms. Is this coat-of-arms, then, sir Thomas Lucy's? Why, no: Malone admits that it is not. For the poet, suddenly recollecting that his ridicule would settle upon the son of his enemy, selects another coat-of-arms, with which his dead enemy never had any connexion, and he spends his thunder and lightning upon this irrelevant object; and, after all, the ridicule itself lies in a Welchman's mispronouncing one single heraldic term – a Welchman who mispronounces all words. [...] This is the very sublime of folly, beyond which human dotage cannot advance.[34]

The tone of this extract is best described in Matthew Arnold's memorable description of the provincial note: 'its approbation weeps hysterical tears and its disapprobation foams at the mouth'.[35] What it now demonstrates is how difficult it is to attack elements of the mythos without at the same time giving them substance. It is true that, as Malone was the first to establish, there was no deer park at Charlecote in Shakespeare's time (although whether the Elizabethan authorities took such a benign view of poaching as De Quincey suggests seems unlikely); but later it was discovered that there were fallow deer on an estate owned by the Lucys which was close to Stratford and that (as I mentioned in Chapter 2) there was at Charlecote itself a 'free warren' with rabbits and perhaps also roe deer. Elizabethan law certainly makes it improbable that Shakespeare was whipped but future commentary was to show how easy it was to adapt or omit that part of the legend without abandoning the whole. De Quincey has a good point about how long Shakespeare seems to have waited to exact his revenge yet, although the coat of arms described in *The Merry Wives* fits several families, it could be that of the Lucys and 'luce', we are told, was pronounced 'louse' in Stratford as well as Wales. The danger of discussing point by point a story for which there is no more real evidence than there would be for hundreds of others is that it thereby acquires credibility – how can there not be 'something in it' when its opponents take so much trouble to contest its various features?

In his treatment of the available information about Shakespeare, De Quincey is like many biographers before and since in that he practises a system of fluctuating rigour, accepting without demur several stories whose provenance is at least as dubious as the one involving Sir Thomas Lucy. A minor advantage of assaulting that one so fiercely is that at least it gives him something to say. This is an important consideration for anyone who was not prepared, or not equipped, to make Shakespeare biography a pretext for writing history – of Catholics in England, for example, local government or economic conditions in Warwickshire, the rise of the public theatre, or Court politics. After he gets his subject to London, De Quincey's biographical account peters out and he falls back, as so many biographers still do, on accounts of the plays, or rather 'of [Shakespeare's] works, of his intellectual powers, and of his station in literature'. This happens quicker than it might have done because he feels that Shakespeare's move to London could not have happened later than 1586 'for already in 1589 it has been recently ascertained that he held a share in the property of a leading theatre'.[36]

The person who had 'recently ascertained' that even by 1589 Shakespeare was already a 'sharer' in the Blackfriars theatre was J. Payne Collier but the documents he produced in support of this claim were bogus. As a forger, Payne Collier was far less picturesque than William Henry Ireland. A genuine scholar who made important contributions to the study of Shakespeare's life (it was he who found the Manningham diary), Payne Collier fabricated additions to the record which were modest in comparison with Ireland's and therefore all the more difficult to detect, and his expertise meant that he knew what not to say. The real story of Blackfriars, as Schoenbaum tells it, is that in 1597 James Burbage paid £600 for 'the old Frater, or refectory, of the dissolved Blackfriars monastery'[37] and then spent several hundred more having it converted into an indoor theatre. But local residents who did not want a theatre in their midst successfully complained to the Privy Council and, although it was afterwards used by the boys' companies, it was not until 1609 that Shakespeare's own company was able to perform there. It was in his *History of English Dramatic Poetry to the Time of Shakespeare*, published in 1831, that Collier first forged a document which suggested they must have used it much earlier and in his *New Facts Regarding the Life of Shakespeare*, which appeared four years later, he produced corroborating evidence in the form of a petition supposedly addressed to the Council by 'the Queen's players' at a time when the Elizabethan authorities were looking to clamp down on the public theatre.

> These are to certifie your right Honble Lordships that her Maiesties poore Playeres, James Burbadge, Richard Burbadge, John Laneham, Thomas Greene, Robert Wilson, John Taylor, Anth. Wadeson, Thomas Pope, George Peele, Augustine Phillips, Nicholas Towley, William Shakspeare, William Kempe, William Johnson, Baptiste Goodale, and Robert Armyn, being all of them sharers in the blake Fryers playehouse, have never given cause of displeasure, in that they have brought into theire playes maters of state and Religion, unfitt to bee handled by them or to bee presented before lewde spectators: neither hath anie complaynte in that kinde ever bene preferrde against them or anie of them. Wherefore they trust moste humblie in your Lordships' consideration of their former good behaviour, being at all tymes readie and willing to yeelde obedience to any command whatsoever your Lordships in your wisdome may thinke in such case meete,' &c.
>
> 'Novr. 1589.'[38]

Collier claimed to have found this document among the manuscripts at Bridgewater House where he worked as the secretary or private librarian of the Earl of Ellesmere; but he had in fact made it up. Beyond the frustration which everyone must have felt at the absence of information about Shakespeare's career, or the fact that the details he provided gave a 'sufficient contradiction to the idle story of Shakespeare having commenced his career by holding horses at the playhouse door' since 'had such been the fact he would hardly have risen to the rank of sharer in 1589', it is hard to see what Collier's motives were for such a colourless yet damaging deception. Everyone who worked on the life of Shakespeare in the early nineteenth century was taken in. Charles Knight, for example, whose popular life of Shakespeare was first published in 1843, repeated Collier's claim and then conscientiously provided potted biographies for all the actors mentioned in the petition, including of course Thomas Greene 'the person who has been conjectured to have been a native of Stratford-upon-Avon, and to have introduced Shakespeare to the theatre'.[39] The frequent presence of Greene in non-fictional and fictional accounts of Shakespeare in the early nineteenth century is at least partly attributable to Payne Collier.

Unlike De Quincey, Charles Knight was able to write at great length on Shakespeare because he gave an account of the historical and, above all, geographical context in which he lived (all the places the dramatist lived in or passed through are elaborately described). Nathan Drake had already shown how it was possible to make Shakespeare's 'times' stand in for his 'life' but he had done so with separate sections on each whereas Knight skilfully wove the two together. A successful and distinguished populariser, he had published from 1838 to 1841 an innovative *Pictorial Edition of the Works of Shakespeare* and his biography was similarly decked out with scores of illustrations designed to increase its popular appeal. It became vulnerable to scholarly criticism in later years in part because of its over-reliance on Payne-Collier but on one topic directly connected with his subject's life he made a contribution which proved lasting. Those in the Victorian period who wanted to think well of a writer whose works gave them so much pleasure – and Knight was certainly one of these – had to negotiate a number of potentially awkward facts. As I shall show in the next chapter, several of these were associated with the sonnets, but one was certainly that his wife was pregnant when he married her and another that all he left her in his will was his 'second best bed'. Knight's challenge to the interpretation which Malone had put on this second fact is something which, on revising his biography twenty years after it first appeared, he felt he could look back on with particular satisfaction. The extract is long but it is worth reproducing because it provides so many details of a dispute which many felt were crucial to thinking about Shakespeare.

> '*Item, I give unto my wife my second-best bed, with the furniture.*' This is the clause of the will upon which, for half a century, all men believed that Shakspere recollected his wife only to mark how little he esteemed her, – to 'cut her off, not indeed with a shilling, but with an old bed' [Malone]. We had the satisfaction of first showing the utter groundlessness of this opinion; and it is pleasant to know, that the statement which we originally published, some twenty years ago, is now fully acquiesced in by all writers on Shakspere. But it was once very different. To show the universality of the former belief in such a charge, we will first exhibit it in the words of one, himself a poet, who cannot be suspected of any desire to depreciate the greatest master of his art. Mr Moore, in his *Life of Byron*, speaking of unhappy marriages with reference to the domestic misfortune of his noble friend, thus expresses himself: –
>
>> By whatever austerity of temper, or habits, the poets Dante and Milton may have drawn upon themselves such a fate, it might be expected that, at least, the 'gentle Shakspere' would have stood exempt from the common calamity of his brethren. But, among the very few facts of his life that have been transmitted to us, there is none more clearly proved than the unhappiness of his marriage. The dates of the births of his children, compared with that of his removal from Stratford, – the total omission of his wife's name in the first draft of his will, and the bitter sarcasm of the bequest by which he remembers her afterwards, all prove beyond a doubt both his separation from the lady early in life, and his unfriendly feeling towards her at the close of it [...]
>
> Steevens, amongst many faults of taste, has the good sense and the good feeling to deny the inferences of Malone in this matter of the 'old bed'. He considers this bequest 'a mark of peculiar tenderness;' and he assumes that she was provided for by settlement. Steevens was a conveyancer by profession. Malone, who was also at the bar, says, 'what provision was made for her by settlement does not

appear.' A writer in *Lardner's Cyclopaedia*[40] doubts the legal view of the matter which Steevens charitably takes: – 'Had he already provided for her? If so, he would surely have alluded to the fact; and if he had left her the interest of a specific sum, or the rent of some messuage, there would, we think, have been a stipulation for the reversion of the property to his children after her decease.' Boswell, a third legal editor, thus writes upon the same subject: – '*If* we may suppose that some provision had been made for her during his lifetime, the bequest of his second-best bed was probably considered in those days neither as uncommon or reproachful.' As a somewhat parallel example Boswell cites the will of Sir Thomas Lucy, in 1600, who gives his son his second-best horse, but no land, because his father-in-law had promised to provide for him. We will present our readers with a case in which the parallel is much closer. In the will of David Cecil, Esq., grandfather to the great Lord Burleigh, we find the following bequest to his wife:

'*Item – I will that my wife have all the plate that was hers before I married her; and twenty kye and a bull.*'

Our readers will recollect the query of the Cyclopaedist, – 'Had he already provided for her? If so, he would surely have alluded to the fact.' Poor Dame Cecil, according to this interpretation, had no resource but that of milking her twenty kye, kept upon the common, and eating sour curds out of a silver bowl.

The 'forgetfulness' and the 'neglect' by Shakspere of the partner of his fortunes for more than thirty years is good-naturedly imputed by Steevens to 'the indisposed and sickly fit.' Malone will not have it so: – 'The various regulations and provisions of our author's will show that at the time of making it *he had the entire use of his faculties.*' We thoroughly agree with Malone in this particular. Shakspere bequeaths to his second daughter three hundred pounds under certain conditions; to his sister money, wearing apparel, and a life interest in the house where she lives; to his nephews five pounds each; to his grand-daughter his plate; to the poor ten pounds; to various friends, money, rings, his sword. The chief bequest, that of his *real* property, is as follows: –

Here Knight reprints the long provision of Shakespeare's will in which he leaves the bulk of his property to Susanna and her husband – see p. 26 above.

Immediately after this clause, – by which all the *real* property is bequeathed to Susanna Hall, for her life, and then entailed upon her heirs male; and in default of such issue upon his grand-daughter, and her heirs male; and in default of such issue upon his daughter Judith and her heirs male, – comes the clause relating to his wife: –

'*Item – I give unto my wife my second-best bed, with the furniture.*'

It was the object of Shakspere by this will to perpetuate *a family estate.* In doing so did he neglect the duty and affection which he owed to his wife? He did not.

Shakspere knew the law of England better than his legal commentators. His estates, with the exception of a copyhold tenement, expressly mentioned in his will, were *freehold.* HIS WIFE WAS ENTITLED TO DOWER. She was provided for, as the wife of David Cecil was provided for, who, without doubt, was not 'cut off' with her own plate and twenty kye and a bull. She was provided for amply, *by the clear and undeniable operation of the English law.* Of the lands, houses, and gardens which Shakspere *inherited* from his father, she was assured of the life-interest of a third, should she survive her husband, the instant that old John Shakspere died. Of the capital messuage, called New Place, the best house in Stratford, which Shakspere purchased in 1597, she was assured of the same life-interest, from the moment of the conveyance, provided it was a direct conveyance to her husband. That it was so conveyed we may infer from the terms of the conveyance of the lands in Old Stratford, and other places, which were purchased by Shakspere in 1602, and were then conveyed 'to the onlye proper use and behoofe of the saide William Shakspere, his heires and assignes, forever.' Of a life-interest in a third of these lands also was she assured. The tenement in Blackfriars, purchased in 1614, was conveyed to Shakspere and *three other persons*; and after his death was re-conveyed by those persons to the uses of his will, 'for and in performance of the confidence and trust in them reposed by William Shakespeare deceased.' In this estate certainly the widow of our poet had not dower. The reason is pretty clear – it was theatrical property. It has been remarked to us that even the express mention of the second-best bed was anything but unkindness and insult; that the best bed was in all probability an heir-loom: it might have descended to Shakspere himself from his father as an heir-loom, and, as such, was the property of his own heirs. The best bed was considered amongst the most important of those chattels which went to the heir by custom with the house. [...]

It is unnecessary for us more minutely to enter into the question before us. It is sufficient for us to have the satisfaction of having first pointed out the *absolute certainty* that the wife of Shakspere was provided for by the natural operation of the law of England. She could not have been deprived of this provision except by the legal process of Fine, – the *voluntary* renunciation of her own right. If her husband had alienated his real estates she might still have held her right, even against a purchaser. In the event, which we believe to be improbable, that she and the 'gentle Shakspere' lived on terms of mutual unkindness, she would have refused to renounce the right which the law gave her. In the more probable case, that, surrounded with mutual friends and relations, they lived at least amicably, she could not have been asked to resign it. In the most probable case, that they lived affectionately, the legal provision of dower would have been regarded as the natural and proper arrangement – so natural and usual as not to be referred to in a will. By reference to other wills of the same period it may be seen how unusual it was to make any other provision for a wife than by *dower*. Such a provision in those days, when the bulk of property was *real*, was a matter of course. The solution which we have here offered to this long-disputed question supersedes the necessity of any *conjecture* as to the nature of the provision which those who reverence the memory of Shakspere *must* hold he made for his wife. [...] We are fortunate in having first presented the true solution of the difficulty.[41]

Knight's certainty that he had settled for ever the problem of the bed recalls the exchange between Dr Johnson and Richard Farmer after the latter had published a book arguing that 'small Latin and less Greek' was a pretty fair estimate of Shakespeare's classical learning. Johnson first congratulated his friend for having put the issue of how much Shakespeare really knew 'beyond all further doubt', but when Farmer pointed that there were still people who remained unconvinced, he responded with, 'Ah! That may be true, for the limbs will quiver and move when the soul is gone'.[42] Critics of Knight's position

21. Title page to Charles Knight's William Shakspere: A Biography, *1843.*

have wondered whether dower right operated equally in all parts of early Jacobean England, but in general his reasoning has been accepted as probable and Shakespeare has therefore often been acquitted, on this score at least, of being mean to his wife.

Knight may have firmly established the tradition of making a narrative of Shakespeare's historical context stand in for the story of his life, but he also relied quite heavily on the methods of those many contemporary writers who were offering fictional portraits of the Bard, inventing certain episodes as well as the dialogue to go with them. There is, thus, at this time inter-penetration between biography helped out with a little fiction, on the one hand, and fiction helped out with a little history on the other. That no new information directly relevant to Shakespeare's life had been discovered was a justification for the first practice but it could also be invoked as a justification for the second. In his preface to his *Merry Wags of Warwickshire*, for example, Henry Curling, who had previously written two novels about Shakespeare,[43] confesses that what he has attempted is a 'presumptuous undertaking'; but, he goes on, while no-one could be more conscious of the imperfections of his play than its author, 'he submits for the indulgent consideration of other worshippers at the shrine of England's *greatest light* whether the very scantiness of our knowledge of the man, apart from his vocation of actor-poet, does not in some degree justify the choice of this mode of depicting his character and the scenes of his early associations'.[44] If scholars are unable to discover the true facts, why then should writers not be entitled to imagine them? Curling had strong military associations and is now best known (if known at all) as the person to whom 'Rifleman Harris' communicated his recollections of the Peninsular war,[45] so it is perhaps not surprising that his idea of Shakespeare is rather like that of the Earl of Sussex in the extract from *Kenilworth* at the beginning of this chapter: 'a stout man at quarter staff, and single falchion'. In an early scene he is shown falling foul of one of Sir Thomas Lucy's foresters even before he takes to poaching that gentleman's deer (Doubletongue and Dismal are described in the cast list as 'citizens of Stratford-upon-Avon').

Enter DOUBLETONGUE *and* DISMAL.

DOUBLETONGUE (*pointing out* ANNE HATHAWAY): Seest thou yonder maiden who was Queen of the May last year – is she not passing fair?

DISMAL: Truly, of exceeding good proportions, and features comely. (*Sighs.*) I have never seen a more perfect form chiselled upon a tomb.

DOUBLE: Out on't, thy voice is like the screech-owl's. Yonder lass on a tombstone, quotha. An' I could get her for a partner, methinks I should like to foot it among the circle.

DISMAL: I would fain dance too; for, by the Mass, this keen wind blows me to an ague. Accost Mistress Anne, good Doubletongue, and I will e'en assay the lass Mopsey.

DOUBLE: You trip it featly, Mistress Anne. Wilt join hands with me?

ANNE: Thanks, gentle Sir.
Enter WILL COTSWOLD *and* BARE.
COTSWOLD: What do you greybeards want with village maidens? Fair Mistress
                    Anne, you must trip it with me.
ANNE *(shrinking back from the Forester)*: Truly, I would fain avoid dancing again.
DOUBLE *(approaching the Forester)*: Thou art a rude companion: the maiden will none of
                    thee.
COTS.:   Why, what a brace of old crones to come to a revel! Go, get thee to
                    the hostel and warm thy doublets with a cup of wine. Dance!
                    Quotha; and with such a lass as Anne Hathaway. Why, there's not a
                    caper in the pair o' ye. Go, ye greybeards, go! or, by my fay, I'll make
                    ye dance to some other tune.
Enter WILLIAM SHAKSPERE, CALIVER, FROTH, *and* CARELESS.
*(*SHAKSPERE *stands aloof in the back-ground leaning on his quarter-staff, and observes*
ANNE HATHAWAY, *whilst his companions mingle with the villagers.)*
DOUBLE: Neighbour Dismal, will you go? This rude companion is a follower
                    of Sir Thomas Lucy - simply the strongest ruffian in Warwickshire.
                    He kept the ring on Kenilworth-green for a twelvemonth.
ANNE *(to* COTSWOLD*)*: If I must take ye for my partner, why then I must: but 'tis ungentle
                    thus to urge me.
COTSWOLD: Thou art ever thus coy with me, Anne. Why use me so, when I have
                    sworn an hundred times I would die to serve thee?
ANNE: I like thee not - would have no further words with thee: I have told
                    thee so I know not how oft. Prithee prove thy love by leaving me.
COTSWOLD: Beware lest I show thee how love, spurned, turneth to hate. Come,
                    you shall dance with me! *(he seizes her hand and drags her towards the
                    revellers.)*
ANNE: Out, insolent! This is cowardly. Ha! Here is one who will not see me
                    wronged.
*(*SHAKSPERE *suddenly comes down and confronts* COTSWOLD.)*
W. SHAKSPERE: Your hand, maiden: I would dance with you. *(Aside)* I will protect
                    you.
ANNE: Nay, William, prithee avoid a quarrel. This is one of the best wrestlers
                    in Warwickshire.
COTS.:   How now, young master; methinks you carry it bravely. But, indeed,
                    I have an old score to settle with thee.
*(*COTSWOLD *attempts to lay his hand on* SHAKSPERE, *who starts back.)*
W. SHAKSPERE: Take your hand from my doublet, sirrah! Words an'ye list; but I brook
                    not thy handling.
COTS.:   Ah! And wherefore not, boy? *(He steps back a pace, and regards*
                    Shakspere *contemptuously.)* By my faith, as likely a youth as e'er I
                    looked upon - well-limbed, strong, and of a goodly favour. Unhand
                    the maiden!
W. SHAK.:   The maiden hath already told thee she will none of thy company.
COTS.:   Nay, then, I will teach thee to brave a follower of 'the Lucy.'
*(*COTSWOLD *attempts to seize* ANNE, *but* SHAKSPERE *places himself before her, and heaves
up his quarter-staff.)*
COTS.:   What! Thou wilt have it, eh? *(He takes off his doublet, assisted by his
                    comrades, whilst the villagers gather round.)*
W. SHAK.:   I pray you make amongst your companions, Mistress Anne; I must

144

	e'en abide this quarrel. (*Re-enter* Grasp.)
Grasp.:	Ha! What, assault and battery here! Keep back, my masters (to Doubletongue *and* Dismal); for, look ye, my wild slip of a clerk, young Shakspere, is about to make a riot.
Dismal:	Truly, this is likely to end in a broken costard: the strong fellow seldom fights but he maims his adversary. Alas!
Cots.:	Come, young Sir, art thou ready to be beaten?
W. Shak.:	I am ready for aught thou canst inflict; so lay on and spare not.

(*A short and rapid combat with quarter-staff.* Shakspere *strikes down his antagonist. The foresters are about to attack* Shakspere, *but the villagers interfere, and all stand in attitude to engage.*) Enter Sir Thomas Lucy, *attended by a couple of serving-men with sword and target.*

All the fictional depictions of Shakespeare after Scott are offered to the public in that 'Elizabethese' he could be said to have invented but, if there were a prize for the worst version of it, then surely Curling would be the winner. In his interpretation of events, marrying Anne Hathaway becomes for Shakespeare a chivalric act not connected with her pregnancy: "Twas to rescue Anne from those fellows, that I married her myself', – he tells his disapproving mother. But the union is unequal and unhappy and young William, who earns his living with Grasp as a lawyer's clerk, is like Prince Hal in running just a little wild with disreputable companions. Hence the deer-poaching and the rhymes pinned on the gates at Charlecote, with in this case the 'lucy/lousy' pun but still without the reference to cuckoldry. Fleeing to London, Shakespeare is again, as in Somerset's play, saved from Sir Thomas's revenge by royal favour, the final scene taking place in 'the interior of the Theatre of Blackfriars' where *Henry IV* is being performed in front of the Queen. There is however a complication to the plot of Curling's play which involves a certain Charlotte Clopton and the young man in love with her called Walter Arderne. By becoming a friend and protector of Charlotte, Shakespeare excites his wife's suspicions. "Tis to her, I suppose', she complains, 'thou dost dedicate the sonnets thou art ever writing.'[46] The line serves as a reminder that, in the middle of what was otherwise desperate penury, there was what must have seemed like at least one rich source of information about Shakespeare's life in his Sonnets. But there were reasons why, at least in the first part of the nineteenth century, that source should have been approached with the kind of ambiguity which Curling demonstrates when he has Shakespeare's wife suspicious of the sonnets which she believes her husband has been dedicating to a female rival, but apparently unaware that most of them were in fact addressed to a man.

Notes

1. *Kenilworth* (London: Walter Scott, 1883), p. 160.
2. *Ibid.*, p. 164.
3. *Ibid.*, pp. 169–72.
4. Katherine Duncan-Jones (ed.), *Shakespeare's Sonnets* (Arden Shakespeare, 1997), p. 184.
5. Nathan Drake, *Noontide Leisure* (1824), vol. 1, p. 80.
6. *Ibid.*, 83.
7. Robert Folkestone Williams, *Shakespeare and His Friends* (Paris: Galignani, 1838), pp. 78–81.
8. *Ibid.*, p. 81. For details of Greene see Edwin Nungezer, A *Dictionary of Actors* (Yale University Press, 1929).
9. T. Earle Welby (ed.), *The Complete Works of Walter Savage Landor*, (1927–36), vol. 10, pp. 270–2.
10. *Ibid.*, pp. 274–8.
11. Ian Jack, *English Literature: 1815–1832* (Oxford University Press, 1963), p. 348.
12. Charles A. Somerset. *Shakespeare's Early Days* (1880). p. 3.
13. See Schoenbaum, A *Documentary Life*, p. 27.
14. *Shakespeare's Early Days*, p. 3.
15. *Ibid.*, p. 5.
16. *Ibid.*, p. 6.
17. *Ibid.*, p. 5.
18. *Ibid.*, p. 8.
19. See Chambers, vol. 2, p. 33. Later in the decade there was a law suit between John Shakespeare and William Burbage. For speculations about the possible connections between this Burbage and the ones in London see Michael Wood, *In Search of Shakespeare* (2003), pp. 108–9.
20. *Shakespeare's Early Days*, p. 11.
21. *Ibid.*, p. 13.
22. *Ibid.*
23 Leigh Hunt, *The Examiner*, 3 May 1820.
24. Douglas Jerrold, *New Monthly Magazine*, 50 (June 1837), pp. 233–4.
25. *Ibid.*, pp. 236–8.
26. Thomas Carlyle, 'Lecture III: the Hero as Poet. Dante; Shakespeare' in *On Heroes, Heroes and the Heroic in History* (London: Chapman and Hall, 1901), pp. 101–2.
27. *Ibid.*, p. 113.
28. David Masson (ed.), *The Collected Writings of Thomas De Quincey* (1897), vol. 4, p. 45.
29. *Ibid.*, pp. 45–6.
30. *Ibid.*, pp. 54–5.
31. J. Dover Wilson, *The Essential Shakespeare: A Biographical Adventure* (Cambridge University Press, 1932), p. 6.
32. There is a full discussion of the Chandos portrait, as well as of several others which it was claimed were also portraits of Shakespeare, in Schoenbaum's *Records and Images*, pp. 156–200.
33. De Quincey, p. 57.
34. *Ibid.*, pp. 58–61.
35. Mathew Arnold, 'The Literary Influence of Academies' in *Essays in Criticism: First Series* (London: MacMillan, 1902), p. 66.
36. De Quincey p. 69,
37. Schoenbaum, *Documentary Life*, p. 153.
38. J. Payne Collier, *New Facts regarding the Life of Shakespeare* (London, 1835), p. 11.
39. Charles Knight, *William Shakspere: A Biography* (1843), p. 299.

40. There is an anonymous life of Shakespeare in a volume devoted to 'Eminent Literary and Scientific Men' which formed part of the Rev. Dionysius Lardner's *Cabinet Cyclopaedia*. The volume in question was published in 1837. By 1849, 133 volumes of Lardner's *Cyclopaedia* had appeared. For details, see Schoenbaum, *Shakespeare's Lives*, pp. 222–3.

41. *Ibid*. (1886 ed.), pp. 534–7.

42. Schoenbaum, *Shakespeare's Lives*, p. 103.

43. They were entitled *Shakespeare; the poet, the lover, the actor, the man (1848)* and *The Forest Youth or Shakepeare as he lived* (1853).

44. Henry Curling, 'To the Reader', *Merry Wags of Warwickshire* (1854).

45. The *Reflections of Rifleman Harris as told to Henry Curling* (1802–1864) were first published in 1848.

46. Henry Curling, *Merry Wags*, pp. 22–5.

22. Shakespeare Composing. *Engraved by H. A. Payne after a painting by
Lilburne Hicks, published by Brain and Payne in 1828.
By permission of the Folger Shakespeare Library.*

Chapter Five

The Sonnets

W HEN THE ORIGINS OF iconic figures are historical, any failure to discover very much about them can be frustrating. The information concerning Shakespeare is more than enough to provide a broad sketch of his career but almost nothing has survived which is relevant to his private life and can tell us about the nature and progress of his relationships or opinions. What this chiefly means is that there are no surviving letters and nothing outside his writings which is in the first person apart from his will and his two dedications to Southampton. Yet within the writings themselves there is a volume of 154 sonnets in which an apparently autobiographical and dramatically revealing 'I' is omnipresent. With the growing interest in the private Shakespeare in the late seventeenth century, and then throughout the eighteenth, it is surprising that more use was not made of the Sonnets. It may be that there was then a more generally diffused sense than there is now of how dangerous it is to extract details of poets' private lives from their writings or (what is more likely) that the poems' obscurities and obsessive word-play discouraged investigation in a period when lucidity and lack of ambiguity were values increasingly prized in literary works. It may be also that those who did read the Sonnets carefully were alarmed by their possible biographical implications. Shakespeare was known to have been married so that, if the Sonnets were to be taken literally, in the final 28 of them especially he was declaring himself an adulterer – and the tone in which he addressed or referred to his mistress was hardly pleasant. Potentially more disturbing was the suggestion of homosexuality in the first 126. Was the warmth of address often found in these not indicative of 'unnatural' passions? But yet another and perhaps more important reason for the relative absence of the Sonnets from discussions of 'Shakespeare the man' until the nineteenth century is that they were not widely available.

Shakespeare must have written some sonnets, independently of those in the plays, before 1598 when Francis Meres refers not only to 'mellifluous and honey-tongued Shakespeare' as witnessed in his two long narrative poems, but also to 'his sugared sonnets among his private friends' (see p. 12 above). His facility in handling the form is evident enough in *Love's Labour's Lost* which is usually thought to have been first performed around 1594 or 5. Most of the young male principals in that play are avid sonneteers and three examples of their work are included in a 'pirated' collection of 20 poems entitled *The Passionate Pilgrim* which was announced to be 'By W. Shakespeare' and published in 1599 by William Jaggard, the man later to be responsible (with his son Isaac) for the First Folio. Three of the poems in this collection are taken from *Love's Labour's Lost* and two more are versions of what would later appear as items 138 and 144 in the first, 1609, edition of *Shakespeare's Sonnets*. None of the other fifteen can be confidently attributed to Shakespeare.

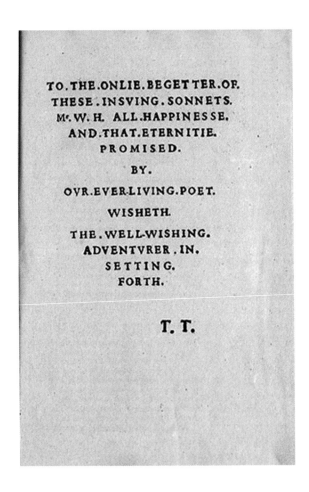

23. *The 'T.T.' conundrum. Title page of the 1609 edition of Shakespeare's Sonnets.*

The 1609 edition of Shakespeare's sonnets was published by Thomas Thorpe who provided it with a dedication the deciphering of which was to become the equivalent, in scholarly terms, of a national parlour game. Its notoriously cryptic wording raises a number of questions. One of these is why it was Thorpe who wrote the dedication and not Shakespeare himself (might it have been because he was no less a pirate than the publisher of *The Passionate Pilgrim?*). Does his 'onlie begetter' refer to the person who procured a copy of the sonnets for him or to the one who inspired them and to whom therefore most of them were addressed? If the latter is the case, what do the initials 'W. H.' stand for? Thorpe may have deliberately set out to mystify his readers but he could have had no idea what a remarkably powerful engine for myth-making he had provided.

There are no records of how the first edition of the Sonnets was received. It is not known whether it dropped like a stone, provoked moves to suppress it, or caused a lively debate, all the evidence for which has now disappeared. The next edition was published in 1640 by John Benson under the title *Poems: Written by Wil Shakes-peare. Gent.* Benson reprinted 146 of the 154 sonnets in the 1609 edition but managed to make only 72 poems out of them by sticking some together. He gave titles to these new poems, changed the pronouns in some so that the addressee became female, and accompanied them with poems by other writers. The preface he provided for this concoction is almost as remarkable as Thorpe's dedication.

To the Reader.

> I here presume (under favour) to present to your view, some excellent and sweetly composed Poems, of Master William Shakespeare, Which in themselves appear of the same purity, the Author himself then living avouched; they had not the fortune by reason of their Infancy in his death, to have the due accommodation of proportionable glory, with the rest of his everliving Works, yet the lines of themselves will afford you a more authentic approbation than my assurance any way can, to invite your allowance; in your perusal you shall find them Serene, clear and elegantly plain, such gentle strains as shall recreate and not perplex your brain, no intricate or cloudy stuff to puzzle intellect, but perfect eloquence; such as will raise your admiration to his praise: this assurance I know will not differ from your acknowledgement. And certain I am, my opinion will be seconded by the sufficiency of these ensuing Lines; I have been somewhat solicitous to bring this forth to the perfect view of all men; and in so doing, glad to be serviceable for the continuance of glory to the deserved Author in these his Poems.[1]

That Benson is perhaps insisting here on the purity of the Sonnets suggests that others had taken a different view, but the most striking aspect of what he writes is his claim that they are 'serene, clear and elegantly plain' and do not 'perplex the brain'. This is about as accurate as pretending that *Ulysses* is light reading and may be the consequence of his having plagiarised much of his

This Shadowe is renowned Shakespear's? Soule of th'age
The applause? delight? the wonder of the Stage.
Nature her selfe, was proud of his designes
And joy'd to weare the dressing of his lines;
The learned will Confess, his works are such,
As neither man, nor Muse, can prayse to much.
For ever live thy fame, the world to tell,
Thy like, no age, shall ever paralell.

24. Title page of John Benson's 1640 edition of the Sonnets, Poems: Written by Wil Shakes-peare. Gent., engraved by William Marshall.

preface from a poem written five years earlier which has nothing to do with Shakespeare.[2]

For the next 140 years most of the rare appearances of the Sonnets were in the form Benson had given them. An exception which did go back to the 1609 Quarto was the edition published in 1709 by Bernard Lintot who falsely claimed in his introduction that all the poems were 'in praise of [Shakespeare's] mistress'.[3] It was not until 1780, in what was described as the *Supplement* to an edition of Shakespeare's works edited by Johnson and Steevens, that Edmond Malone produced a version which was both textually reliable and annotated. One of his annotations was the cause of an exchange of views with Steevens which, as my previous chapter will already have shown, helped set the agenda for very many subsequent discussions of not only the Sonnets, but also of Shakespeare in general. It was attached to the phrase 'like a deceived husband' which occurs in the second line of Sonnet 93.

> *Like a deceived husband*; –] Mr Oldys observes in one of his manuscripts, that this and the preceding sonnet 'seems to have been addressed by Shakespeare to his beautiful wife on some suspicion of her infidelity.' He must have read our author's poems with but little attention; otherwise he would have seen that these, as well as all the preceding Sonnets, and many of those that follow, are not addressed to a female. I do not know whether this antiquarian had any other authority than his misapprehension concerning these lines, for the epithet by which he has described our great poet's wife. He had made very large collections for a life of our author, and perhaps in the course of his researches had learned this particular. However this may have been, the other part of his conjecture (that Shakespeare was jealous of her) may perhaps be thought to derive some probability from the following circumstances. It is observable, that his daughter, and not his wife, is his executor; and in his will, he bequeaths the latter only an old piece of furniture; nor did he even think of her till the whole was finished, the clause relating to her being an interlineation. What provision was made for her by settlement, does not appear. It may likewise be remarked, that jealousy is the principal hinge of *four* of his plays; and in his great performance (*Othello*) some of the passages are written with such exquisite feeling, as might lead us to suspect that the author had himself been *perplexed* with doubts, thought not perhaps *in the extreme*. – By the same mode of reasoning, it may be said, he might be proved to have stabbed his friend, or to have had a *thankless* child; because he has so admirably described the horror consequent on murder, and the effects of filial ingratitude, in *King Lear*, and *Macbeth*. He could indeed assume all shapes; and therefore it must be acknowledged that the present hypothesis is built on uncertain foundations. All I mean to say is, that he appears to me to have written more immediately *from the heart* on the subject of jealousy, than on any other; and it is therefore not improbable he might have felt it. The whole is mere conjecture.[4]

Malone deals firmly here with Oldys' 'misapprehension' as to the addressee of most the sonnets and dismisses what may have been a merely careless assertion that Anne Hathaway was 'beautiful'. He then uses what was, at that time, relatively new information about the will of Shakespeare in order to suggest that he did not get on with his wife, supporting the notion that he had reasons to complain of her behaviour with references to *Othello*. The characteristically tentative nature of these suggestions did not save him from the scorn of Steevens whose reply appears immediately below Malone's note in the 1780 *Supplement*. Beginning with words which are worth reprinting because they became part of a Sceptics' Charter, and then brushing aside the evidence of the will on the grounds that Anne would have been provided for in other ways, the bed may have represented a 'mark of peculiar tenderness', and its apparent appearance as an afterthought could be 'imputed to disease', Steevens proceeds to restate the case which Malone had already made against using the plays as indications of Shakespeare's own temperament and feelings.

> As all that is known with any degree of certainty concerning Shakespeare, is – *that he was born at Stratford upon Avon,– married and had children there,– went to London, where he commenced actor, and wrote poems and plays, – returned to Stratford, made his will, died, and was buried,* – I must confess my readiness to combat every unfounded supposition respecting the particular occurrences of his life. [...]
>
> That Shakespeare has written with his utmost power on the subject of jealousy, is no proof that he ever felt it. Because he has, with equal vigour, expressed the varied aversions of Apemantus and Timon to the world, does it follow that he himself was a Cynic, or a wretch deserted by his friends? Because he has, with proportionable strength of pencil, represented the vindictive cruelty of Shylock, are we to suppose he copied from a fiend-like original in his own bosom? [...]
>
> No argument [...] in my opinion, is more fallacious than that which imputes the success of a poet to his interest in his subject. Accuracy of description can be expected only from a mind at rest. It is the unruffled lake that is a faithful mirror.[5]

Having begun by conceding so much to an imaginary opponent, Malone was nevertheless not prepared to yield completely when he was challenged by a real one. Still in the same note to the phrase in Sonnet 93, he took up his position on what he must have felt was his strongest ground (who after all was more familiar with the documents relating to Shakespeare's life than he was?).

> Our author's forgetfulness of his wife (from whatever cause it arose,) cannot well be imputed to the *indisposed and sickly fit*; for, from an imperfect erasure in his will (which I have seen) it appears to have been written (though not executed) *two* months before his death; and in the first paragraph he has himself told us that he was, at the time of making it, in *perfect health*; words, which no honest attorney, I believe ever inserted in a will, when the testator was notoriously in a contrary state. Any speculation on this subject is indeed unnecessary; for the various regulations and provisions of our author's will show that at the time of making it he had the entire use of his faculties. Nor, supposing the contrary to have been the case, do I see what in the two succeeding months he was to recollect or to alter. His wife had not wholly escaped his memory; he had forgot her, – he had recollected her, – but so recollected her, as more strongly to mark how little he esteemed her; he had already (as it is vulgarly expressed) cut her off, not indeed with a shilling, but with an old bed.

However, I acknowledge, it does not necessarily follow, that because he was inattentive to her in his will, he was therefore jealous of her. He might not have loved her; and perhaps she might not have deserved his affection.

This note having already extended to too great a length, I shall only add, that I must still think that a poet's intimate knowledge of the passions and manners which he describes, will generally be of use to him; and in some *few* cases experience will give a warmth to his colouring, that mere observation may not supply. No man, I believe, who had not felt the power of beauty, ever composed love-verses that were worth reading.[6]

The dispute over whether Shakespeare's feelings for his wife could be inferred from his will would rumble on for the next two centuries and can still be heard. More relevant to this chapter is the question of whether it was legitimate to read the Sonnets autobiographically and, if it was, what conclusions one might have to draw. Malone raises the second half of the issue by referring to 'love-verses'. The Sonnets are undoubtedly often 'love-verses', but ones which, as he insists, were in the main addressed to a man. Although he does not say so, it was perhaps his awareness of this which encouraged Steevens to omit them from a fourth edition of his and Johnson's *Plays of William Shakespeare* published in 1793.

We have not reprinted the Sonnets, etc. of Shakespeare, because the strongest act of Parliament that could be framed, would fail to compel readers into their service, notwithstanding these miscellaneous poems have derived every possible advantage from the literature and judgement of their only intelligent editor, Mr Malone, whose implements of criticism, like the ivory rake and golden spade in Prudentius, are on this occasion disgraced by the objects of their culture. – Had Shakespeare produced no other works than these, his name would have reached us with as little celebrity as time has conferred on that of Thomas Watson, an older and much more elegant sonneteer.[7]

Steevens has here the air of consigning the Sonnets to oblivion when in fact they were just about to emerge from what had been, in comparison with the plays, a long period of obscurity.

The growth of serious biographical interest in the Sonnets runs parallel to the increasing 'Romantic' conviction that even highly stylised forms of writing provide an opportunity for the expression of personal feeling. As Wordsworth put it in the 1820s, in a sonnet of his own: 'Scorn not the sonnet: Critic, you have frowned, / Mindless of its just honours; with this key / Shakespeare unlocked his heart'.[8] The question as to whether the Sonnets are good poems is not the same as the one Wordsworth raises here and the answer he gave to that first question in private, at an early stage of his reading career, is not the same as the one he later provided in public. In the margins of a volume of

155

Anderson's British Poets in which the Sonnets appeared, he said of those addressed to the so-called 'dark lady' that they were 'abominably harsh obscure and worthless' and added that, although those addressed to a man were better, they had heavy faults of 'sameness, tediousness, quaintness and elaborate obscurity'.[9] This must have been before 2 November 1803, the date on which Coleridge replied in the margins of the same volume that 'With the exception of the sonnets to his mistress (and even of these the expressions are unjustly harsh) I can by no means subscribe to the above pencil marks of William Wordsworth'. Addressing himself to his son Hartley, he went on to grapple with the problem of the kind of man the Sonnets revealed.

> These sonnets, then, I trust, if God preserve thy life, Hartley!, thou wilt read with a deep interest, having learned to love the plays of Shakespeare, co-ordinate with Milton, and subordinate only to thy Bible. To thee, I trust, they will help to explain the mind of Shakespeare, and if thou wouldst understand these sonnets, thou must read the chapter in Potter's *Antiquities* on the Greek lovers – of whom were that Theban band of brothers, over whom Philip, their victor, stood weeping; and, surveying their dead bodies, each with his shield over the body of his friend, all dead in the place where they fought, solemnly cursed those whose base, fleshly, and most calumnious fancies had suspected their love of desires against nature. This pure love Shakespeare appears to have felt – to have been in no way ashamed of it – or even to have suspected that others could have suspected it. Yet at the same time he knew that so strong a love would have been made more completely a thing of permanence and reality, and have been blessed more by nature, and taken under her more especial protection, if this object of his love had been at the same time a possible object of desire; for nature is not bad only – in this feeling he must have written the twentieth sonnet, but its possibility seems never to have entered even his imagination. It is noticeable that [there is] not even an allusion to that very worst of all possible *vices* (for it is wise to think of the disposition as a *vice*, not of the absurd and despicable act as a *crime*) not even an allusion to it in all his numerous plays – whereas Jonson, Beaumont and Fletcher, and Massinger are full of them. O my son! I pray fervently that thou mays't know inwardly how impossible it was for a Shakespeare not to have been in his heart's heart chaste. I see no elaborate obscurity and very little quaintness – nor do I know any sonnets that will bear such frequent reperusal: so rich in metre, so full of thought and *exquisitest* diction.[10]

The sonnet Coleridge refers to is the one in which Shakespeare claims that the male addressee was meant to be female until 'nature as she wrought thee fell a-doting, / And by addition me of thee defeated, / By adding one thing to my purpose nothing.' What that 'one thing' was is made clear in the final couplet: 'But since she pricked thee out for women's pleasure, / Mine be thy love, and thy love's use their treasure'.[11] These words would often be referred to much later in a public context in order to argue the same case Coleridge is presenting here: that however fond Shakespeare was of the man to whom most of the poems appear to be addressed, there was no question of any physical relationship with him. It is a tricky topic on which Coleridge is not very clear, even in private; but no hint of it was apparent when Wordsworth, in his 1815 *Essay Supplementary to the Preface*, reversed his previous view of the Sonnets' literary quality.

> There is extant a small volume of miscellaneous poems, in which Shakespeare expresses his own feelings in his own person. It is not difficult to conceive that the editor, George Steevens, should have been insensible to the beauties of one portion of that volume, the Sonnets; though in no part of the writings of this poet is found, in an equal compass, a greater number of exquisite feelings felicitously expressed. But, from regard to the critic's own credit, he would not have ventured to talk of an act of parliament not being strong enough to compel the perusal of those little pieces, if he had not known that the people of England were ignorant of the treasures contained in them: and if he had not, moreover, shared the too common propensity of human nature to exult over a supposed fall into the mire of a genius whom he had been compelled to regard with admiration, as an inmate of the celestial regions – 'there sitting where he durst not soar'.[12]

The opening of this is unequivocal in declaring Shakespeare's Sonnets autobiographical but, in pursuing his assault on his eighteenth-century predecessors, Wordsworth ignores what other reasons, apart from literary quality, might have led Steevens to write in the way he did.

Nathan Drake, the first biographer of Shakespeare to grasp fully the life-saving implications of the phrase 'and his times', and the first author of a novel with Shakespeare at its centre, was also probably the first person to raise with a wider, non-specialised public some of the problems of the Sonnets. The second half of his 'Montchensey' is mostly taken up with finding a noble parentage for the mysterious bandit-chief-cum-minstrel to whom Helen Montchensey is attracted but, at one point, her father calls for a temporary pause while he raises a literary issue.

> 'Let me then, I pray you, turn your attention to another and a better subject; and here, Master Shakespeare,' he continued, taking up a small volume which lay upon the library table, 'is one upon which you, and you only, I apprehend, can throw the light I wish for.' As he said this, he placed in the poet's hands his own Collection of Sonnets, which had been published about six years before. 'Much as I admire these sonnets,' he proceeded, 'and I do assure you I think very highly of many of them in a poetical light, I cannot with any certainty ascertain to whom they are addressed. The point has puzzled sorely both myself and Helen; her curiosity, indeed, is particularly alive on the occasion, and as I promised her to interrogate you on the subject the first favourable opportunity, I left the volume on the table as a memento for that purpose; but I will now, with your permission, call her in, that she may, if you feel no repugnancy to the disclosure, hear the secret from your own lips.'
> 'And so my fair Helen,' cried the poet jocosely, as she re-entered the room with her father, 'you are determined, I find, to bring me to confession. I am

afraid, however, the discovery will be accompanied with some disappointment, when I tell you that, with the exception of about thirty sonnets at the close of the collection, the rest, amounting to more than one hundred, are dedicated to my dearest friend, and earliest patron, my Lord Southampton.'

'There, Helen,' exclaimed Montchensey, with an air of triumph, 'did I not tell you that if to any person more than another these sonnets might be conjectured to have a reference, his Lordship had the best claim?' [...]

Drake's Shakespeare goes on to explain that the first seventeen sonnets were written for Southampton after he had taken a vow of celibacy following the Queen's efforts to frustrate his love for Elizabeth Vernon, and that these and subsequent poems are obscure because it would have been dangerous for him to reveal open support for his patron.

'I must say,' observed Montchensey [...], 'that you have, in my opinion, sufficiently accounted for the obscurity which hangs over this part of your early poetry; but pardon my observing further, that one of the principal obstacles I had to encounter, in cherishing my belief of Lord Southampton being the object you had in view, arose from the terms of familiarity with which you addressed him, and on a topic, too, which required the utmost delicacy of management. Now, considering the great disparity of rank which subsisted between you and your patron, it seemed difficult to conceive that you would venture, or that he would suffer you, "to remonstrate with him on a topic which an equal would scarcely have found himself at liberty to touch upon."'

'It may, I think, be very justly remarked, Master Montchensey,' rejoined Shakespeare, 'that oftentimes many things are endured from an inferior which would not be tolerated in an equal; and more especially is this the case with spirits jealous and quick in resentment, though full of honourable bearing. It is well known, that my Lord Southampton, with a heart alive to every kind and generous feeling, possesses a constitutional warmth and irritability of temper, and an independency of spirit, which brook not the interference of one on his own level, and that what he would not submit to listen to from a Rutland or Montgomery, he would receive with kind and patient consideration from a favourite in humbler life. It is also equally well known that his love for literature, and especially for dramatic literature, is warm, and even enthusiastic: and you compel me to add, that his partiality for myself, however little merited, and his patronage of my efforts, however unworthy of such distinction in the eyes of others, have been, ever since my dedication to him of the *Venus and Adonis*, unparalleled, and, indeed, without bound. Will not all this, my good friend, prove a satisfactory solution of the difficulty which has startled you?'

'I allow it to be so, Master Shakespeare, but I have not done with your little volume yet; for, in the name of wonder, what are we to think of the last twenty-eight sonnets? You have here dropped your noble patron to address one, who is, even on your own confession, the most worthless of womankind. Had I not been assured, from universal report, of the purity of your moral character, I freely confess to you, that I should have condemned these pieces as the production of an unblushing profligate!'

'Most sincerely do I wish, Master Montchensey,' rejoined the poet, 'that, since I find them open to such misconstruction, they had never seen the light! But you will believe me, I have no doubt, when I say, that these sonnets, though apparently written in my own person, are strictly ideal, and were intended solely to express, aloof from all individual application, the contrarieties, the inconsistencies, and the miseries of illicit love.'

'It is impossible to know you, my friend, and to think otherwise,' said Montchensey; 'but as this personal knowledge is necessarily confined to a few, I cannot help wishing either that they had not been published, or that some intimation had been given of the nature of their origin.'

'If I live, Master Montchensey, it shall be done,' cried the bard. 'Indeed,' he continued, 'had it not been for the urgent solicitations of a dear friend of mine, now no more, neither these sonnets, nor the greater part of those which precede them, had come forth; but he wrung from me a reluctant consent, and, having obtained the manuscript, immediately placed it in the hands of Thorpe, whence the edition now lying on your table.'[13]

Drake had first suggested that Southampton must have been the addressee of the Sonnets in *Shakespeare and his times*. The leaden quality of the exchanges in the passage above is in part attributable to the fact that he is using them to counter arguments against this suggestion which had been made by Boswell in his 1821 edition of Malone's *Shakespeare*. (The phrase he puts in quotation marks – 'to remonstrate with him on a topic [...]' etc. – is a direct quotation from Boswell.) Concentration on the problem of identification allows Drake to shift the emphasis away from what the speaker in the Sonnets actually says to his friend (whoever he was). But the thoughts and feelings expressed in the dark lady sonnets cannot be ignored so easily and Drake clearly feels with Montchensey that, for anyone who *knows* Shakespeare, the idea that in these final 28 poems he (as Wordsworth put it) 'expresses his own feelings in his own person' is one which it is impossible to entertain.

Perhaps because he is a character in a novel, or because of the kind of novel in which he figures, Drake's 'Shakespeare' does not offer much detail in support of his explanations. More supporting information is provided by Anna Jameson in a chapter of a volume entitled *The Loves of the Poets* published in 1829. Soon to become well-known for a book on Shakespeare's female characters, Jameson offered to consider the role of women in his life. The way she begins her chapter, called 'On the Love of Shakespeare', illustrates how difficult it would be to reconcile the prevailing bardolotry with any conclusions drawn from the Sonnets which might suggest that, in his private life, Shakespeare was not all he ought to have been.

Shakespeare – I approach the subject with reverence, and even with fear, – is the only poet I am acquainted with and able to appreciate, who appears to have been really heaven-inspired: the workings of his wondrous and all-embracing mind were directed by a higher influence than ever was exercised by woman, even in the plenitude of her power and charms. Shakespeare's genius waited not on Love and Beauty, but Love and Beauty ministered to *him*; he perceived like a spirit; he was created, to create; his own individuality is lost in the splendour, the reality,

25. Southampton in the Tower. *Painting attributed to John de Critz the Elder, 1603. By kind permission of His Grace the Duke of Buccleuch and Queensberry, K.T.*

and the variety of his own conceptions. When I think, what those are, I feel how needless, how vain it were to swell the universal voice with one so weak as mine. Who would care for it that knows and feels Shakespeare? Who would listen to it that does not, if there be such?

It is not Shakespeare as a great power bearing a great name, – but Shakespeare in his less divine and less known character, – as a lover and a man, who finds a place here. The only writings he has left, through which we can trace any thing of his personal feelings and affections, are his Sonnets. Everyone who reads them, who has tenderness and taste, will echo Wordsworth's denunciation against the 'flippant insensibility' of some of his commentators, who talked of an Act of Parliament not being strong enough to compel their perusal, and will agree in his opinion, that they are full of the most exquisite feelings, most felicitously expressed; but as to the object to whom they were addressed, a difference of opinion prevails. From a reference, however, to all that is known of Shakespeare's life and fortunes, compared with the internal presumptive evidence contained in the Sonnets, it appears that some of them are addressed to his amiable friend, Lord Southampton; and others, I think, are addressed in Southampton's name, to that beautiful Elizabeth Vernon, to whom the Earl was so long and ardently attached. [...]

That Lord Southampton is the subject of the first fifty-five Sonnets is sufficiently clear; and some of these are perfectly beautiful, – as the 30th, 32nd, 41st, 54th. There are others scattered through the rest of the volume, on the same subject; but there are many which admit of no such interpretation, and are without doubt inspired by the real object of a real passion, of whom nothing can be discovered, but that she was dark-eyed, and dark-haired, that she excelled in music; and that she was one of the class of females who do not always, in losing all right to our respect, lose also their claim to the admiration of the sex who wronged them, or the compassion of the gentler part of their own, who have rejected them. This is so clear from various passages, that unhappily there can be no doubt of it. He has flung over her, designedly it should seem, a veil of immortal texture and fadeless hue, 'branched and embroidered like the painted Spring', but almost impenetrable even to our imagination. There are few allusions to her personal beauty, which can in any way individualise her, but bursts of deep and passionate feeling, and eloquent reproach, and contending emotions, which show, that if she could awaken as much love and impart as much happiness as woman ever inspired or bestowed, he endured on her account all the pangs of agony, and shame, and jealousy; – that our Shakespeare, – he who, in the omnipotence of genius, wielded the two worlds of reality and imagination in either hand, who was in conception and in act scarce less than a GOD, was in passion and suffering not more than MAN.[14]

Ignoring the unpleasantness of the way in which Shakespeare refers to women in several of the 'dark lady' sonnets, Jameson has two methods for dealing with what might otherwise be an uncomfortable fervour in some of those which precede them. She first of all makes the suggestion, taken up by several commentators afterwards, that some of the poems must have been written in Southampton's name to Elizabeth Vernon. Her second method is simply to assert that other poems were 'inspired by the real object of a real passion' ('real' translating in this context as heterosexual). That her phrase does not refer only to the final batch of poems is made clear as Jameson goes on to identify those in the first 126 which she believes must refer to women. These include numbers 97 and 99 while of 71 ('No longer mourn for me when I am dead') she writes that 'breathing the very soul of profound tenderness', it 'must, I think, have been addressed to a female'.[15]

There is of course nothing in Sonnet 71 to indicate the sex of the person of whom the writer, imagining his own death, says 'I love you so / That I in your sweet thoughts would be forgot, / If thinking on me then should make you woe'. It is only the context in which the poem figures which suggests that it must be addressed to a man yet, since no-one has been able to establish whether Shakespeare or Thorpe was responsible for the order in which the Sonnets appeared, it is possible to imagine that some poems were included in sequences where they did not properly belong. There is (that is) a case – although not a very good one – for the habit which later became wide-spread of invoking various of the poems up to 126 in heterosexual contexts. But Jameson is less concerned with making that case than with relying on her female intuition and in the conclusion to her chapter she implicitly recognises how little logical or scholarly warrant she has for her attributions.

> The period assigned to the composition of these Sonnets, and the attachment which inspired them, is the time when Shakespeare was living a wild and irregular life, between the court and the theatre, after his flight from Stratford. He had previously married, at the age of seventeen, Judith Hathaway, who was eight or ten years older than himself: he returned to his native town, after having sounded all depths of life, of nature, of passion, and ended his days as a respected father of a family, in calm, unostentatious privacy.
>
> One thing I will confess:– It is natural to feel an intense and insatiable curiosity relative to great men, a curiosity and an interest for which nothing can be too minute, too personal. – And yet when I had ransacked all that had ever been written, discovered, or surmised, relative to Shakespeare's private life, for the purposes of throwing some light on the Sonnets, I felt no gratification, no thankfulness to those whose industry had raked up the very few particulars which can be known. It is too much, and it is not enough: it disappoints us in one point of view – it is superfluous in another: what need to surround with commonplace, trivial associations, registers of wills and genealogies, and I know not what, – the mighty spirit who in dying left behind him not merely a name and fame, but a perpetual being, a presence and a power, identified with our nature, diffused through all time, and ruling the heart and the fancy with an uncontrollable and universal sway!
>
> I rejoice that the name of no one woman is popularly identified with that of Shakespeare. He belongs to us all! – the creator of Desdemona, and Juliet, and Ophelia and Imogen, and Viola, and Constance, and Cornelia, and Rosalind, and Portia, was not the poet of one woman, but the POET OF WOMANKIND.[16]

In this passage Shakespeare's eventual return to Stratford, from where after all (the suggestion is) he had been forced to *flee*, is being used by Jameson to extenuate a relationship with a woman other than Anne Hathaway (mistakenly referred to here by the name of his younger daughter). That it is impossible to discover the name of that other woman, she decides, is a matter for celebration rather than regret. This position – 'we know next to nothing about Shakespeare and a good thing too!' — would often be adopted, especially by those who became increasingly dismayed by the lengths to which public curiosity about great men or women could go. As far as the author of the plays is concerned it seems legitimate enough, but when it comes to the Sonnets it is hard not to resist the feeling that we would understand them better if we knew more about the circumstances in which they were written. As D. H. Lawrence put it, 'Even the best poetry, when it is at all personal, needs the penumbra of its own time and place and circumstance to make it full and whole. If we knew a little more of Shakespeare's self and circumstance how much more complete the Sonnets would be to us, how their strange, torn edges would be softened and merged into the whole body.'[17]

The importance of Jameson is that (following Wordsworth) she states so openly and categorically that the Sonnets are the place to go for knowledge of Shakespeare the man, although having done that she then fails to provide any. A writer who took up the same challenge in a more systematic way was Keats's friend Charles Armitage Brown. In 1838 Brown published a book whose full title is, *Shakespeare's Autobiographical Poems, Being his Sonnets Clearly Developed: with His Character Drawn Chiefly from His Works*. Brown was, in fact, no admirer of the Sonnets, complaining of their 'forced metaphors' and 'languid prolixity and monotony of cadence' but, with a missionary certainty which was later to afflict many others, he decided that, if the 1609 printers had 'received efficient directions, and had done their duty', they would have seen that what seemed like individual poems were in fact the stanzas of six long ones. The third poem, for example, consisted of 'stanzas' 27 to 55 and was one in which Shakespeare complained of his friend's coldness and warned him of life's decay. The six divisions he made, Brown claimed, were 'neither arbitrary nor fanciful, but inevitable'.[18] Since the sixth poems was 'To his mistress, on her infidelity', he could hardly slip past the issue of adultery in the way that either Drake or Jameson had; but the defence he feels obliged to provide is peculiarly contorted.

> I fear some readers may be surprised that I have not yet noticed a certain fault in Shakespeare, a glaring one, – his having a mistress, while he had a wife of his own, perhaps, at Stratford. May no person be inclined, on this account, to condemn him with a bitterness equal to their own virtue! For myself, I confess I have not the heart to blame him at all, – purely because he so keenly reproaches himself for his own sin and folly. Fascinated as he was, he did not, like other poets similarly guilty, directly or by implication, obtrude his own passions on the world as reasonable laws. Had such been the case, he might have merited our censure, possibly our contempt. On the contrary, he condemned and subdued his fault, and may therefore be cited as a good rather than a bad example. Should it be contended that he seems to have quitted his mistress more on account of her unworthiness than from conscientious feelings, I have nothing to answer beyond this: I will not join in seeking after questionable motives for good actions, well knowing, by experience, that when intruded on me, they have been nothing but a nuisance to my better thoughts.[19]

The remarkable moral confusion of this could be attributed to intellectual incompetence but it might also be a consequence of the same kind of difficulties Coleridge, Drake and Jameson found in reconciling the divine Shakespeare with the fallible man. When it comes to the nature of Shakespeare's relations with the young man to whom Brown concedes the first five 'poems' are addressed, he quite rightly points out how differently men addressed each other in Elizabethan times but then, like Drake, successfully distracts attention from what the fervour of some of Shakespeare's phrases might nevertheless imply by concentrating on the problem of identification. For Drake and Jameson, Southampton had been the obvious choice for the young man of the Sonnets but in 1837, in a book entitled *On the sonnets of Shakespeare – identifying the person to whom they are addressed; and elucidating several points in the poet's history*, the writer James Boaden (1762–1839) had made out a strong case for the Earl of Pembroke, and it is for Pembroke that Brown (acknowledging Boaden) also plumps.

Southampton had at first seemed the obvious candidate for the addressee of the Sonnets because the dedications to *Venus and Adonis* and (more particularly) *The Rape of Lucrece* strongly suggested that he must at some point have been regarded as Shakespeare's patron. While still a ward of the Crown, he had refused a suitable partner found for him by Burghley, so that there must have been a moment in Southampton's career when he would have been the appropriate recipient of those first sonnets in the 1609 Quarto which urge the young man to marry and procreate. The major stumbling block was that his family name, Henry Wriosthesley, did not correspond to the initials 'W. H.' in Thorpe's dedication. Pembroke's family name, on the other hand, was William Herbert; he also had refused a bride chosen for him (more than one in fact); and a link with Shakespeare could be found in Heminge and Condell's dedication of the First Folio to Pembroke and his brother Philip, who was the Earl of Montgomery. There, the two actors talked of their former colleague having been the Earls' 'servant' and thanked them for the favour they had shown to both Shakespeare and his work. A prominent patron of the arts Pembroke withdrew from a Court performance of *Pericles* in 1619 because 'I being tender hearted could not so endure to see [it] so soon after the loss of my old acquaintance Burbage'.[20]

The struggle between the supporters of Southampton and Pembroke, which begins with Drake and Jameson on one side and Boaden and Brown on the other, went on throughout the nineteenth century. It was only towards the end of it that the Pembroke group gained a distinct advantage thanks to the efforts of Thomas Tyler. In the introduction to a facsmile of the 1609 Quarto published in 1886, Tyler argued as strenuously for Pembroke as he had done before, and dwelt at some length on the affair Pembroke had had around 1600 with one of the Queen's maids of honour (this sort to thing happened with sufficient frequency to make one wonder why Elizabeth did not change their title). Whereas Southampton married his Elizabeth Vernon, Pembroke refused to do the same for Mary Fitton even when she was also pregnant. After the birth and then early death of a baby boy, Mary Fitton retired to live with her sister in the country. Her disgrace, and the reputation she appears to have had at Court before it as a lively flirt, made her an appropriate candidate for the 'dark lady' and thereby strengthened (in Tyler's view) the Pembroke case. One problem was that in the Sonnets it is made reasonably clear that both the young man and Shakespeare had slept with the 'dark lady' who, if she was Mary Fitton, was very well connected (you did not became a maid of honour otherwise).

> But, it may be asked, even though Shakespere may have played before the Court, is it probable that one of the Queen's maids of honour would have formed a *liaison* with a person in the low social rank of an actor? A partial answer to this question is furnished by a fact to which the Rev. W. A. Harrison has lately called attention (*Academy*, July 5, 1884). In 1600, William Kemp, the clown in Shakespere's company, dedicated his *Nine dais wonder* to 'Mistris Anne Fitton, Mayde of Honour to the most sacred Mayde, Royall Queene Elizabeth'. The name of Anne, it can be decisively shown, was inserted by the mistake of some one. Elizabeth had certainly no maid of honour *Anne* Fitton in 1599 or 1600. The lady intended must have been the Mrs Mary Fitton with whom we are at present concerned; and Kemp addresses her in a remarkably familiar manner. This fact is very interesting and important with regard to the probability of Shakespere's intimate acquaintance with this lady.[21]

People agreed with Tyler that Kemp had meant Mary rather than Anne Fitton but not that his dedication was 'remarkably familiar'; and raising the class issue may have made some of them wonder again how it was that in the Sonnets Shakespeare could have addressed in such an intimate way an Earl, whether he was Southampton or Pembroke. An apparently more powerful objection to Tyler's case, however, came from the publication in 1897 of a book entitled *Gossip from the Muniment-Room*, 'transcribed and edited' by Lady Newdigate-Newdegate (it was a provision of her inheritance that the two spellings had to be preserved). This compilation was dedicated to her husband who is described as the 'great-great-great-great-great-grandson' of Anne Fitton, Mary's sister, and it contains portraits of Mary which according to Lady Newdigate-Newdegate show that she 'was fair, not "dun"–complexioned, that her hair was brown, not "black wires", and that her eyes were grey, not "raven black"' (the quotations are, of course, from the Sonnets). 'Nor', Lady Newdigate-Newdegate adds, for good measure, 'have we any hint in the letters that she had any personal acquaintance with Shakespeare'.[22]

Numerous plays or novels of the nineteenth and the early twentieth centuries feature Shakespeare as the intimate friend of either Pembroke or Southampton (just as they often show him chatting in a relatively informal way with Queen Elizabeth). The arbitrary choices novelists and playwrights made was a reflection of continuing scholarly indecision, the failure to arrive at a consensus. A paradigmatic illustration of this indecision was provided by Sidney Lee who in 1898 wrote a biography of Shakespeare which dominated the field for decades. Lee worked with Leslie Stephen on the *Dictionary of National Biography* and for the 1891 edition wrote an excellent entry on Pembroke, one paragraph of which reads:

26. Portrait of Mary Fitton, *from* Gossip from the Muniment Room, *1897.*
Dark-haired, perhaps, but not dark-skinned.

Pembroke shared the literary tastes of his mother and uncle, Sir Philip Sidney. He wrote verse himself, and was, according to Aubrey, 'the greatest Mæcenas to learned men of any peer of his time or since.' Donne was an intimate friend. He was always well disposed to his old tutor Daniel and to his kinsman George Herbert. William Browne lived with him in Wilton House. He was generous to Massinger the dramatist, son of his father's steward. Ben Jonson addressed an eulogistic epigram to him in his collection of epigrams, which is itself dedicated to him. Every New-year's day Pembroke sent Jonson 20l. to buy books (*Conversations with Drummond*, pp. 22, 25). Inigo Jones, who is said to have visited Italy at his expense, was in his service. Chapman inscribed a sonnet to him at the close of his translation of the *Iliad*, and Davison's *Poetical Rhapsody* (1601) is dedicated to him. The numerous books in which a like compliment is paid him, often in conjunction with his brother Philip, amply attest the largeness of his patronage. The two Herberts, William and Philip, are 'the incomparable pair of brethren' to whom the first folio of Shakespeare's works is dedicated (1623); and the editors justify the selection of their patrons on the ground that the Herberts had been pleased to think Shakespeare's plays something heretofore, and had 'prosecuted both them and their author living with so much favour.' Other parts of the dedication prove as clearly that Shakespeare was on friendly terms with Pembroke, and the fact confirms the suggestion that the publisher's dedication of Shakespeare's 'Sonnets' 'to *the onlie begetter* of these insving sonnets, Mr. W. H.,' is addressed to Pembroke, disguised under the initials of his family name – William Herbert. The acceptance of this theory gives Shakespeare's 'Sonnets' an important place in Pembroke's early biography. The 'Sonnets,' though not published till 1609, were written for circulation among private friends more than ten years earlier. The opening series was addressed by Shakespeare to a handsome youth above his own rank, to whom the poet was deeply attached. He advises the youth to marry, is disconsolate when they are separated, and prophesies that his verse will secure his friend immortality. Some of the early sonnets seem to imply that the friend had temporarily robbed Shakespeare of his mistress, and the poet subsequently describes an estrangement between them owing to the young man's corruption by bad company. A reconciliation follows, but the concluding series of sonnets (cxxvi-cliv.) appears to relate how the friend supplanted the poet in the affections of 'a dark lady' associated with the court. Shakespeare's young friend was doubtless Pembroke himself, and 'the dark lady' in all probability was Pembroke's mistress, Mary Fitton. Nothing in the sonnets directly contradicts the identification of W. H., their hero and 'onlie begetter,' with William Herbert, and many minute internal details confirm it (cf. T. Tyler, *Shakespeare's Sonnets*, 1890, passim, and esp. pp. 44–73).[23]

Nine years later, in a revised edition of the *DNB*, a paragraph in Lee's entry on Pembroke appears, the first half of which is identical to the one above. But after the phrase 'and the editors justify the selection of their patrons on the ground that the Herberts has been pleased to think Shakespeare's plays something heretofore, and had "prosecuted both them and their author living with so much favour"', it takes a quite different turn.

Pembroke and his brother knew Shakespeare in his professional capacity of king's servant or member of James I's company of actors. In Pembroke as lord chamberlain the editors of the greatest dramatic publication of the day naturally sought their patron. There is no evidence that Pembroke was Shakespeare's special or personal patron, or came into any direct personal relations with the poet. No value attaches to the suggestion that the dedication of Shakespeare's 'Sonnets' by Thomas Thorpe [q. v.], the owner of the MS., 'to *the onlie begetter* of these insving sonnets, Mr. W. H.,' is addressed to Pembroke, disguised under the initials of his supposed youthful name – William Herbert. Being the eldest son of the earl he was known, from the hour of his birth until his father's death, in all relations of life exclusively as Lord Herbert. When the 'Sonnets' with this dedication were published in 1609, Pembroke's rank and dignity rendered it practically impossible that he should be deprived of those customary formalities of address which formed a prominent part of all extant dedications to him. Thomas Thorpe, the procurer of the MS. of the sonnets for publication, dedicated two books to Pembroke subsequently, but he always approached him in a trembling tone of subservience. There is no good ground for seeking the clue to the mystery of Shakespeare's 'Sonnets' in the publisher's address to 'Mr. W. H.' Thus all the argument which would identify Pembroke with the youth for whom Shakespeare professes affection in the sonnets may safely be neglected [see Wriothesley, Henry, third Earl of Southampton].[24]

What is surprising here is not so much that Lee transferred his allegiance from Pembroke to Southampton but that he gave no explanation for his change of mind. Yet when the evidence for either claim is similarly inconclusive, it is no wonder that even dour scholars become whimsical. The available documentation means that choosing between Southampton and Pembroke will always in the end be a question of guess work.

Not everyone throughout the nineteenth century felt with Wordsworth that Shakespeare had indeed 'unlocked his heart' in the Sonnets. The biographer Alexander Dyce, for example, in an account of Shakespeare's life which appeared in the first volume of an edition of the works published in the 1860s claimed that 'repeated readings of the Sonnets' had 'well nigh' convinced him that most of them 'were composed in an assumed character, on different subjects, and at different times, for the amusement, if not at the suggestion, of the author's intimate friends'; and he went on to insist that, although he would not deny that one or two of them reflected genuine feelings, 'the allusions scattered through the whole series are not to be hastily referred to the personal circumstances of Shakespeare'.[25] Less tentative in his denial that the Sonnets could be read autobiographically was the great Victorian scholar James Halliwell-Phillipps. In the 1887 edition of his modestly entitled *Outlines for the Life of Shakespeare* he commented sternly on those who were more and more taking the autobiographical route.

It was reserved for the students of the present century, who have ascertained so much respecting Shakespeare that was unsuspected by his own friends and contemporaries, to discover that his innermost earnest thoughts, his mental conflicts, and so on, are revealed in what would then be the most powerful lyrics yet given to the world. But the victim of spiritual emotions that involve criminatory reflections, does not usually protrude them voluntarily on the consideration of society; and, if the personal theory be accepted, we must concede the possibility of our national dramatist gratuitously confessing his own sins and revealing those of others, proclaiming his disgrace and avowing his repentance, in poetical circulars distributed by the delinquent himself amongst his own intimate friends.[26]

For Halliwell-Phillipps, the literary quality of the Sonnets is no longer in dispute: at the time of their publication they were 'the most powerful lyrics yet given to the world'; but it is unacceptable to him that the feelings they convey so powerfully could have any direct relevance to Shakespeare's own life. Against what he calls the 'personal theory', he implicitly opposes some version of Dyce's view that the Sonnets are 'dramatic' and involve the adoption of personae. The alternative would have meant radical reassessment of Shakespeare in his role as husband and friend, although whether the 'criminatory reflections' Halliwell-Phillipps refers to are associated with one or both of these roles, is not made clear.

The urge to know more about Shakespeare was so great, and the places where new knowledge might be found so few, that Dyce and Halliwell-Phillipps were necessarily minority voices. Tyler's work held out the hope that correctly identifying the addressee of the Sonnets would bring in its wake the identity of the dark lady; but there were general problems with Pembroke which were equally relevant to Southampton's case. Lee's point about the impossibility of addressing an Earl in public as 'Mr' applied equally to both, as did the difficulties raised by the intimate tone of the Sonnets. Was it possible that a commoner, as well as being so lavish of endearments, could also have hectored and cajoled an aristocrat in that way, whichever aristocrat it had happened to be? It was worries like this which helped to stimulate the search for a Mr W. H. who was less well-born. Enquiries had been given a specific direction, if only for some, by two readings of phrases in the Sonnets, one of which seems more probable than the other. In 135 and 136, it was said, where Shakespeare puns obsessively on his own first name, we learn that the young man's first name was also Will. As early as the eighteenth century, Thomas Tyrewhitt had suggested that his surname could be found in line 7 of Sonnet 20: 'A man in hue, all hues in his controlling' (in the 1609 edition 'hues' appears as *Hews*).[27] But who then was this William Hews or Hughes?

Scholars found in the records of Shakespeare's time one or two more or less possible young men with that name, but there is no documentary evidence at all for the best known candidate. In *The Portrait of Mr W. H.*, Oscar Wilde imagined that *Willie* Hughes (as he insisted in calling him) was a young actor

169

in Shakespeare's company who specialised in female roles. He chose to cast his conjectures in fictional form but often the only difference between him and rival interpreters is that he writes better. Near the beginning of *The Portrait* a lawyer called Erskine explains to the narrator why a dead friend of his called Cyril Graham had not been satisfied with previous attempts to identify the young man of the Sonnets. The framework is certainly fictional but, within it, the engagement with the issues is no different from that in the discursive prose of many of Wilde's predecessors or contemporaries in this area.

> He began by pointing out that the young man to whom Shakespeare addressed these strangely passionate poems must have been somebody who was a really vital factor in the development of his dramatic art, and that this could not be said of either Lord Pembroke or Lord Southampton. Indeed, whoever he was, he could not have been anybody of high birth, as was shown very clearly by Sonnet XXV, in which Shakespeare contrasts himself with men who are 'great princes' favourites'; says quite frankly –
>
> > *Let those who are in favour with their stars*
> > *Of public honour and proud titles boast,*
> > *Whilst I, whom fortune of such triumph bars,*
> > *Unlooked for joy in that I honour most;*
>
> And ends the sonnet by congratulating himself on the mean state of him he so adored:
>
> > *Then happy I, that love and am beloved*
> > *Where I may not remove nor be removed*
>
> This sonnet Cyril declared would be quite unintelligible if we fancied that it was addressed to either the Earl of Pembroke or the Earl of Southampton, both of whom were men of the highest position in England and fully entitled to be called 'great princes'; and he in corroboration of his view read me Sonnets CXXIV and CXXV, in which Shakespeare tells us that his love is not 'the child of state,' that it 'suffers not in smiling pomp,' but is 'builded far from accident.' I listened with a good deal of interest, for I don't think the point had ever been made before; but what followed was still more curious, and seemed to me at the time to dispose entirely of Pembroke's claim. We know from Meres that the Sonnets had been written before 1598, and Sonnet CIV informs us that Shakespeare's friendship for Mr. W. H. had been already in existence for three years. Now Lord Pembroke, who was born in 1580, did not come to London till he was eighteen years of age, that is to say till 1598, and Shakespeare's acquaintance with Mr. W. H. must have begun in 1594, or at the latest in 1595. Shakespeare, accordingly, could not have known Lord Pembroke until after the Sonnets had been written.
>
> Cyril pointed out also that Pembroke's father did not die until 1601; whereas it was evident from the line,
>
> > *You had a father, let your son say so,*
>
> that the father of Mr. W. H. was dead in 1598; and laid great stress on the evidence afforded by the Wilton portraits which represent Lord Pembroke as a swarthy dark-haired man, while Mr. W. H. was one whose hair was like spun gold, and whose face the meeting-place for the 'lily's white' and the 'deep

vermilion in the rose'; being himself 'fair,' and 'red,' and 'white and red,' and of beautiful aspect. Besides it was absurd to imagine that any publisher of the time, and the preface is from the publisher's hand, would have dreamed of addressing William Herbert, Earl of Pembroke, as Mr. W. H.; the case of Lord Buckhurst being spoken of as Mr. Sackville being not really a parallel instance, as Lord Buckhurst, the first of that title, was plain Mr. Sackville when he contributed to the 'Mirror for Magistrates,' while Pembroke, during his father's lifetime, was always known as Lord Herbert. So far for Lord Pembroke, whose supposed claims Cyril easily demolished while I sat by in wonder. With Lord Southampton Cyril had even less difficulty. Southampton became at a very early age the lover of Elizabeth Vernon, so he needed no entreaties to marry; he was not beautiful; he did not resemble his mother, as Mr. W. H. did –

> Thou art thy mother's glass, and she in thee
> Calls back the lovely April of her prime;

and, above all, his Christian name was Henry, whereas the punning sonnets (CXXXV and CXLIII) show that the Christian name of Shakespeare's friend was the same as his own – Will.

As for the other suggestions of unfortunate commentators, that Mr. W. H. is a misprint for Mr. W. S., meaning Mr. William Shakespeare; that 'Mr. W. H. all' should read 'Mr. W. Hall'; that Mr. W. H. is Mr. William Hathaway; that Mr. W. H. stands for Mr. Henry Willobie, the young Oxford poet, with the initials of his name reversed; and that a full stop should be placed after 'wisheth,' making Mr. W. H. the writer and not the subject of the dedication, – Cyril got rid of them in a very short time; and it is not worth while to mention his reasons, though I remember he sent me off into a fit of laughter by reading to me, I am glad to say not in the original, some extracts from a German commentator called Barnstorff, who insisted that Mr. W. H. was no less a person than 'Mr. William Himself.' Nor would he allow for a moment that the Sonnets are mere satires on the work of Drayton and John Davies of Hereford. To him, as indeed to me, they were poems of serious and tragic import, wrung out of the bitterness of Shakespeare's heart, and made sweet by the honey of his lips. Still less would he admit that they were merely a philosophical allegory, and that in them Shakespeare is addressing his Ideal Self, or Ideal Manhood, or the Spirit of Beauty, or the Reason, or the Divine Logos, or the Catholic Church. He felt, as indeed I think we all must feel, that the Sonnets are addressed to an individual, – to a particular young man whose personality for some reason seems to have filled the soul of Shakespeare with terrible joy and no less terrible despair.[28]

Apart from some readings which are strangely contorted or which at least reveal how polysemous the Sonnets are, this is a well-informed, reasonably expert summary of contemporary debate which would not be out of place in an essay, yet it is a story that Wilde is writing. Frustrated in his efforts to convince the world of the truth of his views, efforts which have included the commissioning of the fake Elizabethan portrait alluded to in the story's title, Cyril Graham has committed suicide. The narrator is intrigued by his fate, begins to investigate the issues until, after much research of his own, he becomes as passionately committed to a belief in Willie Hughes as Graham had been himself. He quotes numerous lines from the Sonnets in order to demonstrate that they are not only addressed to an actor but much more concerned with theatrical matters than is usually thought and eventually feels able to reconstruct the story they tell.

> My whole scheme of the Sonnets was now complete, and, by placing those that refer to the dark lady in their proper order and position, I saw the perfect unity and completeness of the whole. The drama – for indeed they formed a drama and a soul's tragedy of fiery passion and of noble thought – is divided into four scenes or acts. In the first of these (Sonnets I–XXXII) Shakespeare invites Willie Hughes to go upon the stage as an actor, and to put to the service of Art his wonderful physical beauty, and his exquisite grace of youth, before passion has robbed him of the one, and time taken from him the other. Willie Hughes, after a time, consents to be a player in Shakespeare's company, and soon becomes the very centre and key-note of his inspiration. Suddenly, in one red-rose July (Sonnets XXXIII–LII, LXI, and CXXVII–CLII) there comes to the Globe Theatre a dark woman with wonderful eyes, who falls passionately in love with Willie Hughes. Shakespeare, sick with the malady of jealousy, and made mad by many doubts and fears, tries to fascinate the woman who had come between him and his friend. The love, that is at first feigned, becomes real, and he finds himself enthralled and dominated by a woman whom he knows to be evil and unworthy. To her the genius of a man is as nothing compared to a boy's beauty. Willie Hughes becomes for a time her slave and the toy of her fancy, and the second act ends with Shakespeare's departure from London. In the third act her influence has passed away. Shakespeare returns to London, and renews his friendship with Willie Hughes, to whom he promises immortality in his plays. Marlowe, hearing of the wonder and grace of the young actor, lures him away from the Globe Theatre to play Gaveston in the tragedy of *Edward II*, and for the second time Shakespeare is separated from his friend. The last act (Sonnets C–CXXVI) tells us of the return of Willie Hughes to Shakespeare's company. Evil rumour has now stained the white purity of his name, but Shakespeare's love still endures and is perfect. Of the mystery of this love, and of the mystery of passion, we are told strange and marvellous things, and the Sonnets conclude with an envoi of twelve lines whose motive is the triumph of Beauty over Time, and of Death over Beauty.[29]

Having rearranged and interpreted the Sonnets to his satisfaction, the narrator writes a long letter to Erskine in which he sets out his reasons for believing Graham's theory and urges him endorse it. Immediately he has done this, however, his own belief evaporates. As he tell Erskine when he pays him a visit in order to apologise for his letter, 'The one flaw in the theory is that it presupposes the existence of the person whose existence is the subject of dispute'.[30] Because he is writing fiction, Wilde can, through his narrator, simultaneously propound and disavow a solution to the problem of the Sonnets, as he was apparently inclined to do in real life. 'You *must* believe in Willie Hughes', a friend reports him as telling her, 'I almost do myself'.[31] But as interesting as this implication of the way Wilde handles his story is the fact that, although the narrator loses faith, his letter has the effect of kindling it in

Erskine who declares himself now ready to devote his life to showing that Graham had been right. It is as if Wilde is recognising biographical interest in the Sonnets as a virus which gets passed from one commentator to another.

As Victorian standards weakened, commentators became increasingly at ease with the idea that Shakespeare may not always have been faithful to his wife. Less easy for them to discuss than adultery was homosexuality, but Wilde's story necessarily raised the question. Not that he ever explicitly suggests that Shakespeare and Willie Hughes were sexual partners. What he does do, however, is remind his readers of the terms in which the young man is addressed.

> For two weeks I worked hard at the Sonnets, hardly ever going out, and refusing all invitations. Every day I seemed to be discovering something new, and Willie Hughes became to me a kind of spiritual presence, an ever-dominant personality. I could almost fancy that I saw him standing in the shadow of my room, so well had Shakespeare drawn him, with his golden hair, his tender flower-like grace, his dreamy deep-sunken eyes, his delicate mobile limbs, and his white lily hands. His very name fascinated me. Willie Hughes! Willie Hughes! How musically it sounded! Yes; who else but he could have been the master-mistress of Shakespeare's passion, the lord of his love to whom he was bound in vassalage, the delicate minion of pleasure, the rose of the whole world, the herald of the spring decked in the proud livery of youth, the lovely boy whom it was sweet music to hear, and whose beauty was the very raiment of Shakespeare's heart, as it was the keystone of his dramatic power?[32]

After the phrase 'master-mistress' there are eight more descriptions of the young man also quoted directly from the Sonnets and Wilde takes care his readers should notice their provenance by providing a reference for each one. He is thereby implicitly asking them what they make of such warm language. What he himself made of it, is suggested in his narrator's conjecture that Willie Hughes was wooed away from Shakespeare by Marlowe in order to play the king's favourite Gaveston in *Edward II* (a play which contains perhaps the most open and extended treatment of a homosexual relationship in the Elizabethan repertoire). But his name on the title page would soon, in any case, become enough to focus minds on the issue.

One of the principal ways in which Shakespeare has manifested himself to posterity is as the great poet of love. To the extent that this image of him lodges in the public mind, it is certainly not because of *Troilus and Cressida* but, above all, *Romeo and Juliet*. Wilde's suggestion that Willie Hughes was Shakespeare's Juliet is not only a reminder that Juliet's lines were written for boys to speak but also a hint that he may be the great poet of love in a way quite different from the usual one. Yet a lot of water would have to pass under this particular bridge before, chiefly because of the Sonnets, Shakespeare could be celebrated by certain groups as a gay icon. Ten years after Wilde had first offered his interpretation of the Sonnets in the number of *Blackwoods Edinburgh Magazine* for July 1889 (my quotations are from the revised and extended version of *The Portrait* which appeared after his death), Samuel Butler published an edition of them. In his long introduction, Butler followed Wilde in dismissing the claims of Southampton and Pembroke and plumping for William Hughes, although his W. H. was not an actor but a sailor. Yet unlike Wilde, Butler was prepared to affirm that what the 'story' of the Sonnets allowed us to glimpse was some kind of sexual encounter between Hughes and Shakespeare. The details he acknowledged as obscure and he gives an exceedingly obscure account of them, but what he felt was involved was a cruel practical joke in which friends of Hughes burst in on him and Shakespeare when they were already or just about to get into bed together.

> Considering, then, Shakespeare's extreme youth, which I shall now proceed to establish, his ardent poetic temperament, and Alas! it is just the poetic temperament which by reason of its very catholicity is least likely to pass scatheless through what he so touchingly describes as 'the ambush of young days'; considering also the license of the times, Shakespeare's bitter punishment, and still more bitter remorse – is it likely that there was ever afterwards a day in his life in which the remembrance of that 'night of woe' did not at some time or another rise up before him and stab him? Nay, is it not quite likely that this great shock may in the end have brought him prematurely to the grave? – Considering, again, the perfect sanity of all his later work; considering further that all of us who read the Sonnets are as men who are looking over another's shoulder and reading a very private letter which was intended for the recipient's eye, and for no one else's; considering all these things – for I will not urge the priceless legacy he has left us, nor the fact that the common heart, brain, and conscience of mankind holds him foremost among all Englishmen as the crowning glory of our race – leaving all this on one side, and considering only youth, the times, penitence, and amendment of life, I believe that those whose judgement we should respect will refuse to take Shakespeare's grave indiscretion more to heart than they do the story of Noah's drunkenness; they will neither blink it nor yet look at it more closely than is necessary in order to prevent men's rank thoughts from taking it to have been more grievous than it was.
>
> *Tout savoir, c'est tout comprendre* – and in this case surely we may add – *tout pardonner.*[33]

This is how Butler dealt with the problem of the National Bard who might have been bisexual. However ludicrous and disagreeable his arguments might now seem, he at least had the courage to put forward a view which in the century just ended had been virtually unpronounceable.

—❖—

If Butler's example suggests that, by the end of the nineteenth century, it had become possible to raise in public the idea of Shakespeare as something other

27. 'Had Shakespeare asked me ... Frank Harris wondering what might have been'.
Cartoon by Max Beerbohm.

than heterosexual, that did not mean he could be easily represented as such in drama or fiction. Frank Harris was one writer iconoclastic enough to have made the attempt but, in spite of the remark I quoted above (p. 36), he was clearly not convinced by a Shakespeare less interested in women than he notoriously was himself. In his play *Shakespeare and His Love*, which dramatises conclusions Harris had previously reached in the succesful biography he had written, there is nothing ambiguous about the last word of the title. In the third act of this dire work, 'Lord William Herbert' is visited by a 'tall and dark' Mary Fitton, who complains he has lost interest in her. While trying to excuse himself, Herbert gives back to Mary a notebook she has lent him, but is then interrupted by knocking. He ushers the woman out of one door while Shakespeare enters by another to the not especially warm greeting of 'Oh, it's you, is it?'. Scene vi then begins:

SHAKESPEARE:	Unbidden; but not, I hope, unwelcome.
HERBERT:	No, no. Come in and be seated. I was half asleep, I think.
SHAKESPEARE:	We have not tasted life together for days and days.
HERBERT:	'Tis true; not since my quarrel with Raleigh. How the old limpet clings to place. He has just come to new honours, I hear; she has made him Governor of Jersey. Curse him!
SHAKESPEARE:	With honour one can always buy honours.
HERBERT [*laughs*]:	Yes! the singular is more than the plural.
SHAKESPEARE [*hesitatingly*]:	When I last saw you I begged your voice. Did you see her?
HERBERT:	I did. I wanted to speak to you about it; but it's not – pleasant.
SHAKESPEARE:	Not pleasant!
HERBERT:	I did my best, talked of your talents – all to no effect. Girls are queer monkeys!
SHAKESPEARE:	No effect!
HERBERT [*looking in the mirror*]:	I mean, though she admires you infinitely, she cannot love you.
SHAKESPEARE:	Cannot love me? Mistress Fitton!
HERBERT:	Who else?
SHAKESPEARE:	She told you she did not love me?
HERBERT [*looking at his profile*]:	She did.
SHAKESPEARE:	Strange!
HERBERT:	Why strange?
SHAKESPEARE:	She does love me.
HERBERT [*waving the mirror*]:	Admire, yes; but love, no!
SHAKESPEARE:	Love, yes!
HERBERT:	Friendship, affection, love if you will, but – but – not passion.
SHAKESPEARE:	Passion.
HERBERT [*throwing down the mirror*]:	Do you mean to say –
SHAKESPEARE:	Yes.
HERBERT [*indignantly*]:	What! What! Ha! Ha! Ha! The damned young minx!
SHAKESPEARE:	Why do you call her minx?
HERBERT:	Because – because she lied to me.
SHAKESPEARE:	No other reason?
HERBERT:	None!

SHAKESPEARE: What object could she have in deceiving you, as to her love for me, you, my friend?

HERBERT [*carelessly*]: In faith I don't know - a girl's whim, I suppose.

SHAKESPEARE: Strange - a girl seldom denies her love - and Mistress Fitton has courage. Most strange!

HERBERT: Well, you must ravel out the tangle at some idle moment; it's too knotty for me. Have you seen Chapman's *Iliad*? I've just been reading it; 'tis as fine as Homer; don't you think?

SHAKESPEARE: I'm not learned enough to judge.

HERBERT: I hear you met Bacon the other day. What did you think of him?

SHAKESPEARE: I know him too little - he's Jonson's friend - she denied me, you say, to you?

HERBERT: She did. But now I must dress: you'll forgive me. [*Takes up his sword-belt and buckles it on: looks for his gloves and cap.* SHAKESPEARE *in the meantime moves to the table and catches sight of the tablets which Herbert has thrown down.*]

SHAKESPEARE [*picking up the tablets.*]: Oh, my divining soul! [*Turns to* HERBERT] I pray you, of your courtesy; when did you see Miss Fitton last?

HERBERT [*arranging his doublet before the mirror*]: Yesterday, today. Why?

SHAKESPEARE [*showing tablets*]: When did she give you these?

HERBERT: Those? where did you find them?

SHAKESPEARE: She gave them to you?

HERBERT: Mary Fitton? Yes.

SHAKESPEARE: And *you* took them, knowing they were my gift to her?

HERBERT: How could I know that?

SHAKESPEARE: She told you. You must have asked where the verses came from: she hates verses, and loves truth - truth!

HERBERT: Don't take it so tragic, man. A girl's kiss, no weightier than a breath.

SHAKESPEARE: A girl's kiss, and a friend's faith. No weightier than a breath.

HERBERT: In love and war, none of us is to be trusted.

SHAKESPEARE: So!

HERBERT: It wasn't all my fault -

SHAKESPEARE [*taking hold of him, and watching his face*]: Not your fault! What? She tempted you - [HERBERT *nods*] - and who could resist her? she tempted you! Oh, let her rot and perish and be damned; the foul thing! I am cold with loathing.

HERBERT: I don't want to put the blame on her; it all came naturally; but you must not think I went about with intent to deceive you.

SHAKESPEARE: She tempted you; when? The first time you saw her; the very night I asked you to plead for me?

HERBERT: I don't wish to excuse myself; you know how such things happen. We danced; she dared me to wait by her when the Queen came; of course I waited - oh, curse it!

SHAKESPEARE: She dared you. That rank pride of hers, the pride that ruined angels and unpeopled heaven! The foul temptress! Damn her, oh, damn her!

HERBERT: Pride's no fault.

SHAKESPEARE: No fault! She swears love to me and then to you; kisses me and kisses you - no fault - she loves the slime that sticks to filthy deeds.

HERBERT: You believe her when you're with her; she seems true.

SHAKESPEARE: O, the world hath not a sweeter creature. She might have lain by an emperor's side. Hang her! I do but say what she is. The public commoner!

HERBERT: Don't blame her, she's so young.

SHAKESPEARE: And so fair! [...] I have lost all – joy, hope, trust – all gone; my pearl of life; my garden of delight!

HERBERT: Think, man: it's not the first time she has slipped, she doesn't pretend it is.

SHAKESPEARE: The pity of it; ah, the pity of it! The sky is all soiled: my lips, too – my hands – ah!

HERBERT: Why can't you be a man, and take what's light lightly!

SHAKESPEARE: Only the light do that! [*To himself*] Is it wrong to kill those light ones?

HERBERT: You would not hurt her.

SHAKESPEARE: No! That's true. I could not hurt her sweet, white flesh. God, how I love her! I'll tear out that love! Oh, the pity of it, the pity of it: all dirtied, all. But I'll not be fond!

HERBERT: Why not? She loves you; she said so: it's true, most likely.

SHAKESPEARE: Trust's dead in me: she has killed it. I think of her, and shudder – the sluttish spoil of opportunity. Faugh!

HERBERT: Put it out of mind, and it's as if it had not been.

SHAKESPEARE: You'll marry her?

HERBERT: I wouldn't marry an angel.

SHAKESPEARE: And yet – she loved you – kissed you – gave herself to you: Damnation!

HERBERT: You make too much of it.

SHAKESPEARE: Too much! I trusted you, your honour: bared my heart to you – Ah! The traitor wound!

HERBERT: Forgive us both and forget: Come. [*Puts his hand out.*]

SHAKESPEARE [*shrinks back*]: Words, words!

HERBERT: I never meant to hurt you.

SHAKESPEARE: That's the Judas curse! They know not what they do; but it's done. I had two idolatries – my friendship for you; I loved your youth and bravery! And my passion for her, the queen and pearl of women. And now the faith's dead, the love's befouled.

HERBERT: In a little while hope will spring again and new love.

SHAKESPEARE: Never, my summer is past! The leaves shake against the cold.

HERBERT: What can I say? What can I do?

SHAKESPEARE: Nothing: I must go. [*Turns to the door*] You have your deeds to live with. [*Exit* SHAKESPEARE][34]

This is the climactic moment in Harris's play. He tries to give it a tragic dimension with the echoes in Shakespeare's speech from *Othello* but, flat though the writing is, the reader is more likely to feel it has considerable comic potential with two essentially Edwardian men-about-town suddenly discovering that they are sleeping with the same woman. So intent is Shakespeare on discovering the truth that he refuses to be distracted – even when he is asked what he thinks of Bacon. The situation being dramatised is taken directly from the Sonnets with the crucial difference that there the speaker is much more concerned with the effect of betrayal on his relations with the young man than on those with the young woman. This is because his love for him is represented as far exceeding that for her. Little of this is evident in Harris's treatment where Herbert and Shakespeare are less like an Earl and a commoner than two former school chums and where the feelings they have for each other are represented as distinctly cool.

A surprising addition to those who, like Harris, insisted that the fervour with which the speaker in the Sonnets addresses the young man has no special sexual significance was Lord Alfred Douglas. In a complicated act of both homage to, and betrayal of, his former friend Oscar Wilde, Douglas proposed an explanation of the tone of the more intimate poems which went out of its way to challenge Butler's. This is part of what he wrote in an edition of the Sonnets which was nonetheless on Butler's model, one (that is) in which the poems were rearranged so that they could more easily support the editor's notion of the story they supposedly tell.

> To avoid misunderstanding it is necessary to emphasize that while Butler distinctly brings the charge of homosexuality against Shakespeare on the evidence of the Sonnets, Wilde in 'The Portrait of Mr. W. H.' refrains from doing anything of the kind, and in a passage in *Dorian Gray* by implication definitely rejects it.
>
> The present writer, while accepting it as perfectly obvious and indisputable that the great majority of Shakespeare's incomparable Sonnets (which comprise among them the finest poetry that has ever been written in this or any language) were written to, or about, a boy whom Shakespeare adored, utterly rejects the notion that Shakespeare was a homosexualist. That this is not a thesis artificially trumped up to cover the exigences of the moment or to make it a little less difficult to write and publish this short essay, is easy to prove.
>
> As long ago as 1921, when I was editing *Plain English*, I wrote an article in that weekly journal called 'Slinging Mud at Shakespeare', in which I defended Shakespeare against this charge [...] Eight years later I touched on the subject again in my *Autobiography* (published 1929), and as what I then wrote contains the gist of what I now wish to repeat and emphasize on this point, I am reproducing it here. I was referring to certain letters written by Wilde:
>
>> The language he used was of course extravagant and unusual. But there is nothing whatever in his letters which could not be matched in Shakespeare's sonnets (also written to a boy), and though I believe it is the fashion nowadays to accuse Shakespeare of having had the same vices as Wilde, this merely shows the ignorance and baseness and stupidity of those who make such accusations on such grounds. Shakespeare, as I have pointed out before, refuted his detractors, by anticipation, in the last six lines of the very sonnet which is generally quoted as the strongest evidence against him. I refer to the sonnet beginning:
>>
>>> *A woman's face with Nature's own hand painted,*
>>> *Hast thou, the Master-Mistress of my passion.*
>>
>> The lines enumerated above (that is to say the last six lines) clearly show, not only that Shakespeare's passion for 'Mr. W. H.' was perfectly innocent,

but that Shakespeare himself had never envisaged the possibility of its being anything else. 'Nature', says he, who intended thee for a woman 'fell a-doting' and 'by addition, me of thee defeated.' Could anything be clearer? 'If you had been a woman [...] but unfortunately you were a boy, so that I was defeated.' To rub it in still more strongly he goes on to say:

> But since she prick'd thee out for woman's pleasure,
> Mine be thy love, and thy love's use their treasure.

(Observe here the tremendous force of the anti-thesis between 'thy love' and 'thy love's use'.)

The effect of the lines referred to is even stronger because they are so obviously not deliberately made in answer to, or in anticipation of, any adverse suggestion. Shakespeare exculpates himself, in the eyes of any reasonable being, quite definitely and quite unconsciously. Obviously it never occurred to him that anyone would put a bad interpretation on his love and adoration for 'Mr. W. H.'

[...] A friend to whom I developed, in conversation, the thesis I have here propounded as to the overwhelming evidence for Shakespeare's innocence in this regard (which is supported by his passionate love of chastity and purity exemplified in the characters of all his heroines, and his hatred and contempt for what would now be considered by many people to be quite venial departures from that standard) said to me: 'Why should you be so anxious to acquit Shakespeare of homosexuality? Supposing he had been a homosexualist, would you have thought any worse of his poetry or his genius? Why get so excited because some people arrive at what appears to them to be a natural conclusion from his own written words?' To which I replied, as I do now, that if it could be proved that Shakespeare was a homosexualist, it certainly would not invalidate my admiration of his poetry, nor would I consider myself qualified to condemn him or to cast stones at him; but if the accusation (or the inference) is not true, and if there really is no evidence at all that he was a homosexualist, and if all the available evidence, such as it is, points utterly against it, why should he be libelled and defamed merely to gratify those who really are tarred with that brush on the one hand, and fools and prudes [...] on the other?

Any honest man who has been at a public school or a university must know perfectly well that young men and boys are liable to fall in love with other young men and boys, and they must also know equally well that some of these relationships are innocent and some are not. In cases where it becomes the legitimate business of any individual to find out into which of the two categories such a state of affairs falls, it is merely a matter of evidence. If Shakespeare is to be convicted of homosexuality on the evidence of his sonnets to Mr. W. H., then David, the Psalmist, who is venerated by Catholics as a Saint and one of the precursors of Christ, must be equally convicted on the strength of his lament for Jonathan. Would anyone in his senses make such a contention, unless he were an 'eminent counsel' speaking from a brief? [...]

[...] The truth is, in spite of Frank Harris and Arnold Bennett and all the other frantic worshippers at the shrine of what they are pleased to call 'the plain facts of life', that Shakespeare was a good deal of a puritan. He was almost certainly brought up a Catholic, and though he undoubtedly succumbed to the pressure of the times in which he lived and outwardly abandoned his religion, he never lost the Catholic view about purity and impurity. Doubtless he had mistresses, we know at any rate that he had one, 'the dark woman (why call her a lady?) of the Sonnets', but he had no romantic feelings about her or about any other woman of easy virtue. All his heroines, with the solitary exception of Cleopatra, were chaste and pure and lovely, and he could not take a 'charitable view' even about Cressida in these regards.

On the other hand he openly adored Mr. W. H. and celebrated his adoration in the most perfect poetry. *Honi soit qui mal y pense.*[35]

Douglas denies that his admiration for Shakespeare's work would be affected by learning that he was homosexual, but the vehemence with which he denounces those who are, makes that seem doubtful. There is a good deal of frank talking in what he says but also uncertainties of tone which illustrate how difficult the topic of Shakespeare and homosexuality remained, even three decades into the twentieth century.

To many, the distinction Douglas establishes may have seemed no more than that between a practising and non-practising homosexual. In the late 1920s and early 1930s, such readers might have felt more comfortable with the version of events offered by G. S. Viereck in the highly successful pot-boiler he wrote in collaboration with Paul Eldridge, *My First Two Thousand Years: the Autobiography of the Wandering Jew.* The Jew of the title, who is known at this point of the narrative as Baron Martini, has come to London in order to bribe Francis Bacon into settling a law suit in his favour:

Lord Verulam listened attentively and meditated. 'Give me a few days' time to consider this, Baron. I believe it can be adjusted – not so easily, perhaps, but it can be.'

He looked at me, his round eyes blinking a little. We understood each other.

He glanced at his watch which hung around his neck by a golden chain, also my gift.

Then, once more philosopher and man of the world, Bacon directed the conversation into other channels.

'Ah, it is time for the play. Is the Baron interested in the theatre?'

'Life's distorted reflection in the mirror of art always amuses me.'

'Will Shakespeare of the Globe Theatre is putting on *Romeo and Juliet* to-day, a charming play though too sentimental. Master Willie Hewes is positively enchanting as Juliet. So consummate is his acting one can hardly believe he's a boy. Would you care to see the performance?'

I accepted the invitation.

The play pleased me mildly. The plot which I had read in several Italian stories, was hackneyed, the end decidedly stupid. But Master Willie Hewes was exquisite.

When had I seen a youth so handsome, so delicately fashioned? Where had I heard so musical a voice? [...]

'How do you like the lad, Baron?' [his Lordship] asked with a smile.

'Willie Hewes, my Lord, resembles a younger brother of mine who died years ago.'

'Should you desire it, Baron, I shall ask Willie to join us over the punch bowl. He is quite a manly fellow, swears, drinks, fences, and makes love to the wenches. If the lad were less enamoured of Shakespeare, he could choose a titled lady for his bride. But his strange passion – '

'A youth's whim, my lord. Besides, is not this Shakespeare the playwright?'

'Yes, of course. Willie's love may be a reflex of his admiration. Meanwhile, however, the scandal sears his character. I told him so, but he would not listen to me. He recited the sonnets Shakespeare dedicated to him. They are not shocking to a classical scholar, but they make ribald tongues wag in London. However,' Bacon laughed, 'I nearly fell in love with the lad myself.'

'The youth intrigues me, my Lord.'[36]

The Jew, who announces himself to Willie Hughes by one of his more traditional names, Cartaphilus, is fascinated by the young actor who reminds him of both a beautiful young boy (Antonio), whom he has previously met in Florence, and of Antonio's equally beautiful sister Antonia. He buys Willie some clothes and they go back to the Jew's lodgings so that the young man can try them on.

> I promised I would not 'peep'. I might arouse his displeasure. It would be a pity. At the beginning of friendship, it might prove disastrous.
>
> But even while these ideas crossed and recrossed my brain, my hand lifted carefully a corner of the curtain.
>
> The long Venetian mirror reflected in gorgeous nakedness – not Antonio, but Antonia – the most beautiful of girls – two small breasts round as apples, a throat as firm and smooth as marble, hips and arms and a torso dazzling like the morning sun. The body was firmly knit as a boy's, but rounded delicately, giving the illusion of softness. The hair, curled and cut at the nape of the neck, resembled that of a Grecian statue.
>
> 'Antonia,' I whispered.
>
> Willie turned around and caught her breath. By an ancient instinct, she covered with one arm her breasts, with the other her femininity. Her face flushed, her lips parted.
>
> 'Cartaphilus! Did you not swear – ?'
>
> I entered the room. 'I swore, but I am happy I perjured myself. Antonia, my dearest, my loveliest maiden!'
>
> She hid her head upon her bosom and sobbed quietly.
>
> I embraced her. 'Is it not infinitely more delectable to find that Antonio is Antonia?'
>
> 'Everybody will hear of it now and I shall have to leave the theatre. I shall have to be merely a woman. No more for me the joy and the recklessness of a boy!'
>
> 'How can you think that, my love? If Antonia desires to be Antonio, shall Cartaphilus frustrate her wish? How much more poignant her beauty, vacillating between boy and girl [...] '
>
> 'Tell me what prompted you to disguise yourself as a boy?'
>
> 'It was the only way I could be near him, since the law does not permit our sex to appear on the stage.'
>
> 'But Shakespeare knew your sex?'
>
> 'Not at first. . . .'
>
> 'He loved you. . . .'
>
> 'Yes. . . . He was completely bewildered . . . at first, but in his heart of hearts

he suspected my secret.'

'How do you know?'

She pouted. 'Because he poured his soul into his sonnets.' Her lips moved, caressing each word affectionately.

> 'And for a woman wert thou first created,
> Till Nature, as she wrought thee, fell a-doting
> And by addition me of thee defeated
> By adding something to my purpose nothing.'

'And when he discovered that nature had not been so cruel? . . .'

'He was overjoyed. It remained a sweet, shameful secret between us. If my true sex were known, I would be banished from the stage, and the Lord Chamberlain would punish Will. In the eyes of the law we are no better than vagabonds.'

'Do you like to play the boy, to be his play-boy?'

She hesitated a minute. Then she said shyly, 'Yes.' She blushed 'He called me master-mistress of his passion. . . .'[37]

This is a recognisable testing to the limits by writers who are always incipiently pornographic but whose 'daring' does not extend to depicting a sexual relationship between a man and a boy. As I have said, it would take many years before gay interest groups could calmly enrol Shakespeare in the Pantheon of gay writers and it is only recently that biographers such as Katherine Duncan-Jones have felt free to entertain in an entirely unembarrassed way the likelihood that Shakespeare had sexual relations, not with Willie Hughes – commonly regarded now as a figment of Wilde's imagination – but with the young Earl of Southampton.[38]

A homosexual or bisexual Shakespeare is not yet, or ever likely to become, the dominant view. The impression it is possible to take from certain of the Sonnets has to battle so hard against those which can be derived from so many other aspects of his work that there is no real difficulty in sustaining the idea of him as the great poet of heterosexual love. Quite how powerfully this idea has been sustained was clear enough from the recent and enormous world-wide success of *Shakespeare in Love*. The writers of that film followed Viereck and Eldridge in having Juliet played by a woman pretending to be a boy, so that fantasies about Shakespeare's own likely involvement with the principal female character in *Romeo and Juliet* could then be free of whatever worrying implications some might discover in remembering that all his female roles were written for males. A handsome lead actor confirmed the general sense that the man who wrote the balcony scene could not have been other than a lover of women and that there must, or ought to have been, some correspondence between the beauty of the verse and its author's appearance.

Shakespeare in Love, about which I say a little more in a later chapter, was a film in the major tradition. The minor one is represented by Derek Jarman's *The Angelic Conversation* (1985) in which Judi Dench's reading in voice-over of fourteen Shakespeare sonnets becomes (in the extravagant words of the publicity release)

> a backdrop for Jarman's trademark visual collages of surreal and haunting images that explore homosexual desire [...] Jarman's painterly non-narrative style explores the hauntingly beautiful passages of the sonnets with a vibrant and intensely homoerotic sensibility that delights in blowing apart the status quo theories on William Shakespeare.

There is no episode in the dreamy and languorous progress of *The Angelic Conversation* which could accurately be accused of blowing anything apart but, in any case, a more recent film that either it, or *Shakespeare in Love*, suggests that the 'theories' referred could never stay blown apart for long. When Emma Thompson adapted Jane Austen's *Sense and Sensibility* for the screen she chose to show Marianne Dashwood's love for Willoughby strengthened by the discovery that he knows by heart Shakespeare's sonnet 116 ('Let not to the marriage of true minds'), just as she does. We watch their mutual attachment confirmed as they take turns to recite various of its lines. This episode is not in Jane Austen's text and not especially appropriate – well-bred young ladies at the very beginning of the nineteenth century were unlikely to have been familiar with the Sonnets – but it confirms a contemporary view of Shakespeare as the poet of heterosexual love, by conveniently ignoring the fact that in Sonnet 116 the subject is almost certainly love between men. It shows the continuing strength of that view, despite the considerable weakening of resistance to the idea that Shakespeare may not have been heterosexual. Whether or not he was is, of course, an entirely different matter from any I have discussed here, and one which there is never likely to be enough evidence to settle. It appeared at one point that the Sonnets might provide such evidence, but when it proved impossible to reach a consensus on the identity of their addressee, the date of their composition, and the circumstances in which they were published, those concerned with the image of Shakespeare found that the poems could reasonably be either ignored or fore-grounded, just as they thought fit.

Notes

1. John Benson, 'Epistle' to *Poems: Written by Wil. Shake-speare. Gent.* (1640).
2. See Hallett Smith, '"No Cloudy Stuffe to Puzzell Intellect". A Testimonial Misapplied to Shakespeare', *Shakespeare Quarterly*, vol. 1 (1950), pp. 18–21.
3. *Shakespeare's Lives*, p. 118.
4. Edmond Malone, *Supplement to the edition of Shakespeare's plays published in 1778 by George Steevens and Samuel Johnson* (1780), vol. 1, pp. 653–4.
5. *Ibid.*, p. 656.
6. *Ibid.*, p. 657.
7. *Plays of William Shakespeare* (1793), vol. 1, pp. vii–viii.

8. *Poetical Works of William* Wordsworth (Oxford University Press, 1904), p. 206.
9. See R. A. Foakes (ed.), *Coleridge's Criticism of Shakespeare: A Selection* (1989), p. 30.
10. *Ibid.*
11. Duncan-Jones (ed.), *Shakespeare's Sonnets*, p. 20.
12. *Poetical Works of William Wordsworth*, pp. 745-6.
13. Nathan Drake, *Noontide Leisure*, vol. 2, pp. 80-88.
14. Anna Jameson, *Lives of the Poets* (1829), pp. 237-41.
15. *Ibid.*, p. 245.
16. *Ibid.*, pp. 246-8.
17. D. H. Lawrence, 'Introductory Note' to *Collected Poems* (1928).
18. C. A. Brown, *Shakespeare's Autobiographical Poems* (1838), p. 47.
19. *Ibid.*, pp. 98-9.
20. Katherine Duncan-Jones, *Ungentle Shakespeare: Scenes from His Life* (Arden, 2002), p. 205.
21. Thomas Tyler, *Sonnets; the first quarto of 1609* (1886), pp. xx-xxi.
22. Lady Newdigate-Newdegate, *Gossip from the Muniment Room* (1897: 2nd edition), p. 36.
23. *DNB* (1891), pp. 227-8.
24. *DNB* (1900), pp. 678-9.
25. Alexander Dyce (ed.), *The Works of William Shakespeare* (1866), vol. 1, pp. 101-2.
26. Halliwell-Phillipps, *Outlines of the Life of Shakespeare*, vol.1, pp. 109-10.
27. See Schoenbaum, *Shakespeare's Lives*, p. 119.
28. *Complete Works of Oscar Wilde*, with an introduction by Vyvyan Hollond (1948), pp. 1153-55.
29. *Ibid.*, p. 1191.
30. *Ibid.*, p. 1198.
31. Richard Ellmann, *Oscar* Wilde (Penguin Books, 1988), p. 281.
32. *Complete Works of Oscar Wilde*, p. 1169.
33. Samuel Butler, *Shakespeare's Sonnets, Reconsidered and in part Rearranged* (1899), pp. 375-6.
34. Frank Harris, *Shakespeare and his Love* (1910), pp. 115-31.
35. Lord Alfred Douglas, *The True History of Shakespeare's Sonnets* (1933), pp. 18-35.
36. G. S. Viereck and Paul Eldridge, *My first two thousand years: the autobiography of the Wandering Jew* (1929), pp, 375-6.
37. *Ibid.*, pp. 380-2.
38. Duncan-Jones, *Ungentle Shakespeare*, pp, 80, 88.

28. *Poster for the sale of the Henley Street house in 1847.*
Courtesy of the Shakespeare Birthplace Trust Records Office.

Chapter Six

Victorians, Edwardians and Some Others

THE SONNETS REPRESENT A special case in the history of Shakespeare's ever-growing iconic status and have taken the story well beyond the nineteenth century. To pick up the threads and note the increasing importance of Stratford-upon-Avon, I need to go back in time. One of the two main centres of interest in the town was Holy Trinity church with its tombstone and memorial bust. Malone did not know that this bust had been multi-coloured in its original state and in 1793 he obtained permission to have it repainted the colour of stone. A witty quatrain published in the *Gentleman's Magazine* in 1815 is a reminder that even Homer nods:

> Stranger, to whom this monument is shown,
> Invoke the Poet's curse upon Malone;
> Whose meddling zeal his barbarous taste betrays,
> And daubs his tombstone, as he mars his plays![1]

Apart from the church there was also of course the Henley Street house, or birthplace. Shakespeare's will had stipulated that his sister Joan Hart should continue to live in a part of this property (even during his life-time another part of it may have been used as an inn[2]), and it was occupied by Harts of one kind or another until, at the end of the eighteenth or beginning of the nineteenth century, John Shakespeare Hart rented it to his cousin Thomas Hornby and his wife. Although in 1806 his widow then sold the property to Thomas Court, the Hornbys continued to live in part of it while the Courts occupied the rest.[3] It was after her husband died that Mrs Hornby ran a trade in Shakespeare relics, and it was this woman whom Washington Irving encountered when in 1815 he made the pilgrimage charmingly recorded in *The Sketch Book*.

To a homeless man, who has no spot on this wide world which he can truly call his own, there is a momentary feeling of something like independence and territorial consequence, when, after a weary day's travel, he kicks off his boots, thrusts his feet into slippers, and stretches himself before an inn fire. Let the world without go as it may; let kingdoms rise or fall, so long as he has the wherewithal to pay his bill, he is, for the time being, the very monarch of all he surveys. The arm-chair is his throne, the poker is sceptre, and the little parlour, some twelve feet square, his undisputed empire. It is a morsel of certainty, snatched from the midst of the uncertainties of life; it is a sunny moment gleaming out kindly on a cloudy day: and he who has advanced some way on the pilgrimage of existence knows the importance of husbanding even morsels and moments of enjoyment. 'Shall I not take mine ease in mine inn? thought I, as I gave the fire a stir, lolled back in my elbow-chair, and cast a complacent look about the little parlour of the Red Horse, at Stratford-on-Avon.

The words of sweet Shakespeare were just passing through my mind as the clock struck midnight from the tower of the church in which he lies buried. There was a gentle tap at the door, and a pretty chambermaid, putting in her smiling face, inquired, with a hesitating air, whether I had rung. I understood it as a modest hint that it was time to retire. My dream of absolute dominion was at an end; so abdicating my throne, like a prudent potentate, to avoid being deposed, and putting the Stratford Guide-Book under my arm, as a pillow companion, I went to bed, and dreamt all night of Shakespeare, the jubilee, and David Garrick.

The next morning was one of those quickening mornings which we sometimes have in early spring; for it was about the middle of March. The chills of a long winter had suddenly given way; the north wind had spent its last gasp; and a mild air came stealing from the west, breathing the breath of life into nature, and wooing every bud and flower to burst forth into fragrance and beauty.

I had come to Stratford on a poetical prilgrimage. My first visit was to the house where Shakespeare was born, and where, according to tradition, he was brought up to his father's craft of wool-combing. It is a small mean-looking edifice of wood and plaster, a true nestling-place of genius, which seems to delight in hatching its offspring in by-corners. The walls of its squalid chambers are covered with names and inscriptions in every language, by pilgrims of all nations, ranks, and conditions, from the prince to the peasant; and present a simple, but striking instance of the spontaneous and universal homage of mankind to the great poet of nature.

The house is shown by a garrulous old lady, in a frosty red face, lighted up by a cold blue anxious eye, and garnished with artificial locks of flaxen hair, curling from under an exceedingly dirty cap. She was peculiarly assiduous in exhibiting the relics with which this, like all other celebrated shrines, abounds. There was the shattered stock of the very matchlock with which Shakespeare shot the deer, on his poaching exploits. There, too, was his tobacco-box; which proves that he was a rival smoker of Sir Walter Raleigh; the sword also with which he played Hamlet; and the identical lantern with which Friar Lawrence discovered Romeo and Juliet at the tomb! There was an ample supply also of Shakespeare's mulberry-tree, which seems to have as extraordinary powers of self-multiplication as the wood of the true cross; of which there is enough extant to build a ship of the line.

The most favourite object of curiosity, however, is Shakespeare's chair. It stands in the chimney nook of a small gloomy chamber, just behind what was his father's shop. Here he may many a time have sat when a boy, watching the slowly revolving spit with all the longing of an urchin; or of an evening, listening to the cronies and gossips of Stratford, dealing forth churchyard tales and legendary anecdotes of the troublesome times of England. In this chair it is the custom of every one that visits the house to sit: whether this be done with the hope of imbibing any of the inspiration of the bard I am at a loss to say, I merely mention the fact; and mine hostess privately assured me that, though built of solid oak, such was the fervent zeal of devotees, that the chair had to be new bottomed at least once in three years. It is worthy of notice, also, in the history of this extraordinary chair, that it partakes something of the volatile nature of the Santa Casa of Loretto, or the flying chair of the Arabian enchanter; for though sold some few years since to a northern princess, yet, strange to tell, it has found its way back again to the old chimney corner.

I am always of easy faith in such matters, and am ever willing to be deceived, where the deceit is pleasant and costs nothing. I am, therefore, a ready believer in relics, legends, and local anecdotes of goblins and great men; and would advise all travellers who travel for their gratification to be the same. What is it to us, whether these stories be true or false, so long as we can persuade ourselves into the belief of them, and enjoy all the charm of the reality? There is nothing like resolute good-humoured credulity in these matters; and on this occasion I went even so far as willingly to believe the claims of mine hostess to a lineal descent from the poet, when, unluckily for my faith, she put into my hands a play of her own composition, which set all belief in her consanguinity at defiance.[4]

The case for 'good-humoured credulity' would be put by others after Irving, but never more engagingly. That the women he encountered in his pilgrimage to the home of 'sweet Shakespeare' was indeed an author is proved by the publication in Stratford in 1819 of *The Battle of Waterloo, a tragedy in five acts* by Mary Hornby who is described on the title page as 'the keeper of Shakespeare's house'. Whether it was that the widow Hornby did too well out of her supposed relics, or that she arrogated too much authority to herself, her landlady and next-door neighbour Mrs Court, now also a widow, evicted her in 1820 and assumed responsibilities for the birthplace herself. When she died in 1846 a committee which included such leading figures as Dickens, and which was to be known as the Shakespeare Birthplace Trust, was formed in order to secure the house for the nation. Thus it was that in the following year, when 'the most honoured monument of the greatest genius who ever lived' was put up for auction, it was secured by the Trust for the tidy sum of £3,000.[5]

In 1847 the Henley Street property still showed signs of previous uses inconsistent with the images which formed in the Victorian mind at the thought of 'the greatest genius who ever lived': one half was after all still a public house and the other had enjoyed a brief incarnation as a butcher's shop. It was a question for the Trust of refurbishment but there were financial difficulties and, if Nathaniel Hawthorne's account of his visit in 1855 is anything to go by - so different in tone from that of his compatriot forty years earlier - 'restoring' the structure of the house and finding appropriate furnishing for the various rooms was a slow process.

We stopt at the Red Lion, a hotel of no great pretensions, and immediately set out on our rambles about town. After wandering through two or three streets, we found Shakespeare's birth-place, which is almost a worse house than anybody could dream it to be; but it did not surprise me, because I had seen a full-sized fac-simile of it in the Zoological gardens at Liverpool. It is exceedingly small – at least, the portion of it which had anything to do with Shakespeare. The old, worn, butcher's counter, on which the meat used to be laid, is still at the window. The upper half of the door was open; and on my rapping at it, a girl dressed in black soon made her appearance and opened it. She was a ladylike girl, not a menial, but I suppose the daughter of the old lady who shows the house. This first room has a pavement of gray slabs of stone, which, no doubt, were rudely squared when the house was new, but they are all cracked and broken, now, in a curious way. One does not see how any ordinary usage, for whatever length of time, should have cracked them thus; it is as if the devil had been stamping on them, long ago, with an iron hoof, and the tread of other persons had ever since been reducing them to an even surface again. The room is white-washed, and very clean, but woefully shabby and dingy, coarsely built, and such as it is not very easy to idealize. In the rear of this room is the kitchen, a still smaller room, of the same dingy character; it has a great, rough fire-place, with an immense passage way for the smoke, and room for a large family under the blackened opening of the chimney. I stood under it, without stooping; and doubtless Shakespeare may have stood on the same spot, both as child and man. A great fire might of course make the kitchen cheerful; but it gives a depressing idea of the humble, mean, sombre character of the life that could have been led in such a dwelling as this – with no conveniences, all higgledy-piggledy, no retirement, the whole family, old and young, brought into too close contact to be comfortable together. To be sure, they say the house used to be much larger than now, in Shakespeare's time; but what we see of it is consistent in itself, and does not look as if it ever could have been a portion of a large and respectable house.

Thence we proceeded upstairs to the room in which Shakespeare is supposed to have been born, and which is over the front lower room, or butcher's shop. It has one broad window, with old irregular panes of glass; the floor is of very rudely hewn planks; the naked beams and rafters at the sides and over head bear all the marks of the builder's axe; and the room, besides, is very small – a circumstance more difficult to reconcile oneself to, as regards places that we have heard and thought much about, than any other part of a mistaken ideal. I could easily touch the ceiling, and could have done so had it been a good deal higher; indeed, the ceiling was entirely written over with names in pencil, by persons, I suppose, of all varieties of stature; so was every inch of the wall, into the obscurest nooks and corners; so was every pane of glass – and Walter Scott's name was said to be on one of the panes; but so many people had sought to immortalize themselves in close vicinity to him, that I really could not trace out his signature. I did not write my own name.

This room, and the whole house, so far as I saw it, was white-washed and very clean; and it had not the aged, musty smell, with which Chester makes one familiar, and which I suspect is natural to old houses, and must render them unwholesome. The woman who showed us upstairs had the manners and aspect of a gentlewoman, and talked intelligently about Shakespeare. Arranged on a table

CHAPTER SIX: VICTORIANS, EDWARDIANS AND SOME OTHERS

and in chairs, there were various prints, views of houses and scenes connected with Shakespeare's memory, editions of his works, and local publications relative to him – all for sale, and from which, no doubt, this old gentlewoman realizes a good deal of profit. We bought several shillings' worth, partly as thinking it the civilest method of requiting her for the trouble of shewing the house. On taking our leave, I most ungenerously imposed on Sophia the duty of offering an additional fee to the lady-like girl who first admitted us; but there seemed to be no scruple, on her part, as to accepting it. I felt no emotion whatever in Shakespeare's house – not the slightest – nor any quickening of the imagination. It is agreeable enough to reflect that I have seen it; and I think I can form, now, a more sensible and vivid idea of him as a flesh-and-blood man; but I am not quite sure that this latter effect is altogether desirable.[6]

Unlike Irving, Hawthorne is a sceptical tourist with curious expectations of what houses built several hundred years ago should provide but the general accuracy of his account here was confirmed a few years later by the Reverend J. M. Jephson whose *Shakespere: His Birthplace, Home, and Grave. A Pilgrimage to Stratford-upon-Avon* was published in 1864. A feature of this book remarkable for its time is that it comes with 'Photographic Illustrations by Ernest Edwards, B.A.'. These show that, although by this period visitors were being charged entry to the Birthplace, they were not getting very much for their money (see plate 29). Jephson planned his book as 'A Contribution to the Tercentenary Commemoration of the Poet's Birth'.[7] Efforts to continue the tradition of celebrating Shakespeare's achievements which Garrick had begun in the anomalous month and year of September 1769 had been made before the tercentenary. In 1824 a Shakespeare club had been formed in Stratford for the annual celebration of his birthday – there is a comic view of the form these celebrations took in the passage from Douglas Jerrold on p. 129 above. The idea was that every third year the festivities should expand into something like a Jubilee, but this only happened in 1827 and 1830.[8] By 1864, however, Stratford had found itself an unusually energetic mayor in Charles Flower, a rich local brewer, and there must have been a feeling that the year required special efforts.

The tercentenary celebrations showed the enduring influence of Garrick in that a magnificent temporary assembly hall was erected (although this time a good way from the river), and that an oratorio, fireworks, a fancy dress ball and a pageant were all on the programme. This time there were performances of Shakespeare's plays and their success strengthened a movement which was to lead to the opening of the first Shakespeare Memorial Theatre in 1879.[9] Both before and after that date the Birthplace Trust grew in strength and effectiveness. A committee led by J. O. Halliwell-Phillipps had secured the grounds of New Place for the Trust in 1862 and the Henley Street property was gradually 'restored'. In 1892 the Trustees bought the cottage where Anne Hathaway was born. According to a graph published in 1972 by Levi Fox, who

29. State of the 'birthplace' in 1864. Photograph by Ernest Edwards in the Rev. J. M. Jephson's Shakespeare: his birthplace, home, and grave: a pilgrimage to Stratford-upon-Avon in the autumn of 1863, *1864*

was then the Trust's director, the number of visitors to the birthplace hovered around the 4,000–5,000 mark until 1860 and then began to increase steadily until by 1900 it had reached 50,000. This may seem a small figure in comparison with the 420,000 it had reached when Fox was writing (and with whatever astronomical heights it has reached now), but as a percentage rise it is impressive.[10] A good many of the visitors must have been Americans, following in the footsteps of Washington Irving and Hawthorne, and one of them was certainly Henry James. Reflecting back on the experience at the beginning of the twentieth century, James wrote a short story entitled 'The Birthplace'. This demonstrates such a luminous (if perhaps occasionally snobbish) intelligence, and such sharp wit, that no survey of Shakespeare's after-life could be without it.

The central characters of 'The Birthplace' are Morris and Isabel Gedge who once ran a preparatory school. Since its failure Morris has tried several things ('the final appearance was of their having tried him no less'), but when the story opens he is in charge of 'the grey town-library of Blackport-on-Dwindle,

30. *State of the 'birthplace' in 1972. By courtesy of the Shakespeare Birthplace Trust Records Office*

all granite, fog and female fiction'. The Gedges are rescued from this sorry situation by the father of a boy Isabel had nursed through a serious illness when he was a pupil in their school. Mr Grant-Jackson has become an important figure in the world and it is thanks to his influence that Morris and Isobel are invited to become the custodians of what is clearly Shakespeare's birthplace in Stratford. The income on offer is hardly an improvement on the library at Blackport-on-Dwindle but what makes the couple thrilled to accept the invitation is the cultural prestige attached to their new post, the honour of being able to show visitors around 'the early home of the supreme poet, the Mecca of the English-speaking race'.[11]

Once installed in lodgings adjacent to the Birthplace, however, Morris Gedge becomes uneasy and dissatisfied. 'His pious, his tireless study of everything connected' with its former inhabitant convinces him that there is nothing left in it with any proven connection with Shakespeare ('There *are* no relics'), and that there is no way of telling, for example, whether the room announced as the one in which he was born had been correctly identified. Prowling through the buildings at night after a day spent 'showing' the property, he comes to feel that nothing in or about them represents a genuine addition to knowledge, yet it is on the assumption of the power of the Birthplace to confer understanding that he is required to guide through its rooms a constant stream of visitors. What his situation requires, James comments, is a 'certain command of impenetrable patience'.

The patience was needed for a particular feature of the ordeal that, by the time the lively season was with them again, had disengaged itself as the sharpest – the immense assumption of veracities and sanctities, of the general soundness of the legend with which everyone arrived. He was well provided, certainly, for meeting it, and he gave all he had, yet he had sometimes the sense of a vague resentment on the part of his pilgrims at his not ladling out their fare with a bigger spoon. An irritation had begun to grumble in him during the comparatively idle months of winter when a pilgrim would turn up singly. The pious individual, entertained for the half-hour, had occasionally seemed to offer him the promise of beguilement or the semblance of a personal relation; it came back again to the few pleasant calls he had received in the course of a life almost void of social amenity. Sometimes he liked the person, the face, the speech: an educated man, a gentleman, not one of the herd; a graceful woman, vague, accidental, unconscious of him, but making him wonder, while he hovered, who she was. These chances represented for him light yearnings and faint flutters; they acted indeed, within him, in a special, an extraordinary way. He would have liked to talk with such stray companions, to talk with them *really*, to talk with them as he might have talked if he had met them where he couldn't meet them – at dinner, in the 'world', on a visit at a country-house. Then he could have said – and about the shrine and the idol always – things he couldn't say now. The form in which his irritation first came to him was that of his feeling obliged to say to them – to the single visitor, even when sympathetic, quite as to the gaping group – the particular things, a dreadful dozen or so, that they expected. If he had thus arrived at characterizing these things as dreadful the reason touches the very point that, for a while turning everything over, he kept dodging, not facing, trying to ignore. The point was that he was on his way to become two quite different persons, the public and the private, and yet that it would somehow have to be managed that these persons should live together. He was splitting into halves, unmistakably – he who, whatever else he had been, had at least always been so entire and in his way, so solid. One of the halves, or perhaps even, since the split promised to be rather unequal, one of the quarters, was the keeper, the showman, the priest of the idol; the other piece was the poor unsuccessful honest man he had always been.
There were moments when he recognized this primary character as he had never done before; when he in fact quite shook in his shoes at the idea that it perhaps had in reserve some supreme assertion of its identity. It was honest, verily, just by reason of the possibility. It was poor and unsuccessful because here it was just on the verge of quarrelling with its bread and butter. Salvation would be of course – the salvation of the showman – rigidly to *keep* it on the verge; not to let it, in other words, overpass by an inch. He might count on this, he said to himself, if there weren't any public – if there weren't thousands of people demanding of him what he was paid for. He saw the approach of the stage at which they would affect him, the thousands of people – and perhaps even more the earnest individual – as coming really to see if he were earning his wage. Wouldn't he soon begin to fancy them in league with the Body,[†] practically deputed by it –

† The Management committee of the Birthplace.

given, no doubt, a kindled suspicion – to look in and report observations? It was the way he broke down with the lonely pilgrim that led to his first heart-searchings – broke down as to the courage required for damping an uncritical faith. What they all most wanted was to feel that everything was 'just as it was'; only the shock of having to part with that vision was greater than any individual could bear unsupported. The bad moments were upstairs in the Birth-room, for here the forces pressing on the very edge assumed a dire intensity. The mere expression of eye, all-credulous, omnivorous and fairly moistening in the act, with which many persons gazed about, might eventually make it difficult for him to remain fairly civil. Often they came in pairs – sometimes one had come before – and then they explained to each other. He never in that case corrected; he listened, for the lesson of listening: after which he would remark to his wife that there was no end to what he was learning. He saw that if he should really ever break down it would be with her he would begin. He had given her hints and digs enough, but she was so inflamed with appreciation that she either didn't feel them or pretended not to understand.

This was the greater complication that, with the return of the spring and the increase of the public, her services were more required. She took the field with him, from an early hour; she was present with the party above while he kept an eye, and still more an ear, on the party below; and how could he know, he asked himself, what she might say to them and what she might suffer *Them* to say – or in other words, poor wretches, to believe – while removed from his control? Some day or other, and before too long, he couldn't but think, he must have the matter out with her – the matter, namely, of the *morality* of their position. The morality of women was special – he was getting lights on that. Isabel's conception of her office was to cherish and enrich the legend. It was already, the legend, very taking, but what was she there for but to make it more so? She certainly wasn't there to chill any natural piety. If it was all in the air – all in their 'eye', as the vulgar might say – that He *had* been born in the Birthroom, where was the value of the sixpences they took? Where the equivalent they had engaged to supply? 'Oh dear, yes – just about *here*'; and she must tap the place with her foot. 'Altered? Oh dear, no – save in a few trifling particulars; you see the place – and isn't that just the charm of it? – quite as *He* saw it. Very poor and homely, no doubt; but that's just what's so wonderful.' He didn't want to hear her, and yet he didn't want to give her her head; he didn't want to make difficulties or to snatch the bread from her mouth. But he must none the less give her a warning before they had gone *too* far. That was the way, one evening in June, he put it to her; the affluence, with the finest weather, having lately been of the largest, and the crowd, all day, fairly gorged with the story. 'We mustn't, you know, go *too* far.'

The odd thing was that she had now ceased to be even conscious of what troubled him – she was so launched in her own career. 'Too far for what?'

'To save our immortal souls. We mustn't, love, tell too many lies.'

She looked at him with dire reproach. 'Ah now, are you going to begin again?'

'I never *have* begun; I haven't wanted to worry you. But, you know, we don't know anything about it.' And then as she stared, flushing: 'About His having been born up there. About anything, really. Not the least little scrap that would weigh, in any other connection, as evidence. So don't rub it in so.'

'Rub it in how?'

'That He *was* born –' But at sight of her face he only sighed. 'Oh dear, oh dear!'

'Don't you think,' she replied cuttingly, 'that He was born anywhere?'

He hesitated - it was such an edifice to shake. 'Well, we don't know. There's very little *to* know. He covered His tracks as no other human being has ever done.'

She was still in her public costume and had not taken off the gloves that she made a point of wearing as a part of that uniform; she remembered how the rustling housekeeper in the Border castle, on whom she had begun by modelling herself, had worn them. She seemed official and slightly distant. 'To cover His tracks He must have had to exist. Have we got to give *that* up?'

'No, I don't ask you to give it up *yet*. But there's very little to go upon.'

'And is that what I'm to tell Them in return for everything?'

Gedge waited - he walked about. The place was doubly still after the bustle of the day, and the summer evening rested on it as a blessing, making it, in its small state and ancientry, mellow and sweet. It was good to be there, and it would be good to stay. At the same time there was something incalculable in the effect on one's nerves of the great gregarious density. That was an attitude that had nothing to do with degrees and shades, the attitude of wanting all or nothing. And you couldn't talk things over with it. You could only do this with friends, and then but in cases where you were sure the friends wouldn't betray you. 'Couldn't you adopt,' he replied at last, 'a slightly more discreet method? What we can say is that things have been *said*; that's all *we* have to do with. "And is this really" - when they jam their umbrellas into the floor - "the very *spot* where He was born?" "So it has, from a long time back, been described as being." Couldn't one meet Them, to be decent a little, in some such way as that?'

She looked at him very hard. 'Is that the way *you* meet them?'

'No; I've kept on lying - without scruple, without shame.'

'Then why do you haul me up?'

'Because it has seemed to me that we might, like true companions, work it out a little together.'

This was not strong, he felt, as, pausing with his hands in his pockets, he stood before her; and he knew it as weaker still after she had looked at him a minute. 'Morris Gedge, I propose to be *your* true companion, and I've come here to stay. That's all I've got to say.' It was not, however, for 'You had better try yourself and see,' she presently added. 'Give the place, give the story away, by so much as a look, and - well, I'd allow you about nine days. Then you'd see.'

He feigned, to gain time, an innocence. 'They'd take it so ill?' And then, as she said nothing; 'They'd turn and rend me? They'd tear me to pieces?'

But she wouldn't make a joke of it. 'They wouldn't *have* it, simply.'

'No - they wouldn't. That's what I saw. They won't.'

'You had better,' she went on, 'begin with Grant-Jackson. But even that isn't necessary. It would get to him, it would get to the Body, like wildfire.'

'I see,' said poor Gedge. And indeed for the moment he did see, while his companion followed up what she believed her advantage.

'Do you consider it's *all* a fraud?'

'Well, I grant you there was somebody. But the details are naught. The links are missing. The evidence - in particular about that room upstairs, in itself our Casa Santa - is *nil*. It was so awfully long ago.' Which he knew again sounded weak.

'Of course it was awfully long ago - that's just the beauty and the interest. Tell Them, *tell* Them,' she continued, 'that the evidence is *nil*, and I'll tell them something else.' She spoke it with such meaning that his face seemed to show a

question, to which she was on the spot of replying 'I'll tell them that you're a – '
She stopped, however, changing it. 'I'll tell them exactly the opposite. And I'll
find out what you say – it won't take long – to do it. If we tell different stories,
that possibly may save us.'

'I see what you mean. It would perhaps, as an oddity, have a success of
curiosity. It might become a draw. Still, they but want broad masses.' And he
looked at her sadly. 'You're no more than one of Them.'

'If it's being no more than one of them to love it,' she answered, 'then I
certainly am. And I am not ashamed of my company.'

'To love *what?*' said Morris Gedge.

'To love to think He was born there.'

'You think too much. It's bad for you.' He turned away with his chronic moan.
But it was without losing what she called after him.

'I decline to let the place down.' And what was there indeed to say? They *were*
there to keep it up.[12]

It is with Morris in the vulnerable state described in this long but brilliant
passage that, just before closing time and with all the crowds gone, a young
American couple arrive at the Birthplace and ask him whether he could give
them a private view. Mr and Mrs Hayes turn out to be sceptics like himself.
They are kindred spirits whose unusually attractive and sympathetic manner
allows Morris to unburden himself: 'I don't say it wasn't', he remarks, as they
linger in the birth room, the 'Holy of Holies', 'but I don't say it *was*'. That they
understand the difficulty of his situation, and regard him with warm, if at the
same time curious, interest, leaves him with feelings of exhilaration in the days
following their visit. In his 'reaction from the gluttony of the public for false
facts' he is tempted by these feelings to sail too close to the wind, even though
he understands well enough what the consequences might be:

The look to be worn at the Birthplace was properly the beatific, and when once
it had fairly been missed by those who took it for granted, who, indeed, paid
sixpence for it – like the table wine in provincial France, it was *compris* – one
would be sure to have news of the remark.[13]

News comes in the form of a visit from Mr Grant-Jackson who reproaches
Morris for ingratitude and issues what is, in effect, a final warning. Faced with
having to choose between his convictions and the sack – 'Have you settled it
that I'm to starve?' Isabel asks him after his interview with Grant-Jackson –
Gedge decides to bury his critical sense and join his wife in support of the
legend. He manages this so effectively, with such panache, that Isabel begins to
worry he has done no more than embrace 'a different perversity': 'There would
be more than one fashion of giving away the show, and wasn't *this* perhaps a
question of giving it away by excess?'[14] But business in brisk, 'the show had
never so flourished', and since so many of the visitors are American, news of
his pyrotechnics travels as far as New York. It is partly this which brings the

Hayes back to the Birthplace curious to learn what has happened to the priest who, when they last saw him, had lost his faith. The performance Morris puts on for them suggests that he would have had a future as a Shakespeare biographer:

> 'It is in this old chimney corner, the quaint inglenook of our ancestors – just there in the far angle, where His little stool was placed, and where, I dare say, if we could look close enough, we should find the hearthstone scraped with His little feet – that we see the inconceivable child gazing into the blaze of the old oaken logs and making out there pictures and stories, see Him conning, with curly bent head, His well-worn hornbook, or poring over some scrap of an ancient ballad, some page of some rudely bound volume of chronicles as lay, we may be sure, in His father's window-seat.'[15]

Like Isabel, the Hayes are also worried that the authorities might find Gedge's new manner more disturbing than the last and, while they are still in the house, Isabel joins them to announce the sudden arrival of Grant-Jackson. She and the Hayes wait anxiously as Morris goes off to what all four of them suspect might be a final interview but when he returns it is to announce that he has not only received congratulations from the authorities Grant-Jackson represents, but also a rise in salary:

> 'The receipts, it appears, speak – '
> He was nursing his effect; Isabel intently watched him, and the others hung on his lips. 'Yes, speak – ?'
> 'Well, volumes. They tell the truth.'[16]

Henry James was one of those who felt that there were not enough facts to warrant serious biographical speculation about Shakespeare. He put the case for scepticism in a direct, non-fictional form when he wrote an introduction for *The Tempest*, published four years after 'The Birthplace' had appeared. This formed part of a new edition of Shakespeare's works whose general editor was Sidney Lee, the leading Shakespeare biographer of the time.

> Let me say that our knowledge, in the whole connection, is a quantity that shifts, surprisingly, with the measure of a felt need; appearing to some of us, on some sides, adequate, various, large, and appearing to others, on whatever side, a scant beggar's portion. We are concerned, it must be remembered, here – that is for getting *generally* near our author – not only with the number of the mustered facts, but with the kind of fact that each may strike us as being: never unmindful that such matters, when they are few, may go far for us if they be individually but ample and significant; and when they are numerous, on the other hand, may easily fall short enough to break our hearts if they be at the same time but individually small and poor. Three or four stepping-stones across a stream will

serve if they are broad slabs, but it will take more than may be counted if they are only pebbles. Beyond all gainsaying then, by many an estimate, is the penury in which even the most advantageous array of the Shakespearean facts still leaves us: strung together with whatever ingenuity they remain, for our discomfiture, as the pebbles across the stream.[17]

For James the absence of information about Shakespeare was a matter for 'discomfiture' but there were ways of considering it in a more positive light. One of these had been articulated more than fifty years earlier by Matthew Arnold. Anyone who examines closely Arnold's famous sonnet on 'Shakespeare' must surely feel that its subsequent fame had less to do with its literary distinction than with the way it alleviated that discomfiture to which James referred, transformed a negative into a positive.

> Others abide our question. Thou art free.
> We ask and ask – Thou smilest and art still,
> Out-topping knowledge. For the loftiest hill,
> Who to the stars uncrowns his majesty,
> Planting his steadfast footsteps in the sea,
> Making the heaven of heavens his dwelling-place,
> Spares but the cloudy border of his base
> To the foil'd searching of mortality;
> And thou, who didst the stars and sunbeams know,
> Self-school'd, self-scann'd, self-honour'd, self-secure,
> Didst tread on earth unguess'd at. – Better so!
> All pains the immortal spirit must endure,
> All weakness which impairs, all griefs which bow,
> Find their sole speech in that victorious brow.[18]

There have been many people since Arnold who have responded to the absence of contemporary testimony about Shakespeare with 'Better so!' Their motives have not always been the same as his. It was probably not quite in the same spirit as Arnold, for example, that Dickens wrote to William Sandys:

It is a great comfort to my thinking that so little is known concerning the poet. It is a fine mystery; and I tremble every day lest something should come out. If he had had a Boswell, society wouldn't have respected his grave, but would calmly have had his skull in the phrenological shop-windows.[19]

The personal anxiety which appears to underlie this remark was more obviously present when Tennyson

thanked God Almighty with his whole heart and soul that he knew nothing about Shakespeare but his writings; and [...] he thanked God Almighty that he knew nothing of Jane Austen, and that there were no letters preserved either of Shakespeare's or Jane Austen's, that they had not been ripped open like pigs.[20]

The tone of this indicates that, prompting Tennyson in his celebration of what Arnold called the 'foiled searching of mortality', is his apprehension, in an age of ever increasing biographical enquiry, that one day soon he himself would be 'ripped open like a pig'. A similar apprehension afflicted Robert Browning whose direct response to Wordsworth's claim that Shakespeare had unlocked his heart in the Sonnets – 'If so, the less Shakespeare he!' – was well known.[21] In 'At the "Mermaid"', composed in 1876, Browning has Shakespeare congratulate himself on the fact that it is impossible to deduce his private character from his work.

> Which of you did I enable
> Once to slip inside my breast,
> There to catalogue and label
> What I like least, what love best,
> Hope and fear, believe and doubt of,
> Seek and shun, respect – deride?
> Who has right to make a rout of
> Rarities he found inside?[22]

Browning's view was that no-one had that right in Shakespeare's case nor, he clearly but vainly hoped, in his own.

While Arnold, Dickens, Tennyson, Browning and James expressed their own very different attitudes to the difficulty of discovering what kind of person Shakespeare was in his private dealings, the biographical scholars soldiered on. Chief among them in the mid and later part of the century was the J. O. Halliwell-Phillipps already mentioned in a different context. A lifetime of extraordinary antiquarian endeavour allowed Halliwell-Phillipps to clarify many details of Shakespeare's family background, his financial dealings, and his life in the theatre; but the end result of all his labours was disappointing. It was not that, like Malone, he failed to finish his biography, but the *Outlines of the Life of Shakespeare* which he first published in 1881 obstinately remained just what the title suggests. In its first manifestation, this work amounted to a little more than a hundred pages but, by the time of the seventh edition in 1887, it had grown to almost nine hundred. The difference was, however, mostly made up with a series of lengthy appendices which dealt with peripheral matters: seventeen large folio pages of 'Notes on the Birth-place', for example, followed by five more on 'The Birth-place cellar' with magnificent illustrations; or thirty-four on 'The History of New Place' with illustrations, architectural drawings and transcriptions of legal documents. The main text continued to be sparse, in spite of an attitude to legends like that of the deer-poaching far more sympathetic than Malone's. What *Outlines* demonstrated was the difficulty which someone of Halliwell-Phillipps's abilities and temperament experienced in saying something both new and interesting about Shakespeare without resorting to the methods of a Payne Collier. Yet there was one matter of interpretation on which Halliwell-Phillipps felt he had something fresh to say and, as his recourse to what might be termed 'the argument from expertise' indicates, he clearly believed that his remarkable knowledge of the Elizabethan period helped him to say it.

The bond given in anticipation of the marriage of William Shakespeare with Anne Hathaway, a proof in itself that there was no clandestine intention in the arrangement, is dated the twenty-eighth of November, 1582. Their first child Susanna, was baptized on Sunday, May the 26ᵗʰ, 1583. With those numerous moralists who do not consider it necessary for rigid enquiry to precede condemnation, these facts taint the husband with dishonour, although, even according to modern notions, that very marriage may have been induced on his part by a sentiment in itself the very essence of honour. If we assume, however, as we reasonably may, that cohabitation had previously taken place, no question of morals would in those days have arisen, or could have been entertained. The precontract, which was usually celebrated two or three month before marriage, *was not only legally recognised, but it invalidated a subsequent union of either of the parties with any one else.* There was a statute, indeed, of 32 Henry VIII., 1540, c. 38, s. 2, by which certain marriages were legalised notwithstanding precontracts, but the clause was repealed by the Act of 2 & 3 Edward VI., 1548, c. 23, s. 2, and the whole statute by 1 & 2 Phil. And Mar., 1554, c. 8, s. 19, while the Act of 1 Elizabeth, 1558, c. I, s. II, expressly confirms the revocation made by Edward the Sixth. The ascertained facts respecting Shakespeare's marriage clearly indicate the high probability of there having been a precontract, a ceremony which substantially had the validity of the more formal one, and the improbability of that marriage having been celebrated under mysterious or unusual circumstances. Whether the early alliance was a prudent one in a worldly point of view may admit of doubt, but that the married pair continued on affectionate terms, until they were separated by the poet's death, may be gathered from the early local tradition that his wife 'did earnestly desire to be laid in the same grave with him.' The legacy to her of the second-best bed is an evidence which does not in any way negative the later testimony.

The poet's two sureties, Fulk Sandells and John Richardson, were inhabitants of the little hamlet of Shottery, and on the only inscribed seal attached to the bond are the initials R. H., while the consent of friends is, in that document, limited to those of the bride. No conclusion can be safely drawn from the last-named clause, it being one very usual in such instruments, but it may perhaps be inferred from the other circumstances that the marriage was arranged under the special auspices of the Hathaway family, and that the engagement was not received with favour in Henley Street. The case, however, admits of another explanation. It may be that the nuptials of Shakespeare, like those of so many others of that time, had been privately celebrated some months before under the illegal forms of the Catholic Church, and that the relatives were now anxious for the marriage to be openly acknowledged.

It was extremely common at that time, amongst the local tradespeople, for the sanction of parents to be given to early marriages in cases where there was no money, and but narrow means of support, on either side. It is not, therefore, likely that the consent of John and Mary Shakespeare to the poet's marriage was withheld on such grounds, nor, with the exception of the indications in the bond, are there other reasons for suspecting that they were averse to the union. But whether they were so or not is a question that does not invalidate the assumption that the lovers followed the all but universal rule of consolidating their engagement by means of a precontract. This ceremony was generally a solemn affair enacted with the immediate concurrence of all the parents, but it was at times informally conducted separately by the betrothing parties, evidence of the fact, communicated by them to independent persons, having been held, at least in Warwickshire, to confer a sufficient legal validity on the transaction. Thus, in 1585, William Holder and Alice Shaw, having privately made a contract, came voluntarily before two witnesses, one of whom was a person named Willis and the other a John Maides of Snitterfield, on purpose to acknowledge that they were irrevocably pledged to wedlock. The lady evidently considered herself already as good as married, saying to Holder, – 'I do confesse that I am your wief and have forsaken all my frendes for your sake, and I hope you will use me well;' and thereupon she 'gave him her hand.' Then, as Maides observes, 'the said Holder, *mutatis mutandis*, used the like words unto her in effect, and toke her by the hand, and kissed together in the presence of this deponent and the said Willis.' These proceedings are afterwards referred to in the same depositions as constituting a definite 'contract of marriage.' On another occasion, in 1588, there was a precontract meeting at Alcester, the young lady arriving there unaccompanied by any of her friends. When requested to explain the reason of this omission, 'she answered that her leasure wold not lett her and that she thought she cold not obtaine her mother's goodwill, but, quoth she, neverthelesse I am the same woman that I was before.' The future bridegroom was perfectly satisfied with this assurance, merely asking her 'whether she was content to betake herself unto him, and she answered, offring her hand, which he also tooke upon th'offer that she was content by her trothe, and thereto, said she, I geve thee my faith, and before these witnesses, that I am thy wief; and then he likewise answered in theis wordes, vid., and I geve thee my faith and troth, and become thy husband.' These instances, to which several others could be added, prove decisively that Shakespeare could have entered, under any circumstances whatever, into a precontract with Anne Hathaway. It may be worth adding that espousals of this kind were, in the Midland counties, almost invariably terminated by the lady's acceptance of a bent sixpence. One lover who was betrothed in the same year in which Shakespeare was engaged to Anne Hathaway, gave also a pair of gloves, two oranges, two handkerchiefs and a girdle of broad red silk. A present of gloves on such an occasion was, indeed, nearly as universal as that of a sixpence.

It can never be right for a biographer, when he is unsupported by the least particle of evidence, to assume that the subject of his memoir departed unnecessarily from the ordinary usages of life and society. In Shakespeare's matrimonial case, those who imagine that there was no precontract have to make another extravagant admission. They must ask us also to believe that the lady of his choice was as disreputable as the flax-wench, and gratuitously united with the poet in a moral wrong that could have been converted, by the smallest expenditure of trouble, into a moral right. The whole theory is absolutely incredible. We may then feel certain that, in the summer of the year 1582, William Shakespeare and Anne Hathaway were betrothed either formally or informally, but, at all events, under conditions that could, if necessary, have been legally ratified.

There are reasons for believing that later in the century cohabitation between the precontract and the marriage began to be generally regarded with much disfavour, but the only means of arriving at an equitable judgment upon the merits of the present case lay in a determination to investigate it strictly in its relation with practices the legitimacy of which was acknowledged in Warwickshire in the days of the poet's youth. If the antecedents of Shakespeare's union with Miss Hathaway were regarded with equanimity by their own neighbours, relatives and friends, upon what grounds can a modern critic fairly impugn the propriety of their conduct? And that they were so regarded is all but indisputable. Assuming, as we have a right to assume, that the poet's mother must have been a woman of sensitive purity, was she now entertaining the remotest apprehension that her son's honour was imperiled? Assuredly not, for she had passed her youth amidst a society who believed that a precontract had all the validity of a marriage, the former being really considered a more significant and important ceremony than the other. When her own father, Robert Arden, settled part of an estate upon his daughter Agnes, on July 17th, 1550, he introduces her as *nunc uxor Thome Stringer, ac nuper uxor Johannis Hewyns*, and yet her marriage was not solemnized until three months afterwards. '1550, 15 October, was maryed Thomas Stringer unto Agnes Hwens, wyddow,' Bearley register. Let us hope that, after the production of this decisive testimony, nothing more will be heard of the suspicions that have hitherto thrown an unpleasant cloud over one of the most interesting periods of our author's career.[23]

Charles Knight had shown that it was not necessary to conclude from the fact that Shakespeare only left his wife his second-best bed in his will that he did not appreciate her, and now Halliwell-Phillipps suggested that it was wrong to draw the conclusion which would usually be drawn from the birth of Shakespeare's daughter only six months after his marriage. Both offered the Victorians a more comfortable national Bard than the facts might at first seem to warrant. Knight's scenario has had much more success with subsequent biographers than that of Halliwell-Phillipps although, given our ignorance of the circumstances surrounding both Shakespeare's marriage and his death, there seems no compelling reason why one is not as plausible as the other.

The natural successor to Halliwell-Phillipps was the Sidney Lee for whom James wrote his introduction to *The Tempest*. His 1898 biography of Shakespeare was later much revised and enlarged. The edition of 1915 runs to 776 pages, only partly for reasons like those which filled out the *Outlines* of Halliwell-Phillipps. There were in it (that is) ten appendices, but eight of these dealt with some aspect of the *Sonnets*, and in the body of the work itself there were chapters on 'Quartos and Folios', 'The Editors of the eighteenth century and after', 'Shakespeare's posthumous reputation in England and America', and 'Shakespeare's foreign vogue'.[24] Lee was much more of a *literary* historian than his predecessor and also much more of a literary critic. His book can be as long as it is because he accompanies a measured, intelligent summation of all the biographical facts which were available by 1915 (including the Belott/Mountjoy deposition) with a chronological account of all Shakespeare's dramatic writings and three chapters on the Sonnets. Partly because he writes much better than Halliwell-Phillipps, his is an exhaustive, well-constructed, well-balanced account which must have left many contemporaries feeling that there was no more to be said. Yet for many of them what could be said amounted to so little, was so removed from what one might really have wanted to know, that it left the situation very much as Arnold had described it in 1849. In 1916 Oxford University Press published a massive and handsome *Book of Homage to Shakespeare* in celebration of the tercentenary of his death. This included, along with short academic studies by leading Shakespeare scholars, tributes from representatives of the allies of Britain in the Great War and of countries of the Empire, as well as from the great and good at home. Close to its beginning there is a poem by Austin Dobson which is called 'Riddle' and which ends on a recognisably Arnoldian note.

> Men may explore thy secret still, yet thou,
> Serene, unsearchable, above them all,
> Look'st down, as from some lofty mountain-brow,
> And art thyself thine own Memorial.[25]

Similar feelings are expressed in a more distinctive manner by Thomas Hardy in a poem which had the honour of introducing the volume: 'To Shakespeare: After three hundred years':

> Bright baffling Soul, least capturable of themes,
> Thou, who display'dst a life of common-place,
> Leaving no intimate word or personal trace
> Of high design outside the artistry
> Of thy penned dreams,
> Still shalt remain at heart unread eternally.
>
> Through human orbits thy discourse today,
> Despite thy formal pilgrimage, throbs on
> In harmonies that cow Oblivion,
> And, like the wind, with all-uncared effect
> Maintain a sway
> Not fore-desired, in tracks unchosen and unchecked.
>
> And yet, at thy last breath, with mindless note
> The borough clocks in sameness tongued the hour,
> The Avon just as always glassed the tower,
> Thy age was published on thy passing-bell
> But in due rote
> With other dwellers' deaths accorded a like knell.
>
> And at the strokes some townsman (met, maybe,
> And thereon queried by some squire's good dame
> Driving in shopward) may have given thy name,
> With, 'Yes, a worthy man and well-to-do;

Though, as for me,
I knew him but by just a neighbour's nod, 'tis true.

'I'faith, few knew him much here, save by word,
He having elsewhere led his busier life;
Though to be sure he left with us his wife.'
'Ah, one of the tradesmen's sons, I now recall . . .
Witty, I've heard. . . .
We did not know him. . . . Well, good-day.
Death comes to all.'

So, like a strange bright bird we sometimes find
To mingle with the barn-door brood awhile,
Then vanish from their homely domicile –
Into man's poesy, we wot not whence,
Flew thy strange mind,
Lodged there a radiant guest, and sped for ever thence.[26]

For Hardy and many like him there were commonplace facts one could learn about Shakespeare but, because he left 'no intimate word or personal trace', there was no way outside the writings of reading his heart; yet that of course could be part of the appeal.

For those who were not content to celebrate our ignorance of Shakespeare, or wanted a livelier sense of him than Halliwell-Phillipps or Lee could provide, there was the continuing resource of prose fiction and drama. Plays and novels in which Shakespeare figures appeared throughout the latter half of the nineteenth century but at the beginning of the twentieth there is a flurry of them and an interesting contrast between two figures who could both be described as late-Victorian in their literary sensibility. The first of these is Richard Garnett who, by 1904, was nearly seventy and the author of innumerable essays, biographies and poems most of which were written while he was fully employed as the Assistant Keeper and then Keeper of Printed Books at the British Museum. 1904 was the year of his *William Shakespeare: Pedagogue and Poacher* the third of three 'poetic dramas' for which he was responsible. This final drama was given a concert performance or reading on 8 November with Florence Farr, the favoured actress of Shaw and Yeats, in one of the roles.[27]

As its title suggests, Shakespeare is a schoolmaster in Garnett's play and one unfortunate enough to have led his pupils on a deer-poaching expedition and been caught. The second of the two acts is thus the trial scene which Landor dramatised (in a similarly undramatic way), but what makes Garnett's treatment so distinctive is the way he introduces and handles his female characters. If Sir

31. Shakespeare with his family at Stratford. *Painting of Shakespeare reading to his wife, children and parents published in* The Eclectic, *and also by F. Sala and Co, Berlin. Date and provenance unkown, although the manner strongly suggests the mid- to late nineteenth century.* (The Eclectic, *an American journal, ran in one form or another from 1841–1898). By permission of the Folger Shakespeare Library.*

Thomas Lucy is shown as having a particular animus against Shakespeare it is because his wife is attracted to the young man. When it comes to the matter of punishment, Anne Shakespeare requests that her husband should be whipped rather than imprisoned so that she can then look after him, but Lady Lucy wants him banished so that he can escape his shrewish wife and make the most of his talents. Sir Thomas, doubly angered by the threat to his deer and his marriage, decides that the culprit should be whipped, imprisoned *and* banished but at this juncture the Earl of Leicester arrives with an urgent message from the Queen. Shakespeare has sent a play based on his marital experiences to London and Elizabeth has liked *The Taming of the Shrew* so much that she wants to see him in the capital right away. He is therefore released while Sir Thomas is instructed to provide for Shakespeare's wife and children.

The plot of *William Shakespeare: Pedagogue and Poacher* is Victorian melodrama but not the treatment. In the first act, for example, Sir Thomas is reproaching his wife for the interest she takes in Shakespeare.

SIR THOMAS LUCY: What, alack!
        Well, well, I will not doubt all's honesty.
        Yet somewhat doth it stir my noble stomach
        To mark you thus concerned about a vassal.
LADY LUCY: Merely as one may watch a struggling fly
        Drowning in clammy milk, or muddy beer,
        Scarce caring if he scapes or perishes,
        Yet indolently sorry for his plight,
        And, haply, scornful of aerial wings
        Soused in a stuff so gross.
SIR THOMAS LUCY: If this be all,
        Wherefore so fiery-hot against the woman?
LADY LUCY: The virtuous lady much abhorreth vice,
        Abhors the vicious more, and most detests
        The leman crept into the matron's place.
        What! Would she eat her cake and have it too?
        Infringe the rules, and yet be free of the guild?
        Cannot she be one thing or else the other?
        If Anna were no worse than a light woman,
        Despised she were, but not abominated;
        But being what she is, is child of wrath.
        I see thou know'st not her enormities.
        This mirror of the maidenhood of Stratford,
        This wan ungathered rose, this vestal ogress,
        Sets cap and trap for Shakespeare, he is caught,
        And frequent seeks her cot past toll of curfew.
        There rapture reigns, till, one autumnal even,
        Sudden the chamber swarms with angry brothers,
        And cousins in a most excited state.
        Poor Shakespeare hangs his head, a manifest villain,
        And creeps like snail unwillingly to church,

207

Wishing his godsire in his infancy
Had brought him to the gallows, not the font.
And ill continues what was ill begun.
The crab upon the peach so crossly grafted
Grows none the sweeter, and the course of wedlock
Runneth no smoother than the course of love.[28]

It is always an option for those juggling with the few known facts of Shakespeare's life to blame Anne Hathaway for his early and (as far as one can tell) precipitate marriage. The incipient misogyny of that position is partly veiled here by having a woman make the complaint; but later in the play Shakespeare himself discourses on the same theme.

SHAKESPEARE: The venom clamours of a jealous woman
Poison more deadly than a mad dog's tooth.
I should abhor thee, Anna, knew I not
Thy mood the black reflection of thy conscience.
Thou knowest thou hast wronged me, and dost deem
That I am like to pay thee back again.
Thou sawest thyself a sallow rose, with petals
So faded, it were better they were fallen:
Nor refuge could'st thou find in any bosom
Save one, where dwelt what I am bold to call
A gentle spirit, who did bend to soothe
The anguished soul with breathings of soft pity;
Which thou wert ready to mistake for love,
Imagination's fool. I fain would hope so.
For sure it were the office of a fiend
To rob me of my boyish innocence,
Marring the fair intent of kindly Nature,
Blighting the young unbudded rose of love,
And binding on my ignorance a burden
Then illy borne, now insupportable.
Nor way but one see I to loosen it.

ANN SHAKESPEARE: Innocent babe! And what of her who rules
The roost at Charlecote?

SHAKESPEARE: Ye both played for me,
Thou in dire earnest, she as for a counter:
And thou had'st wit to triumph in the game,
But not the wisdom well to ward thy winnings.
Much water since hath flowed 'neath Stratford bridge,
And now the counter shines a gem, more rich
Than coffered hoards of royal treasuries,
Poor to one love throb of a trusting heart.
Anna! If women knew a bosom's wealth!
But fools are they, whose trivial shallow spirits,
Nought giving, nought receive. Weak wanton Cupid
Shall quench his torch for me, and fall to slumber
By a cold valley fountain of the ground,

208

And I will seek a manly soul, and wear him
In my heart's core, even in my heart of hearts.
And in high verse I will eternise him,
Blazoning his beauty forth, his name concealing
To set the wide world wondering who he was,
And sharp debate shall drain the inky stands
Of sage and scholar labouring to divine
If worth it was of his, or wit of mine.[29]

It may just be possible that Garnett *meant* his readers or listeners to regard Shakespeare as a loathsome prig, as well as a bad poet, but it seems unlikely. The explanation of how he came to write the Sonnets would be uncomfortable in the mouth of any other character but, in his own, it is both psychologically and dramatically impossible. With its stilted verse and unconvincing characterisation, *William Shakespeare; Pedagogue and Poacher* is not an attractive work, yet Garnett's biographer says that prominent figures such as Dowden, Gosse, Hardy and Sidney Lee were unanimous in their praise of the play's 'youthful verve and humour' and that it 'exemplifies Richard's style at its best'.[30]

Interestingly different from Garnett's play is the title piece in a collection published the year following its first performance. *'Shakespeare's Christmas' and Other Stories* was advertised as being by 'Q', the pseudonym of Arthur Quiller-Couch. As prolific in fiction and anthologies as Garnett was in his own kind of writing, Quiller-Couch was also to combine his literary career with a scholarly activity when in 1914 he was appointed to the chair of English Literature at Cambridge. His academic bent is already in evidence in 'Shakespeare's Christmas' which is otherwise very much in the adventure-story manner of Stevenson or John Buchan. It opens at a final performance of *2 Henry IV* in James Burbage's Shoreditch 'Theatre' – final because, after it is over, all the company begin dismantling the structure in which they have just performed in order to ferry it across the river to Bankside where the Globe would be built. This is an event which took place on 28 December 1598 but Quiller-Couch shifts it back a few days for dramatic effect. Present at the performance is a remarkably large, voluble and energetic old man from the country who turns out to be Shakespeare's father. Quiller-Couch may have been influenced in this presentation by the first publication in 1904 of the notes of an obscure late seventeenth century arch-deacon in which John Shakespeare is described as a 'merry cheeked old man',[31] but it is, in any case, an original touch to assume that the father of England's greatest writer must have been a force of nature, or at least it seems original, after so many assumptions about the refinement and sensitivity he must have inherited from his well-born mother.

While watching his son's play, John Shakespeare makes the acquaintance of a stage-struck apprentice whom he invites to supper with the actors. Together therefore with Richard Burbage, Thomas Nashe, and Shakespeare himself the old man and his new young friend make their way to 'Mistress Witwold's at the corner of Paris Gardens' on a Bankside which is seen through the apprentice's eyes as an area both exciting and threatening, full of illicit and dangerous pleasures. As they enter the room where many of the company are already eating, its occupants stand and cheer Shakespeare who bows 'to the homage as might a king'.[32] In the next section of the story three hours have passed (the 'epilogue' referred to here is the removal of the theatre from Shoreditch to Bankside):

Three hours the feast had lasted: and the apprentice had listened to many songs, many speeches, but scarcely to the promised talk of gods. The poets, maybe, reserved such talk for the Mermaid. Here they were outnumbered by the players and by such ladies as the Bankside (which provided everything) furnished to grace the entertainment; and doubtless they subdued their discourse to the company. The Burbages, Dick and Cuthbert, John Heminge, Will Kempe – some half-a-dozen of the crew perhaps – might love good literature: but even these were pardonably more elate over the epilogue than over the play. For months they, the Lord Chamberlain's servants, had felt the eyes of London upon them: to-night they had triumphed, and to-morrow London would ring with appreciative laughter. It is not everyday that your child of pleasure outwits your man of business at his own game: it is not once in a generation that he scores such a hit as had been scored to-day. The ladies, indeed, yawned without dissembling, while Master Jonson – an ungainly youth with a pimply face, a rasping accent, and a hard pedantic manner – proposed success to the new comedy and long life to its author; which he did at interminable length; spicing his discourse with quotations from Aristotle, Longinus, Quintilian, the *Ars Poetica*, Persius, and Seneca, authors less studied than the Aretine along Bankside. 'He loved Will Shakespeare. . . . A comedy of his own (as the company might remember) owed not a little to his friend Will Shakespeare's acting. . . . Here was a case in which love and esteem – yes, and worship – might hardly be dissociated. . . . In short, speaking as modestly as a young man might of his senior, Will Shakespeare was the age's ornament and, but for lack of an early gruelling in the classics, might easily have been an ornament for any age.' Cuthbert Burbage – it is always your quiet man who first succumbs on these occasions – slid beneath the table with a vacuous laugh and lay in slumber. Dick Burbage sat and drummed his toes impatiently. Nashe puffed at a pipe of tobacco. Kempe, his elbows on the board, his chin resting on his palms, watched the orator with amused interest, mischief lurking in every crease of his wrinkled face. Will Shakespeare leaned back in his chair and scanned the rafters, smiling gently the while. His speech, when his turn came to respond, was brief, almost curt. He would pass by (he said) his young friend's learned encomiums, and come to that which lay nearer to their thoughts than either the new play or the new play's author. Let them fill and drink in silence to the demise of an old friend, the vanished theatre, the first ever built in London. Then, happening to glance at Heminge as he poured out the wine – 'Tut, Jack!' he spoke up sharply: 'keep that easy rheum for the boards. Brush thine eyes, lad: we be all players here – or women – and know the trade.'

It hurt. If Heminge's eyes had begun to water sentimentally, they flinched now with real pain. This man loved Shakespeare with a dog's love. He blinked, and a drop fell and rested on the back of his hand as it fingered the base of his wine-glass. The apprentice saw and noted it.

'And another glass, lads, to the Phoenix that shall arise! A toast, and this time not in silence!' shouted John Shakespeare, springing up, flask in one hand and glass in the other. Meat or wine, jest or sally of man or woman, dull speech or brisk – all came alike to him. His doublet was unbuttoned; he had smoked three pipes, drunk a quart of sack, and never once yawned. He was enjoying himself to the top of his bent. 'Music, I say! Music!' A thought seemed to strike him; his eyes filled with happy inspiration. Still gripping his flask, he rolled to the door, flung it open, and bawled down the stairway –

'Ahoy! Below, there!'

'Ahoy, then, with all my heart!' answered a voice, gay and youthful, pat on the summons. 'What is't ye lack, my master?'

'Music, an thou canst give it. If not – '

'My singing voice broke these four years past, I fear me.'

'Your name, then, at least, young man, or ever you thrust yourself upon private company.'

'William Herbert, at your service.' A handsome lad – a boy, almost – stood in the doorway, having slipped past John Shakespeare's guard: a laughing, frank-faced boy, in a cloak slashed with orange-tawny satin. So much the apprentice noted before he heard a second voice, as jaunty and even more youthfully shrill, raised in protest upon the stairhead outside.

'And where the master goes,' it demanded, 'may not his page follow?'

John Shakespeare seemingly gave way to this second challenge as to the first. 'Be these friends of thine, Will?' he called past them as a second youth appeared in the doorway, a pretty, dark-complexioned lad, cloaked in white, who stood a pace behind his companion's elbow and gazed into the supper-room with eyes at once mischievous and timid.

'Good-evening, gentles!' The taller lad comprehended the feasters and the disordered table in a roghish bow. 'Good-evening, Will!' He singled out Shakespeare, and nodded.

'My Lord Herbert!'

The apprentice's eye, cast towards Shakespeare at the salutation given, marked a dark flush rise to the great man's temples as he answered the nod.

'I called thee "Will",' answered Herbert lightly.

'You called us "gentles,"' Shakespeare replied, the dark flush yet lingering on either cheek. 'A word signifying bait for gudgeons, bred in carrion.'

'Yet I called thee Will,' insisted Herbert more gently. ''Tis my name as well as thine, and we have lovingly exchanged it before now, or my memory cheats me.'

''Tis a name lightly exchanged in love.' With a glance at the white-cloaked page Shakespeare turned on his heel.

'La, Will, where be thy manners?' cried one of the women. 'Welcome, my young Lord; and welcome the boy beside thee for his pretty face! Step in, child, that I may pass thee round to be kissed.'

The page laughed and stepped forward with his chin defiantly tilted. His eyes examined the women curiously and yet with a touch of fear.

'Nay, never flinch, lad! I'll do thee no harm,' chuckled the one who had invited him. 'Mass o' me, how I love modesty in these days of scandal!'[33]

In Garnett's play Shakespeare turns to the idea of friendship with a man because his relationships with women are so unsatisfactory. In Quiller-Couch's story the suggestion that the 'dark flush' which the apprentice sees on Shakespeare's face when 'Lord Herbert' enters has an homosexual origin, is mitigated by the fact that the 'dark complexioned' page who has come with him turns out to be a woman in disguise, the implication being that the estrangement between his lordship and Shakespeare is a result of rivalry in heterosexual love. The gender of the page is revealed when she faints as an exotic dancing girl performs a dance which involves two pet snakes. This dancer is accompanied by two male companions on drum and flageolet both of whom look as foreign as she does. One of these companions is later observed by the horrified apprentice stabbing the other in the neck as they quarrel over the dancing girl's favours. By this time Shakespeare and Nashe are once more crossing the river.

Dawn was breaking down the river; a grey dawn as yet, albeit above the mists rolling low upon the tide-way a clear sky promised gold to come - a golden Christmas Day. The mist, however, had a chill which searched the bones. The red-eyed waterman pulled as though his arms were numb. Tom Nashe coughed and huddled his cloak about him, as he turned for a last backward glance on Bankside, where a few lights yet gleamed, and the notes of a belated guitar tinkled on, dulled by the vapours, calling like a thin ghost above the deeper baying of the hounds.

'Take care of thyself, lad,' said Shakespeare kindly, stretching out a hand to help his friend draw the cloak closer.

'Behoved me think of that sooner, I doubt,' Nashe answered, glancing up with a wry, pathetic smile, yet gratefully. He dropped his eyes to the cloak and quoted -

'Sometime it was of cloth-in-grain,
'Tis now but a sigh-clout, as you may see;
It will hold out neither wind nor rain -

And - and - I thank thee, Will -

But I'll take my old cloak about me.

There's salt in the very warp of it, good Yarmouth salt. Will?'
'Ay, lad?'
'Is't true thou'rt become a landowner, down in thy native shire?'
'In a small way, Tom.'
'A man of estate? With coat-of-arms and all?'
'Even that too, with your leave.'
'I know - I know. Nescio qua natale solum - those others did not understand: but I understood. Yes, and now I understand that fifth act of thine, which puzzled me afore, and yet had not puzzled me; but I fancied - poor fool! - that the feeling was singular in me. 'Twas a vile life, Will.' He jerked a thumb back at Bankside.
'Ay, 'tis vile.'
'My cough translates it into the past tense; but - then, or now, or hereafter - 'tis vile. Count them up, Will - the lads we have drunk with aforetime. There was Greene, now - '

Shakespeare bent his head for tally.

' – I can see his poor corse staring up at the rafters: there on the shoemaker's bed, with a chaplet of laurel askew on the brow. The woman meant it kindly, poor thing! . . . She forgot to close his eyes, though. With my own fingers I closed 'em, and borrowed two penny pieces of her for weights. 'Twas the first dead flesh I had touched, and I feel it now. . . . But George Peele was worse, ten times worse. I forget if you saw him?'

Again Shakespeare bent his head.

'And poor Kit? You saw Kit, I know. . . . with a hole below the eye, they told me, where the knife went through. And that was our Kit, our hope, pride, paragon, our Daphnis. Damnation, and this is art! Didst hear that blotch-faced youngster, that Scotchman, how he prated of it, laying down the law?'

'That Jonson, Tom, is a tall poet, or will be.'

'The devil care I! Tall poet or not, he is no Englishman and understands not the race. Art is not for us. We have dreamed dreams, thou and I: and thy dreams are coming to glory. But the last dream of a true Englishman is to own a few good English acres and die respected in a dear, if narrow, round. Dear Will, there is more in this than greed. There is the call of the land, which is home. For me – thou knowest – I had ne'er the gift of saving. My bolt is shot, or almost: two years at farthest must see the end of me. But when thou rememberest, bethink thee that I understood the call. Wilt guess what I am writing, now at the last? A great book – a sound book – and all of the red-herring! Ay, the red-herring, staple of my own Yarmouth. Canst never, as an inland man, rise to the virtues of that fish nor to the merit of my handling. But I have read some pages of it to my neighbours there and I learn from their approving looks that I shall die respected. Yet I, too, forgot and dreamed of art. . . .'[34]

The verse Nashe quotes here is from a sixteenth–century ballad which in 1919 Quiller-Couch was to include in his most enduring publication, the *Oxford Book of English Verse*; the Latin quotation concerning the appeal of one's native land or territory is from Shakespeare's favourite Ovid; and Nashe's 'great book' appeared in 1599 as *Nashe's Lenten Stuff* [...] *with a new play never played before, of the praise of the red herring*. The Shakespeare portrayed is someone who now wants to turn his back on bohemian life, just as Hal turns his back on Falstaff in the fifth act of *2 Henry IV*; but rather than having him announce the change himself, as Garnett's figure himself announces his alienation from women, Quiller-Couch has Nashe do it for him. The contrast is between the short and turbulent lives of many of Shakespeare's contemporaries and his own apparently steady progress (*apparently* steady because that impression may only be the consequence of an absence of information).

Prose fiction and drama are not the only literary genres in which posterity dramatised the life of Shakespeare. In the nineteenth and early twentieth centuries there are innumerable, largely celebratory poems along the lines of Arnold's sonnet, but poetry could also be used to tell stories in which Shakespeare was involved. Quiller-Couch was some thirty years younger than Richard Garnett and Alfred Noyes some twenty years younger than Q, but all three breathe what is recognisably the same literary atmosphere. Noyes's *Tales of the Mermaid Tavern* were published in 1914 and mostly feature contemporaries of Shakespeare rather than Shakespeare himself. Yet in a 'Coiner of Angels' the deer-poaching episode is dealt with when Ben Jonson supposedly composes and recites a ballad in which the deer are characterised as phantoms since it would have been impossible '*To steal a deer in Charlecote wood / Where never deer was seen*' (like Q's and so many other stories about Shakespeare, Noyes's poem has an extra level of meaning for those familiar with the scholarly literature). The meat of the deer is so exceptionally fine because '*this buck was born in Elfin-land / And fed upon sops-in-wine*'.[35]

More interesting than this reference to the deer-poaching, is the way Noyes deals in 'A Coiner of Angels' with the best known report on Shakespeare: Greene's attack on him as 'upstart crow' in his *Groats-worth of wit*. The topic is introduced with the appearance at the Mermaid of Richard Bame, the government spy whose denunciation of Marlowe led to his having to appear before the Privy Council. Bame is characterised as a ferocious Puritan who carries with him, '*A message from a youth, who walked with you / In wantonness, aforetime, and is now / Groaning in sulphurous fires!*'.[36] This is, of course, Greene, the sub-title of whose *Groats-worth of wit* is *Bought with a Million of Repentence*. Bame has brought with him Greene's pamphlet and it is while Marlowe and Jonson are reading and commenting on it that Shakespeare enters.

> And there, unseen by them, a quiet figure
> Entered the room and beckoning me for wine
> Seated himself to listen, Will himself,
> While Marlowe read aloud with knitted brows.
> '*Trust them not; for there is an upstart crow*
> *Beautified with our feathers!*'
>   – O, he bids
> All green eyes open! – '*And being an absolute*
> *Johannes fac-totum is in his own conceit*
> *The only Shake-scene in a country.*'
>
>   'Feathers!'
> Exploded Ben, 'Why, come to that, he pouched
> Your eagle's feather of blank verse, and lit
> His Friar Bacon's little magic lamp
> At the Promethean fire of Faustus.[†] Jove,
> It was a faëry buck, indeed, that Will
> Poached in that green-wood.'
>   'Ben, see that you walk
> Like Adam, naked! Nay, in nakedness
> Adam was first. Trust me, you'll not escape
> This calumny! Vergil is damned – he wears
> A hen-coop round his waist, nicked in the night

[†] Greene was the author of a play entitled *Friar Bacon and Friar Bungay*.

From Homer! Plato is branded for a thief,
Why, he wrote Greek! And old Prometheus, too,
Who stole his fire from heaven!'
                                    'Who printed it?'

'Chettle! I know not why, unless he too
Be one of these same dwarfs that find the world
Too narrow for their jealousies. Ben, Ben,
I tell thee 'tis the dwarfs that find no world
Wide enough for their jostling, while the giants,
The gods themselves, can in one tavern find
Room wide enough to swallow the wide heaven
With all its crowded solitary stars.'

'Ah, but the Mermaid, then, must swallow this,'
The voice of Shakespeare quietly broke in,
As laying a hand on either shoulder of Kit
He stood behind him in the gloom and smiled
Across the table at Ben, whose eyes still blazed
With boyhood's generous wrath. 'Rob was a poet.
And had I known . . . no matter! I am sorry
He thought I wronged him. His heart's blood beats in this.
Look, where he says he dies forsaken, Kit!'
'Died drunk, more like,' growled Ben. 'And if he did,'
Will answered, 'none was there to help him home,
Had not a poor old cobbler chanced upon him
Dying in the streets, and taken him to his house,
And let him break his heart on his own bed.
Read his last words. You know he left his wife
And played the moth at tavern tapers, burnt
His wings and dropt into the mud. Read here,
His dying words to his forsaken wife,
Written in blood, Ben, blood. Read it. "*I charge thee,
Doll, by the love of our youth, by my soul's rest,
See this man paid! Had he not succoured me
I had died in the streets.*" How young he was to call
Thus on their poor dead youth, this withered shadow
That once was Robin Greene. He left a child –
See – in its face he prays her not to find
The father's, but her own. "*He is yet green
And may grow straight,*" so flickers his last jest,
Then out for ever. At the last he begged
A penny-pott of malmsey. In the bill,
All's printed now for crows and daws to peck,
You'll find four shillings for his winding-sheet.
He had the poet's heart, and God help all
Who have that heart and somehow lose their way
For lack of helm, souls that are blown abroad
By the great winds of passion, without power
To sway them, chartless captains. Multitudes ply

215

Trimly enough from bank to bank of Thames
Like shallow wherries, while tall galleons,
Out of their very beauty driven to dare
The uncompassed sea, founder in starless nights,
And all that we can say is – "They died drunk!"' [...]
                            'As for that scrap of paper,'
The voice of Shakespeare quietly resumed,
'Why, which of us could send his heart and soul
Thro' Caxton's wooden press and hope to find
The pretty pair unmangled. I'll not trust
The spoken word, no, not of my own lips,
Before the Judgment Throne, against myself
Or on my own defence; and I'll not trust
The printed word to mirror Robert Greene.
See – here's another Testament, in ink,
Written, not printed, for the Mermaid Inn.
Rob sent it from his death-bed straight to me,
Read it. 'Tis for the Mermaid Inn alone;
And when 'tis read, we'll burn it, as he asks.'
Then, from the hands of Shakespeare, Marlowe took
A little scroll, and, while the winds without
Rattled the shutters with their ghostly hands
And wailed among the chimney-tops, he read: –

> Greeting to all the Mermaid Inn
> From their old Vice and Slip of Sin,
> Greeting, Ben, to you, and you
> Will Shakespeare and Kit Marlowe, too.
> Greeting from your Might-have-been,
> Your broken sapling, Robert Greene.
>
> Read my letter – 'tis my last,
> Then let Memory blot me out,
> I would not make my maudlin past
> A trough for every swinish snout.
> First, I leave a debt unpaid.
> It's all chalked up, not much all told,
> For Bread and Sack. When I am cold,
> Doll can pawn my Spanish blade
> And pay mine host. She'll pay mine host!
> But . . . I have chalked up other scores
> In your own hearts, behind the doors,
> Not to be paid so quickly. Yet,
> O, if you would not have my ghost
> Creeping in at dead of night,
> Out of the cold wind, out of the wet,
> With weeping face and helpless fingers
> Trying to wipe the marks away,
> Read what I can write, still write,
> While this life within them lingers.

216

Let me pay, lads, let me pay.
Item, for a peacock phrase,
Flung out in a sudden blaze,
Flung out at his friend Shake-scene,
By this ragged Might-have-been,
This poor Jackdaw, Robert Greene.

Will, I knew it all the while!
And you know it – and you smile!
My quill was but a Jackdaw's feather,
While the quill that Ben, there, wields,
Fluttered down thro' azure fields,
From an eagle in the sun;
And yours, Will, yours, no earth-born thing,
A plume of rainbow-tinctured grain,
Dropt out of an angel's wing.
Only a Jackdaw's feather mine,
And mine ran ink, and Ben's ran wine,
And yours the pure Pierian streams.

But I had dreams, O, I had dreams!
Dreams, you understand me, Will;
And I fretted at the tether
That bound me to the lowly plain,
Gnawed my heart out, for I knew
Once, tho' that was long ago,
I might have risen with Ben and you
Somewhere near that Holy Hill
Whence the living rivers flow.
Let it pass. I did not know
One bitter phrase could ever fly
So far through that immortal sky
 – Seeing all my songs had flown so low –
One envious phrase that cannot die
From century to century.

Kit Marlowe ceased a moment, and the wind,
As if indeed the night were all one ghost,
Wailed round the Mermaid Inn, then sent once more
Its desolate passion through the reader's voice: –

Some truth there was in what I said.
Kit Marlowe taught you half your trade;
And something of the rest you learned
From me, – but all you took you earned.
You took the best I had to give,
You took my clay and made it live;
And that – why, that's what God must do! –
My music made for mortal ears
You flung to all the listening spheres. [...]

217

Yet – through all the years to come –
Men to whom my songs are dumb
Will remember them and me
For that one cry of jealousy,
That curse where I had come to bless,
That harsh voice of unhappiness.
They'll note the curse, but not the pang,
Not the torment whence it sprang.
They'll note the blow at my friend's back,
But not the soul stretched on the rack.
They'll note the weak convulsive sting,
Not the crushed body and broken wing. [...]

Item, – one groatsworth of wit,
Bought at an exceeding price,
Ay, a million of repentance,
Let me pay the whole of it.
Lying here these deadly nights,
Lads, for me the Mermaid lights
Gleam as for a castaway
Swept along a midnight sea
The harbour-lanthorns, each a spark,
A pin-prick in the solid dark,
That lets trickle through a ray
Glorious out of Paradise,
To stab him with new agony.
Let me pay, lads, let me pay!
Let the Mermaid pass the sentence:
I am pleading guilty now,
A dead leaf on the laurel-bough,
And the storm whirls me away.

Kit Marlowe ceased; but not the wailing wind
That round and round the silent Mermaid Inn
Wandered, with helpless fingers trying the doors,
Like a most desolate ghost.[37]

Like Quiller-Couch, Noyes offers his reader a Shakespeare who is warm and generous towards his less fortunate contemporaries. He has him apologise for Greene but then allows us to hear Greene's own apology for his hasty words, several of the less hasty and more touching ones having been quoted *verbatim* in Shakespeare's account of A *Groats-worth of wit*. Unlike the more intemperate Jonson and Marlowe, Noyes's Shakespeare exhibits that magnanimity which was often felt to be a central feature of his writing. This is part of the satisfaction Noyes provides but another is that he disposes of the uncomfortable feeling that there was at least one contemporary of Shakespeare who did not like him very much.

What helps to make Garnett, Quiller-Couch and Noyes now look so broadly similar is the literary revolution which took place during and immediately after the first World War. Between their dealings with England's national poet and those of Stephen Dedalus, as he expounds his theories about Shakespeare's life to a handful of listeners in Dublin's national library, there is an obvious gulf in literary technique. *Ulysses* is an impractical novel to quote from but what deserves mention is how characteristically well-informed James Joyce must have made himself in order to write this ninth episode of his novel. He has Stephen repeat a number of familiar facts or legends: that Shakespeare was a butcher's son, for example, that he was whipped by 'lousy Lucy', began his London life by minding horses outside a theatre, and was the father of William Davenant; but he also shows him in possession of several details which are far from obvious. Stephen knows about the Mountjoy/Belott deposition and the malt census of 1598, but he is also aware that in 1601 the will of Thomas Whittington, who had worked for Anne Hathaway's father as a shepherd, revealed that she owed him 40 shillings. He knows that in 1613 Shakespeare's elder daughter Susanna successfully prosecuted another Stratfordian who had accused her of promiscuity and that in 1614 the Stratford Corporation paid Shakespeare 20d as a contribution to the entertainment of a guest preacher at New Place.[38] These are recondite matters and so is some of the reading it appears Stephen has been doing: of D. H. Madden's study of *Shakespeare and Elizabethan sport* (1897), for example, in which it is shown that the degree of familiarity with hunting terminology manifested in the plays must mean that their author was an aristocrat; or Maurice Clare's *A Day with William Shakespeare* (1913) where it is suggested that Shakespeare would have known the great Elizabethan herbalist, John Gerard. Like Wilde before him Joyce is speculating playfully about Shakespeare but, again like Wilde, with a depth of knowledge which makes his speculations scarcely distinguishable from contemporary, non-fictional treatments of the same topics.

The Shakespeare Stephen presents to his readers would be hard to summarise. A good deal in what he says revolves around the issue of paternity. *Hamlet*, he notes, was written shortly after its author's father died. When Shakespeare played the ghost and addressed the Prince of Denmark was he not also speaking to his recently deceased son Hamnet? Does not a writer father a whole world in the same way as God is the creator of all? For Stephen, the seduction of the eighteen-year-old Shakespeare by the much older Anne Hathaway was a major traumatic event in the playwright's life which he illustrates with numerous references to *Venus and Adonis*. Where he differs most from previous commentators is in the emphasis he places on sibling rivalry. One of Shakespeare's brothers was called Richard and in *Richard III* the character with that name seduces a woman with the same name as Shakespeare's wife. His brother Edmund lay dying when his name was used for an evil and yet attractive character in *King Lear*. The force of speculations like these is diminished by Stephen's confession that he doesn't believe in them, so perhaps the main significance of his talk in this present context is the extent to which it is critical of Shakespeare. As previous extracts may have shown, a tradition had grown up in the nineteenth century of lauding what were considered the Bard's typically English virtues of financial acumen and prudence, and of using him as a symbol of the country's imperial greatness. No wonder then if some people, and especially some people in Ireland, eventually began to feel that an attack on him could be an attack on English Establishment values. Joyce is one of the first to suggest through Stephen that Shakespeare was a typical English snob who went toadying for a coat of arms; that he pandered to anti-Semitism by writing *The Merchant of Venice* after the trial and execution of Elizabeth's Jewish doctor Roderigo Lopez; and that, in addition to being a hoarder of malt, he was also a moneylender relentless in his pursuit of debtors.

Joyce used four main sources for Stephen's portrait of Shakespeare. One was a book published in the mid 1870s by his compatriot Edward Dowden, *Shakespeare: A Critical Study of His Mind and Art*, but much reprinted afterwards; another a long and detailed critical study by the Danish academic George Brandes, first published in the 1890s; and the third, the biography of Sidney Lee. But a fourth source was the biography of Shakespeare by Frank Harris. This began life in the late 1890s as a series of articles in the *Saturday Review* and was published in 1909 under the title *The Man Shakespeare and His Tragic Life-story*. Nearly all previous biographers of Shakespeare had used the plays in apparent support of their discoveries. The originality of Harris was to spend 350 pages of his book deducing Shakespeare's life-story from the plays and only then to devote a mere 50 to showing how his deductions were 'borne out by the known facts'.[39] In his view, the advantage of having learnt to know Shakespeare through his writings meant that he was able to accept or reject the various items of the mythos with 'some degree of confidence'. It also meant that he could say of Shakespeare's mother, for example, 'the poet, as we learn from *Coriolanus*, held her in extraordinary esteem and affection'.[40] With phrases marked by his characteristic self-confidence or swagger, Harris defended his method in his preface and the beginnings of his first chapter.

> I read Shakespeare's plays in boyhood, chiefly for the stories; every few years later I was fain to re-read them; for as I grew I always found new beauties in them which I had formerly missed, and again and again I was lured back by tantalizing hints and suggestions of a certain unity underlying the diversity of characters. These suggestions gradually became more definite till at length, out of the myriad voices in the plays, I began to hear more and more insistent the accents of one voice, and out of the crowd of faces, began to distinguish more and more clearly the features of the writer; for all the world like some lovelorn girl, who, gazing with her soul in her eyes, finds in the witch's cauldron the face of the beloved.

I have tried in this book to trace the way I followed, step by step; for I found it effective to rough in the chief features of the man first, and afterwards, taking the plays in succession, to show how Shakespeare painted himself at full-length not once, but twenty times, at as many different periods of his life. This is one reason why he is more interesting to us than the greatest men of the past, than Dante even, or Homer; for Dante and Homer worked only at their best in the flower of manhood. Shakespeare, on the other hand, has painted himself for us in his green youth with hardly any knowledge of life or art, and then in his eventful maturity, with growing experience and new powers, in masterpiece after masterpiece; and at length in his decline with weakened grasp and fading colours, so that in him we can study the growth and fruiting and decay of the finest spirit that has yet been born among men. [...]

As it is the object of a general to win battles so it is the life-work of the artist to show himself to us, and the completeness with which he reveals his own individuality is perhaps the best measure of his genius. One does this like Montaigne, simply, garrulously, telling us his height and make, his tastes and distastes, his loves and fears and habits, till gradually the seeming-artless talk brings the man before us, a sun-warmed fruit of humanity, with uncouth rind of stiff manners and sweet kindly juices, not perfect in any way, shrivelled on this side by early frost-bite, and on that softened to corruption through too much heat, marred here by the bitter-black cicatrice of an ancient injury and there fortune-spotted, but on the whole healthy, grateful, of a most pleasant ripeness. Another, like Shakespeare, with passionate conflicting sympathies and curious impartial intellect cannot discover himself so simply; needs, like the diamond, many facets to show all the light in him, and so proceeds to cut them one after the other as Falstaff or Hamlet, to the dazzling of the purblind.

Yet Shakespeare's purpose is surely the same as Montaigne's, to reveal himself to us, and it would be hasty to decide that his skill is inferior. For while Montaigne had nothing but prose at his command, and not too rich a prose, as he himself complains, Shakespeare in magic of expression has had no equal in recorded time, and he used the lyric as well as the dramatic form, poetry as well as prose, to give his soul utterance.

We are doing Shakespeare wrong by trying to believe that he hides himself behind his work; the suspicion is as unworthy as the old suspicion dissipated by Carlyle that Cromwell was an ambitious hypocrite. Sincerity is the birth mark of genius, and we can be sure that Shakespeare has depicted himself for us with singular fidelity; we can see him in his works, if we will take the trouble, 'in his habit as he lived.' [...]

Even had Shakespeare tried to hide himself in his work, he could not have succeeded. Now that the print of a man's hand or foot or ear is enough to distinguish him from all other men, it is impossible to believe that the mask of his mind, the very imprint, form and pressure of his soul should be less distinctive. Just as Monsieur Bertillon's whorl-pictures of a thumb afford overwhelming proofs of a man's identity, so it is possible from Shakespeare's writings to establish beyond doubt the main features of his character and the chief incidents of his life. The time for random assertion about Shakespeare and unlimited eulogy of him has passed away for ever: the object of this inquiry is to show him as he lived and loved and suffered, and the proofs of this and of that trait shall be so heaped up as to stifle doubt and reach absolute conviction. For not only is the circumstantial evidence overwhelming and conclusive, but we have also the

221

testimony of eye-witnesses with which to confirm it, and one of these witnesses, Ben Jonson, is of rare credibility and singularly well equipped.[41]

The paradox here is that Harris makes his method seem as subjective as it undoubtedly is, by comparing himself to a lovelorn girl finding the face of her beloved in a witch's cauldron and then claims objective, scientific status for it by talking of Bertillon and thumbprints. But a thumbprint remains the same whoever takes it while the portrait of Shakespeare drawn from the plays changes from reader to reader.

The usual way of finding Shakespeare in his plays involves assuming that he expressed his own thoughts and feelings through this or that character, or that the theme of a particular work reveals what preoccupied him at the time of its composition. In the first part of the twentieth century more complicated means of using these old methods began to emerge. One of these derives from what Stephen Dedalus calls at one point in his disquisition 'the new Viennese school'.[42] Taking his hint from a note in Freud's *Interpretation of Dreams*, Ernest Jones argued in studies which began to appear in 1910 that an examination of *Hamlet* allowed one to say a good deal about Shakespeare's own state of mind and the effect on him of the deaths of his father and only son. It must have been a shock to Jones, therefore, when in 1923 Freud first read and was converted by the book in which J. Thomas Looney argued that the author of the plays was not in fact Shakespeare but the Earl of Oxford, since then the biographical details which had supported the original note in the *Interpretation* could no longer apply. But Jones wisely chose to ignore this change of mind in his mentor. An alternative and more literary method for decoding the plays was developed by Caroline Spurgeon who in the early 1930s began publishing work on Shakespeare's imagery. It occurred to her that, if writers do not necessarily reveal themselves easily through their characters, or through their choice of subjects and ways of treating them, a lot could nonetheless be learned from the kind of images they favoured. In the book she published in 1935 on *Shakespeare's Imagery and What It Tells Us* she summed up what Shakespeare's imagery had told her about (her own phrase) 'Shakespeare the Man'.

> As I have collected and examined these many thousands of images, and have pondered over them during the last nine or ten years, there has gradually emerged before my eyes a very definite figure of the man who was the author of them. [...]
>
> I propose therefore to make the bold attempt in this chapter to set down some of his characteristics as they strike me, or as they have been borne in upon me after long study of him from this particular angle. Naturally some of the characteristics which I point out have been suggested or surmised before. The interest of their appearance here is that they are confirmed from evidence never before systematically examined; evidence from Shakespeare's own lips, which is all the time being measured up against the same kind of unconscious self-revelation in a number of his contemporaries. [...]

The figure of Shakespeare which emerges is of a compactly well-built man, probably on the slight side, extraordinarily well co-ordinated, lithe and nimble of body, quick and accurate of eye, delighting in swift muscular movement. I suggest that he was probably fair-skinned and of a fresh colour, which in youth came and went easily, revealing his feelings and emotions. All his senses were abnormally acute, especially – probably – those of hearing and taste.

He was healthy in body as in mind, clean and fastidious in his habits, very sensitive to dirt and evil smells. Apart from many indirect proofs of these facts in the plays, no man could have written his images on sickness, surfeit, gluttony, dirt and disease, who had not naturally a strong feeling for healthy living, a liking for fresh air and 'honest water' (*Timon*, I. 2. 58), and who was not himself clean, temperate and healthy. [...]

One of the first things we notice in his collected 'sickness' and 'food' images is how far ahead of his age he is in his belief – implied and stated – that we bring upon ourselves a great deal of our own bad health by ill-regulated living, and especially by over-eating.

This physical alertness and well-being is but a part of Shakespeare's intense vitality, which goes to make him an almost incredibly sensitive and amazingly observant man. Probably he was a quiet one – he does not like noise – though not, it would seem, a dreamer, but practical and watchful, all the time absorbing impressions and movements like a sponge, registering them like a sensitive plate.

We see he is a countryman through and through, that it is the sights and sounds of boyhood which chiefly remain with him, and that half a lifetime spent in the midst of a great city has never deflected by one iota his interest from the pageant of the English country-side to that of the streets, which latter, indeed, he seems, in comparison, scarcely to notice. What he does notice and rejoice in are the sky and clouds, the revolving seasons, the weather and its changes, rain, wind, sun and shadow, and of all the outdoor occupations what he loves most is to walk and saunter in his garden or orchard, and to note and study the flight and movements of the wild birds. This persistent preoccupation with country things bears out the probable truth of Aubrey's report: 'He was wont to goe to his native Country once a year'.

He was, one would judge, a competent rider, and loved horses, as indeed he did most animals, except spaniels and house dogs. These he disliked probably because his fastidious senses revolted from the dirty way they were kept and fed at table. He was almost certainly an expert archer (as probably were most able-bodied young men of his day) and enjoyed the sport. Of all games, bowls would seem to be the one he knew most intimately and played with keenest zest.

He had, in short, an excellent eye for a shot, with bowl or with arrow, and loved exercising it. He was, indeed, good at all kinds of athletic sport and exercise, walking, running, dancing, jumping, leaping, and swimming. He had an extraordinarily sensitive ear for time, and what he seems to notice most about riding is the pace and rhythm of the horses' movement; plodding, tired, ambling, trotting and galloping, the peculiar ambling action of the countrywoman's horse going to market (*A.Y.L.I.* 3. 2. 100), or the rough uneven paces of the young untrained colt (*M.N.D.* 5. I. 119).

He was deft and nimble with his hands, and loved using them, particularly in the carpenter's craft, and, contrary to our idea of most poets, he was probably a practical, neat and handy man about the house, as we know that he was a 'Johannes Factotum' about the stage.

223

Next to his delight in outdoor life, he was, one would gather from the images, most interested in the homely indoor occupations and routine, eating, drinking, sleeping, the body and its clothes, light, fire, candles and lamps, birth and death, sickness and medicine, parents and children; while that which, next to an orchard and garden, has registered itself most clearly and continuously upon his mind is the picture of a busy kitchen, and the women's work for ever going on in it, preparing food, cooking, washing up, scouring, dusting, knitting, darning and patching. We see that in that kitchen, he has enjoyed much, and has also suffered from many things, from smoky chimneys, stopped ovens, guttering evil-smelling candles and ill-trimmed lamps, as well as greasy badly cooked food and tainted or musty meat. In fact it is his acute sensitiveness to these things of which we are continually becoming aware to such an extent that it makes one wonder how he managed to survive the dirt and smells of Elizabethan England.

For the rest of him, the inner man, five words sum up the essence of his quality and character as seen in his images - sensitiveness, balance, courage, humour and wholesomeness. We see, on the one hand, sensitiveness; on the other, balanced poise, amounting at times almost to aloofness. His sensitiveness is quick and abnormal, to a depth and degree rarely found in any human being. It is this side of his nature, revealed chiefly in those images bearing on sport and animals, which enables him to enter into the hearts of so many different characters. The other side of him, calm, detached, even ironic, keeps him steady and balanced in the midst of the whirlpool of passion he calls into being. There is another salient quality, naturally not to be seen in his images (except in some of Falstaff's), which must be mentioned, for it is the salt and savour of his whole being, and keeps it ever fresh and wholesome. This is his sense of humour. And above and surrounding all these, we find one other constant characteristic - his passion for health, for soundness, cleanliness and wholesomeness in all realms of being, physical, moral and spiritual. In this, as in humour, his whole nature seems to be steeped. If it were anyone but Shakespeare, I might use the words 'purity' and 'holiness', but for one so firmly rooted in things material and concrete as he, the physical terms best fit the facts.

These, then, as I see them, are the five outstanding qualities of Shakespeare's nature - sensitiveness, poise, courage, humour and wholesomeness - balancing, complementing and supporting each other. If he is abnormally sensitive, he is also unusually courageous, mentally and spiritually. The intense sensitiveness, the vividness of the imagination, make the courage the more remarkable. In his own outlook on life he is absolutely clear-eyed, but rarely bitter. In looking at evil, he sees it, not in terms of sin or a sinner, nor does he attach blame to it, but he views it with concern and pity as a foul and corrupt condition or growth produced by the world order, yet alien to it, as disease is to a body; which, if health is to be attained, must at all costs be expelled. That which he prizes most in life is unselfish love, what he instinctively believes to be the greatest evil is fear; which, far more than money, is, in his view, the root of all evil. Fear drives out love, as love drives out fear. What most rouses his anger is hypocrisy and injustice, what he values supremely is kindliness and mercy.

He is indeed himself in many ways in character what one can only describe as Christ-like; that is, gentle, kindly, honest, brave and true, with deep understanding and quick sympathy for all living things. Yet he does not seem to have drawn any support from the forms and promises of conventional religion, nor does he show any sign of hope or belief in a future life. But he does show a passionate interest in this life, and a very strong belief in the importance of the way it is lived in relation to our fellows, so that we may gain the utmost from the ripening processes of experience and of love.[43]

This is a remarkably comprehensive portrait but it seems to have more to do with how Spurgeon would like to think about Shakespeare than with what can be reliably deduced from his imagery. An assumption of her method is that Shakespeare reveals himself more inadvertently, and therefore more truly, in his images than he does when supposedly speaking through his various characters. Characters come and go but the same images reoccur from play to play forming, as it were, the ground notes of his nature. Like an analyst listening to the free associations of a patient, Spurgeon is alert to habits of language which are idiosyncratic, tell-tale repetitions. One problem for her is the familiar one: that the path from what Shakespeare wrote back to what he directly experienced is unlikely to have been straight, and that we have no available means of confirming whether it was or not. Another is that, to the extent that she wants her enquiry to be as systematic as she claims, it needs to be conducted in as an objective spirit of possible, avoiding that circularity which consists in gathering a general impression of Shakespeare from long and deep immersion in his plays and then seeking to confirm it later through more analytic study. Confirmation is rarely lacking in these cases because the rich diversity of Shakespeare's writings can support almost any initial impression we might form of him. Examining Shakespeare's imagery Spurgeon found him Christ-like, but it is not difficult to imagine another examination of exactly the same material resulting in quite different conclusions.

What tends to happen in the effort to discover Shakespeare's character, what he was 'really like', is that fiction constantly aspires to the condition of scholarly enquiry while scholarly enquiry constantly, if often accidently, aspires to the condition of fiction. A writer who found a successful way to negotiate between the desire for discovery on the one hand, and the lack of information on the other, was Hugh Kingsmill in whose 1929 novel, *The Return of William Shakespeare*, the mix between fiction and biography is an unusually interesting one. The story concerns an amateur scientist, Alfred Butt, who has learned how to bring figures from the past back to life, to 'reintegrate' them. His shady associate, Gustavus Melmoth, blackmails a high-ranking dignitary of the Anglican Church into providing money for Butt's researches by implicitly promising that one of the figures who *won't* be reintegrated is Jesus, but that leaves him with the problem of whom to choose. 'The hundred per cent. agreement about Shakespeare's gentleness is what finally fixed me for Shakespeare', Melmoth explains but the consequences are disappointing – 'Gentle Shakespeare! Thank you, I've been there!'[44] The more particular problem he experiences highlights an issue all biographers of Shakespeare face. The 'character' of individuals, whatever it is that creates our dominant impressions of them, is not static from birth to death but alters or develops over time. Melmoth has to decide which Shakespeare he should ask Butt to reintegrate, the Shakespeare of which particular moment, or at least period, in his life. Having read Sidney Lee's biography he plumps for the beginning of 1607 only to discover that the Shakespeare of that time was not the calm, successful, accommodating individual Lee had described him as being. 'How was I to know', he complains, tapping a copy of Lee's biography, 'Shakespeare was all to bits in the early part of 1607?'.[45]

Because the reintegrated Shakespeare is not feeling well, he is sent into the country to recuperate, while one of Melmoth's associates, Guy Porter, agrees to placate the immense public interest which the return of the Bard has excited by impersonating him. In a scene in which the narrator Arthur Haigh and a journalist called Evelyn Craye advise Porter on how best to manage the impersonation, Kingsmill wittily reviews various of the options for presenting Shakespeare which were current in his time.

> Accent was the first problem discussed. Shakespeare's fine ear, we all felt, would quickly accommodate itself to modern usage both in accent and language. A kind of northern burr, 'sea' pronounced 'say,' and a few oddities of that sort, would be sufficient. No Wardour Street locutions. Porter, Evelyn Craye, and myself found we agreed without argument on these points. Evelyn Craye began to strike me as not unintelligent. Melmoth, meanwhile, seemed a little lost. His suggestion that Porter should spot his talk with an occasional 'pri'thee' or 'by your favour' was ignored.
>
> How much Porter should remember of his past and of the Elizabethan age generally was a more difficult question. Shakespeare's own memory, according to Melmoth, seemed to have almost vanished under the shock of re-birth, but an imitation Shakespeare could not take the same liberties. It was finally agreed that Porter should remember as much as was required by the line he proposed to adopt. But what was the line to be?
>
> 'Evelyn,' said Porter, 'wants me to be the lover broken by passion – the Frank Harris idea. Sex-exhaustion. To hell with women. The pity of it, Iago. But does the public want that? I doubt it. Not the big public, anyway.'
>
> 'All right,' Evelyn Craye retorted. 'Try a Victorian Shakespeare on them, Guy, bland and mild, getting a little nest-egg together in London for the wife and kiddies down at Stratford. My dear boy, you won't last twenty-four hours on *that* tack. The public may be bloody fools, but they move with the times to some extent.'
>
> 'But who reads Harris?'
>
> 'Damn Harris! It's not Harris. There are a hundred others. It's the general feel of the thing. You can't put that bland-and-mild pap across nowadays. Can you, Mr Haigh?'
>
> 'I must say I agree with Miss Craye. At the same time, it seems to me, you ought to conciliate some big organised section of public opinion right from the start. The stricken lover can emerge later. If I were you, the first thing I should remember was that I was a Catholic.'
>
> 'I don't see that,' said Porter. 'England, I understand, is Protestant now, and

was Protestant in Shakespeare's time.'

'Yes, but the Protestants won't object to a Catholic Shakespeare. They'll put it down to domestic reasons, the family faith, the fact that the Reformation was only just beginning, a dozen reasons. They'll be profoundly grateful that he was a Christian at all; one in the eye for all these brilliant moderns – Shaw, Wells, etc.'

'Sound, that,' said Evelyn Craye. 'What about the Catholics?'

'The Catholics will, of course, not care whether Shakespeare was a Christian or not. Private whims, if not obtruded, don't interest them. What they'll value is the evidence supplied by Shakespeare's Catholicism of how the English Reformation struck the biggest mind of the age.

'It seems to me that if you say you were a Catholic, but had to keep quiet about it in your work, you'll have all the Catholics and most of the Protestants behind you.'

Porter reflected for a little. 'I think you're right,' he said finally. 'What do you say, Evelyn.'

'I agree with Mr Haigh; and being a Catholic won't cramp your style with Mary Fitton.'

'Any Catholic references in the plays, Haigh?'

Porter poised his fountain-pen, and I gave him Friar Laurence and Isabella. [...]

'I like that,' Porter said, [...] 'That should hold them. Now what about my politics? My own idea about Shakespeare is that he'd control labour with a machine-gun, if he got half a chance.'

'The greasy plebs.,' said Miss Craye.

'He was a gentleman, of course,' Melmoth remarked. 'Very much "born", at any rate on the spindle side.'

'But his father was a tradesman,' Porter mused.

'Decayed gentry, Porter. Shakespeare was received at Court. Coat-of-arms revived by James's special order and consent. There or thereabouts, if my memory serves.'

'What's your view, Haigh?' Porter asked.

'I think it would be a great mistake to antagonise democratic sentiment. Except for a handful of die-hards and a few actor-managers, you won't get any definite backing for a Shakespeare with strong aristocratic sympathies. The ordinary public-school or army type will feel uncomfortable if you're markedly class-conscious. One takes that sort of thing for granted. Poor style to rub it in. They'll put you down as a bit of an outsider, especially when they gather you were only at a grammar-school yourself. And everyone else will be very sore about it. You're the great national poet. You must represent all classes.'

'And how does one do that?'

'By representing none. Your sympathies are equally divided between king and peasant. Both are human, that's enough for you.'

'A trifle vague. Can't you give me a more definite line?'

'Well, you might say that when you came up to London as a young man, the magnificence of the Court and the aristocracy naturally took your eye. Refer to the defeat of the Spanish Armada, and the big-drum sentiment in *King John* and *Henry V*. Heat of youthful enthusiasm. You might stroke your beard and smile a little wistfully. Later on, you felt differently about things. Gradual change in your values. You saw the suffering masses behind the glory and power of the few. Quote Lear – "Poor, naked wretches, wheresoe'er you are . . ." '

'One minute.' He raised his pen. '"Poor, naked" - how much? . . . Thanks. I've got it now.' [...]

'Melmoth,' I said, 'feels there's not much kick in it, up to now. But we've got the decks cleared. All religious and political complications disposed of. Shakespeare, the man and the poet, is now ready for action.'

'Absolutely,' Evelyn Craye exclaimed. 'I see it now, it's the only way to work it. I hope you agree with me, Mr Haigh, that Mary Fitton . . .'

'Let's begin at the beginning,' Porter interrupted. 'There's a person called Anne Hathaway. How shall we handle her, Haigh?'

'She doesn't count,' Evelyn Craye exclaimed. 'An impossible country wench. Eight years older than Shakespeare. No style, no ideas, nothing! Bored Shakespeare to tears before he was twenty, and simply ceased to exist for him as soon as he'd got away to London.'

'Wives, my dear Evelyn, don't simply cease to exist,' Porter murmured, gently stroking his beard.

Miss Craye glared at Porter. It occurred to me that Porter was in danger of a third wife. 'Personally,' I said, a little hurriedly, 'I think it would be impolitic to antagonise the general sentiment, especially strong among married women, in favour of a good husband as opposed to a bad husband.'

'But, great God, Mr Haigh - ' Evelyn Craye regarded me with astonished horror. 'You said, you quite definitely said . . .'

'Don't worry, Miss Craye. I entirely agree about Mary Fitton. But you don't wish to wreck the whole show for want of a little care at the delicate points, do you?'

Miss Craye nodded. She seemed reassured, but the recent shock had deprived her of speech.

After a long discussion, it was finally agreed that Shakespeare had continued to look after his wife's interests, when he was in London, that he visited Stratford regularly, and was devoted to his children. To balance this, Mary Fitton was the supreme love of his life, the source of the passion and suffering in the great plays, from *Hamlet* to *Antony and Cleopatra*.

'But don't forget,' I continued, 'that *Anthony* was written after the date at which you are reintegrated. You will have read it for the first time this week.'

Other points discussed were Shakespeare's attitude towards his work, which we decided was to be less deprecating than the Victorian tradition maintained; his business faculty, which was to be more considerable than Frank Harris allowed, but less imperious than Sidney Lee imagined; and finally a rough classification of his plays according to his own preference. Here I suggested that Shakespeare should supply some original information, should, for example, complain at the wretched modern versions of *Timon*, *All's Well*, and *Macbeth*. I suggested, too, that Porter should corroborate some, at any rate, of the traditions about Shakespeare: the poaching–Sir Thomas Lucy one, the tradition that he acted Adam in *As You Like It*, and possibly the story of the city dame, in love with Burbage, but captured by Shakespeare.

'The nineteenth-century notion,' I said, 'that a tradition about an event conclusively disproves its occurrence is beginning to wear thin. You'll make a hit if you show this notion up in your own case. Neo-Catholic opinion will be especially conciliated.'

It was now lunch-time. After a light meal, Melmoth left us for Torrington Square, while Porter went over the results of the morning's conference, clearing up every point he had not quite grasped with a thoroughness that exacted my admiration, though it was rather wearisome.[46]

While Porter is holding the fort in London, the real Shakespeare is talking about himself to Melmoth's brother-in-law, Cecil Wilkinson, who owns the farm where the Bard has been sent to rest. From his conversations with Wilkinson, the reader gathers how conscious Shakespeare was of having a well-born mother and a father who failed in trade. What he says reveals his fascination with the upper-classes but also the disillusionment he came to feel once he had penetrated aristocratic circles. Although the portrait of Shakespeare which Kingsmill offers is very different from that of Frank Harris, it is like his in being largely based on the Sonnets and plays. The two Antonios of *Twelfth Night* and *The Merchant of Venice*, for example, are described by Shakespeare as the means by which he was able to convey the bitterness he felt at being abandoned by Pembroke (identified here as the addressee of the Sonnets); behind his portrayal of Julius Caesar, he says, lay disgust with Queen Elizabeth because of her treatment of Essex; and through the figure of Timon of Athens he claims he was able to express his own rage at life. So many characters are identified as mouthpieces for Shakespeare's own thoughts and feeling that at one point Wilkinson mildly protests, 'now Achilles, no longer Pistol, or Silvius, or Malvolio?' Although this remark has no effect on Shakespeare, it allows Kingsmill to indicate to his reader that he understands the weakness of his method while still continuing to employ it. More generally, the fictional framework means that he can offer an intelligent, well-informed speculation as to the course of Shakespeare's life without ever being in danger of believing or, more importantly, having his readers believe, that he is writing history. Gradually the reintegrated Shakespeare begins to weaken and fade away, Porter's attempts at impersonation are exposed, and the novel ends with the failure of all Melmoth's schemes. Yet like Wilde and Joyce before him, and with at least as much success as either, Kingsmill had found a way of reconciling natural curiosity about Shakespeare with the recognition that we do not, and almost certainly never will, know much about him. Readers are conscious of where they stand with Kingsmill because he himself appears to have no doubts about what can or cannot be established with any certainty.

Notes

1. *Gentleman's Magazine*, vol. 85 (1815), p. 390.
2. See R. B. Wheler, *An Historical Account of the Birthplace of Shakespeare* ed. J. O. Halliwell (1863) and Chambers, vol. 2, p. 34. (Halliwell changed his name to Halliwell-Phillipps when he inherited an estate.)
3. See F. E. Halliday, *The Cult of Shakespeare* (1957), p. 120.

4. Washington Irving, *The Sketch Book of Geoffrey Crayon, Gent.* (Paris, 1825), vol. 2, pp. 143-8.

5. Levi Fox, *In Honour of Shakespeare: The History and Collections of the Shakespeare Birthday Trust* (1972), p. 7.

6. R. Stewart (ed.), *The English Notebooks of Nathaniel Hawthorne* (1962), pp. 131-2.

7. J. M. Jephson, *Shakespere: his birthplace, home, and grave: a pilgrimage to Stratford-upon-Avon in the autumn of 1863* (1864), p. v.

8. F. E. Halliday, pp. 135-6.

9. See Richard Foulkes, *The Shakespeare Tercentenary of 1864* (Society for Theatre Research, 1984).

10. Levi Fox, p. 12.

11. Leon Edel (ed.), *The Compete Tales of Henry James* (1964), vol. 11, p. 405. 'The Birthplace' was first published in *The Better Sort*, (1903).

12. *Ibid.*, pp. 424-30.

13. *Ibid.*, p. 442.

14. *Ibid.*, p. 453.

15. *Ibid.*, pp. 451-2.

16. *Ibid.*, pp. 465-6.

17. Morris Shapira (ed.), *Selected Literary Criticism of Henry James* (1963), pp. 298-300. James's introduction appeared in vol. XVI of the Renaissance edition of *The Complete Works of William Shakespeare* (1907).

18. *The Poetical Works of Mathew Arnold* (Oxford, 1950), pp. 2-3.

19. Madeleine House, Graham Storey and Kathleen Tillotson (eds), *Letters of Charles Dickens* (Oxford, 1974), vol. 3, p. 512.

20. See Robert Bernard Martin, *Tennyson: The Unquiet Heart* (Oxford, 1980), p. 552.

21. *Poems of Robert Browning* (Oxford Standard Authors, 1905), p. 530.

22. *Ibid.*, p. 528.

23. Halliwell-Phillipps, *Outlines*, vol. 1, pp. 61-7.

24. Sidney Lee, *A Life of Shakespeare* (1915).

25. Israel Gollancz (ed.), *1916: A Book of Homage to Shakespeare* (Oxford University Press, 1916), p. 13.

26. *Ibid.*, pp. 1-2.

27. Barbara M. McCrimmon, *Richard Garnett. The Scholar as Librarian* (American Library Association, 1989), p. 157.

28. Richard Garnett, *William Shakespeare: Pedagogue and Poacher* (1905), pp. 20-22.

29. *Ibid.*, pp. 48-50.

30. McCrimmon.

31. Chambers, vol. 2, p. 247.

32. 'Q', *'Shakespeare's Christmas' and Other Stories* (1905), p. 39.

33. *Ibid.*, pp. 39-44.

34. *Ibid.*, pp. 59-62.

35. Alfred Noyes, *Tales of the Mermaid Tavern* (1914), p. 17.

36. *Ibid.*, pp. 21-2.

37. *Ibid.*, pp. 25-33.

Chapter Seven

Shakespeare in Our Time: Fiction

W HAT MAY NOT BE entirely clear from the previous chapter is that the
traditional, reverential attitude to Shakespeare, which is so much a
part of most nineteenth-century representations of him, persisted
well into the twentieth. A curious and interesting illustration of this is *With
Golden Quill. A cavalcade, depicting Shakespeare's life and times* by E. Hamilton
Gruner, published in 1936. It is hard to see how this play in three long acts,
with a not especially brief 'Epilogue', could ever have been performed since
the list of 'characters in sequence of their appearance' with which it begins
comprises well over a hundred names; and yet that list is immediately followed
by a 'music key' which carefully itemises the musical accompaniments required
for each scene. *With Golden Quill* was published by the Shakespeare Press in
Stratford and prefaced with a six-paged 'Tudor Cameo' by William Jaggard
who gives his address as 'Rose Bank, Stratford-on-Avon'. This is no doubt the
Captain William Jaggard (1868–1947) who was responsible for several scholarly
publications in the early part of the century, including an important *Shakespeare
Bibliography*; and who, in running the Shakespeare Press at Stratford, sometimes
announced himself as 'William Jaggard, publisher, second of that name'. In
Act 2, scene 18 of his play Gruner has the first William Jaggard complaining
bitterly to his son Isaac about pirated editions of Shakespeare's plays: 'The law
should protect authors from these pirates. They go to the Globe Theatre and
note down the words of the play, and what they fail to write down they make
up . . . Pshaw! Rogues!';[1] and it then shows him indignantly rejecting the offer
of a pirated manuscript of *King Lear*. The intention is clearly to celebrate the
father and son who would eventually be responsible for the printing of the
First Folio and at the same time pay a graceful tribute to the Captain Jaggard
whom a *Times* obituary describes as their 'direct lineal descendant'.[2] But Gruner
is too well informed not to know that the first William Jaggard's publishing
career did not necessarily began as respectably as it ended and too conscientious

therefore not to have one of the shady individuals who is trying to unload the *King Lear* manuscript say, in response to Jaggard's accusations of theft: 'And they do say, sir, that there is something mighty queer about your *Passionate Pilgrim*'.[3]

Recommending Gruner's play in his 'Tudor Cameo' (an evocation of life in Shakespeare's times) Jaggard writes:

> In this attractive volume our author presents a moving picture of the Empire's hero, from cradle to grave, relating what happened, actually or conceivably, during that crowded half-century, to himself, family, friends, and fellow-actors. This drama is not an unreasonable coinage of the brain, or mere flight of fancy, as might, in error, be hastily assumed, but a careful and finely-conceived narrative in dramatic form, based throughout on actual fact. Where possible, Shakespeare's own words and songs are quoted, invigorating the recital with his puissant and incomparable English.[4]

Shakespeare is here not just England's or Britain's hero but the Empire's and there is praise for the use of Shakespeare's own words when it is precisely those which help to ruin so many efforts like Gruner's, either because they make what accompanies them seem trivial by comparison or because there is something inherently peculiar in, for example, having the young Shakespeare say, when he hears that the Earl of Leicester's Men are in town: 'My chance . . . maybe . . . There is a tide in the affairs of men, which, taken at the flood . . .' (1.xi).[5] Yet what is perhaps most noteworthy about Jaggard's recommendation is his description of Gruner's play as based on 'actual fact'. So to a large extent it is and some of the facts appealed to are like the reference to *The Passionate Pilgrim* in not being of the most obvious variety. When, for example, in the 'Prologue' Shakespeare is born his father greets the occasion with, 'The Lord be praised, at last we have an heir to Mary's ancestral estate of Asbies'.[6] Asbies is the name of a property which was left to Mary Arden in her father's will. Many have believed that it was on this bequest John Shakespeare raised £40, by mortgaging it in 1579 to his brother-in-law Edmund Lambert. When he could not pay the money back (the story goes), the Lamberts hung on to the land even after Edmund's death, despite a law suit. This is why, when William is trying to persuade his wife that he ought to try his luck in London, Gruner has him say, 'Shall Asbies remain in the grasp of the Lamberts?'[7] In his courting of Anne Hathaway, Shakespeare is shown relying a good deal on the Hathaways' shepherd, Thomas Wittington, who (as Joyce knew) left to the poor '40s, that is in the hand of Anne Shaxspere, wife unto Mr Wyllyam Shaxspere or his assigns'.[8]

The young Shakespeare is anxious to leave Stratford with Leicester's Men but he is in any case driven to do so because Sir Thomas Lucy is about to prosecute him for deer-stealing. Gruner's treatment implies that he may be innocent of this charge and he has John Shakespeare refer to Lucy as 'Our dear enemy!' (1.xiii), reminding his readers in a note that 'Sir Thomas Lucy took a prominent part in the arrest of the ill-fated Sir Edward Arden, head of the Arden family, to which the poet's mother belonged'.[9] Act Two opens in Southampton's country house in Titchfield where the Earl is providing for both John Florio and Shakespeare. With Southampton are two younger men who were also at the specified time, 1593, wards of Lord Burghley: Edward Russell, the Earl of Bedford and Roger Manners, the Earl of Rutland. Reference is made in their conversation to 'Master Gobbo', Southampton's falconer. This is because, a decade or two before Gruner wrote, there had been claims that the name Gobbo could be found in the Titchfield parish register of Shakespeare's time. But as G. P. V. Akrigg records, in what is still the standard biography of Southampton, 'Unfortunately this information is incorrect. The present writer, searching for Shakespearean names, has transcribed the Titchfield parish register from its beginnings in 1587 to the burial entry for Southampton in 1624. There are no Gobbos. The names misread as 'Gobbo' were Holte and Hobbes'.[10]

Southampton is shown by Gruner impatiently looking forward to his majority on 5 October 1594. In the meantime he complains (with historical accuracy) that his father had left him in his will an obligation to pay numerous generous bequests, and build a princely tomb, but insufficient money to cover the cost. All three young Earls are fervent admirers of Essex who had also been one of Burghley's wards and who drops in to see his old friends. So also do Southampton's neighbours, the Danvers brothers, one of whom has just killed another neighbour, Sir Henry Long, and therefore requests the help of the company (Shakespeare included) to help him escape. From the way he deals with this historical incident[11] it is clear that Gruner shared the common view that the feud between the Danvers and the Longs, with its tragic outcome, influenced Shakespeare in his presentation of the Montagues and Capulets (*Romeo and Juliet* is the play he is shown to be writing while the action at Titchfield whirls round him).

More striking proof that Gruner was well-informed can perhaps be found when the action switches to the Bell Inn and Richard Quiney is discovered about to write that single surviving letter to Shakespeare in which he requests a loan of £30 (2.vi). Before he does that, he opens a letter from his eleven-year-old son which he is pleased to declare is in 'in excellent Latin'. This is a document which can still be consulted in Stratford and which Stanley Wells has recently used to suggest that 'it is quite possible that, if letters written by Shakespeare ever did turn up, they may well be in Latin.'[12] The Essex rebellion is dramatised by Gruner with Shakespeare shown trying to persuade his patron to withdraw before it is too late and later he is found lodging with the Mountjoys and regretting the fate of the rebels, that of Southampton in particular. A comparatively original feature of Gruner's treatment is that he represents Shakespeare as angry with the 'old and miserable' Queen (2.xv) because of her treatment of Southampton and not prepared, therefore, to lament her death in public (an omission that some scholars have found puzzling). There is a joyful reunion between Shakespeare and Southampton when the latter is released from the Tower on James I's accession.

As this only partial summary may indicate, Gruner's dealings with the Shakespeare mythos are not entirely business as usual although most of the usual episodes are included. An exception is anything that relates to the so-called dark lady. This omission appears to be in the interests of an unusually sanitised representation of Shakespeare's marriage. No-one could tell from the play, for example, that Anne Hathaway was pregnant at the time of her wedding (the only hint of that fact being a note attached by Gruner to a melodramatic portrayal of her father's death which reads: 'Richard Hathaway's dying words are taken from his will. Perhaps his illness and death delayed Anne's marriage'[13]). The Shakespeares are shown to be a devoted couple and the spirit which governs the way they are presented is typified in the play's finale. This takes place in 1623 at the unveiling of what the stage directions knowledgeably describe as a 'coloured bust' of Shakespeare in Stratford parish church (my italics), a memorial which Anne says has been her 'constant thought for seven years'.[14] When the ceremony is over, Jonson, Heminge and Condell exit leaving Anne alone on the stage.

> [... *Stage grows dark. Light floods rear of stage, where the altar has been replaced by a golden staircase in radiant light. Enter* W. S. *at head of staircase, in white, Tudor court dress, with silver cloak. He is once more a youth of eighteen, as in Act 1.*
> *Organ plays 'On wings of song' by Mendelssohn.*
> W. S. *gazes at* ANNE; *he descends slowly, step by step. He advances towards her, then stops, holding out both hands.* ANNE *rises and gazes at him, speechless with wonder. Her black cloak slips from her and she advances solemnly towards him, arrayed all in white. She is a young maiden once more, as in Act 1. Their hands join; he stoops and kisses both her hands. He takes her left hand with his right, and they ascend the steps slowly, one by one, he pointing upwards with his left hand.*
> *Darkness returns ... Altar reappears.*
> *Enter* SUSANNA *and* DR HALL. SUSANNA *approaches* ANNE, *now a black figure lying on ground before bust. Music ceases.*]
> SUS. [*cries loudly*]: John, John. Mother's ill ... Oh! ... she is very ill indeed ... Mother! Curtain.[15]

This is not a finale within the reach of even a very enthusiastic amateur dramatic society or student acting group. It would take Busby Berkeley to do justice to it, or perhaps Mel Brooks.

The name of Mel Brooks seems appropriate here because there is a degree of reverence in *With Golden Quill* which encourages comic treatment. A comic approach to Shakespeare was not new in the twentieth century. Parodies of his plays were common in the nineteenth and there was a similar if less evident

234

tradition, which Jerrold illustrates, of making comedy out of what was known of the man himself. In 1941, only five years after Gruner published his play, there appeared *No Bed for Bacon* by the gifted comic duo Caryl Brahms and S. J. Simon. In its first and only edition, *With Golden Quill* was 'limited to 500 sale copies', but *No Bed for Bacon*, reprinted by Penguin Books in 1948, was by comparison a huge, popular success.

Whereas the reader of Gruner's play immediately encounters a testimony to its historical accuracy, Brahms and Simon preface their book with a 'warning to scholars' which reads: 'This book is fundamentally unsound'.[16] Yet because it parodies the historical novel, there is inevitably a good deal of accurate historical information in it. One of its many running jokes, taken up more than half a century later in the film *Shakespeare in Love*, is Shakespeare's inability to decide how his own name ought to be spelt. That there are several different ways in which it is written in the surviving records is hardly specialist knowledge but this is not quite the case with another joke of this kind, Shakespeare's recurrent, but always failed, attempts in the novel to get down to writing *Love's Labour's Won*. This title appears in Francis Meres's 1598 check-list of Shakespeare's plays (see p. 12 above), and a record of a quarto edition in 1601 suggests it did once exist;[17] but no-one has yet been able to discover what happened to it.

This same mixture of common with relatively recondite knowledge is evident in the way Brahms and Simon deal with the general historical background. They have great fun with Queen Elizabeth's notorious indecisiveness but they also dramatise a crucial moment in her relationship with Essex when she refused to renew his monopoly on sweet wines.[18] Thus, like so many other fictional treatments of Shakespeare's times, their novel works on two levels, one of which is for the cognoscenti. On both there is plenty of accurate historical information yet, operating in the mode they do, Brahms and Simon feel free not only to invent but also to make deliberate mistakes. Because there is a reference in the second paragraph to the defeat of the Armada 'six years ago', the reader must assume that the action opens in 1594; even though Sir Philip Sidney and Richard Tarleton, both of whom died in the 1580s, are included in it. The plot revolves chiefly around the efforts of the theatrical entrepreneur Henslowe to close down his rival Burbage. Using his political contacts, Henslowe is able to prompt the Puritan City fathers into closing Burbage's 'Theatre' and it is this setback, rather than the difficulties Burbage did in fact have with the owner of the land on which 'The Theatre' was built, which is seen as prompting the move to Bankside, outside the city limits. Whether it was a real or deliberate mistake of the authors to forget that the land on which 'The Theatre' was built lay just as much outside the city's jurisdiction as the Bankside is not important in the comic context in which they operate.

Burbage's move south of the river did not take place until the end of 1598 and the play which in *No Bed for Bacon* Shakespeare and his colleagues are shown rehearsing while the new theatre is still being erected, was not the first to be put on there, but the last. Brahms and Simon choose *Henry VIII*, however, so that the famous accident which took place during a performance of that play, and which burnt down the Globe, can be attributed to the scheming of the envious Henslowe.[19] It is after this disaster that Shakespeare and Burbage, still dressed in the parts they had played in *Henry VIII*, make the obligatory visit to the Mermaid where one of the habitués is Sir Walter Raleigh absorbed in lamenting the ruin of another new cloak by a servant who had doused him with water because he found him smoking, and the failure of the banquet where the Queen and her courtiers had been invited to taste the first potato.

> There was a stir round the doorway. The rugged face of Henry the Eighth appeared in it. Behind him came the Bishop of St Asaph. Taking care not to disturb the sleeper by the door, they advanced upon Ben Jonson.
>
> The room was awed to complete silence. How to chatter in the face of such great grief?
>
> The silence was broken with a thwack.
>
> It was Burbage walloping Ben Jonson on the back.
>
> 'What ho! You beer-swilling old dragon,' he roared.
>
> Shakespeare's arm was already raised to thwack Sir Walter Raleigh. Just in time he pulled it back.
>
> 'Good evening, Master Raleigh,' he cried, trying his best to imitate Burbage's deep boom. 'Come to drown your sorrows?'
>
> Raleigh leapt to his feet.
>
> 'Too much of water have I had, O Shakespeare!' he announced passionately.
>
> 'A pentameter,' said Shakespeare approvingly. 'Iambs. Anapestic substitution.' He made a note with much flourish.
>
> The tavern gasped. Here indeed was the right kind of courage to bear outrageous fortune.
>
> 'Boy', boomed Burbage. 'Ale. For everyone,' he added largely.
>
> 'You are very generous to-night,' said Ben Jonson.
>
> 'And why not?' roared Burbage, draining his pewter and holding it out for more. 'The doctor has forbidden me ale, but what do I care to-night? To-night I would drink with the whole world, I would drink with you, I would drink with Master Polonius, I would even drink with Philip Henslowe. Ah, here he comes.' He waved a welcoming arm. 'A *moi*, you plotting old weazel!'
>
> Philip Henslowe looked slightly surprised. He advanced warily.
>
> 'He called you a weazel,' hissed Edward Alleyn, advancing warily behind him.
>
> 'Hist,' said Henslowe. 'Admit nothing.'
>
> They came forward.
>
> 'Drink, Master Henslowe,' boomed Burbage, passing a pewter. 'Refresh yourself at my expense. You will not even have to make an entry in your account book.'
>
> Edward Alleyn sniggered. His father-in-law's account book was easily the most unpleasant feature of his life.
>
> 'Drink deep, Master Henslowe,' said Shakespeare. 'Fear not. It is no Greek

236

who brings you this gift.'

Henslowe blinked. He had always been given to understand that Master Will was weak on the classical side.

'Drink deep, Master Alleyn,' said Ben Jonson, puzzled, but unwilling to be left out of the conversation any longer. 'It is good ale - I can vouch for its quality, even if I do not understand why it is offered.'

'Maybe,' said Sir Walter Raleigh sourly, 'they have poisoned it.'

Edward Alleyn dropped his pewter. Henslowe, whose nerves were stronger, merely stopped drinking.

'I have great news,' boomed Burbage, clambering on to the table. 'I want the tavern to drink a toast with me.'

There was a pushing back of stools. [...]

'Gentlemen,' said Burbage, lifting up his pewter. 'I give you my new playhouse. I have acquired the Whitefriars Theatre.'

They drank.

If ever a look said 'Silly old bungler - I told you so', it was the look which Edward Alleyn shot at his father-in-law.

'Great news', said Ben Jonson, clapping Shakespeare on the back. 'I rejoice for you. There is not a playwright in the theatre,' he assured him, 'whose talent pleases me more. Provided,' he added severely, 'you keep off sonnets.'

Shakespeare smiled. 'And you, Master Jonson,' he said, 'take my advice and stop writing plays. *Volpone!*' he roared.

'Congratulations, Master Burbage,' said Henslowe, holding out his hand. 'I am very glad to hear of your good fortune.' Already his conspirator's brain was turning over at high speed seeking for schemes to wreck it.

'Congratulations, Master Burbage,' said Sir Philip Sidney. 'Raleigh and I will come to your opening. In a new cloak - eh, Raleigh?'

The chaff was getting on Raleigh's nerves. 'Never again,' he muttered, 'shall I go forth without my cloak.'

'C-L-O-K-K,' muttered Shakespeare.

'Not in a sonnet, Will,' warned Ben Jonson.

But Shakespeare was already searching round for parchment and quill. 'It is the very line I needed to begin one - ah!' He pounced on the blank side of Jonson's composition.

'Not that, Will,' said Ben Jonson quickly. 'I don't want you to read that.'

Shakespeare promptly turned it over. 'What is it?' he asked. 'A play?'

Ben Jonson fidgeted. 'No, Will,' he said. 'It is an epitaph.'

'My epitaph?' said Shakespeare.

He read it.

'This figure that thou here seest put,
It was for gentle Shakespeare cut;
Wherein the graver had a strife
With Nature to outdo the life:
O, could he have but drawn his wit
As well in brass, as he hath hit
His face: the Print would then surpass
All, that was ever writ in brass.
But, since he cannot, Reader, look,
Not on his Picture, but his Book.'

He read it again. He frowned.

'Is it not good?' asked Ben Jonson uneasily.

'It is good,' said Shakespeare. 'But untimely.'

Out in the courtyard the prentice boys were waiting, lovely lads singing to tavern lattices. Their voices, like fledgling bells, came floating through the open window and hushed the babble of congratulation that had been surging round Burbage.

> 'Drink to me only with thine eyes
> And I will pledge with mine.'

'Listen,' said Ben Jonson. He pushed aside his pewter. The voices sang on.

> 'I sent thee late a rosy wreath
> Not so much honouring thee
> As giving it a hope that there
> It could not withered be.
> But thou thereon didst only breathe
> And sendst it back to me
> Since when it grows and smells, I swear,
> Not of itself but thee.'

The voices died away.

'O rare Ben Jonson,' said Shakespeare. He was weeping.

Ben Jonson nodded sadly.

'God', he said. 'What genius I had then!'[20]

Much of what is characteristic of *No Bed for Bacon* is on display here. The account book of which Henslowe's son-in-law complains is, of course, authentic and the most important surviving source of information about the Elizabethan theatre, while Jonson's famous remark in the First Folio concerning the extent of Shakespeare's classical learning may well suggest that the topic had been discussed in literary circles before he made it. On the other hand, while the Whitefriars was a real theatre, there is no record of the Lord Chamberlain's Men playing there, although when the Globe burnt down they did have the *Blackfriars* to fall back on. 'Hist' is an archaism used in Gruner's play where it sounds just as absurd as his having one of his characters say, 'A murrain on her'; but in this context there are no difficulties. The comedy is addressed to a highly literate audience, some of whom might have been expected to recognise that here Shakespeare responds to the discovery of his own epitaph (or rather the verses which appear in the First Folio opposite the Droeshout engraving) with the words which were eventually to provide Jonson's own. It makes fun of English literary history, while at the same time never suggesting that Jonson's famous lyric is anything other than beautiful.

Shakespeare emerges from *No Bed for Bacon* as a bad speller and a rotten actor – the Bishop of Asaph is hardly the most important part in *Henry VIII* – but otherwise a hard-working Company author, composing lines for his next or current play while being continually pestered for literary advice or a new

32. 'William Shakespeare: His Method of Work', cartoon by Max Beerbohm from Poet's Corner, 1904. The other figure is presumably Bacon.

poem amid all the chaos of backstage. There is no mention of the dark lady and no inclination to associate him with homosexuality. The only hint of this last topic comes in the figure of Francis Bacon who is presented as a mincing sycophant consumed with the ambition of acquiring one of the beds the Queen has slept in during this or that Progress (hence the novel's title), and already upset, when the action begins, at having missed out during the Progress to Cheltenham. 'What went wrong there?', Shakespeare asks him:

> Bacon blushed. 'The arrangements', he admitted. 'It was delivered to some place at Stratford. It was the second-best bed, too'. He sighed.
> Shakespeare looked elaborately out of the window.
> 'There seems to be quite a mode for Gloriana's bedsteads', he observed.
> 'Enormous', said Bacon. Every noble in the land covets one to leave to his children. Prices are soaring daily.'
> 'Quite an investment', said Shakespeare.[21]

The rivalry between Burbage and Henslowe is the chief plot device in *No Bed for Bacon* but subsidiary to it is one which Viereck and Eldridge had used in *My First Two Thousand Years*, and which was to turn up again in *Shakespeare in Love*. A gentlewoman - Brahms and Simon make her one of Elizabeth's maids of honour - is passionate about the theatre and disguises herself as a boy actor. In the final chapter of their novel Shakespeare nobly turns his back on the love which has developed between him and the disguised gentlewoman and sends her off to learn more of her newly adopted trade with Henslowe and Alleyn. This is partly because he wants her to be ready to play the part of Cleopatra in a play which he has not yet written and which 'needs a woman and cannot be acted by some prancing boy'; and partly also because he feels that the provincial tour to which he is now condemned, with its 'one-night stands in rough places', is 'no life for a girl'. The girl in question is called Viola and protests: 'You want to get rid of me. [...] You have always wanted to get rid of me. [...] Why, you have never so much as written a single sonnet to me.' Shakespeare holds fast to his decision, but when the young woman has gone, he once again puts aside *Love's Labour Wunne*, with only 'Act 1. Scene 1. The Garden of Eden. Enter a serpent' completed, and begins a poem about Viola whose first line - 'Shall I compare thee to a summer's day' - is also the last line of the novel.[22]

The Shakespeare Brahms and Simon depict is a thoroughly decent chap. They make fun of the world Gruner celebrates but the final effect of what they write is not so very far from his own, as far at least as Shakespeare himself is concerned. What is probably important here is that their novel was published during the Second World War. In by far the longest episode, Hawkins, Drake and Frobisher are anachronistically brought together in order to reminisce with Elizabeth about the defeat of the Armada and Shakespeare is part and parcel of the national identity which these reminiscences, and the novel in general, celebrate. It was perhaps only after the war was over that English writers would feel free to attack Shakespeare precisely because of his relation to that national identity, or allow their comic treatment radically to affect how their readers were meant to view him.

A good example of a freer comic treatment which is nonetheless still amiable and easy-going can be found in the 'Flook' strip cartoon which appeared for many years in *The Daily Mail*. The episodes in which Flook encounters Shakespeare ran during July, August and September 1964, in parallel with, or in competition to, the many events in that year which celebrated the fourth centenary of Shakespeare's birth. They were the work of Wally Fawkes (drawings) and George Melly (words and story), both of whom were also well known as jazz musicians; and they made the most of what is known as the 'authorship controversy'. Faint intimations that Shakespeare might not have written the plays commonly attributed to him occur in the eighteenth century, but the idea only began to take hold in the middle of the nineteenth with the efforts of Delia Bacon to show that they were really the results of a group of aristocratic or well-connected figures spear-headed by her namesake, Francis. Although Delia Bacon went mad and died in England in 1859, many others, most of them from her native America, took up the cause and made extraordinary efforts to show that encoded in the plays and poems were clear messages to prove that their author was not Shakespeare. It was not however until 1920 that a schoolmaster from the north east of England, J . Thomas Looney, in the book which so impressed Freud, gave the Baconians what Schoenbaum wittily calls a 'run for their madness'[23] by proposing that the real author hiding behind Shakespeare's name was Edward de Vere, the seventeenth earl of Oxford. Later still, others would suggest it was Marlowe. A major difficulty with these last two candidates is that both died well before Shakespeare, Marlowe in 1593 and the Earl of Oxford in 1604; but in the first case it could be suggested that Marlowe's murder was faked by Walsingham for obscure reasons of State and in the second that, when Oxford died, he left behind unfinished manuscripts which were then prepared for performance by other, lesser lights.

As I pointed out in the first chapter, to suppose that Shakespeare, the existence of whom is never challenged by the so-called anti-Stratfordians, merely provided a convenient cover for someone better born, better connected or at least (in Marlowe's case) better educated, means supposing, among other feats of logic, that Heminge, Condell, Jonson and all those associated with the First Folio were involved in a conspiracy of silence. There are two major but contradictory reasons why people might want to do this. One of these has often been described as snobbish: how could the son of a provincial glover whose formal education was limited to a few years at the local grammar school, and whose opportunities must always have been limited for mixing in the kind of aristocratic company often depicted in Shakespeare's plays, have possibly written them? The second is something like the opposite of snobbish in that it involves a protest against an intellectual Establishment which, the anti-Stratfordians feel, is not even willing to entertain suggestions which might diminish Shakespeare's reputation (and certainly not those, therefore, which would destroy it entirely). Those who hold this latter view would find an all too clear reflection of what they have to fight against in Gruner's 'Epilogue' to *With Golden Quill*. There, a couple called Anne and Will are seen attending the opening of the new Stratford Memorial Theatre in 1932 (the previous building having burnt down in 1926).[24] They are engaged but the young woman threatens to break the engagement when Will suggests that Oxford might have been the real author of the plays: 'Lord Oxford? . . . You thief! . . . You would steal the laurels from England's dead poet? and besmirch his honoured name?'[25] For Fawkes and Melly a name honoured in this way is too tempting a target.

Their Shakespeare episodes begin with Colonel Cordite-Smith, one of the cartoon's recurrent characters, asking Flook to go down to Stratford and prevent his wife from breaking open Shakespeare's tomb (as Delia Bacon had wanted to do in the nineteenth century[26]). Describing his wife as a 'rampant feminist', the Colonel explains how she has become convinced that the real author of the plays was Anne Hathaway. When, however Flook and his young friend Rufus arrive in Stratford, they are immediately identified as her husband's spies by Mrs Cordite-Smith (that she should have no difficulty in spotting them is hardly surprising when Flook looks like a Koala bear with a trunk). In order to gain her confidence, Flook pretends to be convinced by Mrs Cordite-Smith's views with the consequence that he and Rufus find themselves having to stick notices which read 'Anne Hathaway wrote the lot' on various of Stratford's cultural monuments. This naturally attracts the attention of the police, acting on behalf of what Mrs Cordite-Smith calls 'the vested interests in bardolatry'. When Rufus asks what this phrase means, Flook replies, 'Matchboxes with pictures of Shakespeare on them. Things like that', when he might also have mentioned stamps, shops, bank notes, tea-towels, beer mats, mugs, street signs and of course hundreds of English pubs.

The police chase Flook and Rufus into an exhibition of Shakespeare's life and times where there is a scuffle which results in Flook being knocked unconscious by a flying copy of the First Folio. When he wakes up, he is in Elizabethan England, the clown of the Lord Chamberlain's Men, and wondering with his fellow actor Will Shakespeare how he is going to get through the summer now that a 'Puritan plot' has closed their theatre and the plague is on the way. Hope appears in the shape of young Lord Rufus who is just about to attain his majority, writes plays and wants to be patron of his own company. For the next ten weeks of so, readers of the *Daily Mail* were able to follow Flook and Shakespeare as they visited Lord Rufus's family seat in

242

34. *'The First Plague Victims', Flook cartoon by Wally Faulkes and George Melly, 1964*

Runcorn where his very recently widowed mother has married his uncle. This is the cue for a parody of *Hamlet* (with echoes of *Macbeth* thrown in for good measure). The climax comes with the play within the play, performed not only in front of Rufus's mother and his guilty uncle, but also Queen Elizabeth whose latest 'progress' has stretched as far as Runcorn. After Rufus has stabbed the uncle who, in addition to having murdered his brother, was about to poison the Queen so that she could be replaced by Mary Queen of Scots, Elizabeth asks what reward he would like. When Rufus replies that he wants to be a patron of an acting company which could perform his own plays, she accedes to his request on condition that his own, aristocratic name should not appear on the playbills. After some toying with the unsatisfactory idea of '*Hamlet* by Flook', it is agreed that Shakespeare's name would look and sound better.

Back in London, Shakespeare is found rehearsing Flook in the gravediggers' scene from *Hamlet*, using the First Folio which Lord Rufus has given him as a prompt book. When Anne Hathaway bursts in complaining of neglect ('How did I?', Shakespeare has previously mused, 'I must have been very drunk') an altercation ensues which results in Flook again being knocked unconscious by a flying First Folio. 'Look what you've done, dear,' Shakespeare says, 'You've

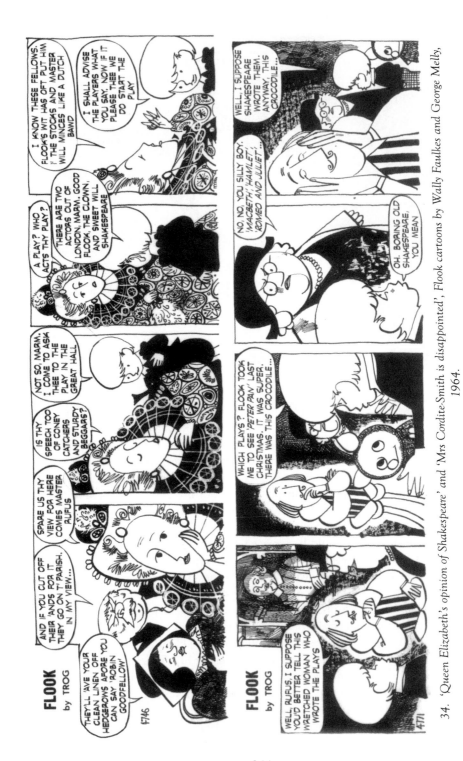

34. 'Queen Elizabeth's opinion of Shakespeare' and 'Mrs Cordite-Smith is disappointed', Flook cartoons by Wally Faulkes and George Melly, 1964.

knocked out me clown. Just for that I'll leave you me second-best bed.' When Flook wakes up back in Stratford, Rufus has already explained the real reason of their visit to Stratford to the police who are full of apologies: 'I 'ope you don't intend taking no action, sir, on account of us rendering you unconscious with the First Folio, but we did think as how you believed the immortal bard an impostor, and Stratford Corporation's very down on that'. He and Rufus rush off and are just in time to find Mrs Cordite-Smith prising open Shakespeare's tombstone in spite of the famous words written on it cursing those who would move its bones. The ghost of Shakespeare rises from the opened tomb fully expecting to be exposed as a fraud but fortunately for him Rufus has no memory of his former Elizabethan self and the secret is therefore safe.

Very unlike Gruner, Fawkes and Melly clearly enjoy tweaking the tail of the Establishment and playing with the idea that Shakespeare was a fraud, partly because they understand so well why the Stratford authorities should be 'down on' it. Stratford-upon-Avon is an attractive and well-situated town but it would hardly have the appeal it does for millions of tourists if it were not in fact the birthplace of the author of *Hamlet*. Not that it is these authorities alone who would be concerned if it could be shown that he wasn't. As Douglas Lanier has put it in the important chapter of his recent book on *Shakespeare and Modern Popular Culture* which deals with the man rather than his works:

> Shakespeare's face offers an easy means for attaching commercially useful connotations to products, among them quality craftsmanship, *gravitas*, trustworthiness, Britishness, antiquity, cultural sophistication, intellectuality and artsiness.[27]

Some of these connotations would be less easy to attach – trustworthiness in particular perhaps – if it could be proved that the face in question masked someone else. Although it does not make the case of the anti-Stratfordians any stronger, it is true that huge commercial forces are necessarily ranged against them.

Flook and Rufus began life in a cartoon meant for children and although, with the arrival of George Melly in particular, they later became the vehicles for social and political satire there was always a charming ingenuousness in Wally Fawkes's depiction of both figures which ensured that the satire could never be too sharp. This is as true for the implicit attack on the Shakespeare industry as it is for the glancing blow at feminism or the presentation of Shakespeare as a homosexual. Looking back nostalgically to the fifteen years of his association with Fawkes, George Melly has said of the effort to imagine new stories, 'Sometimes I was reduced to a sort of despair and said, "Why not a story about the past?" They were quite fun to do and often very successful. We had Shakespeare as a screaming poove, and there were others';[28] but 'screaming poove' seems too strong an expression for a figure who is above all what would be now be called camp, the stereotypical, limp-wristed actor of so much subsequent comic writing. As in the 1960s, the so-called 'satire boom' gathered force, there was much less public resistance to seeing Shakespeare in this way than there would have been earlier and not yet the unease about ridiculing homosexuals which would develop in many quarters later.

⎯⋇⬦⋇⎯

The material in Chapter 5, makes clear that it was, above all, the Sonnets which were responsible for the idea that Shakespeare may have been homosexual. Reconciling that belief with his marriage, and the references in the poems to the dark lady, became increasingly inviting material for novelists as the limits to what could be said about Britain's national bard were extended. It was while the fourth centenary of his birth was being celebrated, and in the same year therefore as the Flook cartoon, that in *Nothing Like the Sun. A story of Shakespeare's love-life* Anthony Burgess made the first of his several attempts to imagine what the historical record is too sparse and inadequate to tell us. This account of how it was that Shakespeare came to have sex with Anne Hathaway, from a work which Harold Bloom has called 'the only successful novel written about Shakespeare',[29] gives a fair indication of its predominant literary manner. It is May Day in Stratford and young Will Shakespeare, who has been disappointed to see the dark-haired girl in whom he has declared an interest go off with a miller's son, has consoled himself with drink.

> He went out to piss and near fell over a dribbling drunkard who lay snoring at the moon. The moon had risen, then. He saw them in his mind's eye, buttocks moon-besilvered, rising and falling. The roar of the ale within, rage athirst for enactment, he would rail, send them on their ways stark naked, lash them with a birch-bough, sob, plain at unfaith, tear, kill. But he would drink first, drink out his sixpence.
>
> Drink, then. Down it among the titbrained molligolliards of country copulatives, of a beastly sort, all, their browned pickers a-clutch of their spilliwilly potkins, filthy from handling of spade and harrow, cheesy from udder new-milked, slash mouths agape at some merry tale from that rogue with rat-skins about his middle, coneyskin cap on's sconce. Robustious rothers in rural rivo rhapsodic. Swill thou then among them, O London-Will-to-be, gentleman-in-waiting, scrike thine ale's laughter with Hodge and Tom and Dick and Black Jack the outlander from Long Compton. [...]

In the alehouse a discharged soldier hits the drunken Shakespeare in the belly so that he vomits. He is then jostled and finally pushed outside where he vomits again before passing out.

> Yet, an eternity of nothing after, he woke warm. The dawn birdsong was deafening. He smelt grass and leaves and his mother's comforting and comfortable

smell, the faint milk and salt and zest and new-bread odour of a woman's bosom. He sighed and burrowed deeper his head. His mouth was foul, it was as if he had licked rust. He squinnied, frowning, to see that the ceiling had become all leaves, that the house-beams had returned to their primal tree-state. There was white sky, in leaf-beguiled patches, over. He gave in wonder to this world a pair of tormented eyeballs. She smiled, she kissed his brow in gentleness. Her shoulders and arms and bosom were naked beneath the rough coverlet, a pair of cloaks. Beneath was some hairy blanket-like protector against the ground's damp, through which odd harmless needles of roots and stubble pricked. He was in his clothes, though they were unbuttoned, untied in disarray. He dredged memory and found naught. It was the wood, it was Shottery, but what woman was this? To ask, when twined so in early morning and near-nakedness – would not that be ungentle? He must needs smile back to her smile and murmur some formula of good-morrow. It would come out, he would learn all if he waited. In God's name, though, what had he done in that great void of unmemory? Never never never never would he come more to that. He would be a moderate man. But then she whispered, in a fierce sort, 'Anon will it be full light and all stirring. *Now*.' And she lay upon him, a long though not a heavy woman, and it was in vain for him to protest that his mouth was not yet, not till some cleansing and quickening draught had done its office, at all ready for kissing. And so he sought to avoid her lips, lithely (though with aches and dumbed groans) turning her to the posture of Venus Observed and giving his mouth to her left breast, his stiff and wooden tongue playing about its rosy pap till she panted hard like poor Wat pursued by hounds. He arose for air, his hand now at work in darkness, an eye on each finger-end, to observe with his true, though cracked, eyes this country Venus-head, its straight bound red-gold locks, brow deep and narrow and bony, twittering scant pale lashes, the mole on the neck's long pillar gazing steadily back at his wavering light-wounded wonder, Will at work, WS thinking that perhaps he knew her (since she must belong hereabouts), though certain he had not, in the other sense, known her before. Was she not approaching carrotiness, Arden pallor? But, as the early light stretched and yawned, time spoke of the need for but one thing, and the ale's residuum, like lusty flesh-meat, fed that cock-crow Adam to bursting. ('This,' he told himself, 'is hate of her, that other, faithless with her roaring miller's son'.) And she made him like a madman, for she gripped him with powerful talons and let forth a pack of words he had thought no woman could know. So then he cracked open, going aaaaaaah, all in the tender morning, and loosed into her honey his milk, shuddering like a puppy, whinnying like a horse.

He felt, to his surprise, no shame after, no *tristitia*. They lay quietly as the morning advanced its little way, hid snug in their greenwood coign. She talked and he listened, ears pricked houndlike for a clue of the quarry. '. . . So', saith she, 'if Anne will not then maybe one of the boys, her brothers . . .' So she was Anne, then, fair and English smelling of mild summers and fresh water. She was not young, he thought: past twenty five. She was no plum-plump pudding of the henyard, roaring the health of burning air and an ample plain cottage diet, nor was there in her voice the country twang of such as Alice Studley. The thin song of would-be ladyship (she would turn her blushing face away, no doubt, from the cock's treading) beat smartly in her neck's pulse as he fingered it. It in no wise congrued with her lying near-bare against him nor with that horrible steaming-out, some few minutes past, of a mouthful apter for a growling leching collier pumping his foul water into some giggling alley-mort up by the darkling wall of a stinking alehouse privy. What could he do but smile in secret, still queasy as he was? But he must be on his feet soon and away, saying I-thank-you-perhaps-we may-meet-again-Anne. But he said 'Anne' softly, to taste that name in an unsisterly context,[†] though posthumous, posthumous. . . .

Speaking her name, it was as if he spake pure cantharides. 'Quick,' she panted. 'There is time before they are all about. *Again.*' She thrust bold hot long fingers, lady-smooth, down at his root in its tangled nest. 'If thou wilt not –' And she lay on him as before, to woman him, her tongue's tip near licking his little grape, her kneading fingers busy at his distaff which, all bemused, rose as it were in sleep.

And so the Maypole was brought home.[30]

The linguistic virtuosity of this passage is a reminder that Burgess was a great admirer of Joyce. Nearly all the unfamiliar words it contains are archaic and come mainly from his reading in Elizabeth literature, particularly the pamphlets of writers like Nashe, although there are echoes here too of Shakespeare's own writing and in particular ('poor Wat') *Venus and Adonis*, that tale of a mature woman trying to oblige a youth to make love to her. The alternative image the episode offers of WS is, to say the least, less glamorous than Gruner's. After it is over Will becomes interested in the seventeen-year old, dark-haired Anne Whateley (Whateley being the name that appears in the record of Shakespeare's special marriage licence in the Bishop's *Register* at Worcester, presumably by mistake for Hathaway[31]); but news of the pregnancy of the other Anne forces him to redirect his attention elsewhere. Married and a father, he then seizes an opportunity to move away from Stratford to become a private tutor in Gloucestershire but, after a while in the job, is dismissed for being too physically intimate with one of his young male charges. Once he is in London, physical intimacy with Southampton is no barrier to advancement (although the details of their relationship are never made very specific). As Shakespeare slowly establishes himself as a successful poet and playwright so also does he become obsessed with a black courtesan of possibly Moorish origins whom he suspects he first saw on visit to a brothel in Bristol when he was working as a tutor and whose name is now Mistress Lucy. Burgess, who gives to Lucy certain Malayan characteristics with which he had become familiar during his time as a teacher in the Far East, works up this character from a reference in the *Gesta Grayorum*, an account of the Christmas celebrations at Grays Inn at the end of 1594. In addition to the claim that a performance of *The Comedy of Errors* formed part of these celebrations, there is a mention in this text of a local prostitute known as 'Lucy Negro, abbess de Clerkenwell'. It was the Shakespearean scholar J. B. Harrison who first proposed a link between this figure and the dark lady of Shakespeare's Sonnets.[32]

At one early point in the action of Burgess's novel, Southampton and

---

[†] Shakespeare had a sister called Anne who died in childhood.

Shakespeare have become such close friends that the young Earl, who is infatuated with the wife of a tavern-keeper in Islington, wants to take his favourite poet to see her. Shakespeare agrees to go, chiefly because he knows that Chapman is living in this same tavern and he is curious to meet the poet who, he suspects, is becoming his rival for his patron's attention. In what seems to be a very loose adaptation of the Manningham anecdote, the night they decide to spend in the tavern results in Southampton pining for love of the landlord's wife while Shakespeare actually sleeps with her. The young Earl has his revenge later however when, in line with the situation implied in the Sonnets, he steals Lucy from his poet; and Shakespeare's miseries are then compounded when he makes an unexpected trip home only to find his wife in bed with his brother Richard. (Burgess gives Richard a limp, perhaps to remind himself or his readers of the way Stephen Dedalus derived this possibility from *Richard III*.) Back in London, Shakespeare recovers Lucy who has been abandoned by Southampton, but then discovers he is infected with syphilis. The extent to which, in the depiction of all these dramatic events, Burgess remains as close as possible to the little that is known about Shakespeare, can be gauged from this account of Shakespeare and Southampton talking together. What this passage also illustrates is that *Nothing Like the Sun* has its quieter moments and is not always ablaze with linguistic fireworks.

> 'I said it would come to this. All along I said it. Yet you would not have it so.'
> Harry screamed and threw the book to the floor. It was a thin book, ill-bound, the cover already coming away. WS, calm, in many ways glad, picked it up. It was an anonymous poem called *Willobie His Avisa or The True picture of a modest maid and of a chaste and constant wife* – anonymous, but he could guess who had written it or, at least, was behind the writing of it. It was not weighty enough for Chapman, slim stuff; belike he had sold the theme to some drunken hack, master of arts. It was sure of good sales. WS turned and turned the pages to a hunk of prose, as indigestible as cheese-and-black-bread: [...]

Burgess now transcribes most of the 'Argument' from *Willobie His Avisa* reproduced on p. 11 above.

> 'You can expect talk now,' said WS, putting the little book down on the table by the casement. Outside the plane tree was yellowing. The swallows twittered in loud companies. Another autumn, a sere fall, but now perhaps the end of his servitude. Not of friendship, no. He felt himself as close to this lord as to a son, as to himself. But the end of hugging, of that secret love that June's frenzy and self-hatred had seemed to quell. He thought it must be so. As for Harry, he was more openly busy now among the Queen's glories. WS twisted the knife in further. He said:
> 'My lord Burghley will be told, doubtless.' Harry gave a maniacal smile, saying:
> 'Oh, my lord Burghley knows everything. My lord Burghley has issued a table-thumping threat.'
> 'Threat? When was this?' for WS had been busy, these last weeks, with other

matters, player's matters.

'I am given my last chance. Either I marry dear Lady Liza, God curse her poxy face, or pay the penalty. And the penalty is by way of a damages, for my guardian's ravaged heart and the time wasted in waiting by this pocked bitch.'

'A penalty? Money? You must pay money?'

'Five thousand pound.'

WS whistled in Stratford tradesman's vulgar astonishment. 'So what will you do?'

'Oh, I shall find the money. It will not be easy. But I will pay ten times that rather than mingle my bare legs with hers. I refuse to marry.'

WS spoke carefully. 'You may, if all I hear is true, be hurled still into marriage against your desire. Love is pleasant, but nature sees that it will have consequences that are naught, or little, to do with love.'

'Do not paste your own past on to my future. Because you were forced into marriage by the baring of a fat belly – '

'Yes? Great lords are different from Stratford glovers?'

Harry went to the wine-table and poured himself a beaker of the bloody ferrous brew of Vaugraudy; he liked it; these days he was growing faint ruby with it; he did not offer any to his friend.

'I do not think you should speak to me,' he said. 'There are times when I feel I may compass mine own disaster through over-much familiarity. Not through disobedience to them that are set over me but through mine own free behaviour with – Ah, it is no matter.' He drank thirstily.

'You have never had cause,' said WS, 'nor will you ever have cause to complain of any indiscretion of mine. I never took you tavern-hunting. I sought to discourage your Islington venture with a trick. I would never be so foolish as to place myself in a posture that could earn just rebuke. We are friends when we are alone, and when we are in company I am as tame an adjunct to your house as Master Florio. And now I cease to be that. This book tells me what to do.' He held *Willobie His Avisa* in both hands, as he would tear it. 'You need five thousand pound now, you say. Would that I were in a position to let you have it. It is not right that you mortgage ancestral land. I go now to seek the way of substance, and that lies not in pretty poetry. When we meet again it must be more as equals.'

'You cannot make such equality,' said Harry with a sort of foxy sneer. 'You will never earn yourself an earldom. Earldoms are not earned in playhouses or by the buying of flour against famine or by the foreclosing of mortgages. Degree remains and may not be taken away.' He poured himself more wine, but this time he offered a cup to his friend. His friend shook his head, saying:

'I foresee a time when gold will buy anything. Gold already rules this city. I foresee a time of patched nobles seeking alliance with dirty merchant families. As for myself, my way up leads to the estate of gentleman. For you, the way up can lead only to disaster.'

'Meaning?'

'I say no more now. But let us consider the example of my lord of Essex.'

'I will not consider his example nor anybody's,' said Harry in a sudden passion. 'I will not have country nobodies speaking of great lords as though they were subject to the rule of ordinary men. Play with your plays and leave state matters to statesmen.'

'So my lord Essex is no longer merely a soldier and a courtier but a statesman too? And what is the next step?'

'I think,' said my lord Southampton, 'you had best leave now. And take that filthy book with you. No,' he said, 'I will read it again. We shall meet this evening when perhaps we are both more in our right minds.'

WS grinned at that. 'Alas, my lord, I have other business. Player's business. But tomorrow I shall be much at your service if you would wish to come to my lodging. See, I have writ it on this paper, the house and street. Bishopsgate is not far from Holborn.'

Harry threw the book once more, this time at his friend. The cover that had threatened to come away now did so; it was a piece of cheap and unskilful binding, not the work of Richard Field, that other ascending Stratfordian.[33]

Burgess's use here of *Willobie His Avisa*, for which he has previously taken the trouble to provide a background with the episode in Islington, suggests a high degree of familiarity with the by-ways of twentieth-century Elizabethan scholarship. He knows that the sum which Burghley exacted from his ward for refusing to marry the woman chosen for him, Burghley's own granddaughter, Lady Elizabeth Vere, was £5,000 (although our only surviving evidence for that happens to be from Father Garnet, the superior of the English Jesuits, who was hardly one of Burghley's greatest supporters).[34] With 'baring of a fat belly' he has Shakespeare look forward to the difficulties Southampton would encounter from having made Elizabeth Vernon pregnant (the major consequence of which was no different from that which followed the Stratford glover's impregnation of Anne Hathaway); and the future dangers of association with Essex are also hinted at. Burgess knows that the tax records suggest that Shakespeare must, at some point, have lived in Bishopsgate and there are the near-obligatory references to his possible association with Florio and John Field, the fellow Stratfordian who printed both *Venus and Adonis* and *The Rape of Lucrece*. Armed with knowledge which makes his text have the double nature characteristic of nearly all fictional accounts of Shakespeare, Burgess sets out to meet two major creative challenges. One is to decide when and why Shakespeare gave up living or attempting to live as a poet with a patron and went back to the theatre. The other, much more difficult one, is to imagine how a middle-class writer and an Earl who were, or had been intimate friends, might talk to one another.

In addition to publishing a biography of Shakespeare in 1970, Burgess persevered with imagined portraits until his death in 1993, including him as a character in at least two more novels and one short story.[35] He was not alone in this activity but rather only one of the more intellectual, 'high-brow' members of a group keen to have Shakespeare as a character in their novels and plays. As I suggested in my introduction, depictions of Shakespeare become so numerous as time progresses that, whereas in the earliest periods the choice of illustrative material could hardly be called 'choice' at all, in the later ones the question of what to select is subject to influences which are ever more arbitrary. Throughout the twentieth century, 'Shakespeare' makes an increasing number of appearances in crime fiction and popular novels of romantic love. He is present in many works of science fiction and often depicted in stories primarily aimed at children or adolescents.[36] If, to all the works in these genres by British authors were added similar ones by North Americans, the number of appearances Shakespeare makes would seem more than ever unmanageable. To help make sense of all the many, often very different attempts to imagine Shakespeare, Douglas Lanier has evoked a distinction proposed by Paul Franssen and Ton Hoenselaars in their introduction to *The Author as Character: Representing Historical Writers in Western Literature* (1999). This is between the *vie romancée*, the kind of biographical fictions I am chiefly discussing, and the *vie imaginaire*, that is to say a life 'freely reimagined or depicted in anachronistic or fantastic contexts', one whose representation is not constrained by what Lanier calls, in his post-structuralist fashion, 'the illusion of historical fidelity'.[37] Yet since it is hard to imagine any representations of Shakespeare which did not rely on *some* historical data, another way of imposing a semblance of order on an unwieldy mass of material would be to categorise each representation according to the extent to which their authors were willing to ignore or stray from the known facts. Then there would be no sudden break between one kind of fiction and another but rather a continuum. By this criterion, Burgess, for all of what might reasonably be called his wild imaginings, is very much at the conservative end of the spectrum.

A novelist who has sometimes been hailed as Burgess's successor, as far as the representation of Shakespeare is concerned, is Robert Nye. In his *The Late Mr Shakespeare*, published in 1998, an old actor looks back to his days with the Lord Chamberlain's Men and tells stories which provide solutions to most of the usual puzzles of Shakespeare's life; but in *Mrs Shakespeare: the complete works*, which appeared in 1993, it is Anne Hathaway who acts as the reader's informant, proving that no man is a hero to either his valet or his wife. The persona Nye adopts in this earlier novel takes him well away from Burgess's usual literary manner. Mrs Shakespeare is plain-speaking and commonsensical, not at all interested in literature. She describes the moment during her courtship when she had to explain to her future husband that, although she had been irritated by his behaviour, she did not really hate him, and prints the sonnet that he was then prompted to write (the one now known as 145, '*Those lips that love's own hand did make . . .*' etc.), thoughtfully providing a commentary for those who, like herself, are 'not accustomed to the kind of riddling speech you find in poesy'.

> The line, by the way, which Mr Shakespeare was especially pleased with himself for writing was the thirteenth:
>
> '*I hate*' *from hate away she threw ...*
>
> When I first read the sonnet, I made no comment on this particular line,

which annoyed him hugely.

Whereupon he read the whole thing aloud, stressing the *'I hate' from hate away* bit.

I fear that I still failed to get the point.

Then Mr Shakespeare cried:

'Hate away! Hathaway! Don't you see? A play on your name, Anne!'

I suppose that *is* clever.

As clever as a monkey's tricks.

But then I don't like monkeys.

Mr Shakespeare also boasted:

'One day someone will read it and know it was you! That I hid your name there! The name of my love who said and did these things to me!'

I suppose he might be right.

But that's another trouble with poesy.

When poets are not caressing themselves with their own words, they're busy a-courting posterity.[38]

Anne Shakespeare is writing after her husband's death and what Nye has her describe is the week in April 1594 when, for the first and only time, she went to meet Shakespeare in London. He is conspicuously well-dressed and explains that he has been writing more sonnets but this time been paid for them. Her curiosity aroused, Anne forces Shakespeare to tell her that the man for whom he wrote these new sonnets was called Risley. They go back to her husband's lodgings where there is a magnificent new bed and where Shakespeare reveals just how much money Risley has been willing to pay.

I stared at Mr Shakespeare.

Mr Shakespeare did not smile.

He was looking hard at me.

'What did you do?' I breathed. 'What did you do that was worth a thousand pounds?'

Mr Shakespeare was naked now.

His member stood up stiff as any poker.

'You want to know,' he said. 'You really want to know.'

It wasn't a question.

It was a statement of fact.

'I want to know,' I whispered. '*What did you do?*'

'Why, I buggered him, my dear,' Mr Shakespeare said softly.

'And what is that?' I enquired. 'What does it mean?'

Mr Shakespeare answered nothing.

His eyes were like burning coals.

He was biting his lip.

When he stopped biting his lip, he kissed me hard on my lips. Then he stroked my cheeks with his fingers and kissed me gently on the eyelids.

Once my husband had kissed me on my eyelids, I chose to keep my eyes shut, and I waited.

I felt Mr Shakespeare move behind me.

I felt the bed shift as he knelt upon it.

I could feel him crouched behind me in the dark.

His hands came down and he clasped my hips tight from behind.

Then I felt his engorged member smack-smacking at my bottom cheeks.

'She wants to know,' he said coldly. 'I do believe she really wants to know.'

His voice sounded far away. But I could feel him hot and hard between my bottom cheeks.

'I do!' I cried eagerly. 'Yes, please, I do! *How do you do it?*'

Then:

'Like this,' said Mr Shakespeare.

And then he did it to me.

It hurt me at first.

Then it didn't hurt.

Hurt me or not, once Mr Shakespeare had started there was no stopping him.

'Good?' he cried. 'Like it?'

'No!' I cried. 'No, I don't, no, I won't, no, no . . .'

But, then, after some more of it:

'*Yes!*' [...]

When we had done, Mr Shakespeare started talking about the money.

That bed had not cost so very much, he said.

He had plenty of the thousand pounds left over.

He was going to buy shares in a new playhouse which Mr Burbage was building on the Bankside.

His plays would be performed there, my husband said.

That way he would get paid for the plays, and also receive a percentage of their profits.

Money made money, Mr Shakespeare said.

Soon he would purchase property as well.

The day would come, my clever husband promised, when we would live in the finest house in Stratford. . . .

(Well, it didn't.

We had to settle for the second-best.)

I grew tired of his talking.

So I touched him.

'You want it again?' Mr Shakespeare asked wonderingly. 'You want it again up there?'

I wanted it.

I wanted it again up there.

And Mr Shakespeare proved more than willing to give it to me where and how I wanted it.

I fell asleep at last.

I fell asleep worn out by what he'd done to me.

A very great peace came over me.

I do not think I was ever so pleased or contented.

254

It started to rain as I fell asleep, I remember that.
I could hear the April rain falling gently upon the roof.
Mr Shakespeare was still talking about the money as I fell asleep.
But it was not about the money I dreamt.[39]

The idea that Southampton (and Risley is certainly how his family name is pronounced) gave Shakespeare £1,000 which he was then able to use to buy a share in the Lord Chamberlain's Men dates back to the seventeenth century,[40] but the relation here proposed between Shakespeare's marriage and his supposed homosexual involvement with Southampton is all Nye's own. Anne has found her husband an inadequate sexual partner in the past – but not any more – and she spends the rest of the week playing sex games on the new bed with Shakespeare. These are all related to the plots of Shakespeare's plays and they all end with acts of anal intercourse. Some people have always wondered whether Anne Hathaway read Shakespeare's Sonnets, what she made of them if she did, and how what they imply affected her marriage. Nye provides a humorous response to at least the last part of this question but in terms so characteristically of our time that they would have given E. Hamilton Gruner heart-failure.

As I have said, it was inevitable that the reverence which has been accorded Shakespeare from the eighteenth century onwards should eventually invite comic treatment, what Douglas Lanier calls 'carnivalesque inversion';[41] and that the questions about his sexual life raised by the Sonnets should attract special attention when it became possible to speak more freely about sexual matters and when a general assumption developed, largely because of Freud, that sexual feelings are central to the story of any life. But the concentration on sex which Burgess and Nye exemplify does not mean that they, and in particular modern authors more 'popular' than they are, ignore other questions: whether or not Shakespeare's marriage was unhappy, for example, what his religious views were, how he first became an actor, what his relations were with his fellow actors and writers, how focused he was on the pursuit of gentility, when he 'retired', and so on. A large number of writers, operating in very different literary modes or traditions, offer answers to these questions which, according to their various levels of skill, it becomes possible to imagine as correct. They can do this because even the most attentive regard to the historical record leaves plenty of room for manoeuvre; although there is of course no special compulsion on the writers concerned to *be* attentive. The well-informed to whom all the authors already discussed in this chapter address the odd flattering aside or in-joke will always be outnumbered by a class of more 'general' readers whose knowledge of the details of Shakespeare's life, or the Elizabethan period, is necessarily sketchy.

Writing in defence of these more general readers Lanier says:

To speak censoriously of the public's ignorance of the historical record is to miss
how Shakespeare the mythic character provides a way of articulating popular
notions of authorship and cultural hierarchy, collective ideas, attitudes,
aspirations, desires, and anxieties that have a variety of political inflections;

and he later adds, 'popular portrayals of Shakespeare (and scholarly ones as
well) inevitably serve ideological ends'.[42] In this, the most general sense of the
word, all fictional depictions of Shakespeare are 'political' but there are some
distinctly more political than others. Of all those who, in recent times, have
made their portrayal of Shakespeare serve more distinctly ideological ends, the
best known is perhaps the dramatist Edward Bond. His play *Bingo*, with its
rather more immediately informative sub-title *Scenes of money and death*, was
first performed in 1973 and takes Shakespeare as necessarily representative of
a cruel and oppressive social order. In his introduction to the published text,
Bond says that however much Shakespeare's plays may show a need for justice,
his own 'behaviour as a property-owner made him closer to Goneril than Lear.
He supported and benefited from the Goneril-society – with its prisons,
workhouses, whipping, starvation, mutilation, pulpit-hysteria and all the rest
of it.'[43] The focus in the play is on an episode from Shakespeare's later life
briefly described in Chapter 1 above: the proposal to enclose some of the land
from which he drew tithe income. Bond takes care to itemise in his
introduction all the changes which he feels he has had to make to the historical
record for dramatic convenience: giving Shakespeare only one daughter instead
of two, making one of his known associates, William Combe, alone responsible
for the enclosure proposals, omitting Drayton from the 'last binge' with Jonson,
or shifting the date of the fire at the Globe from 1613 to 1616. He says he
mentions these changes because he wants 'to protect the play from petty
criticism. It is based on the material historical facts as far as they are known,
and on psychological truth as far as I know it'.[44] Some of the force of his play
depends on his public's awareness of the iconic status of its central figure and
he clearly feels that this force might be less, if petty critics could complain that
the real Shakespeare was nothing like the figure they saw depicted.

Bingo opens in 1615 with Shakespeare in his garden at Stratford, gloomily
laconic and alienated from his daughter Judith and from his bed-ridden wife
(who is referred to quite often in the play but never seen). The appearance of a
female vagrant more or less coincides with the arrival of Combes to discuss the
enclosure project and, because he is a local magistrate, she is sent off to be
whipped. The second scene takes place six months later in the same location
when Combe arrives to secure Shakespeare's signature on the document
indemnifying him against any loss should the enclosure project go ahead. In
the meantime the female vagrant has been driven distracted by her whipping.
Hidden and protected by an old man who works for Shakespeare and whose

wife is also his servant, she has taken to lighting fires in the area. That her appearance at New Place again coincides in this second scene with that of Combes hastens her arrest and in the third she has been hanged and her body exhibited on a gibbet. Scene 3 takes place in front of this gibbet with Shakespeare contemplating both the young vagrant's fate and the cruelty of life in general. As will have been evident on many occasions already, a major problem for all those who offer fictional portraits of Shakespeare, and who resist the temptation to have him speaking lines from his own plays, is to give him dialogue which corresponds to the reader's or listener's sense of his intellectual and linguistic distinction. That apparent divorce between artist and work which Proust is so fond of dramatising, may mean that the expectation of always hearing something special from Shakespeare is unreasonable, but there is an inevitable discomfort when the author of *Macbeth* is made to sound as if nothing but banalities could ever pass his lips. For most of his play, Bond solves this problem by having a Shakespeare who is so preoccupied with his own gloomy thoughts, and so alienated from his immediate physical and human environment, that he hardly says anything. But in Scene 3, as his daughter tries to bring him away from the gibbet and take him home, he soliloquises at some length on what his experience of life has taught him.

JUDITH:	Come home.
SHAKESPEARE:	Later. (*He sits.*)
JUDITH:	You're hungry.
SHAKESPEARE:	Why do . . . ? I thought I knew the questions. Have I forgotten them?
JUDITH:	People will stroll out here to look after work. They'll talk if you sit there. We know what she was. (SHAKESPEARE *doesn't react.*) You were out all yesterday. Did you see her hang?
SHAKESPEARE:	The baited bear. Tied to the stake. Its dirty coat needs brushing. Dried mud and spume. Pale dust. Big clumsy fists. Men bringing dogs through the gate. Leather collars with spikes. Loose them and fight. The bear wanders round the stake. It knows it can't get away. The chain. Dogs on three sides. Fur in the mouth. Deeper. (*The* OLD WOMAN *comes on upstage right.*) Flesh and blood. Strips of skin. Teeth scrapping bone. The bear will crush one of the skulls. Big feet slithering in dog's brain. Round the stake. On and on. The key in the warder's pocket. Howls. Roars. Men baiting their beast. On and on and on. And later the bear raises its great arm. The paw with a broken razor. And it looks as if it's making a gesture – it wasn't: only weariness or pain or the sun or brushing away the sweat – but it looks as if it's making a gesture to the crowd. Asking for one sign of grace, one no. And the crowd roars, for more blood, more pain, more beasts huddled together, tearing flesh and treading in living blood.
JUDITH:	You don't like sport. Some bears dance.
SHAKESPEARE:	In London they blinded a bear. Called Harry Hunks. The sport was to bait it with whips. Slash, slash. It couldn't see but it could hear. It grabbed the whips. Caught some of them. Broke them. Slashed back at the men. Slash, slash. The men stood round in a circle slashing at

it. It was blind but they still chained it to the ground. Slash, slash. Then they sent an ape round on a horse. A thin hairy man or a child. You could see the pale skin under its arm when it jumped. Its teeth. The dogs tore it to pieces. The crowd howled. London. The queen cheered them on in shrill latin. The virgin often watched blood. Her father baited bears on the Thames. From boat to boat, slash, slash. They fell in and fought men in the water. He was the man in a mad house who says I'm king but he had a country to say it in.

JUDITH: I must go down. Someone must watch the house, count the glasses, knives, spoons. I shan't ask you to listen any more. You're only interested in your ideas. You treat us as enemies. (JUDITH *walks upstage to the* OLD WOMAN. *The* OLD WOMAN *puts her arm round her and silently tries to comfort her.*)

SHAKESPEARE: What does it cost to stay alive? I'm stupefied at the suffering I've seen. The shapes huddled in misery that twitch away when you step over them. Women with shopping bags stepping over puddles of blood. What it costs to starve people. The chatter of those who hand over prisoners. The smile of men who see no further than the end of a knife. Stupefied. How can I go back to that? What can I do there? I talk to myself now. I know no one will ever listen.

(*The* Old Woman *comes down to* SHAKESPEARE.)

OLD WOMAN: A gen'man's come from London. At the Golden Cross. (*She hands a note to* SHAKESPEARE.) He sent this up by me.

SHAKESPEARE: There's no higher wisdom of silence. No face brooding over the water. (*The* OLD WOMAN *glances helplessly up at* JUDITH.) No hand leading the waves to the shore as if it's saving a dog from the sea. When I go to my theatre I walk under sixteen severed heads on a gate. You hear bears in the pit while my characters talk.

OLD WOMAN: Now, sir. That's bin a longish winter. That's brought yo' down.

SHAKESPEARE: No other hand . . . no face . . . just these . . .

OLD WOMAN (*to* JUDITH): I'll bring him hwome. (JUDITH *goes out.*)

SHAKESPEARE: Stupid woman! They stand under a gallows and ask if it rains. Terrible. Terrible. What is the right question? I said be still. I quietened the storms inside me. But the storm breaks outside. To have usurped the place of god, and lied . . .

OLD WOMAN: Why torment yo'self? You'm never harmed no –

SHAKESPEARE: And my daughter?

OLD WOMAN: No, no. Yo' yont named for cruelty. They say yo'm a generous man. Yo' looked arter me an'father. Give us one a your houses t' live in.

SHAKESPEARE (*points*): There's a coin. I saw it when I came up. Glittering in the grass.

OLD WOMAN (*goes immediately to where* SHAKESPEARE *pointed*): Here?

SHAKESPEARE: Perhaps the hangman dropped it.

OLD WOMAN (*picks up the coin*): We'm put a little by for later. Times change. Read your note.[45]

It has often disturbed more recent admirers of Shakespeare that his theatre flourished alongside such a sport as bear-baiting and that the highly educated Queen perhaps enjoyed it more than she did watching plays (see the extract from *Kenilworth* above). Bond associates its cruelty with social injustice by having Shakespeare speak in front of the body of the gibbeted woman and by references like those to 'the shapes huddled in misery that twitch away when you step over them.' With severed heads on gates, this is the everyday barbarity of Elizabethan life (although the 'Women with shopping bags' sounds an incongruously modern note). In Bond's depiction Shakespeare has reached a stage in his life when injustice and cruelty strike with a force which alienates him from those around him, those whose main concern is keeping an eye on the family silver or saving for the future; and he appears to be regretting that he did nothing in his own work to protest against the status quo ('To have usurped the place of god, and lied . . .').

The note which the old woman has given Shakespeare announces a visit from Ben Jonson. In the fourth scene the two dramatists are in the local tavern, much the worse for drink. Jonson has brought news of the fire at the Globe and finds it hard to believe that his companion is not still writing. He delivers a humorous harangue, describing his own troubled career and contrasting it bitterly with what he regards as the serenity and calm of Shakespeare's progress through life. In response Shakespeare hardly speaks and eventually slumps forward unconscious across the table. Neither writer is therefore in a condition to notice much when four local farmers come in after having just filled in the ditches which Combe has had dug as a preliminary to the enclosure process or when Combe himself then enters, rightly suspecting that these four are the culprits. It is only in scene 5, when he is wandering in the snow after his meeting with Jonson, looking towards his own house but reluctant to go in it, that Shakespeare finds much to say.

SHAKESPEARE:	The door's opened. I drank too much. I must be calm. Don't fall about in front of them. Why did I drink all that? Fool! Fool! At my age . . . Why not? I am a fool. Why did I come back here? I wanted to meet some god by the river. Ask him questions. See his mouth open and the lips move. Hear simple things that move mountains and stop the blood before it hits the earth. Stop it so there's time to think. I was wrong to come - mistakes, mistakes. But I can't go back. That hate, anger -
	(JUDITH *comes in. She wears a green cloak.*)
JUDITH:	Walk all night in the fields if you like. I don't mind. But not when it's snowed. Mother's crying.
SHAKESPEARE:	Who woke her?
JUDITH:	It's late and I'm tired.
SHAKESPEARE:	Who?
JUDITH:	Another scene.
SHAKESPEARE:	Why did you do it? What can she do? Cry!
JUDITH:	When you behave like a child you'll be treated like one.
SHAKESPEARE:	Listen. You'll get my property between you when I'm dead. When I ran away from your mother and went to London - I was so bored, she's such a silly woman, obstinate, and you take after her. Forgive me, I know that's cruel, sordid, but it's such an effort to be polite

259

any more. That other age when I ran away, I couldn't cut you out, you were my flesh, but I thought I could make you forgive me: I started to collect for you. I loved you with money. The only thing I can afford to give you now is money. But money always turns to hate. If I tried to be nice to you now it would be sentimental. You'd have to understand why I hate you, respect me for it, even love me for it. How can you? I treated you so badly. I made you vulgar and ugly and cheap. I corrupted you.

JUDITH: Go on. I'm not listening. I'm young and this coat's warm. I'll wait till you drop and then have you dragged in.

SHAKESPEARE: Don't be angry because I hate you, Judith. My hatred isn't angry. It's cold and formal. I wouldn't harm you. I'll help you, give my life for you - all in hatred. There's no limit to my hate. It can't be satisfied by cruelty. It's destroyed too much to be satisfied so easily. Only truth can satisfy it now. I don't think all this matters to you, I can't hate you more than when I say that. (*Judith goes out.*) The last snow this year. Perhaps the last snow I shall see. The last fall. (*He kneels on the ground and picks up some snow.*) How cold. (*He half smiles.*) How perfect, but it only lasts one night. When I was young I'd have written on it with a stick. A song. The moon over the snow, a woman stares at her dead . . . What? In the morning the sun would melt it into mortality. Writing in the snow - a child's hand fumbling in an old man's beard, and in the morning the old man dies, goes, taking the curls from the child's fingers into the grave, and the child laughs and plays under the dead man's window. New games. Now *I'm* old. Where is the child to touch me and lead me to the grave? Serene. Serene. Is that how they see me? (*He laughs a little.*) I didn't know. (*The dark* FIGURES *run back across the top of the stage. Their heavy breathing is heard. They go off left.*) Snow. It doesn't melt. My hand's cold. (*He breathes on the snow in his hand.*) It doesn't melt. I must be very cold. Serene. How? When you're running from hangers and breakers and killers. The mad clown still nurses the child.

> *Far upstage a shot and a spurt of flame.*

Every writer writes in other men's blood. The trivial, and the real. There's nothing else to write in. But only a god or a devil can write in other men's blood and not ask why they spilt it and what it cost. Not this hand, that's always melted snow . . . (SHAKESPEARE *lies forward on the ground. A dark* FIGURE *appears upstage. It cries and whimpers weakly and then vanishes.*) I didn't want to die. I could lie in this snow a whole life. I can think now, the thoughts come so easily over the snow and under my shroud. New worlds. Keys turning new locks - pushing the iron open like lion's teeth. Wolves will drag me through the snow. I'll sit in their lair and smile and be rich. In the morning or when I die the sun will rise and melt it all away. The dream. The wolves. The iron teeth. The snow. The wind. My voice. A dream that leads to sleep. (*He sits up.*) I'm dead now. Soon I shall fall down. If I wasn't dead I could kill myself. What is the ice inside me? The plague is hot - this is so cold. The truth means nothing when you hate. Was anything done? Was anything done? I sit in a wound as large as a valley. The sides are smooth and cold and grey. I sit at the bottom and cry at my own death.[46]

During his harangue at the inn, Jonson has described how he has come to hate Shakespeare because of the apparent simplicity of his life, which contrasts so much with his own. The implication is that it is this simplicity which has given Shakespeare his serenity. Bond here has his central character giving the lie to Jonson but also to that image of Shakespeare calmly floating above the troubles of the world which partly derives from Arnold's famous sonnet. He retreats for the last time to his bedroom in New Place an angry and disappointed man. When his daughter and his hysterical wife try to see him he sends them away by slipping the pages of his will under the door and accepts only the attentions of the old woman whose feeble-minded husband, wandering in the snow at the same time as Shakespeare, has been accidentally shot by his own son (one of the active anti-enclosure protesters). In their tavern talk, Jonson had boasted of a poison bottle which he always carried with him and which it now turns out Shakespeare has borrowed. Asking himself frequently 'Was anything done?', he is thus able to commit suicide, a bitterly disenchanted man. All his writing success, and the money that it brought, has come to seem meaningless in comparison with the human suffering he sees all around and in which he is implicated indirectly or perhaps even directly – although this is a point Bond does not seem anxious to stress – because of his signature on the indemnity document.

Terence Hawkes, an academic whose political convictions are similar to those of Bond, has criticised him for being simple-minded. 'The question to be asked,' he writes in *That Shakespeherian Rag* (1986), 'is not the rather naïve one posed by Edward Bond's play *Bingo*: how could a man who wrote the great tragedies behave as he did in the face of suffering humanity? The more probing enquiry asks how could he not?'[47] Whether or not the question Hawkes reports Bond as asking is in fact naïve, that word would hardly be a fair description of how he treats it. Scrupulous in giving at least some dramatic force to the case for enclosure, Bond refuses to sentimentalise its putative victims, and, unlike Hawkes in the account he offers of the episode, he convincingly suggests that the opposition of the Stratford Corporation to the proposals was not merely humanitarian but a result of anxiety about a greater number of poor people becoming an increasing burden on the already over-stretched Corporation funds. At no point does he imply that those who drew up the document which promised to indemnify Shakespeare (should that have become necessary) ever intended its terms to be in exchange for his active support. He sees complexity in the enclosure issue whereas what is complex in Hawkes are the methods he employs to ensure that he can pursue a parallel between Shakespeare and Prospero as both tellers of tales and rack-rent landlords. And yet Hawkes's 'how could he not?' remains a potent challenge. However much some might like to feel that Shakespeare was a man with liberal views on all social issues, fully conversant with the work of the Hammonds on the evils of enclosure, he was necessarily (*pace* Jonson) a man of his own age rather than ours. To judge properly his attitude on what are now politically sensitive issues, one would have to have developed, from deep immersion in the period and comparison with his contemporaries, a sense of the range of possibilities for a man of his time. Yet even with that sense, judgement would not be feasible because, in most cases, there is not enough surviving evidence to tell us what Shakespeare's attitude actually was.

The use which Bond makes of the known or supposed details of Shakespeare's life is 'political' in the more narrowly defined sense of that word and one of the inevitable implications of *Bingo* is that it represents the kind of drama which would have enabled Shakespeare to look back on his life with more satisfaction had he himself chosen (or been able) to write it. The manner in which he exploits his subject's iconic status is unusual but not unique. In the field of drama, for example, a later representation of Shakespeare which is broadly in the tradition of Bond can be found in Frank McGuinness's *Mutabilitie*. This has Shakespeare and two fellow actors (Richard and Ben) washed up in Ireland around 1598, soon after the Munster wars, and meeting there Edmund Spenser who spends much of the play pondering the ethics of bringing Protestant enlightenment to the benighted Catholic Irish. Like *Bingo*, *Mutabilitie* is concerned with the responsibilities of writers in an environment of political oppression and injustice, although quite what McGuinness wants to say on that topic is made difficult to understand by his choice of a dramatic mode which seems to owe more to Yeats than Brecht. Certainly many of the critics of its first performance in London in 1997 were baffled by it.[48]

Mutabilitie could perhaps be cited as an example of the *vie imaginaire* rather than the *vie romancée* in that there is no historical justification for placing Shakespeare in Ireland, nor any solid evidence that he ever met Spenser (who spent most of his professional life there). But our knowledge of Shakespeare's movements is so poor that trips to Ireland (or Italy) can never be *completely* ruled out and evidence that Spenser at least admired his younger contemporary, and may therefore have sought to meet him, has been found in these once much discussed lines from his *Tears of the Muses*:

> And he the man, whom Nature self had made
> To mock her self, and Truth to imitate,
> With kindly counter under Mimic shade,
> Our pleasant Willy, ah is dead of late:
> With whom all joy and jolly merriment
> Is also deaded, and in dolour drent.[49]

The general context here is a complaint about the decline of comedy from its muse, Thalia, but although Shakespeare's first name was certainly William neither he himself nor (an alternative meaning) his productive powers could be described as 'dead of late' in 1591 when *The Tears of the Muses* was first published. As a consequence, Chambers was able to describe the idea that there is an allusion to Shakespeare in these lines as 'universally rejected',[50] yet it is one any author might feel entitled to develop in a work where the practice is not to produce an imaginary portrait of Shakespeare out of nothing but rather to work with the accumulated mass of known fact, legend and conjecture. It is this practice which explains why McGuinness's Shakespeare, who is never given his second name and who is presented as homosexual, secretly Catholic and cut off from the world around him, is in one sense controversially different but in another reassuringly recognisable and familiar.

Like Bond, and like also his fellow, contemporary playwright Peter Whelan,[51] McGuinness takes what might be described as an avant-garde view of certain elements in the historical record or the mythos. Although their interests are not similarly political in any narrow sense, the same is true of Burgess and (to a lesser extent) Nye. More representative of the mainstream is John Mortimer whose *Will Shakespeare* was published in 1977. Instead of concentrating on one particular phase, this novel encompasses the whole of its subject's career, using the known facts as a framework, filling the gaps with imaginative reconstructions but also, since the chief aim is after all entertainment, making free use of the myths and legends. Thus it is that the narrator, a former boy actor who is writing at the time of the Interregnum when the theatres have been closed, can say, 'When I first knew Shakespeare, he tended horses outside the old Rose theatre', and then go on to describe how the stage-struck young man from Stratford was given his first chance in the theatre because of his ability to imitate a cock-crow.[52] Like many before him, Mortimer finds it convenient to assume that Shakespeare collaborated with Marlowe on the *Henry VI* plays since that allows him an easy method for introducing into the action a particularly colourful figure. In his version, Shakespeare is obliged to take over more and more of the writing of *Henry VI* because Marlowe is increasingly involved in spying. It is through Marlowe that Shakespeare is introduced to the Elizabethan underworld, one of whose denizens, a young horse thief called Hal, turns out to be the disguised Earl of Southampton in search of excitement. This is to say the least highly improbable, but the account of Southampton's background which Mortimer then offers is more or less straight from the history books and he does face squarely a question which all those who assume there was some close relation between Southampton and Shakespeare have to ask themselves (in his old age the narrator of *Will Shakespeare* has become a sexton at a local church).

> What manner of friendship was it then, between this poet and that Lord? It is a question that must be enquired into, although only at night, and behind the

locked door of this vestry; but I can tell you only what I know of it, and what I have heard, and the final answer must be yours to decide on as you will.

First may be asked what drew them together, when their stations in life were so different. There was a learned Doctor here, caught in a hay loft with his serving wench, a girl but thirteen with no letters in her head, who yet denied adultery. Asked what drove him to this chit's company he answered, 'Why, only that we discussed the wisdom of Seneca together.' He was not believed. But it can well be thought that Poet and Peer had much to talk of, besides their common experiences of the world of thieves. And it's certain Hal thought himself in need of a verse-maker who could cheat death for him, and Shakespeare found in the company of such lively beauty of form and person that which made him careless of whether his verses made either one of them immortal or no.

During this time Hal was often summoned to appear at Court and coming back reported all that had been said by the Queen and the Great Lords and those sweet Ladies, tumbled as often as nine-pins in the Royal Gardens, who were called the Queen's 'Glories'. All this was necessary information to Will, who would make Kings and Queens and Great Lords in the Theatre, and where could he better learn their tongue than at the Earl of Southampton's table? When I think of the plays, I remember he could write Panders and Princes, Rogues and Royalty well; but there are few solid burghers or honest shop-keepers there. So his characters seem to come either from the Jolly Struggler or Titchfield Abbey. So may his long friendship with Hal be explained other then by lusts and passion.

When at Titchfield, Shakespeare also had occasion to meet Hal's mother, who had become a garrulous old dame and, perhaps because of her light behaviour in the past, found it no shame to prattle to a Poet and a Playmaker (unlike some of the well-born guests who sat above the salt and would not think it at all befitting to talk to one who came from the brothel world of the London Theatres. Such a proud Popinjay was Southampton's exquisite cousin Anthony Browne, who thought it an insult that any servant should turn his back upon his master's roast while it was a'cooking. Him Will Shakespeare frightened so by dressing as an old woman whom the first Earl had burned at the stake come back to haunt Titchfield, that Master Browne ran screeching out of the Abbey one Twelfth Night and was never there more.) As I say the old Countess spoke much to Shakespeare of her longing to see her Hal with an heir, and he repeated her advice, somewhat improved as to the expression, in the verses he wrote her son: but I question whether he was mightily concerned as to his friend's feats of fatherhood, I think he rather wrote these lines to calm an old lady whose past had been too exciting and whose present too dull.

It is true that in one of the poems he wrote to Hal, Shakespeare spoke of that addition which doting nature bestowed upon his patron (whom he there called his 'Master-Mistress') whereby he was defeated of the enjoyment of his beloved who, he agrees, was 'prickt' out for women's pleasure. Some may think this verse closes the door on all speculation; but I, who know all the stir and scandal caused when these same sonnets first became public, think this may be a verse added to silence those who might suspect that Hal, though 'prickt', was not thereby placed beyond the full reach of him whose passion is therein made clear. On the other side I must agree that Shakespeare, unlike his teacher Marlowe, would rather lie with a girl or a woman if one could be had, and although he may have been bewitched by some boys, he never, by a nod, a wink, or a hand to the waist, far less to the buttock, made me a suggestion when I was young and parted as all his

Fairest Ladies. This I find most strange.

And what of Hal? He at that time set his face most stubborn against breeding, and was so firm against obeying his guardian's command to marry with Lady Vere, that old Burghley, as he was empowered to do by law, fined him £5,000 all to be paid at once. This Hal did, although it left his estate sorely maimed, and Lady Vere earned fame through England as the woman it cost most not to tumble. I believe Hal thought all women then as false as his mother, and, in his heart, Shakespeare had no rival.

So I sit here, a chilly old man writing in a blanket and mittens, who has less chance of sporting between silken sheets with a young Earl than of becoming Lord Chief Justice of England. And it seems to me I must be done with this key-hole spying and there shall be no more of it. If they did not the act of darkness, which is the act of loving, they could not have loved each other more; and if they did it they could not thereby have loved each other less.

I hold to the opinion, all things being considered, that they did. Let us say no more upon the subject but proceed with our history.[53]

In support of his narrator's assertion that Shakespeare would 'rather lie with a girl or a woman if one could be had' Mortimer gives a good deal of space to the 'dark lady'. She turns out to be the young wife of an old judge whom Shakespeare first sees when his company is performing *The Two Gentlemen of Verona* in the Middle Temple. In order to see his plays in the public theatre, the wife disguises herself a boy and meets him later at a room in the shop of apothecary where she is, however, reluctant to grant him the final favours. In a manipulation of the Manningham anecdote, it is Southampton who secures these instead and arranges that Shakespeare should come to the shop just as he is in enjoying them. This is in revenge for what he thinks of as Shakespeare's disloyalty in not having told him about the dark lady.

More than most of his predecessors, Mortimer is concerned with the fate of Hamnet. When Shakespeare goes home to see his family (stopping off on the way to see Mistress Davenant in Oxford, the mother of his other son), Hamnet refuses to speak. It turns out that he has taken a vow to remain silent until his father returns to his family permanently but this fact only emerges after Shakespeare has been obliged to take his son to London; so that it is there, rather than in Stratford, that Hamnet dies. After his death Mortimer cannot resist the Essex rebellion (why indeed should he?). In his account a group of the Lord Chamberlain's Men, which fortunately includes the narrator, is taken by Southampton to Essex house where the two Earls positively plead with Shakespeare to put on *Richard II*. Although this episode stretches the known facts, it is in keeping with the tradition of bringing Shakespeare as close as possible to the major actors in Elizabethan public life, and it is in accordance with that same tradition that Mortimer has him meet the Queen twice. On the second occasion, which comes after the failure of the rebellion, Shakespeare pleads for Southampton's life which is assumed to be still in danger after he has been confined to the Tower.

One of the major puzzles of Shakespeare's career is what the addressee of the Sonnets, always supposing there was such a person, would have thought of their publication, and how Anne Shakespeare might have reacted had she been able to read them. In Mortimer's novel the Sonnets are stolen and piratically published in a cheap version which predates the text of 1609 and which reaches as far as Stratford.

In Stratford on Avon there was, as elsewhere, loyal rejoicing at the Coronation of James, that great and wise Christian Monarch. Citizens who had never seen him fiddle or dribble lit bonfires, danced Morrises, held fairs and drank rivers of bastard ale. There was a fair at Stratford and Judith Shakespeare, twin of the deceased Hamnet, now eighteen, was attracted to the tray of a pedlar. From him she bought ribbons, buttons, a love charm and a vilely-printed pamphlet to which she was attracted by reading on the front of it her father's name, and further interested by a notice saying it contained Sundry Sonnets of Love. So she took the pamphlet home.

Many years after, Hamnet Sadler remembered the explosion that then took place, and how he sat at the Shakespeares' table trying to calm his nerves with a cup of mulberry wine whilst Mistress Anne stalked the room in her outrage, and ever and again flourished the dreadful printing in his face.

'Two loves I have of comfort and despair . . .'

Anne was giving Hamnet a dramatic reading.

'Which like two spirits do suggest me still
The better angel is a man right fair!'

She paused, appalled at the confession.

'The worser spirit a woman coloured ill . . .'

'My child Judith bought this off a pedlar!'

'Why, no man should have two loves, truly!' Hamnet was suitably shocked.

'If he had stopped at two! How many are there? A dark, dusky woman. Moorish? Do you think she's Moorish, Hamnet?' Having read so far Anne thought anything possible.

'Not Moorish, surely!' Hamnet was not exactly sure what being Moorish might imply.

'And a light gentleman. It makes me sick to read it!'

'Some painted player, surely, that apes a petticoat,' said Hamnet with disgust.

'He has done some wickedness. Great wickedness, as do all those who haunt playhouses and bear-baits and bowling alleys.'

'Aye, men will do wickedness, round the bowling alleys.'

Hamnet spoke from his knowledge of the world.

'But not to brag of it!' Anne released her rage. 'Not to blast a trumpet and have it called out by the town Crier to shame his wife and daughters! I could burn to death with this humiliation. To have it printed out in a broadsheet like a vulgar ballad. Who knows how much more of this Devil's handiwork may be a'printing? What then, will Master Parson read it? Or the Mayor and Aldermen? Or all our neighbours? What will lady Lucy think?'

'We may get the printing stopped. We may complain to the Justices.' Hamnet saw that some step must be taken.

'I'd be ashamed to have the Justices see this. What, Sir Thomas Lucy and old Squire Dawson, him who once stood my godfather, should I go and tell them I am betrayed for a Moorish doxie and an actor in petticoats?'

'We need a power! Some Great Lord who Will's afraid of, to make him keep this silent!' Hamnet had the first inkling of an inspiration.

'A man who could write this fears neither his God nor his wife, nor any Great Lord either. Oh, Hamnet, Neighbour Hamnet, why did he seek to wound us so?' Anne's rage softened to tears.

'Danged if I know, neighbour Anne.' Hamnet finished his mulberry wine. 'It's a mystery. Why, a man may sin; all men do sin a little. But why, in the name of Lucifer, must they needs write poetry about it?'[54]

This effort to evoke provincial life in Elizabethan England, just as it becomes Jacobean, is typical of *Will Shakespeare* as a whole. There is here the historical friend after whom it has always been reasonably presumed Hamnet Shakespeare was named, and 'real' local gentry like the Lucys; but there is also part of that period paraphernalia with which thousands of novels and films have made the general public familiar: Morris dancing, bastard ale and mulberry wine. This goes together with forms of address (Master Parson, neighbour Anne) which, whatever their degree of authenticity, do as much to say 'Elizabethan' as the fringe famously said 'Roman' for Roland Barthes.[55] This is period writing of a popular kind, although whether Hamnet Sadler finishing his mulberry wine does enough to offset his saying 'Danged' is doubtful, since the *OED* does not record a use of 'dang' as a euphemism for 'damn' before 1793.

The status of *Will Shakespeare* as a 'popular' text is confirmed by the fact that it was also a six-part television series. This guaranteed that the image of Shakespeare which Mortimer presented should be widely disseminated, although the scale of that dissemination was as nothing compared with the success achieved twenty years later by the film I mentioned briefly in the chapter on the Sonnets, John Madden's *Shakespeare in Love* (1998). Like *Bingo*, this Oscar-winning film concentrated on a particular moment in Shakespeare's career, but one from the beginning rather than the end. Bond took his subject at the close of his life, after he had become wealthy, and one way of describing his treatment is to say that he is asking a question which had been provocatively raised by Pope as early as the eighteenth century:

> Shakespear (whom you and ev'ry Play-house bill
> Style the divine, the matchless, what you will)
> For gain, not glory, wing'd his roving flight,
> And grew Immortal in his own despight.[56]

This notion of a Shakespeare who wrote only for money was uncomfortably confirmed for some by the bust in Stratford church (Dover Wilson's 'self-satisfied pork butcher'), but the makers of *Shakespeare in Love* turned not to that image but to the Chandos portrait, presenting a Shakespeare who in his early days lived from hand to mouth, a bohemian with a touch of the gypsy. Theirs is the traditional Romantic view of the artist, needing money only so that body and soul can be kept together and more art produced. At the end of the film Shakespeare's acquisition of the £50 which will allow him to become a sharer in Burbage's company, and to thereby embark on that career of bourgeois authorship which interests Bond, is entirely incidental to its hero's main concerns.

Shakespeare in Love begins in a manner very like *No Bed for Bacon* (certain resemblances were noted at the time of its first showing). Typical of jokes which Brahms and Simon would have appreciated is the appearance of a young boy who, before feeding a live mouse to a cat, explains that the only kind of plays he likes are those with rapes and killings and who then says that his name is John Webster; or Shakespeare's visit to an Elizabethan doctor of the Simon Forman variety who doubles as a Freudian analyst. These are a reminder of the two levels on which fictions about Shakespeare usually operate (one of them for those in the know) but also that the film was co-authored by Tom Stoppard, a name which suggests how difficult it would be to attempt any rigorous definition of the word 'popular'. Shakespeare's visit to the doctor is necessary because he has become impotent, in his sexual dealings, perhaps, but above all in his creative life. What he lacks, it emerges, is the kind of inspiration which will shortly be provided by the young woman played by Gwyneth Paltrow. It is with her appearance that the film starts to mutate from a comedy of the Brahms and Simon variety into a romantic love story. Although humour remains present throughout, it becomes increasingly secondary as the love interest develops.

Douglas Lanier's defence of modern popular culture in its dealings with Shakespeare, which I quoted earlier on p. 256, is often in conflict with other features of his general, ideological position. In the chapter in which he discusses *Shakespeare in Love*, for example, he notes how resistant popular culture has been to 'the insights of contemporary criticism'.[57] What he is thinking of in particular is the insistence of Barthes, Foucault and others on the death of the author. Certainly in Madden's film, any idea that literary expression might not be a direct consequence of an author's own personal experience is discounted. Once he has seen and fallen in love with Viola de Lesseps, as Paltrow's character is called, Shakespeare is inspired to transform the pot-boiler he is listlessly trying to write into *Romeo and Juliet* and, from then on, extracts from the rehearsals of that play alternate so often with scenes in which he enacts with Viola its chief love story that it becomes hard to tell the difference. This is the Romantic view of authorship according to which language is freely chosen by writers rather than speaking through them, and a play is written from pressing personal need and not because its author has listened to various colleagues, consulted antecedents or responded to public expectation.

35. *Joseph Fiennes as Shakespeare. Note the ear-ring. Still from the film,* Shakespeare in Love, *1998. Photograph used under licence from Miramax FIlm Corp. All rights reserved.*

Sexuality is another area in which Lanier's enthusiasm for manifestations of popular culture appears to be in conflict with the very principles which inspire it. 'An unfortunately typical feature of Shakespeare romances', he writes, 'is the depiction of Shakespeare's love-life as conventionally heterosexual (if he is allowed an erotic life at all), a portrayal which closes off other forms of desire to which his plays and the cross-dressed stage clearly seem addressed).'[58] As he later notes, *Shakespeare in Love* is 'unfortunately typical' in this way. There is in the film one kiss between the disguised Viola and Shakespeare while she is still in male clothing. But in the first place it is she who kisses him and, in the second, Shakespeare learns almost immediately her true identity so that shock is succeeded in him by the feeling that all is right with the world after all. Not that his love for Viola could ever run smoothly: there is too much social difference between the two parties for that and, in any case, Viola's rich, merchant father has promised her to an unpleasant nobleman, in an exchange of money for status. Even Queen Elizabeth, who plays in the film a similar *dea ex machina* role to that she performs in many nineteenth-century novels or plays,

269

cannot prevent this business arrangement going ahead, although a dream-like finale intimates that the love between a common playwright and wealthy gentlewoman has perhaps not been quite as doomed as that between the two young lovers in the play Shakespeare has been writing. A completely sad ending would not do. *Shakespeare in Love* benefited from a witty screenplay, was exceptionally well acted and skilfully shot. Its huge success, which may have been helped by that of Buz Luhrmann's *Romeo and Juliet*, is not therefore too surprising. What it reinforced was a public belief that the author of the world's greatest love story could not but have been a lover himself, and a pretty good-looking one at that. This is why Joseph Fiennes, in the role of Shakespeare, sports the earring of the Chandos portrait rather than the doublet of the Trinity church bust or, more significantly since the bust clearly represents a Shakespeare in middle age, the wired collar of the Doeshout engraving.

Of these three portraits it is of course only the bust and the engraving which have any real claim to authenticity, but it is hard to find a romantic lover in either of them. At the beginning of the chapter in Lanier's book from which I have been quoting, however, he does suggest how the engraving at least, because it lacks the usual 'classicizing and allegorical paraphernalia', can serve the purposes of icon construction.

> Whether or not Droeshout captured Shakespeare's likeness accurately, what he conveys is Shakespeare's compelling, mature, self-possessed but finally enigmatic intellect. The Droeshout portrait inaugurates the myth of Shakespeare the self-made author, a man whose literary stature springs not from divine inspiration, patronage connections, or classical education, but rather from the productions of his own formidable brain. Part of the portrait's appeal may be that it provides an icon for the then-emergent, now-dominant ideology of the bourgeois subject, the notion, most famously formulated by Descartes, that the mind is the sole determinant and source of one's identity, a notion that, when translated into 'I can be what I want', accords perfectly with middle-class upward mobility and the rise of advanced capitalism.[59]

Here then is the money-making Shakespeare which *Shakespeare in Love* denies, or which it post-dates, although whether this way of 'reading' the Droeshout engraving accurately represents how it was read in the past, or is merely a reflection of Lanier's own perspective on the history of Western culture, is a matter for debate.

Notes

1. E. Hamilton Gruner, *With Golden Quill* (Stratford-upon-Avon, 1936), p. 165.
2. *The Times*, 30 April, 1947.
3. Gruner, p. 166.
4. *Ibid.*, p. x.

5. *Ibid.*, p. 64.

6. *Ibid.*, p. 13.

7. *Ibid.*, p. 63.

8. See Chambers, vol. 2, p. 42. Why Anne Shakespeare should have been holding some of Whittington's money has never been made clear. There is some dispute as to whether the land mortgaged to the Lamberts was indeed Asbies or some other property.

9. Gruner, p. 202.

10. G. P. V. Akrigg, *Shakespeare and the Earl of Southampton* (1968), p. 223.

11. *Ibid.*, pp. 41-6 for a full account of how Southampton helped the two Danvers brothers to escape abroad after the death of Long.

12. Stanley Wells, *Shakespeare for All Time* (Oxford University Press, 2003), p. 14.

13. Gruner, p. 202.

14. *Ibid.*, p. 184.

15. *Ibid.*, p. 186.

16. Caryl Brahms and S. J. Simon, *No Bed for Bacon* (Penguin Books, 1948), p. 6.

17. See Michael Dobson and Stanley Wells (eds), *The Oxford Companion to Shakespeare* (Oxford University Press, 2001), p. 261.

18. The importance of the sweet wine monopoly to Essex is described in great detail in Paul E. J. Hamer, *The Polarisation of Elizabethan Politics. The Political Career of Robert Devereux, 2nd Earl of Essex, 1585-97* (Cambridge University Press, 1999).

19. For details of the fire which destroyed the Globe see Schoenbaum, *A Documentary Life*, p. 224.

20. *No Bed for Bacon*, pp. 131-5.

21. *Ibid.*, p. 14.

22. *Ibid.*, pp. 255-6.

23. Schoenbaum, *Shakespeare's Lives*, p. 431.

24. See Ivor Brown and George Fearon, *The Shakespeare Industry. Amazing Monument* (1939), pp. 272-85.

25. Gruner, p. 197.

26. For an excellent account see Schoenbaum, *Shakespeare's Lives*, pp. 386-93.

27. Douglas Lanier, *Shakespeare and Modern Popular Culture* (Oxford University Press, 2002), p. 112.

28. *Flook at 30: A Celebration* (University of Kent: Centre for the Study of Cartoons and Caricature, 1979), p. 12.

29. Harold Bloom, *The Western Cannon: The Books and Schools of the Ages* (1995), p. 416.

30. Anthony Burgess, *Nothing Like the Sun* (Penguin Books, 1966), pp. 33-6.

31. See Schoenbaum, *A Documentary Life*, pp. 70-1.

32. See Schoenbaum, *Shakespeare's Lives*, p. 497.

33. *Nothing Like the Sun*, pp. 135-8.

34. Akrigg, *Shakespeare and the Earl of Southampton*, p. 39.

35. See *Enderby's Dark Lady* (1984), *A Dead Man in Deptford* (1993), 'A Meeting in Valladolid' in *The Devil's Mode* (1989).

36. Douglas Lanier gives brief accounts of several of these works in *Shakespeare and Modern Popular Culture*.

37. Lanier, p. 127.

38. Robert Nye, *Mrs Shakespeare: the complete works* (1993), pp. 102-4.

39. *Ibid.*, pp. 168-72.

40. The story of the £1,000 can be found in Rowe's *Life of Shakespeare*, p. 441.

41. Lanier, p. 112. The concept is derived from the work of Mikhail Bakhtin on Rabelais.

42. *Ibid.*, pp. 112-3.

43 Edward Bond, *Bingo* (1974), p. ix.

44. *Ibid.*, pp. v-vi.

45. *Ibid.*, pp. 24-7.

46. *Ibid.*, p. 41-3.

47. Terence Hawkes, *That Shakespeherian Rag* (1986), pp. 21-2.

48. Compare Nicholas de Jongh, *Evening Standard,* 21 Nov., John Peter, *The Times,* 30 Nov., or Robert Butler, *The Independent,* 23 Nov. All in 1997.

49. The lines are quoted and discussed in Chambers, vol. 2, pp. 186-7.

50. See Chambers, vol. 1, p. 27.

51. Whelan has included Shakespeare or members of his family in *The School of Night* (1992) and *The Herbal Bed* (1996).

52. John Mortimer, *Will Shakespeare* (1977), pp. 14, 36.

53. *Ibid.*, pp. 112-4.

54. *Ibid.*, pp. 230-2.

55. Roland Barthes, 'Les Romains au cinema', *Mythologies* (Paris: Seuil, 1957), pp. 27-30.

55. Alexander Pope, 'First Epistle of the Second Book of Horace Imitated' ll. 69-72, *Poetical Works,* ed. Herbert Davis (Oxford University Press, 1966), p. 363.

57. Lanier, p. 114.

58. *Ibid.*, p. 115.

59. *Ibid.* pp. 110-11.

Chapter Eight

Shakespeare in Our Time: Biography

UP UNTIL NOW IN this book I have been inclined to consider fictional representations of Shakespeare along with those which are non-fictional (the ones which occur in biographical writing). Yet all the illustrations I provided in the last chapter were from fictional texts. I suggested that the most sensible method for beginning a categorisation of them would not be to posit some absolute distinction between *vie romancée* and *vie imaginaire* but rather consider the degree to which their authors felt free to abandon or contradict the historical record. A difficulty in discussing the biographical writing on Shakespeare in the twentieth or twenty-first centuries is that no addition of significance was made to that record after 1909 (when the Mountjoy papers were discovered). The question which therefore arises is how biographers could satisfy the ever-growing demand for a 'life' of someone who was not only England's best-known writer, but also an icon of the national culture, when there was no new material. Instead of merely illustrating here, in the largely descriptive mode I have previously adopted, the fact that they did indeed satisfy it, and in abundance, I want instead to identify six different methods biographers have adopted to compensate for the absence of evidence, illustrating these methods from works published mostly, although not exclusively, in the last ten years.

The Argument from Absence

Since the major impediment to writing a life of Shakespeare is a lack of information, more often than not biographers who set out to investigate a particular aspect of their subject find themselves staring into a black hole. This seems at first a crippling disadvantage for who, after all, can make bricks without straw? Yet there are ways in which biographers of Shakespeare are able to ensure that their ignorance works for them. How this is so, is perhaps easiest to see by considering the possibility that Shakespeare was a secret Catholic. From a biographer's point of view there are considerable advantages in presenting him in this light. To do so ties him in with high-profile and well-researched events such as Father Edmund Campion's Jesuit mission to England in 1580 or the Gunpowder Plot a quarter of a century later. Both these episodes have Warwickshire connections which I shall discuss later in a different context, but the point here is that by associating Shakespeare with them, biographers can transform his life into a drama of concealment, danger and strained loyalties. The difficulty is that most of the evidence available on this topic is not only dubious but related to Shakespeare's father rather than himself. There is no equivalent in his own life of John Shakespeare's supposed 'Spiritual Testament' or the documents which list him as absent from his local church. In the plays there are certainly manifestations of sympathy with the Old Faith but also expressions of hostility towards it. On no occasion, in either the writings or the documentary record, is there an unequivocal declaration of support for Catholicism which can be taken as coming from Shakespeare himself.

How far this is from being the end of the matter is suggested by a phrase which has become proverbial in our own time, 'Well, he would, wouldn't he?' The Shakespearean scholar Gary Taylor states the issue in a clearer, more pertinent form when he writes, 'I can't prove Shakespeare was a Catholic. But then, if he were one, he would have had strong incentives to prevent *anyone* from being able to prove it.'[1] It is easy to see how close this is to being able to say that it is precisely because Shakespeare never reveals he was a Catholic that we know he must have been one. This is what I have called the 'argument from absence' and its use in all presentations of Shakespeare as a Catholic is ubiquitous and multiform. Michael Wood, for example, in the book which accompanied his BBC TV series (2003), has applied it successfully to the connection with Southampton. Like E. Hamilton Gruner, he notes that, through his mother, Shakespeare was related to the Edward Arden executed for his supposed involvement in a Catholic plot to kill the Queen in 1583, and that Southampton's father was a notorious recusant. In the past, it has been assumed by scholars that Mary Arden's connection to Edward was either too distant or too dubious to be significant; and that Shakespeare's Southampton – brought up from an early age as a ward of Lord Burleigh and a member, when he came to Court, of Essex's fervently anti-Spanish and therefore anti-Catholic faction – did not necessarily hold the same views as his father. But if we suppose that the Shakespeares were close to the rich Ardens of Castle Bromwich and that the dedicatee of *Venus and Adonis* was a chip off the old bloc, then,

> There may even have been family connections between Southampton and the Warwickshire Shakespeares. Back in 1583, members of the Arden family had

been found sheltering in Southampton's houses. The contacts that led to Shakespeare seeking Southampton's patronage would no doubt be revealing but it is in the nature of the times that we are never likely to know about them: these were not the sort of things people talked about.[2]

We can see here how it is precisely the absence of any evidence of a specifically Catholic connection between Shakespeare and Southampton which suggests there must have been one.

What I have called the 'argument from absence' is known by theologians as the 'argument from silence'. Katherine Duncan-Jones, whose *Ungentle Shakespeare* appeared in 2001, is perhaps the only recent biographer of Shakespeare to make explicit reference to it. This is in her support of the tradition that there was an ongoing feud between Shakespeare and Ben Jonson. As the material in my second chapter will have suggested, there is scant evidence for anything so biographically interesting as a feud in Jonson's contributions to the First Folio or in *Timber*, but he does make disparaging references to Shakespeare's history plays and to *Titus Adronicus* in two of his prologues, and many have felt that there is a mocking reference to Shakespeare's aspirations to gentility in *Every Man Out of his Humour*. It is in support of the notion that Sogliardo's 'not without mustard' in that play is indeed a reference to the Shakespeare family's motto 'non sans droict' that Duncan-Jones offers what she specifically terms 'an argument from eloquent silence':

> From the 1616 folio of Jonson's works we learn that Shakespeare, his name listed top left, took the leading position among the 'principal comedians' in the original 1598 performance of *Every Man In*. Probably he played the poetical Ed Knowell, opposite Burbage as the versatile Brainworme. In *Every Man Out* the top left position is occupied, instead, by Burbage, and Shakespeare's name does not appear. The fact that the leading player in Jonson's first 'Humour' play took no part in his second is rather striking.[3]

Duncan-Jones is here using the argument from silence to suggest that there must be an uncomplimentary reference to Shakespeare in *Every Man Out* because he declined to act in it; but it is perhaps not such a good idea for her then to mention reasons for the absence of Shakespeare's name from the cast list other than the one she favours. She admits, for example, that the usual interpretation of the omission is that he was too busy writing plays to act in them, and she herself suggests that Shakespeare may have shrunk from more collaboration with 'the newly stigmatised' Jonson because he had so recently escaped execution for killing a fellow actor in a duel.[4] This is to invite readers to find yet more reasons of their own – are we dealing with a printer's error? Was Shakespeare indisposed? The protection for the newly-arrested which for many centuries was part of the English legal system was presumably there because it was recognised that silence can mean many things. The argument from silence (or from absence) clearly works best when those using it contrive to leave their readers with a single option.

If the biographer of Shakespeare avoids drawing attention to the potential flaws in the argument from absence, it is remarkable how useful it can be. It has become almost customary, for example, to assume that if Shakespeare did not actually die of syphilis, then this was the complaint from which he was suffering towards the end of his life. At this distance in time it would of course be foolish to hope to prove that this was the case and the only items of evidence usually presented are therefore the fairly frequent allusions to venereal disease in the plays and sonnets. It so happens, however, that Shakespeare's son-in-law John Hall, a doctor well known in the Stratford area, kept notes on his patients. Anthony Burgess was one of the first to imply that the very absence of references to Shakespeare in these notes strengthens the case for syphilis because it suggests that 'decency prevailed over clinical candour'.[5] Duncan-Jones makes the same point, without, in this instance, any distracting references to alternative explanations, when she suggests that, 'the absence or excision of Hall's notes may well be a consequence of his father-in-law's syphilis'. 'As a doctor who ministered to the aristocracy and the landed gentry,' she goes on, 'Hall may have been habitually careful to avoid explicit mention of this shaming condition, even when he observed it'.[6] Of course Duncan-Jones does not positively state that Hall observed Shakespeare's syphilitic condition but there is considerable skill in making the reader feel that he did and in suggesting that the blank which scholars have drawn when they have investigated Hall is positive rather than negative.

A less specific illustration of the way the argument from absence works can be found in general accounts of Shakespeare's character. If there is one word in these which appears more often than others, it is 'discreet': here was someone, the impression given usually is, who liked to keep his head down. It will be clear immediately how this way of presenting Shakespeare transforms the fact that we know virtually nothing about him from a weakness into a strength. Viewed from this perspective the absence of information is not so much a result of the passage of time, accident or Shakespeare's social status (whether or not aristocrats wrote more letters than ordinary people, those they did write were more likely to be preserved), but of particular patterns of behaviour. If, in his private capacity, he left little mark on his age, it is because he did not want to. This conclusion is open to challenge from those who say that it cannot be drawn without reference to some standard of comparison, but such a standard is not far to seek. In his *Shakespeare: A Life* (1998), Park Honan is one of many to indicate what that standard is when he insists that,

> As a man [Shakespeare] would lack a quirky egotism, as seems clear from his relatively peaceful career in the theatre, a hive of tension. He was not involved in Ben Jonson's kind of embroilments, or Marlowe's. He has a calm, fine control of

emotive materials, and his Sonnets, in the artfulness of their structures, reveal a lordly, easy play over feelings.[7]

The final phrases in this extract may be questionable, but what the whole of it illustrates is the freedom for calling Shakespeare discreet, peace-loving and the like which can be derived from the fact that he was never on trial for his life, as both Jonson and Marlowe certainly were. However true it may be that not all manifestations of violence, aggression and unpleasantness end up in the courts, the failure to uncover a trace of any legal difficulties comparable to those suffered by his two great contemporaries has allowed biographers to arrive at conclusions about his character which are otherwise hard to draw. Once again, therefore, an absence which might in other contexts be deplored comes to the rescue.

Perhaps the most sustained use of the argument from absence is to be found in Ernst Honigmann's treatment of Shakespeare's will. In one of his many academic essays on the life of Shakespeare, Honigmann has noted that, unlike several of his contemporaries, Shakespeare left no money for the repair of his local church, or a funeral sermon, and has therefore been able to suggest that, commemorated though he was to be in Holy Trinity (with a tombstone in the chancel), he was not as committed a parishioner as he might have been. He finds it significant that there is no mention in the will of cancelling debts or at least reducing the sums owed. 'A gentleman', he also writes, 'usually remembered his servants in his will'. Since in the documents which survive Shakespeare did not do so, there is an obvious conclusion to be drawn: far from being the 'gentle Shakespeare' of tradition he was at the time of his death an angry, bitter man, 'totally self-centred and shockingly tight-fisted'.[8] Here is a whole character sketch conjured up from absence and the three examples I have given – nothing for the church, failure to forgive debts and nothing for the servants – make it easy to see how the near absence of Shakespeare's wife from his will can be exploited.

One of the problems of interpreting Shakespeare's will lies in reaching a consensus as to what can be regarded as usual in his time. Everyone agrees, for example, that in leaving the bulk of his property to his elder daughter and relatively little therefore to his younger one, he was not being unjust, but merely following the practice of every other Jacobean gentleman; yet Honigmann describes the £10 Shakespeare left to the poor as 'generous' whereas for Duncan-Jones it was 'minimal'.[9] The advantage might be thought to lie with Honigmann here in that he has edited, with Susan Brock, over 130 wills of men and women associated with the theatre between 1588 and 1642. It is on these that he is able to call when examining the provisions for Judith Shakespeare's second £150 and the question of whether these were deliberately designed to keep her new husband's hands off the money? In arguing that they were, Honigmann cites the widow of Shakespeare's colleague Condell who says in her will of a certain bequest, 'yet so I do intend the same that my son-in-law Mr Herbert Finch shall never have possession of the same'; and also the theatrical entrepreneur Jacob Meade who insisted in his that a sum of money should be retained by his executors for his daughter's use 'so long as it shall please almighty God that she shall live with the husband Michael Pyttes, whom I will shall have nothing to do or meddle therewith'. These phrases certainly suggest strong animus against sons-in-law, yet according to Honigmann, Thomas Quiney was 'put in his place even more humiliatingly'. That was because 'he was not mentioned by name, his very existence was not acknowledged, even though the most carefully hedged clauses of the will were clearly devised in response to his unwelcome arrival in the bosom of the family'.[10] Of all examples of the argument from absence in recent Shakespeare biography, this must be the most notable.

Honigmann is not the first scholar to have thought of contextualising Shakespeare's will. More than sixty years ago, for example, in what is still the most detailed and exhaustive study of it ever to appear, B. Roland Lewis claimed to have based his enquiries on 'a critical examination of several thousand wills, from that of Alfred the Great (†901) to that of Sir Walter Raleigh (†1618)' as well as 'firsthand acquaintance with the legal treatises of the day, particularly those bearing on testamentary documents, and with the activities of Probate and Prerogative Courts'. The widow Condell did not escape his broad sweep and he felt that, in comparison with what she said about her son-in-law, there was 'certainly in Shakespeare's will [...] not the least hint of a dislike for Thomas Quiney'.[11] The absence of any hint might be taken here to be precisely Honigmann's point, yet it is sometimes hard, when looking at the way all Shakespeare's recent biographers have employed the argument from absence, not to recall the memorable example of its use which is described by Robert Graves in his novel *They Hanged My Saintly Billy*. This tells the story of Dr William Palmer who was executed in 1856 for the murder by strychnine of his betting partner John Cook. Everyone believed that Palmer had committed this crime as well – very probably – as several others of the same type. The difficulty lay in finding proof of his guilt but the prosecution managed to persuade the jury that, since strychnine is very rapidly absorbed, the absence of any hint of it in Cook's body showed that Palmer must certainly have used it to poison him.[12]

Minding your Language

Because so little is known about Shakespeare and all authors of his 'life' are obliged to speculate, one of their problems is how to acknowledge this uncomfortable fact without giving their readers the impression that they might just as well have opened an historical novel. Part of the solution lies in phraseology: finding the right expressions and knowing how to put them in the right places. Those weasel words 'perhaps', 'if', 'probably', 'could have', 'may' etc. are difficult to avoid in any biography, but no biographer of Shakespeare can do without them. Skilfully handled they can function to recall that moment in many American court-room dramas when the handsome defence attorney suddenly suggests to a witness the scenario that makes him or her responsible for the murder of which his own client stands accused. Although the prosecuting counsel leaps to his feet with an objection, the idea of that witness as the murderer is firmly lodged in the jury's mind well before the judge can say 'Sustained'. The weasel words I mention have this same function of 'sustained' in that they acknowledge the rules in the very moment when they are being broken. They announce an intellectual responsibility which would make writing yet another life of Shakespeare very difficult while at the same time presiding over what is – if the work is to get written – its very necessary abandon.

I can demonstrate how this process works by considering the way Duncan-Jones deals with the intractable issue of which theatre company Shakespeare joined when he first became an actor. The Lord Chamberlain's Men, to which we know he belonged, only surfaces in 1594, but in the 1580s the most famous company was the Queen's Men. Since this is a group about which something is known it would be convenient to be able to attach Shakespeare to it, but the only presentable evidence of his involvement is the close familiarity he was later to show with several plays which were in its repertoire, and there are more ways of becoming familiar with plays than acting in them. The something which is known about the Queen's Men is, above all, that in June 1587 one of its members (William Knell) killed another in a brawl.[13] This would have meant that when they played Stratford a few weeks later, they were almost certainly a couple of actors short. 'As Shakespeare's own English history plays were to show', Duncan-Jones writes, 'one man's sudden death is very often the occasion of another man's sudden promotion. *So it may perhaps have been* for Shakespeare himself in the summer of 1587.' She knows of course that an élite company like the Queen's Men was only likely to engage new actors who already had some training and suggests therefore that it was '*perhaps* [...] from among Leicester's Men' that Shakespeare was 'drafted in June or July 1587'.[14] In this way she avoids offending against common sense while at the same time not entirely depriving her reader of the dramatic scenario in which the depleted Queen's Men trundle into Stratford and find in a local boy the answer to all their needs.

'*If*' Shakespeare was 'for a time among Leicester's Men', Duncan-Jones continues, his service '*may have been* fairly brief'. She points to one document which '*may conceivably* link Shakespeare both with [Sir Philip] Sidney and with

Leicester's men'. This is a well-known letter from Sidney to his father-in-law Walsingham which contains the phrase, 'I wrote to you a letter by William my Lord of Leicester's jesting player, enclosed in a letter to my wife, and I never had an answer thereof.' It has usually been assumed that the jesting player in question was the famous clown Will Kemp, but Duncan-Jones raises the 'exciting possibility' that it may been Shakespeare. Although she goes on later to say that, 'Definite proof that Sidney's blundering messenger was William Shakespeare is lacking. Possibly the messenger was, after all, William Kempe', the point at which this concession is made means that it has an effect similar to 'objection sustained' or at least by the time readers come to it, though they may not be certain that Shakespeare was Sidney's messenger, they probably have it firmly fixed in their minds that he was one of Leicester's Men.[15] Focusing the attention on a minor point has always been a useful way of ensuring that the right answer to the main one is taken for granted.

A Shakespeare who had served his time in Leicester's company would certainly have been qualified to become a Queen's Man but how did he make his first breakthrough? 'My *conjecture is*', Duncan-Jones writes, and she then goes on to describe the Sir Fulke Greville who lived only a dozen miles to the west of Stratford. She supposes that he saw Shakespeare performing in the town, took him into his service and later, since he was 'very closely allied to the Dudleys' (Leicester's family name), passed the young man on to the Earl. Thus 'as a member of Leicester's Men for some time between 1584 and 1586, Shakespeare *would have* quickly shown his versatility both in writing and performing. He *would have* been a natural choice to supply one of the gaps left by Knell's death in June 1587'.[16] What is so effective here is that in English 'would have' so often has the mere appearance of the conditional.

The idea that Shakespeare replaced Knell is so confidently expressed that it is hardly necessary for Duncan-Jones to say at this point in her chapter that the rest of it 'will be based on the *supposition* that from about 1588 Shakespeare was indeed a Queen's Man'. How could he be anything other when all the genuinely interesting information about this company which she then offers would be redundant if he weren't? Duncan-Jones has paid her dues to the intellectual conscience in the words I have italicised, but that has not prevented her from convincing her readers that there is only one possible solution to the problem of what Shakespeare did before he became a member of the Lord Chamberlain's Men. So assured is she in her handling of this issue that she can refer a little later to the work Shakespeare did for the Queen's Men 'while he was a full-time member of the company in the later 1580s'[17] and later still, in relation to the absence of Shakespeare's name from the title page of *Venus and Adonis*, deal confidently with the lack of any relevant documentary record,

As a playwright, Shakespeare was well used to having his works identified by the title and subject matter only. Even as a 'sharer' in the Queen's [...] Men [...] his name was not recorded, and yet, as we saw in chapter 2, there is little doubt of his membership.[18]

In demonstrating the way in which Duncan-Jones manipulates the weasel words of biography, I inevitably began to touch on methods which are not simply linguistic. I can come back to those which are, by showing how much can be achieved by that familiar device, the rhetorical question. Noting that the theme of sleep is 'obsessive' in *Macbeth* Anthony Holden asks in his 1999 biography, 'Is it entirely idle to wonder if Shakespeare himself was suffering sleepless nights while writing *Macbeth*?' and he then goes on, 'He had cause enough, as papist families of his long acquaintance went to the gallows in the wake of the "Powder Plot"'.[19] The obvious answer to the question Holden first asks is 'yes' but the context he then goes on to provide prevents the reader from giving it.

More extensive use of the rhetorical question is made by Holden in his treatment of Mrs Mountjoy. As was made clear in chapter 1, Shakespeare must have been a lodger at the Mountjoys prior to the marriage of their daughter Mary in 1604 but it was all of seven years previously that Mrs Mountjoy (also called Mary) had consulted Simon Forman because she was worried that her affair with a local tradesman, Henry Wood, might have resulted in pregnancy. Holden solves the difficulty of uniting these two facts by approaching them via the composition of *Othello*. 'Who might have caused [Shakespeare] such powerful emotions at this particular time', he asks, 'feeding the frenzy behind Othello's "goats and monkeys"? Who, for one, but the indirect cause of his future legal woes, Mary Mountjoy senior?'[20] 'For one' protects Holden from the absurdity of claiming that Mrs Mountjoy was the sole inspiration for Othello's jealous rages and, by describing an appearance as a witness in a civil law suit in 1612 as a 'legal woe', he suggests the trouble she would bring; but the main work here is being done by the interrogative form.

> Was Mary senior flighty enough to seduce her lodger [...] and then to torment him with her attentions to Wood or indeed her husband? Had she and Shakespeare secretly been lovers for five years or more before he moved in, the name of Mountjoy in *Henry V* being his coded thanks for her flirtatious help with the play's adventures in French?[21]

Perhaps it does not so much matter here that the chronology is potentially confusing and that, if Shakespeare had indeed been Mrs Mountjoy's secret lover for five years, she would not have had to 'seduce' him when he became her lodger. What clearly counts is being able to plant in the reader's mind the idea that there was certainly something going on between the two figures. The rhetorical question does that, but Michael Wood achieves a similar effect by very different linguistic means. 'Shakespeare was perhaps close to Mrs Mountjoy', he writes, 'though to suggest he might have been responsible for her pregnancy in 1597 is perhaps to over-stretch the evidence'.[22] Here again is 'perhaps' (twice) but more significant is the reference to 'over stretching' the evidence when in the past no-one has ever thought there was any.

There is a feature of Wood's reference to non-existent evidence which is worth noting in passing. All Shakespeare's biographers have at their disposal a number of anecdotes more or less equal in their unverifiability. Between the idea that he was Mrs Mountjoy's lover, the father of Sir William Davenant, a deer-poacher in Stratford, or a Catholic schoolmaster in Lancashire there is, from an evidential point of view, very little to choose. What can be regarded as important, therefore, is that the biographer should be like Wood in the case of Mrs Mountjoy and convey an impression of tough-minded discrimination. One of the simplest way to achieve this is to choose one or two of the traditional stories for arbitrary rejection. This may be a sacrifice, but it is one which makes it easier to gain acceptance for those stories not rejected.

A more specifically linguistic method for dealing with the unverifiable is to suggest that, although you yourself may not be able to prove what you are saying, there is no one able to *disprove* it either. This is a common enough move, often seen in recent biographies, although its most notable exponent was probably A. L. Rowse. Of the notion that William Davenant was Shakespeare's son, for example, Rowse writes that there is 'no reason why this should not be so'.[23] This invites any readers inclined to disagree with him to a challenge they are almost bound to fail and obscures the fact that the burden of proof is usually on people who propound a thesis rather than their listeners. A variation on the method is made clear by Honigmann when he says of claims made by Shakespeare's first biographer Nicholas Rowe and by John Aubrey, 'In the absence of evidence to the contrary, we must be grateful for both of these statements as to Shakespeare's early career.'[24] Implicitly inviting your reader to disprove what you say is a shrewd move because the kind of material involved is always likely to make disproof impossible. The only effective response to conjectures based on a minimum of verifiable facts, most of which can be interpreted or amplified in a wide variety of ways, is what is known as the *reductio ad absurdum*. In his biography of Macauley, Trevelyan describes how his subject met in India a clergyman who said he could prove that Napoleon was the Beast of the Apocalypse. This was because if you write Napoleon Bonaparte in Arabic and leave out only two letters the numerical values of the remainder will give you 666. Macauley told the clergyman that he must be wrong because he himself had already discovered the real Beast to be the House of Commons: 'There are 658 members of the House and these, with their chief officers – the three clerks, the Sergeant and his deputy, the Chaplain, the doorkeeper, and the librarian – make 666'.[25] There is no doubt that this is an cogent rejoinder but, if biographers after Macauley are still found inviting disproof rather than struggling to offer the opposite, it is because *reductios* are very hard to think up, and the chances of a biographer of Shakespeare meeting anyone with Macauley's gifts for doing so are in any case very slim.

Once again my discussion has moved away from more strictly linguistic matters. Part of the reason for this is that 'minding your language' is not like the argument from absence, a technique or method which can be learned. It is rather a matter of attitude, of the prospective biographer remaining alert to all the various possibilities the English language offers for appearing to be tentative while gratifying fully the reader's curiosity. The only way it can be satisfactorily described is through example. A useful final illustration, therefore, would be Holden's treatment of the Davenant story. Although I have just said that all the traditional stories concerning Shakespeare are more or less unverifiable, the idea that he was Davenant's father is certainly on the 'more' side of the equation and yet not to include it might well deprive a biographical narrative of much needed colour. Holden begins by boldly ignoring the question of John Aubrey's reliability and repeating that writer's assertion that Shakespeare 'would always break his two-day ride' between Stratford and London by staying at the same tavern in London where 'John and Jeanette Davenant were long-standing friends'. He concedes that Davenant was an engaging rogue, and that his boast that he was Shakespeare's son may therefore have been wishful thinking, but he then moves to dispel the doubts he has raised by noting that 'four centuries of detective work have failed to disprove' the relationship. On the question of why 'our poet did not mention Sir William Davenant in his will' he has his own variation on the argument from absence: 'he would no more have told his wife about an illegitimate child by his regular Oxford hostess [...] than he would have regaled her with gory details, not least the clap, of his nocturnal adventures in London.'[26] What has happened here is that Holden has transformed an objection which is difficult to answer into one to which the reply is easy. If William Davenant was publicly recognised as Shakespeare's *godson* then the inclusion of him in the will could hardly have shocked Shakespeare's widow and his omission from it is perhaps puzzling; but to have acknowledged him there as an illegitimate son would (as Holden suggests) have been a quite different matter.

Yet the use of language with which I am here chiefly concerned is more in evidence in Holden's treatment of the Davenant affair when he writes that, according to Plutarch, Cleopatra was thirty-eight at the time of her 'tempestuous fling' with Mark Antony, 'exactly the same age as Jeanette Davenant while Shakespeare was writing *Antony and Cleopatra*'. Unfortunately for symmetry, Shakespeare himself was forty-three, 'some ten years younger than Antony'. Still, 'Was it pure coincidence, if he was bedding the wife of the Oxford tavern-keeper, that he now chose to conjure – through the besotted eyes of an older man – the most alluring, highly-sexed woman ever to emerge even from his capacious and libidinous imagination?'[27] This is of course the rhetorical question again, but the particular language use I want to illustrate is that of being able to so encapsulate the word 'if' in a general speculation about the relation of literature to life that it loses its conditional force. Something similar occurs when, a little later in his book, Holden is discussing Shakespeare's situation in 1608. 'Over the last four years,', he writes, '[Shakespeare] had put himself under tremendous strain: if his private life had remained adventurous, if indeed he had suffered the stress of an eventful extra-marital affair, he had also produced three of his mightiest tragedies'.[28] Although the presence of two 'if's in this sentence suggests that Holden is keeping open the possibility that all he has had to say about Shakespeare and Jeanette Davenant is conjectural, readers know in their heart of hearts that it is not because the meaning which has in fact been given to that word is 'even though'.

Using the Plays

Drama provides what is, perhaps, the most unpromising terrain on which to play hunt the author. It is not hard to believe that when Hamlet talks about acting we are hearing Shakespeare's own thoughts but does that then mean we have access to his own views or feelings when Falstaff pronounces on honour or Othello on women? The plays tell us what he read, and they may show him preoccupied with certain themes, but when it comes to their capacity for revealing distinct features of Shakespeare's own life, it is hard to disagree with Henry James.

> The man himself, in the Plays, we directly touch, to my consciousness, positively nowhere: we are dealing perpetually with the artist, the monster and magician of a thousand masks, not one of which we feel him drop long enough to gratify with the breath of the interval that strained attention in us which would be yet, so quickened, ready to become deeper still.[29]

Any biographer who took these words to heart would have to renounce 'using the plays', but for most of them the sacrifice has always seemed too great.

Anthony Holden demonstrates the blithe way of ignoring the difficulties James raises when he writes that 'we know more about the life of Shakespeare than about that of any of his literary contemporaries bar Ben Jonson', and then goes on, 'And the rest is there for all to see, in and between every line he wrote – as well as the order in which he wrote them.'[30] The more academically inclined Jonathan Bate, the first part only of whose *Genius of Shakespeare* (1997) is biographical, refers to the effort of trying to deduce details of Shakespeare's youth from the plays as a 'dubious procedure', and Duncan-Jones says that 'in general, it is a risky literalism that seeks originals or analogues in "real life", so-called, from exceptionally powerful passages of Shakespeare's writing'.[31] But these are disclaimers which have much the same function in Shakespeare biography as 'perhaps' or 'probably' since they in no way prevent both these authors from relying on the plays a good deal.

Once radical difficulties of the kind hinted at by Bate and Duncan-Jones have been side-stepped, or simultaneously acknowledged and ignored, the way is open for the myriad ways in which the plays can be used. Although some of these have nothing to do with the kind of person Shakespeare might have been, they all bear on the question of how his life can still be written. It might be reasonably assumed, for example, that his biographers would have most trouble filling their pages when they were dealing with that youth Bate mentions, but quite the opposite is the case, as I shall show later. The really difficult period for the biographer comes between the time when Shakespeare is well established, in full flow, and the preliminaries which lead up to his death: those years during which all he seems to be doing is writing the plays which have made him famous. It is then that plot summaries accompanied by a few critical commentaries can be most useful. Nearly every biography of Shakespeare is filled out around its middle with accounts of the plays. This is the kind of material which might be difficult to publish in any other context but which can always pass muster in a biography. Why after all should we be interested in Shakespeare if it is not for what he wrote?

A second use of the plays which also has no direct bearing on the discovery of Shakespeare's character or nature is to add colour to the narrative. When dealing with his schooldays, for instance, it is useful to be able to quote Jaques's famous lines from 2.vii of *As You Like It* about the 'whining schoolboy, with his satchel / And shining morning face, creeping like snail / Unwillingly to school'; there are many lines in *Romeo and Juliet* which can be associated with his courtship of Anne Hathaway; and several plays (*King Lear, The Tempest, Pericles*) will illustrate a reasonable variety of possible relationships with his two daughters. With the help of a good concordance, any aspect of Shakespeare's life which the biographer sets out to describe can be bolstered and enlivened with quotations from the plays without the claim for any close relationship between those quotations and Shakespeare's own personal experience being anything more than implicit. But when there is a call to be explicit, there are many directions in which to go.

In spite of Caroline Spurgeon, the first and most obvious is still to find Shakespeare's thoughts and feelings in the utterances of a particular character. As I have suggested, few people have ever objected to taking Hamlet's thoughts on the acting profession as Shakespeare's own and Holden maintains the tradition of claiming that 'when writing Prospero's farewell to arms' – in those famous lines from 5.1 of *The Tempest* about breaking his staff and drowning his book – 'Shakespeare was consciously writing his own'.[32] Rather surprisingly, Touchstone has often been designated as Shakespeare's spokesperson and the bitterness which it is assumed he began to feel in later life has frequently been heard in Timon of Athens. Othello has been thought to express the jealousy Shakespeare felt, if not on account of Mrs Mountjoy then when his dark mistress was stolen by the addressee of the Sonnets; for some we eavesdrop on his political opinions in Ulysses' great speech on 'degree' in *Troilus and Cressida*; and if Park Honan is right in saying that Volumnia is 'not entirely different from what is known of Mary Arden',[33] then it may be that (as Frank Harris thought) we have an insight into Shakespeare's relations with his mother in *Coriolanus*. The channel of communication for revealing how he himself thought and felt does not have to be male. Many biographers have believed that in Queen Constance's lament for her son Arthur in 3.iv of *King John* Shakespeare is expressing his response to the death of his only son Hamnet in August 1596. The advantage of this method which I am now illustrating for enrolling the plays in the biographical enterprise is that it is limited only by the finite number of characters in them. Almost any state of mind, opinion or feeling which biographers can conjecture in Shakespeare himself will be expressed by someone, somewhere in the plays (it is for convenience only that my examples are limited to major figures). That expression will represent confirmation of the conjecture, even when it was also what first suggested it. It is hardly surprising that many biographers refuse to deny themselves this all-purpose tool when otherwise, on the question of Shakespeare's inner life, they are more than likely to flounder in the dark.

Having Shakespeare express his thoughts and feelings through a particular character is the simple way of finding him in the plays and of thereby making them serve the aims and purposes of biography; but there are very many others which are more sophisticated. Jonathan Bate, for example, has discovered that the William in *As You Like It* is its author's 'wittily self-deprecatory portrait of himself as tongue-tied country bumpkin' and that it is 'deliciously ironic because Shakespeare's true wit and verbal facility are amply on display in the character of Touchstone.'[34] A similarly indirect route to the mystery of Shakespeare's nature is taken by those who also follow the clue provided by a Christian name and identify as self-portraiture young William Page in *The Merry Wives of Windsor*. It is in 4.i of this play that William is put through his paces by the Welsh parson and schoolmaster, Sir Hugh Evans. When this scene is invoked, it is not for the merely descriptive purposes of Jaques's lines in *As You Like It* about the schoolboy, but because it can be taken to represent a direct comment by Shakespeare on the nature and quality of his own education. As Bate is not alone in pointing out, one of the schoolmasters at Stratford Grammar School at the time of Shakespeare's early youth was also Welsh.[35]

The belief that Shakespeare speaks through a particular character, or represents himself in one of them, offers almost as many biographical opportunities as there have been, are, or ever will be, biographers. If no-one can ever say for certain whether this or that identification is accurate neither can it ever be proved that it is false. What makes the possibilities additionally rich in this area is that on occasions Shakespeare's personal concerns have also been found reflected less in the lines his characters speak than in an episode. It is well known, for example, that around the middle or late 1570s John Shakespeare, after initially prospering in his trade as a glover, fell on hard times. One consequence seems to have been that he stopped attending meetings of the Stratford Corporation even though, in 1568, he had been the town's bailiff or mayor. His fellow aldermen were very patient, but after ten years of non-attendance, they elected someone in his place and struck him off the aldermanic role. Honan intimates how John's son must have felt about all this by inserting into his description of the scene in *Richard III* where Richard contrives to have himself offered the crown (3.vii): '(The playwright's father having been dismissed by his brother aldermen, the gallery drama obliges an audience to scorn aldermen as fools, just as Richard does.)'[36] As I have noted in discussing E. Hamilton Gruner, one consequence of John Shakespeare's financial misfortunes was that in 1578 he borrowed £40 by mortgaging a house and some land which had been part of his wife's inheritance. When he tried later to recover this property he could not do so. Holden is able to link this misfortune to *Hamlet* by telling us how Shakespeare was 'still mindful' of it when he wrote about Fortinbras's efforts to recover his lost heritage.[37] In both cases, it could be argued that we would not know that Shakespeare resented how his father had been treated, or was concerned about that part of the family estate which could no longer be his, were it not for the plays.

Apart from helping biographers to describe aspects of Shakespeare's inner life, and to justify the inclusion in a biography of accounts of plays which might otherwise seem banal, these links between the life and the writing (or the writing and the life) also allow them to develop their special interests. Duncan-Jones, for example, has paid special attention to the Shakespeare family's coat of arms. It is not known precisely why, three years after having secured his own arms, John Shakespeare's attempt to have them combined with those which he claimed belonged to his wife's family failed (or was not pursued) but, as I have already said, it may have had something to do with the difficulty of establishing the relationship between her and the Ardens who lived at Park Hall in Castle Bromwich, not far from Birmingham. As Schoenbaum notes, this question has resisted the most 'intense genealogical zeal'[38] but, whatever its answer, the Shakespeares' coat of arms remained the same. Duncan-Jones is able to suggest how this might have upset – or at least annoyed – Shakespeare by linking his father's application and its 'defence of the legitimacy of descent through the female line' to the Archbishop of Canterbury's lengthy 'Salic law' speech in *Henry V*. As she says, that a personal interest is reflected here is not something which 'any uniformed spectator or reader would guess', nor is the link one which any mere apprentice biographer would be expected to perceive. It does not take much biographical experience, on the other hand, to propose that the frequent references to venereal disease in *Troilus and Cressida* means that Shakespeare must have had it. 'Deeply rooted in [...] the desperate struggle to make one's voice heard before disease destroys both pen and phallus', is how Duncan-Jones describes this play, and she suggests that Shakespeare's visits to Turnbull Street, where his fellow playwright George Wilkins is reputed to have kept a brothel, 'may have left him with an unwanted legacy of chronic and humiliating sickness.'[39]

In the past, one powerful objection to relying on the plays when describing Shakespeare's inner life or his more personal affairs, has been that they can be made to prove anything; but then this is precisely the method's strength. If anyone setting out to write his life were to spend a week drawing up a list of his possible thoughts and feelings and then matching each item with lines from the plays, it would be the equivalent of those warm-up exercises which athletes perform before a big game. One very obvious danger is apparent in Holden's somewhat ungainly reference to discovering Shakespeare 'in and between every line he wrote, as well as the order in which he wrote them'. It is not so much the order in which Shakespeare wrote his lines which can be problematic but the order in which he wrote his plays. When it became clear that *The Tempest* was not his final play but that it was followed by *Henry VIII* and one or two other collaborations, Prospero's retirement speech was made to look a little premature.[40] Shakespeare could only have been mourning the death of Hamnet through the speech of Constance in *King John* if that play belongs to 1596, rather than (as Honigmann has suggested[41]) to 1591. Chronology can be a tricky business. Duncan-Jones describes *The Merry Wives* as a play which 'can be dated with unusual precision' and says that in his representation of young William Page, Shakespeare was assimilating his grief at Hamnet's loss 'into what he happened to be writing in the spring after his death'. Her book bears the Arden imprint, but when Giorgio Melchiori came to edit *The Merry Wives* in Arden's 'Third Series' he decided it belonged to 1599 or later.[42] This does not of course matter very much. Shakespeare could still have been grieving for his son three of four springs after his death but it does suggest why many are inclined to adopt the motto: *when in doubt, keep it general.* This is what Holden does by attributing to Hamnet's death 'the personal grief which now becomes a recurring strain in [Shakespeare's] work [...] lifting his history to quite another poetic plane, floating on a cloud of personal grief.'[43] Generality at this level is additionally useful in that some of the plays which follow Hamnet's death (including *The Merry Wives*) are after all fairly cheerful. Michael Wood illustrates its usefulness even better than Holden when he also describes the effect on Shakespeare's writing of losing his only son:

Within the next year or two a change gradually came about not only in Shakespeare's themes but also in his way of writing, in his language and imagery. The great tragedies followed, plumbing 'the well of darkness'. This was not only a personal tragedy but a powerful intimation of mortality.[44]

It stands to reason that Shakespeare must have been profoundly affected by the death of Hamnet, but it is a smart move to let the reader decide exactly where in the plays this is evident, in case one of them was written before it took place, but also because relevant quotations which readers themselves recall have more effect than any the biographer could choose for them.

Using the Sonnets

As chapter 5 suggests, the difficulties for biographers of using the Sonnets are not quite the same as those they encounter when dealing with the plays but they equally formidable. To ignore them requires a good deal of nerve and no biographer in the twentieth century has shown more of that than A. L. Rowse. For him, the Sonnets were 'autobiography throughout' and, as a result, Shakespeare was the 'most autobiographical of all the Elizabethan dramatists'. 'When these autobiographical sonnets were published years after they were written', he explained, 'the *publisher*, Thomas Thorp, dedicated them to 'Mr W. H.', from whom he had got them. So Mr W. H. was the publisher's man, *not* the young lord within the Sonnets – the obvious person, Shakespeare's patron, Southampton'. Rowse went on to point out that 'no-one hitherto had noticed this obvious point, and for lack of it had made a complete muddle of Shakespeare's life and work'. He thought it 'pitiable' that people had not realised how Shakespeare had written his sonnets 'in the course of his duty to the young lord upon being accepted as his poet', and he believed that the story they told was 'perfectly clear', although 'the key was lost for so long'. This key was the identity of the dark lady and Rowse felt he had eventually found it in Emilia Lanier, the daughter of Court musicians who were of Italian extraction (hence the swarthy complexion). He noted how he had always been convinced that if the identity of the dark lady was one day discovered, she would prove to be a member of the Southampton set. 'This turns out to be true', he wrote, '– a complete vindication of fact and argument uncovered by rigorous dating and proper chronological method instead of absurd conjectures *in vacuo*, devoid of any historical reality'.[45]

The confidence of Rowse is a quality which later biographers of Shakespeare have only felt able to display intermittently. Jonathan Bate begins the chapter on the Sonnets in his *Genius of Shakespeare* with a convincing account of why they ought *not* to be read as if they were autobiographical (and why they are therefore unsuitable material for biography). He goes on the refer to the 'wonderfully circular' logic of Rowse and ironically offers several examples of that writer's unusual 'assurance'. But then, with an appeal to the example of William Empson, the direction of his argument shifts. In a well-known essay, Empson had linked one of the most apparently impersonal of the Sonnets ('They that have power to hurt and will do none') to Shakespeare's feelings of dismay at being betrayed by Southampton and hence to Hal's rejection of Falstaff in 2 Henry IV.[46] Encouraged by this precedent, Bate replaces the identifications of Rowse (and others) with his own. Although in the same year his book was published, Duncan-Jones produced an edition of the Sonnets which argued that Pembroke was their addressee, he felt that 'the case for Southampton as the original patron/youth to whom the Sonnets were addressed looks irrefutable'. For him, the dark lady is not Emilia Lanier but rather the sister of Samuel Daniel, author of a sonnet sequence published in 1592 and therefore a candidate for the Sonnets' 'rival poet'. Avoiding the difficulties which proponents of Mary Fitton had encountered, Bate points out that in Elizabethan times 'darkness' should not necessarily be taken literally but is rather an indicator of social status, and that 'one thing we do know about Miss Daniel is that she was a low-born Somerset lass'. At the time Shakespeare could have known her, this woman was the wife of John Florio, a member of Southampton's household, and the mother of four children, two of whom, Edward and Elizabeth, were born in 1588 and 1589 respectively. Thus: 'The simile in sonnet 143 whereby "Will" compares himself to his mistress's "neglected child" would gain added poignancy if Mrs Florio really were neglecting young Edward and Elizabeth as she lay in bed with Will'. The initial rival for Southampton's favour to whom Shakespeare refers in the Sonnets thus becomes Florio himself and Bate is then able to suggest that a notoriously obscure reference in Sonnet 125 to a 'suborned informer' indicates Florio, since he is thought to have been planted in the Southampton household by Lord Burghley who was anxious to keep an eye on his former ward. As for Mr W. H., Bate takes up the old suggestion that the initials are a misprint for W. S. so that the dedication then becomes a tribute which Thorpe wanted to pay to the Sonnets' author.[47]

Towards the end of his chapter, Bate admits that he began work on the Sonnets with 'a determination to adhere to an agnostic position on the question of their autobiographical elements', but that the poems have 'wrought their magic' on him.[48] Because they can be invoked in support of so many different biographical speculations, it is not surprising to find their effect has been magical on many others also. Their flexibility is priceless but means there is a risk that any particular interpretation which the biographer adopts will seem arbitrary. This risk is diminished by an informal consensus among biographers as to which readings can be regarded as more or less fixed. My extract from Scott's Kenilworth shows that in the early nineteenth century, chiefly because of the third line in Sonnet 37 – 'So I, made lame by fortune's dearest spite', it was generally assumed that Shakespeare limped, that he was 'a halting fellow'. Anyone who offered this reading now might unfairly be regarded as simple-minded when their real weakness was a failure to acquaint themselves with what, in their own time, it has become customary to take literally. Most biographers of Shakespeare are now agreed, for example, that the eclipse of the mortal moon in Sonnet 107 is a reference to the death of Elizabeth (rather than, as Leslie Hotson thought, to the battle formation of the ships of the Spanish Armada[49]). Fixing that meaning provides an invaluable point of chronological reference since it would have been impossible for Shakespeare to have alluded to this event before it happened. Most of them are also agreed that the interrogative form at the beginning of Sonnet 125 – 'Were't ought to me I bore the canopy / With my extern the outward honouring' – can be ignored, and that the lines can therefore be associated with Shakespeare's likely involvement in the ceremonies welcoming James I into London in 1604.

These two readings may not be any less inherently speculative than that of line 4 in Sonnet 37 but, as I have suggested already, in areas where everything is more or less equally dubious, firmly rejecting some options usefully conveys an impression of tough discrimination and gives all the more authority to those which the biographer does decide to take up. The two readings I mention are by now almost traditional, but there are several relating to Shakespeare's love life which are more recent. One of them is of a line in Sonnet 145, the only poem in the collection written in eight rather than ten syllable lines. The feelings in this sonnet seem simple in comparison to those in the often contorted and violent sonnets around it. It was Andrew Gurr who in 1971 suggested that in the final couplet – 'I hate from hate away she threw / And saved my life, saying not you' – there might well be a punning allusion to the maiden name of Shakespeare's wife.[50] This has been picked up by Robert Nye (see pp. 252–3 above) but also provides licence enough for Michael Wood to acknowledge 'a growing consensus that William composed [the sonnet] for his marriage day and that it is his earliest surviving work'.[51] Perhaps even newer as a fixed interpretation which biographers can use to structure their narratives is the meaning now given to the two final Sonnets. Both these poems are loose translations of a Greek epigram which describes how the nymphs of love wanted to extinguish the torch of love but only succeeded in boiling the water into which they plunged it. In his first version of this epigram, Shakespeare refers to a 'seething bath, which yet men prove / Against strange maladies a sovereign cure'; and in the second to a 'cool well' which 'from love's fire took heat perpetual, / Growing a bath and healthful remedy / For men diseased'.[52] This example is different from the other three in that there is no ambiguity in the lines themselves which quite clearly refer to the contemporary method of treating syphilis with very hot baths. What is new therefore, and a growing part of that common narrative structure which is now generally agreed can be extracted from the Sonnets, is the assumption that a man who talks about this remedy must have undergone it. Since (as Duncan-Jones puts it) 'disturbingly graphic images of sweating tubs and venereal infection close both *Troilus and Cressida* and Shakespeare's Sonnets',[53] the obvious conclusion is not hard to draw.

One question on which it has been vital for recent biographers to agree is that Shakespeare was himself responsible for the way in which the Sonnets appeared. In 1612 Thomas Heywood referred to Shakespeare having published them 'in his own name' and about two years later Jonson's friend, William Drummond, wrote of him having 'lately published [his work]' (by which he meant the Sonnets).[54] It is important to assume that both these people knew what they were talking about and were not just using a familiar expression ('Oh, I see he's published his poems') loosely. This is what Michael Wood assumes when, with Rowse-like confidence, he writes, 'Shakespeare, then, was responsible for the selection, punctuation, italicization, and, crucially, the order of the 154 sonnets, of which the last two are versions of the same one' (this final detail is included because, in further exemplification of Shakespeare's Catholicism, Wood wants to point out that '153 is the number of prayers in the Catholic rosary').[55] Once these matters are clear, individual sonnets which are otherwise obscure can be interpreted by reference to their neighbours and the sequence as a whole can be made to tell a story which, since it can include both homosexuality and adultery, will brighten up the pages of any biography. Arguing that Shakespeare and his wife did not get on, Honigmann has said that, 'Biographers are now pretty well agreed that the poet's relationship with the dark lady of the Sonnets cannot be waved away as just a literary exercise'[56] and since he has provided much of the scholarly material for several of the biographers concerned, he speaks with authority. In his *Shakespeare for All Time*, Stanley Wells writes of 'reasons to suppose that Shakespeare had extramarital affairs' and suggests that Sonnet 31 indicates that he took pride in them.[57] The speaker in this poem refers to the addressee as '*the grave where buried love doth live, / Hung with the trophies of my lovers gone*'.[58] That the addressee and the departed lovers here appear to be male only shows that the Sonnets can support the idea of extra-marital affairs with either men or women, as it can, of course, with both.

Wells is for the most part admirably conservative in his biographical speculations so that his use of Sonnet 31 is a departure from the norm. Wood on the other hand is always willing to take a risk and has the knack of finding new things to say about familiar matters. Sonnet 33, for example, ('*Full many a glorious morning have I seen / Flatter the mountain top with sovereign eye,*') has generally been taken as expressing disappointment that the addressee, after delighting the speaker with his friendship, has somehow let him down. Although his 'sun one early morn did shine' it was 'but one hour mine' and is now obscured with 'basest clouds'. This has in no way altered the way the speaker feels about the young man, however, since 'Suns of the world may stain, when heaven's sun staineth'. 'It is hard to imagine', Wood writes,

> that poetry of this intensity is only about separation from the beautiful young nobleman, however much loved. Shakespeare here has run together loss of the young man, loss of his own sun/son and the loss of God's son. It would not have escaped an Elizabethan reader that the number of the sonnet, 33, was Jesus's age at the time of the crucifixion; and, coincidentally or not, it was also Shakespeare's age in 1597.
>
> The sonnets have been the subject of many bizarre theories but it is surely inconceivable, if this sonnet was written in 1597, that it is not also about his son.[59]

This illustrates nicely the importance of insisting that the ordering of the poems was Shakespeare's own; the room for manoeuvre which their puns and metaphors allow a biographer; and that effective device I described in my section on language of incorporating a disclaimer ('*if* this sonnet was written in 1597') in a way which ensures that it does not spoil the general effect. It shows how open the Sonnets are to multiple readings and the way that they can be used to illustrate almost any aspect of Shakespeare's life which his biographer chooses to emphasise. As my illustrations show, they are an invaluable resource even if more than two hundred years of intense scholarly enquiry has failed to establish with any certainty when they were composed (or revised); the person or persons to whom they were addressed; the degree to which they are fictional; and whether their publication was either approved or supervised by Shakespeare. On these and other questions the evidence is so sparse that biographers who want to use the Sonnets inevitably find themselves playing the same game as novelists or dramatists.

History to the Rescue

There is always an initial difficulty in offering to write the biography of someone whose life has been written many times before. In theory, there are as many possible biographies as there are people willing to write them: new perspectives on the same old material; but in practice the public like to be given the impression that their biographers have been driven to composition by material which is new. This is perhaps why the blurb for Michael Wood's 2003 book talks of 'a wealth of unexplored archive evidence' and 'fascinating new discoveries'; or the first sentence of the preface to Park Honan's biography reads: 'Research into the Elizabethans is of such quality today that new material about Shakespeare, his town, his parents, his schooling, his friendships, or his career comes to light continually'.[60]

The reference here to new material about *Shakespeare* may be puzzling but there is a way in which information about his town (for example) can be considered a kind of information about the man himself. Although Nathan Drake had been there before, Schoenbaum credits the Victorian biographer Charles Knight with being the first person properly to 'associate Shakespeare with the circumstances around him' and thus triumph over the 'limitations of his data'.[61] No new information directly relevant to Shakespeare himself may have come to light since 1909, but historians are always discovering more details about the age in which he lived. This means that most lives of Shakespeare are not what they say on the cover, but rather history books disguised as biographies; and often very interesting history books at that.

'This is the moment', wrote Anthony Burgess at the beginning of the fifth chapter of his 1970 biography of Shakespeare, 'for the traditional florid cadenza to mark Will's first glimpse of London'[62] and being a gifted writer he then obliged better than have most biographers before or since. The narrow, bustling streets, the vile smells emanating from primitive sanitary arrangements, the small scale in comparison with present-day London, its spectacular population growth in the fifty years before Shakespeare arrived there . . . all biographers worth their salt are able to fill several pages with these features of English social history, although it is perhaps not a good idea to follow Burgess and reveal that this is precisely what all biographers do. But then Burgess wrote both fiction and biography about Shakespeare and was therefore more aware than most of how thin the dividing line is between the two. When he writes, only a few pages before this allusion to the cadenza: 'I find if convenient to imagine that [Shakespeare] knew Anne Hathaway carnally, for the first time, in the spring of 1582'[63] he may also be showing that his experience on both sides of the line makes him more alert than others to the moments when he crosses it.

Shakespeare's first arrival in London is a relatively circumscribed topic but there are other ways of shifting the burden of writing biography to history which allow much more room for manoeuvre. After all, Shakespeare presumably came to the capital to be an actor and the rapid growth of the public theatre in the late sixteenth century, its relatively sudden and spectacular development out of the old mystery and morality plays into a thriving commercial enterprise, is a fascinating topic. So also is the status of actors in those days and the way they needed to protect themselves from being classified as vagabonds by working under the patronage of some aristocratic figure, or of the monarch herself. It is a pity, of course, that we have no idea which theatrical company or companies Shakespeare joined before he became a member of the Lord Chamberlain's Men, but Duncan-Jones shows that there are ways of circumventing that difficulty. It must in any case have been one or several of them so it could be said that descriptions of one or several are relevant to the story of his career.

Neither social nor theatre history is what the general reader usually understands by the second word in both terms, but there are dozens of ways of making Shakespeare the trigger for pages of history in the more traditional sense. The continuing wars in the Low Countries, for example, can be linked to Shakespeare through the number of discharged soldiers in his plays; when he writes of England's past he can frequently be taken as reflecting on contemporary Court intrigues; and anxiety over the Succession, which so dominated people's thinking in Elizabeth's later years, can be seen as often transposed by him to a domestic level. In the depiction of Shylock in *The Merchant of Venice*, there is a particular opportunity for the biographer to talk about the trial in 1594 of Elizabeth's Jewish doctor, Roderigo Lopez, on a charge of attempted poisoning. There are many fascinating and page-filling aspects to this episode as there are to what is perhaps the most celebrated event of Elizabeth's reign, the defeat of the Armada. This took place inconveniently early, but most lives of Shakespeare manage to incorporate some of its details, using them to indicate the mood of national optimism in which he began his career, or as an example of how ambivalent a crypto-Catholic might feel at witnessing the humiliation of Spanish power. A biography is traditionally the story of the subject's life and times and where information about the life is sparse, the times will always be there to take up the slack. Pondering his investigation of Shakespeare's 'lost years', Michael Wood has to admit that it has involved 'a long search with many blind alleys. But none, I think, are fruitless. All are revealing about his times.'[64]

An episode whose surrounding details are almost as dramatic as those associated with the Armada can be linked much more easily than it can with Shakespeare and, indeed, no biographer has failed to provide an account of how, in 1601, an exasperated Earl of Essex staged a minor rebellion against Elizabeth and was then arrested, tried and executed. The special licence which this event gives to Shakespeare's biographers for shifting their burden to history derives from the fact that one of Essex's fellow conspirators was the Earl of Southampton and Shakespeare is of course linked to Southampton by the dedication he had attached to *The Rape of Lucrece* seven years earlier. What provides an additional link is that two days before the rebellion took place one of Essex's followers paid the Lord Chamberlain's Men forty shillings to stage *Richard II*, complete (one assumes) with the scene in which the sovereign is deposed. The follower who negotiated with the actors was not Southampton but Sir Gilly Meyrick and the Lord Chamberlain's man who afterwards defended the behaviour of his company was not Shakespeare but Augustine Phillips; yet this has not deterred biographers from closely involving Shakespeare, any more than it has novelists and dramatists, and it is a peculiarly self-denying writer of Shakespeare's life who does not presume (as Duncan-Jones does) that it was 'the long-standing connection with Essex's close friend and confederate Southampton that constituted the first and most compromising link between the players and the two malcontent Earls'.[65]

Imprisoned for the rest of Elizabeth's reign, Southampton was only pardoned when James I came to the throne. The story of James's accession, and the early years of his rule, make useful copy for a biographer. In an interesting example of the argument from absence, Duncan-Jones is able to exploit the fact that Shakespeare did not compose a poem lamenting the passing of Elizabeth (or celebrating the arrival of James), and writes several pages about the efforts of those who did.[66] The issue of the patent which transformed the Lord Chamberlain's into the King's Men was one of the first administrative acts of the new monarch's reign. In an admirable study, Leeds Barroll has poured cold water on the notion that this indicates how enthusiastic James was about the drama, Shakespeare's theatrical company and Shakespeare himself;[67] but, as I pointed out in Chapter 2, Sir William Davenant was thought to have possessed a letter which James wrote to Shakespeare and it has traditionally been assumed that *Macbeth* was written to flatter not only the king's dynastic pride but also his interest in witches. These indications of a special relationship between dramatist and monarch may not seem much to justify those biographers who allow details of James's reign to take the strain in the second half of their lives of Shakespeare, but they are no less substantial than those which encourage them to allow the history of Elizabeth to do the same in the first half. For those who present Shakespeare as a secret Catholic, of course, there is a special advantage in describing how enthusiastically members of the English Catholic community welcomed James (whose wife was known to practise their faith), why he was gradually led to break the promises he appeared to have made to them, and the degree of disappointed expectation in the anger which fuelled the Gunpowder Plot.

I indicate only very briefly here the uses which the astute biographer can make of histories of London and the theatre, and of history *tout court*; but there are other resources of a similar kind at least as rich as these three. What biography of Shakespeare does not after all begin with a history of Stratford-upon-Avon, or of the whole of Warwickshire if need be? So much more information is available on that topic than on Shakespeare himself that it is tempting not to use it. The rationale for doing so is that we are most of us products of a regional background and that – where there is no alternative – the history of that background can always tell one kind of story of our lives. Even today it seems to be generally accepted that a person from the rugged North of England will have a quite different character from someone brought up in the Home Counties. Shakespeare was of course, in the words of the song, 'a Warwickshire lad'. The advantage of his being born there, Duncan-Jones points out, is that the number of major writers who had been bred either in Warwickshire or in the six counties which surrounded it made the West Midlands 'much the likeliest region of England to produce a major secular poet or playwright'.[68]

From general matters like these, the biographer can move smoothly to the more immediate and particular historical features of Shakespeare's background. Park Honan has offered a striking, if somewhat idiosyncratic, illustration of how to do this. He notes, as most of his predecessors have done, that shortly after Shakespeare was born there was an outbreak of plague which carried off almost twenty percent of the Stratford population, in spite of the authorities' valiant efforts to contain it. A description of this event certainly makes for interesting reading but its biographical relevance has always seemed to be no more than that Shakespeare survived. Yet, argues Honan, the special care which Mary Shakespeare must have lavished on her new-born son in order to achieve this outcome set the pattern for the rest of his life. The confidence he later showed, Honan claims, 'cannot be dissociated from the emotional support he must have found at home.'[69] This is an unusual illustration of the use of local history. The more typical direction in which biographers can move is suggested by Michael Wood when he writes, 'The young Shakespeare was shaped by family, work, church and environment. And although we have few details of the poet's early life we can access these influences through other sources.'[70] What he seems to mean is that the knowledge we now have of Shakespeare's local environment can compensate for our ignorance of his more personal experience. A good example here, missing from Wood's list even though it is an influence as shaping in its way as family or church, is education. No records survive from the Stratford Grammar School of Shakespeare's time, but it is virtually certain he went there and, thanks to the historians, we now know what he is likely to have been taught. This means that biographers can spend considerable space discussing Elizabethan grammar-school education, which is relatively uniform, secure in the knowledge that what they are talking about was Shakespeare's daily experience during a good proportion of his early life.

Yet some people might complain here that the history I am describing is only useful for describing *collective* experience. It may tell us what books the young Shakespeare was made to read along with the rest of his class but not what he himself thought of them, nor whether he was an unruly, dutiful or especially precocious student. It cannot give us the flavour of his personal involvement any more than the other kinds of history I have mentioned can tell us how he responded to first seeing London, or what he felt about the Essex rebellion. All this is unfortunately true and there are general problems here about the use of history in biography which need to be confronted. No-one could write a biography of Shakespeare without knowing a good deal about his times but can knowledge of those times always take biographers all the way they need to go? Is there not a danger of writing *Hamlet* without the Prince of Denmark, of making it too obvious that the word 'Shakespeare' is no more than a pretext for a description of various aspects of Elizabethan or Jacobean life? The question is one of transitions, of how to make the reader feel that Shakespeare is firmly linked to the material being discussed. One method biographers of Shakespeare have for overcoming this problem constitutes such an important weapon in their armoury, and is a topic relevant to so many matters other than those which normally fall under the rubric of 'history', that it deserves a separate section of its own.

The Argument from Proximity: Joining up the Dots

Michael Wood's reference to 'church' as a shaping influence is a reminder that, because his father was a prominent public official, the young Shakespeare must have attended the Stratford parish church with his family. Historical scholarship can tell us the kind of things he would have listened to there, just as it can reconstruct the usual curriculum in an Elizabethan grammar school; but it can no more discover what he thought as he sat in his pew than help us describe how he responded to his grammar-school teachers. The problem for biographers is to make the connection between the fascinating history of religion in Elizabethan times and Shakespeare's own religious opinions, to find ways of persuading the reader into thinking that talking about one is talking about the other.

As I have already indicated on several occasions, it has been the fashion in more recent times to present Shakespeare as Catholic. This is a tricky word to use about people in the sixteenth century during more or less half of which it described what everybody more or less was. For those not deeply interested in theological questions, the English Reformation could hardly have come in with a rush and there must have been thousands who, while outwardly conforming to the changes, kept the substance of their old beliefs. It could well be that Shakespeare's parents were among these and that Shakespeare himself always retained not merely an familiarity with the old ways but a positive fondness for them. That would not however be very interesting from a biographical point of view. What one wants to know is whether Shakespeare was one of those Catholics who accepted in full the implications of the Pope's excommunication of Elizabeth in 1571 and believed, not only that the old ways were the best, but that they ought to be restored, something which could only have happened under a different sovereign. Catholics of that variety were inevitably regarded as enemies of the State which is why they preferred to keep their degree of commitment secret. I have already noted how the absence of any indication from Shakespeare himself that he belonged to this group can be used as evidence of his affiliation, but there are other ways of making the link.

An exemplary instance of these other ways is provided by Ernst Honigmann who notes that the man appointed as the Stratford Grammar School master in

1579 was John Cottam. Cottam had a brother called Thomas who was a Catholic priest and a member of Campion's 1580 mission. Like Campion, he was eventually arrested, tried and then executed in that peculiarly sadistic manner of the Elizabethans. Soon after his brother's arrest, John Cottam retired to his home ground in Lancashire where he lived only ten miles from a certain Alexander Hoghton. It is in the will which Hoghton made about the time of the Campion mission that, first Oliver Baker in 1937, and then E. K. Chambers in 1944, felt that they might have found a reference to Shakespeare. Hoghton left his musical instruments and his play clothes to his brother:

> if he be minded & do keep players. And if he will not keep & maintain players, then it is my mind & will that Sir Thomas Hesket knight shall have the same instruments & play clothes. And I most heartily require the said Sir Thomas to be friendly unto Fulk Gillom & William Shakeshafte now dwelling with me & either to take them unto his service or else to help them to some good master [...][71]

It is chiefly these words which allow Honigmann to speculate that, recommended by Cottam, the fervently Catholic young Shakespeare went to work for the Hoghtons, in the first instance perhaps as a tutor – Catholic families felt a special need for private tuition for their children – and that he then discovered his gift for acting before returning to Stratford in 1582 to marry Anne Hathaway and father his three children. To those who object that 'Shakeshafte' is not the same as 'Shakespeare', Honigmann can point out that there was a great deal of fluidity in the spelling of family names in Elizabethan times; and to those who have tried to discredit his claim by showing that Shakeshafte was a common name in Lancashire, he can retort that this is all the more reason why the clerk who drew up Houghton's will should have copied down Shakespeare's name wrongly. Honigmann further supports his case by noting that John Weever, the author of the highly complimentary sonnet 'Ad Gulielmum Shakespeare' published in 1599, was related to the Hoghtons.[72] Thus there is a line running from Shakespeare, to Cottam, Houghton, Weever and then back to Shakespeare so all that it then remains for the biographer to do is run a narrative charge through the circuit.

The suggestive force of the connections Honigmann is able to make has often been more that sufficient to overcome objections such as the fact that by the time John Cottam came to Stratford Grammar School in 1579, the fifteen-year-old Shakespeare had probably left it. He himself is one of those scholars who appears to have derived little commercial advantage from his researches and is therefore an invaluable resource for biographers past, present or to come. The third chapter of Anthony Holden's biography, for example, is based on Honigmann and Katherine Duncan-Jones takes her title (*Ungentle Shakespeare*), and therefore the overall scheme of her book, from Honigmann's efforts to show that by the time he made his will, Shakespeare was a bitter, angry and reproachful man. A recent biographer who has probably benefited as much from Honigmann's work on Shakespeare and Catholicism as they have is Michael Wood. He has not only been able to extend the method Hongimann employs but also find uses for it in an area which has been familiar to Shakespeare scholars for years but the possible significance of which many of them have passed by.

In the past, showing that Shakespeare was a crypto-Catholic has usually meant demonstrating that his father was one too. This has involved rejecting the official reason given at the time for John Shakespeare's absences from church in the early 1590s (that he was fearful of being arrested for debt), and attributing them instead to a late twinge of Catholic conscience. It has also meant accepting that the 'Spiritual Testament' described in Chapter 2 had in fact been signed by him and was not another example of the eighteenth-century penchant for literary forgery (the latter part of the testament could not have been forged, but John Shakespeare's name on it may have been). These are such inviting topics to discuss that there has been a tendency to ignore, or at least downplay, the religious affiliations of Shakespeare's *mother*.

By following E. Hamilton Gruner and bolding assuming that the Edward Arden executed in 1583 for his supposed involvement in a Catholic plot to assassinate the Queen was 'the head of Shakespeare's mother's family', Wood immediately adds drama to his narrative. After Arden's arrest, the houses of many of his relatives and known associates were searched so that, although there is no record of searches at Henley Street, it becomes easy for Wood to present Shakespeare as anxiously keeping his head down and hoping to escape detection, just as he was to do later at the time of the Gunpowder plot whose principal organisers (Wood notes) 'Catesby, Tresham, and Winter – all had Stratford connections, indeed, the Catesbys were distantly related to [Shakespeare's] mother'.[73] By making these links, Wood is able to escape one common and rather boring characterisation of Shakespeare as a man who stood to one side of the political and religious life of his time in order to write plays which made him a lot of money and show him instead as someone with a dangerous secret, perpetually in danger of being exposed.

There are several more threads to Wood's presentation of Shakespeare as entangled in a Catholic network. He notes, for example, that the Robert Debdale who was arrested at much the same time as Campion and John Cottam's brother was a native of Shottery, Anne Hathaway's village; and that he was also another distant relation of Shakespeare's mother, and a former pupil of Stratford Grammar School. Debdale was one of the Catholic priests attacked in Samuel Harsnett's *Declaration of Egregious Popish Impostures*, a book which it is clear from *King Lear* Shakespeare must have read. In the printed account of Shakespeare's life, Wood decides that the jury is still out on the question of whether he ever went to Lancashire; but in the television version he finds the clinching detail in information initially discovered by Hotson and then refined by Honigmann, namely that the Thomas Savage who acted as a trustee for Shakespeare and four of his colleagues when the Globe was being built, came from the same village in Lancashire as the Thomas Hesketh to whom Alexander Hoghton recommended William Shakeshafte.[75]

My aim here is not to describe a particular way of presenting Shakespeare, but rather to identify a method which can be used whatever idea of him the biographer wants to convey. Clearly enough, therefore, this method has no inherent connection with the question of Shakespeare's religious views. Wanting to strengthen the case for his association with the Queen's Men, for example, Duncan-Jones points out that the widow of the unfortunate actor who was killed before they arrived in Stratford later became the wife of Shakespeare's colleague in the Lord Chamberlain's Men, John Heminge; and she suggests that 'solid evidence' for Shakespeare's personal closeness with fellow playwright John Marston (about whom she writes a great deal) can be found in the fact that Marston and his father were the sponsors at the Middle Temple for the Thomas Greene who, during the Welcombe enclosure affair, refers to Shakespeare as his cousin.[75] I have called the method with which I am concerned here the 'argument from proximity' because it consists of drawing the reader's attention to people who were related to Shakespeare (however distantly); with whom he had dealings of some kind; or who were in the same place at more or less the same time as he was. Of course we know that in our own case we may have relations who in no way impinge upon our lives; that having commercial dealings with communists or Plymouth brethren does not necessarily mean that we share their views; and that sometimes it is only in retrospect that we realise that a person who has since become famous went to our school or used to drink every Friday in the same pub. We know also that when this method is used to denigrate people it is known as 'guilt by association' and not considered respectable. But none of the biographers set out to denigrate Shakespeare and in any case it is clear both that kinship was much more important in the sixteenth century than it is now and that England was much more thinly populated. Just as it sometimes seems impossible today to meet a second New Zealander who does not know the first, so in those days it is possible that most of the people living in the same towns or practising the same trades were acquainted. This at least is the assumption biographers tend to rely on as they accumulate around Shakespeare a number of figures whom they can use to draw him out of the deep obscurity in which he would otherwise languish.

As a final example of how this method works, it is useful to take the case of Richard Field. Two-and-a-half years older than Shakespeare, Field was a Stratford boy who would also have attended Stratford Grammar School and whose family must have known Shakespeare's (in 1592 his recently deceased father's goods were evaluated by Shakespeare *père*[76]). Apprenticed to a London printer, he took over the business when his master died and married the widow. That Field printed both *Venus and Adonis* and *The Rape of Lucrece* is the reason all the biographers have felt justified in describing him as Shakespeare's friend, usually his close friend. This is despite the fact that he was one of those local residents who in 1597 successfully petitioned against James Burbage making any use of a large room in the former priory at Blackfriars after he had spent £600 converting it into an indoor theatre.[77] (Friendship is one thing, having your sleep disturbed by rowdy theatre-goers quite another.) But the chief usefulness of Field is that his master had been a Huguenot refugee and that he therefore provides a link with the Mountjoys. This link is strengthened by the fact that in c. 1600 he moved from Blackfriars to a house near the Mountjoys and that he and Mrs Mountjoy were both at one time or another patients of Simon Forman, the same Simon Forman who has left us the best surviving account of going to a Shakespeare play. He is therefore one pathway into the Mountjoy/Belott milieu and to George Wilkins who was called to testify in the case Stephen Belott brought against his father-in-law and in one of whose brothels (Duncan-Jones believes) Shakespeare may first have contracted the syphilis which he talks about so much in *Measure for Measure* or *Troilus and Cressida*. The Mountjoy/Belott affair offers a number of figures or events which are interestingly juxtaposed; but merely by juxtaposing them the biographer will be able to suggest to the reader that they are connected. Given the dearth of information, what I term 'joining up the dots' has become an obligation for anyone who wants to write an exciting life of Shakespeare and an important method for making a little, or even nothing, go a long way.

Throughout the last century biographies of Shakespeare continued to appear and there is no sign of the flow diminishing in the early years of this. Of all Britain's national icons he is the one for whose 'life' there will always be a ready welcome. Biographies distinguish themselves in the public mind by making a claim to truth. That is that they carry with them the implication that every effort has been made to establish how it probably was, what is most likely to have happened. They differentiate themselves from novels and plays by claiming not just casual, but intimate, association with history. But in its traditional form at least, history only works with information and the relative absence of it in Shakespeare's case means that without the methods I describe, and others like them, biographies of him could not continue to be written. That they are, is a further indication of Shakespeare's iconic status. Sales figures suggest that there is an on-going demand from the public for the life of a writer whose works are so much enjoyed and whose image is visible everywhere. What the public continues to want, it usually continues to get, so that perhaps the only thing which is then left to consider is the price it has to pay.

Notes

1. Gary Taylor, 'Forms of Opposition: Shakespeare and Middleton', *English Literary Renaissance*, vol. 24, no. 2 (Spring, 1994), p. 298.

2. Michael Wood, *In Search of Shakespeare* (2003), p. 147.

3. Katherine Duncan-Jones, *Ungentle Shakespeare* (2001), pp. 118-9.

4. *Ibid.*, p. 119.

5. Anthony Burgess, *Shakespeare* (Vintage Books, 1996), p. 214.

6. Duncan-Jones, p. 266.

7. Park Honan, *Shakespeare: A Life* (1998), p. 18.

8. E. A. J. Honigmann, 'Shakespeare on his deathbed: the last will and testament' in *Myriad-minded Shakespeare* (Manchester University Press, 1998), pp. 225-6.

9. 'Shakespeare on his deathbed', p. 223; Duncan-Jones, p. 262.

10. 'Shakespeare on his deathbed', p. 224.

11. B. Roland Lewis, *The Shakespeare Documents* (Stanford University Press, 1940), vol. 1, p. 486.

12. *They Hanged My Saintly Billy* was first published in 1957.

13. For a full account of the Queen's Men see Scott McMillin and Sally-Beth Maclean, *The Queen's Men and Their Plays* (Cambridge University Press, 1998).

14. Duncan-Jones, p. 28. The italics in this and the next three quotations are mine.

15. *Ibid.*, pp. 31-4.

16. *Ibid.*, p. 35-6.

17. *Ibid.*, 36, 43.

18. *Ibid.*, p. 60. The words omitted have no bearing on my argument.

19. Anthony Holden, *William Shakespeare: His Life and Work* (1999), p. 237.

20. *Ibid.*, pp. 217-8.

21. *Ibid.*, p. 218.

22. Wood, p. 246.

23. A. L. Rowse, *Shakespeare the Man* (1988), p. 119.

24. E. A. J. Honigmann, *Shakespeare: the 'lost years'* (Manchester University Press, 1985), p. 3.

25. G. O. Trevelyan, *Life and Letters of Lord Macauley* (1908), p. 268.

26. Holden, pp. 240, 242, 247.

27. *Ibid.*, p. 248.

28. *Ibid.*, p. 260.

29. M. Shapira (ed.), *Selected Literary Criticism of Henry James*, p. 300.

30. Holden, p. 2.

31. Jonathan Bate, *The Genius of Shakespeare* (1997), p. 6; Duncan-Jones, p. 152.

32. Holden, p. 286.

33. *Ibid.*, p. 346.

34. Bate, p. 7.

35. Shakespeare's Welsh schoolmaster was called Thomas Jenkins and appears to have been at the Stratford Grammar School from 1575 to 1579. See Schoenbaum, *A Documentary Life*, p. 53.

36. Honan, p. p. 143.

37. Duncan-Jones, p. 40.

38. Schoenbaum, A *Documentary Life*, p. 15.

39. Duncan-Jones, pp. 110, 221-2.

40. Before the publication of Stephen Greenblatt's *Will in the World*, Anthony Holden appeared to be the only recent biographer willing to maintain the tradition of hearing Shakespeare announce his retirement in Prospero's speech. Greenblatt has no doubt that Shakespeare did indeed 'retire' and has him contemplating the prospect of doing so as early as 1604, in the opening scenes of *King Lear* (see p. 356).

41. E. A. J. Honigmann (ed.), *King John* (Arden, 1954), p. lviii.

42. *Ibid.*, p. 97, 99. See also Giorgio Melchiori, *The Merry Wives of Windsor* (Arden, 2000), pp. 18-30.

43. Holden, p. 151.

44. Wood, p. 166.

45. Rowse, pp. 38, ix, 56-7, 88.

46. See William Empson, *Some Versions of Pastoral* (1935), pp. 89-115.

47. Bate, pp. 49-64.

48. *Ibid.*, p. 58.

49. See Leslie Hotson, *Mr W. .H.* (1964), pp. 73-84.

50. Andrew Gurr, 'Shakespeare's first poem; Sonnet 145', *Essays in Criticism*, vol. 21 (1971), pp. 221-6.

51. Wood, p. 87.

52. Duncan-Jones (ed.), *Shakespeare's Sonnets* (1997), pp. 153-4.

53. Duncan-Jones, p. 224.

54. See Chambers, vol. 2, pp. 218, 220-1.

55. Wood, p. 305.

56. 'Shakespeare on his deathbed', p. 229.

57. Stanley Wells, *Shakespeare For All Time* (2002), p. 83.

58. *Shakespeare's Sonnets*, p. 31.

59. Wood, p. 185.

60. Honan, p. ix.

61. Schoenbaum, *Shakespeare's Lives*, p. 277.

62. Burgess, p. 65.

63. *Ibid.*, p. 53.

64. Wood, p. 109. A whole chapter in Stephen Greenblatt's *Will in the World* is organised around possible links between Shakespeare and the Lopez who, immediately before his execution, provoked laughter when he declared that he loved the Queen as well as he loved Jesus Christ. 'This laughter', Greenblatt comments, 'welling up from the crowd at the foot of the scaffold, could well have triggered Shakespeare's achievement in *The Merchant of Venice*' (p. 277).

65. Duncan-Jones, p. 127.

66. *Ibid.*, pp. 161-6.

67. See Leeds Barroll, *Politics, Plague, and Shakespeare's Theater: The Stuart Years* (Cornell University Press, 1991).

68. Duncan-Jones, p. 1.

69. Honan, p. 18.

70. Wood, p. 35.

71. See Honigmann, *Shakespeare: the 'last years'*, p. 136.

72. *Ibid.* The debate as to whether Shakespeare could have been Shakeshafte is on-going. See Robert Bearman's claim that he was not, in '"Was William Shakespeare William Shakeshafte?" Revisited', *Shakespeare Quarterly*, 53, (2002), pp. 83-94 and Honigmann's reply, 'The Shakespeare/Shakeshafte Question, Continued', *Shakespeare Quarterly*, 54, (2004), pp.83-6.

73. Wood, p. 283.

74. The claim comes in the second part of Wood's four part TV series ('The lost years').
75. Duncan-Jones, pp. 31, 145.
76. Schoenbaum, *Documentary Life*, p. 29.
77. See Halliwell-Phillipps, *Outlines*, vol. 1, p. 304.

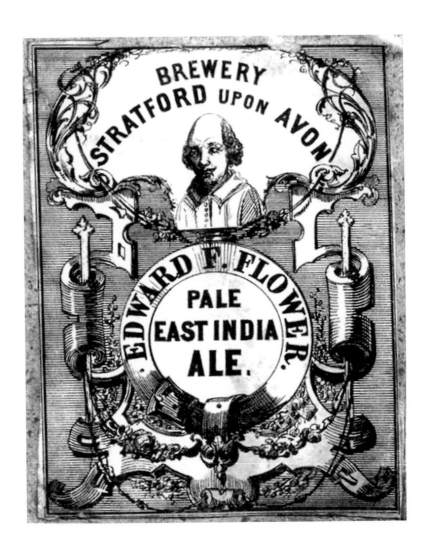

36. *Label from a bottle of beer brewed in Stratford by the Flower Brewery (founded in 1831) who used a bust of Shakespeare as their trademark. Here the bust is based on the Chandos portrait, but on other labels they used a bust based on the Janssen monument in Holy Trinity Church. By courtesy of the Shakespeare Birthplace Trust Records Office.*

Chapter Nine

Conclusion

THE FOCUS IN THE previous chapter was on biography but, insofar as they are concerned with the effort to reconstruct or imagine the life of a national icon, that is true of all my other chapters also. In the 'General Editor's Preface' at the beginning of this volume, I say that icons come in all shapes and sizes and imply that one method of categorisation would be to concentrate on origins and make a distinction between those which belong to history and those frankly acknowledged as mythological. In the latter instance, the mind is free to conjure up whatever seems pleasing and appropriate but in the former it may be trammelled by a sense of obligation to the documentary record. It is then that the role of the scholar becomes more important and conflicts can develop between those who operate either within or without a particular scholarly environment. In *The Late Mr Shakespeare*, the second of his Shakespeare novels, Robert Nye presents the case for the outsiders with considerable eloquence and force.

Reader, there are, in truth, as I would now make clear for your better understanding of this sorry mad book of mine, two kinds of history, as different from each other as chalk and cheese.

There is town history and there is *country* history.

Town history is cynical and exact. It is written by wits and it orders and limits what it talks about. It relies on facts and figures. It is knowing. Dry and sceptical and clever, it is ruled by the head. Beginning in the shadow of the law courts, at the end of the day your town history tends to the universities – it becomes academic. Town history is believable and reliable. Offering proofs it never strains credulity. But sometimes it can't see the Forest of Arden for the trees. And it falls probably short of the mark when it comes up against Mr Shakespeare.

Your country history is a different matter. Country history is faithful and open-ended. It is a tale told by various idiots on the village green, all busy contradicting themselves in the name of a common truth. It exaggerates and inflames what it talks about. It delights in lies and gossip. It is unwise. Wild and mystical and passionate, it is ruled by the heart. Beginning by the glow of the hearth, at the end of the night your country history tends to pass into balladry and legend – it

307

becomes poetic. Country history is fanciful and maggoty. Easy to mock, it always strains belief. But sometimes it catches the ghostly coat-tails of what is otherwise ungraspable. It is the only possible way of accounting for Mr Shakespeare.[1]

Nye is in part relying here on the frequently expressed belief that there is more essential truth in poetry than in history, and he clearly wants to mark off his own efforts from those of academics whose supposed commitment to 'facts and figures' deprives them of the imaginative insight which provides the only avenue to an understanding of what Shakespeare was really like. By calling country history 'maggoty', he is recalling Anthony Wood's well known description of John Aubrey, that richly entertaining and quintessential gossip, as a 'shiftless person, roving and maggoty-headed'.[2] His town history is clearly academic biography in the tradition of Malone, Halliwell-Phillipps or Chambers, yet the country version includes not only Aubrey but also novelists like himself. The distinction he wants to make is therefore not so much between fiction and its opposite but the academic and non-academic.

The authors of the mostly very recent biographies which I have used in chapter 8 to illustrate how those who want to respond to the public demand for ever more 'lives' of Shakespeare are able to do so, come from both sides of Nye's demarcation line. Anthony Holden, Michael Wood as well of course as Anthony Burgess are, or were, professional writers while Duncan-Jones, Bate, Honigmann and Honan are distinguished academics who, like Rowse and Hotson before them, hold or have held senior positions in British universities. A similar distinction between the more or less academically inclined has no doubt always existed, but it has become much more marked with the expansion of university education throughout the twentieth century: certain scholars who may in the past have seemed very different from each other now always tend to share at least the one defining characteristic of being, or having been, university teachers. The books these two classes of authors write are in many ways recognisably different in character but that they both use the same methods for overcoming the 'limitations of data' relating to Shakespeare's life, suggests that the differences between them are not clear-cut and that it is now impossible to mark a strict divide between Nye's town and country history, one kind of writing about Shakespeare and another.

The divide is certainly fuzzy, but it can be made to seem less so by viewing matters from the point of view of readers: ordinary, common or otherwise. When any of them pick up a novel they freely grant its author a licence to 'make things up' and even when faced with a representative of that rapidly rising sub-genre of 'fictionalised biography', such as David Lodge's very recent book on Henry James[3], they know that a good deal of what they read will be invented. What they expect from their biographers, on the other hand, is that they should adhere to a number of traditional standards, only saying what their information allows them to believe is probable or likely. The relevant point here is that, in our time, this expectation of readers is likely to be greater, the closer the biographer concerned is associated with the university. A consequence is that, although that sharing of methods between academic and non-academic biographers which I have demonstrated in my last chapter might well be celebrated as an example of how biography is the one literary form which has managed to bridge what is otherwise an ever increasing gap between the universities and the common reader, it could also be regarded as a serious betrayal of trust. After all, there is a perspective from which each and every one of the methods I have described will seem intellectually reprehensible. Absence (or silence), their critics say, cannot prove anything without an appropriate context and replacing biographical foreground with historical background means having to assume that Shakespeare's behaviour, thoughts and feelings were always representative when the indications are that he was an exceptional person. Proximity, they go on, is not always a sure sign of a relationship and certainly will not tell us its nature. These are the critics who claim that it is impossible to use Shakespeare's writings to uncover his private thoughts and feelings because the plays give out so many conflicting signals while the poems are so dominated by literary convention (as well as often being quite deliberately enigmatic) that to draw biographical conclusions from them is worse than foolish. Besides, there is still no firm chronology for either. If all this is true, does not the participation of university intellectuals in the highly profitable business of writing Shakespeare biographies represent a monstrous *trahison des clercs*? What after all are the universities *for*, if it is not to renounce and denounce false reasoning, shoddy speculation, and to refuse to feed a public appetite when there are no intellectually respectable means available for doing so?

One reply to at least a part of this criticism relates to the nature of all biography. Shakespeare's academic biographers may often be accused of unwarranted speculation but a cursory examination of recent lives of other figures will show that all biographers speculate, more or less. Every one of them is forced into speculation at some point because, regardless of the number of documents they may have at their disposal, what the understanding of another human being always requires at some point is imagination. Stendhal was fond of comparing his memory of the past to a decaying fresco. Fragments had fallen from the wall but it was still possible to visualise the whole picture. Constructing a life is like fresco restoration, or less nobly perhaps, struggling with a jigsaw puzzle. The missing pieces can be imagined because their shape can be conjectured from those which surround this or that gap. It is unfortunately true that, in Shakespeare's case, there is so much gap that the honest-minded, or the faint-hearted, might sometimes be tempted to feel that the only sensible thing to do is put the few available pieces back in the box; but that would be to shrink before the imaginative challenge of piecing together (as it were) a dash of blue sky, a fragment of a finger or big toe, the pattern of a dress. If all 'lives' need the help of their authors' imagination, the argument runs, why complain that in Shakespeare's case the help required is greater than usual.

A more general response to the critics of academic biography of Shakespeare, and one which also bears directly on the general issue of icons, comes very much from the university itself. Schoenbaum has divided speculations about Shakespeare's life into three categories, the probable, the possible, and the preposterous[4] and those three figures I have already mentioned who had what might be called a traditional interest in biographical scholarship, Malone, Halliwell-Phillipps and Chambers, were always very concerned to confine themselves to the first two. Although they no doubt understood very well that different kinds of questions allowed for different kinds of certainty and that (for example) the date of Shakespeare's christening and his feelings about the Gunpowder plot are objects of enquiry which can never be considered in the same light, these three scholars would have described themselves as aspiring to give as true an account of his life as possible. But in more recent times this concern for 'truth' has been characterised as both philosophically naïve and unhealthy. Taking their inspiration from Nietzsche and Heidegger, many have argued that since we habitually construct our understanding of past events by imposing on them a narrative form, and expressing that narrative in a language which inevitably carries with it the ideological presuppositions of the present, the 'truth' of the past is an illusion which no amount of information could render otherwise. An influential proponent of this approach in the United States has been Hayden White who has argued that all history books and therefore, by an extension which can operate in this context, all biographies also, are really literary texts best analysed in literary terms. In France Michel Foucault has taken a similar view claiming, in what are admittedly complicated contexts, that his own work on punishment or madness is fiction while, in that country also, Michel de Certeau has presented an aggressive case for the illusionary nature of history in the traditional sense.[5] According to the positions defined by these academics, and very many others working in the same direction, those who criticise Shakespeare's recent biographers are the unknowing victims of the illusion of truth in history, unconsciously measuring what they read against an ideal 'true' account which is not merely currently unavailable but could never possibly exist.

The unfinished biography of Edmond Malone, the first of my trio of typical seekers after 'truth' in the old style, has already been cited as an illustration of what happens to those who want everything they say to be verifiable. A recent scholar who has sought to demonstrate the folly of Malone's methodology, and by implication therefore that of all those who might be inclined to express dissatisfaction with today's biographical writing, is Margreta De Grazia. She is chiefly interested in attacking the tradition of textual scholarship which Malone may be said to have founded and which has resulted in the habit of calling certain quartos of Shakespeare's plays 'bad' or 'corrupt' when (as a witty commentator points out) all they really are is textually challenged.[6] But she sees the same bad habit of always wanting to go back to the source or origin in the study of a Shakespeare text as also vitiating investigation of his life. 'The same preoccupation with authenticity', De Grazia writes, 'characterized Malone's account of Shakespeare's life as it did his treatment of Shakespeare's text'. As she points out, the legends or 'traditionary tales' which Malone found in Rowe could be credited by him 'only if the facts were accurate to begin with and were then entrusted to responsible transmitters'; it was, that is, only when a particular story had been (in his own words) 'handed down, by a very industrious and careful inquirer, who has derived it from persons most likely to be accurately informed concerning the facts related and subjoins his authority' that he was prepared to believe it. Any reader must feel that if this was Malone's attitude to the stories which necessarily make up biographies of Shakespeare, it was no wonder he never finished his own. Yet for De Grazia, the very fact that a story such as the deer-poaching episode was so improbable shows that it was really concerned 'not with recording facts but with commemorating "the occasion" that introduced Shakespeare to his brilliant theatrical career'. It indicated 'not an historical and datable event but a significant occasion'. Other items in the mythos, she believes, were also not concerned with 'actual and verifiable occurrences' but were rather methods which people in the seventeenth and eighteenth centuries employed to meet the 'peculiar problem posed by Shakespeare's art' (in particular how plays which broke all the classical rules came to be so great). According to her therefore, by 'linking Shakespeare to a past defined by facts and documents Malone cut him off from the traditional context that made his life relevant to those who discussed it'; 'by rejecting the traditional tales in favour of the authentic documents, [he] abstracted the life from the broader social and moral concerns and sealed it in an historically remote past constructed of authentic papers'.[7] He set a bad example not merely by perversely refusing to base his own endeavours on the traditional tales in Rowe but also by attempting with his criticisms to inhibit other people's enjoyment of them.

De Grazia sees Malone as the personification of unhelpful 'Enlightenment' values. She regrets that, in advancing her own views, she has been forced to rely on 'such positivistic mainstays as logic and evidence', but feels that, 'if these procedures can be used to disclose their own past construction in history, they can also be used to accelerate their eventual dismantling in history'.[8] Some are likely to feel that, as far as evidence or logic is concerned, she has less to apologise for than she thinks; but De Grazia certainly succeeds in providing a riposte to critics of Shakespeare biography which is both full of vigour and also highly sophisticated, suggesting that, like Malone, they are not only kill-joys but deniers of our rich cultural heritage. Most of her arguments, loosely associated as they are with those that challenge the definition of history as a search for truth, are perhaps too complicated for general use, but there is in Jonathan Bate's book what might be regarded as a domesticated version of them, or at least one which is more adapted to a non-academic public. Quoting the anecdote which I reprinted in Chapter 2 about Shakespeare saying that, in his capacity as godfather, he would give Jonson's newly born son a dozen latin/ latten spoons so that Ben could then translate them, Bate comments, 'Regardless of its factual origin, this story has the authentically representative truth of anecdote'.[9] To understand quite what this means the reader has to go to the introduction of Bate's book where he says,

> Most of the records we have concerning Shakespeare as an actor-dramatist are anecdotal, but the representative anecdote, like the horoscope, is precisely a form of which the purpose is to distil someone's characteristic disposition, their 'genius'. The point of the anecdote is not its factual but its representative truth.[10]

It may not be a good idea for biographers to encourage their readers to believe that there could be any connections between what they want to do and writing horoscopes, and it might be asked how it is possible to tell whether or not anecdotes are representative in the absence of non-anecdotal information about the subject. Yet Bate's championing of representative over factual truth is an obviously useful step for an academic biographer and, if necessary, De Grazia could always be invoked to justify it. There are perhaps important differences here between Bate and a non-academic colleague like Holden who is willing to describe the Manningham anecdote as 'one of those unverifiable vignettes too good to discard on the grounds of merely dubious provenance',[11] but whether the reasons for relying on what Chambers so aptly called the mythos are crude or sophisticated, the important point is that it should be brought into play. This is because if the mythos were ignored on the grounds that it consists of rumour, gossip and innuendo, all of it unverified and unverifiable, there would then be no means of satisfying public curiosity about what kind of person Shakespeare was.

As this book has shown, interest in the author whose plays quickly came to comprise the core of serious theatre in Britain developed to a crescendo during the eighteenth century and it was then that he became part of that notion of Britishness about which there has been so much discussion recently.[12] Here was a writer, conveniently born in the very middle of the country, who could represent all that was best about the nation and compete successfully with other countries' national bards. The French may have had their Molière and Racine but, on the principle that one Englishman is always a match for two foreigners, Britain was satisfied with Shakespeare. Most of the known facts of his life appeared to contradict the belief fostered by the careers of contemporaries like

Jonson or Marlowe, that genius could never be associated with respectability, and his financial success proved that he had been lucky enough to have been born in a country which knew how to reward talent. Shakespeare was therefore a writer whose name could become synonymous with his home country (think of the one and you think of the other), and who could later function as a tool of its imperial mission as well as a cultural justification for it.

This 'official' image of Shakespeare illustrates what is very obvious: that icons are constructed differently at different times according to the needs of particular interests and groups. It supports the view of those philosophers whom I have mentioned and who insist that we have no unmediated access to the past but are necessarily condemned to constructing it according to our own desires and value systems. The image I describe was partly derived, of course, from a selective reading of Shakespeare's plays: passages whose implications were inconvenient would be ignored or attributed to other hands. But to the extent that its origins were biographical, there was not only the danger of hostile interpretations of the available data, but also of the sudden appearance of skeletons in the cupboard. What would have removed anxiety was an authoritative, soundly-based 'life' yet that was no more available to those who favoured the official view than to those inclined to deviate from it. The situation has hardly changed, but in a society which has become increasingly and rightly proud of its scientific and technological achievements, it has often been found unacceptable. How is it possible for a people to have the determination and expertise to conquer major diseases or send men to the moon and not be able to discover the details of the life of a solitary individual? This refusal to accept failure and make an accommodation with ignorance, or to make do in fiction with what non-fiction is in no position to supply, appears to me to have become stronger the more 'Shakespeare' has mutated from being an icon into what is now more a trademark or an advertising logo.

A recent book edited by Mary Cross is called *A Century of American Icons*.[13] The reader who might be expecting from it accounts of Abraham Lincoln, Buffalo Bill or Marilyn Monroe would be quickly undeceived by its sub-title: '100 products and slogans from the twentieth-century consumer culture' and its concern is not, in fact, with figures around whom have gathered all kinds of national aspirations, feelings and beliefs but with the histories of such universally recognised brands as Coca Cola, Kellogg's corn-flakes, Heinz beans or Levi's jeans. Icons in this now perhaps most easily understood sense of the term are like countries without a hinterland and very different from what is meant by calling Shakespeare an icon. Yet, insofar as the name, image or idea of Shakespeare is used as a marketing tool, there is a certain convergence. From almost the very beginning he was used to sell things: those snuff-boxes of mulberry wood on sale in Stratford in the eighteenth century are proof of that; but his use in this way is a process which has accelerated rapidly in keeping

*37. Advertisement on the internet. Around the bottle neck is a copy of a page from
Shakespeare's will bearing his signature and on the reverse is an excerpt from* Macbeth.
*With permission of High Street Trading Company owner of William Shakespeare's
Whisky Liqueur.*

with rapid developments in economic life so that now there are many areas of
our national culture in which his greatest value is as a brand-name. When
commentators talk of the 'Shakespeare industry' part of what they must mean
is that there is money to be made from every feature of him, including accounts
of his life (or even, on very rare occasions, accounts of accounts of his life).
Because one of the reasons why, in spite of the dearth of information, new
Shakespeare lives have been and will continue to be written, is because they
will always sell, the last word here ought perhaps to go, not to Margreta De
Grazia and Jonathan Bate in their sophisticated concern for truth, but to
James's Morris Gedge in 'The Birthplace'. Once a 'poor honest unsuccessful
man' it is Gedge who admits, at the end of the passage from which this
description of him comes (quoted on p. 198 above), 'The receipts, it appears,
speak – [...] Well, volumes. They tell the truth'.[14]

314

Notes

1. Robert Nye, *The Late Mr Shakespeare* (1998), p. 67–8.
2. See *Shakespeare's Lives*, p. 62.
3. David Lodge, *Author, Author* (2004).
4. *Ibid.*, p. 42.
5. For 'I am well aware that I have never written anything but fictions', see Colin Gordon (ed.), *Michel Foucault, Power/Knowledge: Selected Interviews and Other Writings 1972–1977* (New York: Pantheon Books, 1980), p. 182. De Certeau's book is called *L'Ecriture de l'Histoire* (Paris: Gallimard, 1975).
6. I am indebted to Howard Mills for this remark.
7. Margreta De Grazia, *Shakespeare Verbatim: The Representation of Authenticity and the 1790 Apparatus* (Oxford University Press, 1991), pp. 71–8.
8. *Ibid.*, p. 12.
9. Bate, p. 31.
10. *Ibid.*, p. 5.
11. Holden, p. 100.
12. See especially Linda Colley, *Britons: forging the nation. 1707–1837* (1992).
13. Mary Cross (ed.), *A Century of American Icons* (Westport, CT: Greenwood Press, 2004).
14. Leon Edel (ed.), *Complete Tales of Henry James*, vol. 11, p. 466 (my italics).

38. Portal of the HSBC bank at the corner of Ely and Chapel Streets in Stratford-upon-Avon.

Envoi

'pete the parrot and shakespeare'

DOM MARQUIS

i got acquainted with
a parrot named pete recently
who is an interesting bird
pete says he used
to belong to the fellow
that ran the mermaid tavern
in london then i said
you must have known
shakespeare know him said pete
poor mutt i knew him well
he called me pete and i called him
bill but why do you say poor mutt
well said pete bill was a
disappointed man and was always
boring his friends about what
he might have been and done
if he only had a fair break
two or three pints of sack
and sherris and the tears
would trickle down into his
beard and his beard would get
soppy and wilt his collar

i remember one night when
bill and ben jonson and
frankie beaumont
were sopping it up

here i am ben says bill
nothing but a lousy playwright
and with anything like luck
in the breaks i might have been
a fairly decent sonnet writer
i might have been a poet
if i had kept away from the theatre

yes says ben i ve often
thought of that bill
but one consolation is
you are making pretty good money
out of the theatre

money money says bill what the hell
is money what i want is to be
a poet not a business man
these damned cheap shows
i turn out to keep the
theatre running break my heart
slap stick comedies and
blood and thunder tragedies
and melodramas say i wonder
if that boy heard you order
another bottle frankie
the only compensation is that i get
a chance now and then
to stick in a little poetry
when nobody is looking
but hells bells that isn t
   what i want to do
   i want to write sonnets and
   songs and spenserian stanzas
   and i might have done it too
if i hadn t got
into this frightful show game
business business business

grind grind grind
what a life for a man
that might have been a poet
well says frankie beaumont
why don t you cut it bill
i can t says bill
i need the money i ve got
a family to support down in
the country well says frankie
anyhow you write pretty good
plays bill any mutt can write
plays for this london public
says bill if he puts enough
murder in them what they want
is kings talking like kings
never had sense enough to talk
and stabbings and stranglings
and fat men making love
and clowns basting each
other with clubs and cheap puns
and off colour allusions to all
the smut of the day oh i know
what the low brows want
and i give it to them

well says ben jonson
don t blubber into the drink
brace up like a man
and quit the rotten business
i can t i can t says bill
i ve been at it too long i ve got to
the place now where I can t
write anything else
but this cheap stuff
i m ashamed to look an honest
young sonneteer in the face
i live a hell of a life i do
the manager hands me some mouldy old
manuscript and says
bill here s a plot for you
this is the third of the month
by the tenth i want a good

script out of this that we
can start rehearsals on
not too big a cast
and not too much of your
damned poetry either
you know your old
familiar line of hokum
they eat up that falstaff stuff
of yours ring him in again
and give them a good ghost
or two and remember we gotta
have something dick burbage can get
his teeth into and be sure
and stick in a speech
somewhere the queen will take
for a personal compliment and if
you get in a line or two somewhere
about the honest english yeoman
it s always good stuff
and it s a pretty good stunt
bill to have the heavy villain
a moor or a dago or a jew
or something like that and say
i want another
comic welshman in this
but I don t need to tell
you bill you know this game
just some of your ordinary
hokum and maybe you could
kill a little kid or two a prince
or something they like
a little pathos along with
the dirt now you better see burbage
tonight and see what he wants
in that part oh says bill
to think i am
debasing my talents with junk
like that oh god what i wanted
was to be a poet
and write sonnet serials
like a gentleman should

well says i pete
bill s plays are highly
esteemed to this day
is that so says pete
poor mutt little he would
care what poor bill wanted
was to be a poet

archy

Bibliography

Akrigg, G. P. V., *Shakespeare and the Earl of Southampton* (London: Hamish Hamilton, 1968).

Allen, Don Cameron (ed.), *Francis Meres's treatise 'Poetrie'* (University of Illinois studies in language and literature, 1933).

Anon (ed.), *Shakespeare's Garland, Being a Collection of New Songs, Ballads, Roundelays, Catches, Glees, Comic-Serenatas, etc. Performed at the Jubilee at Stratford-upon-Avon. The music by Dr. Arne, Mr. Barthelimon, Mr. Ailwood, and Mr. Dibdin* (London: P. A. de Hondt, 1769).

Anon, *Memoirs of the Shakespear's-Head in Covent Garden: in which are introduced many entertaining adventures, and several remarkable characters. By the ghost of Shakespear* (London: F. and J. Noble, 1759). 2 vols.

Arnold, Matthew, 'The Literary Influence of Academies', *Essays in Criticism: First Series* (London: Macmillan, 1902).

Arnold, Matthew, *Poetical Works* (Oxford University Press, 1950).

Avery, Emmet L., 'The Shakespeare Ladies Club', *Shakespeare Quarterly*, vol. 7 (Spring, 1958).

Barroll, Leeds, *Politics, Plague, and Shakespeare's Theater: The Stuart Years* (Cornell University Press, 1991).

Barthes, Roland, 'Les Romains au cinéma', *Mythologies* (Paris: Seuil, 1957).

Bate, Jonathan, *The Genius of Shakespeare* (London: Picador, 1997).

Beerbohm, Max, *The Poet's Corner* (London: Heinemann, 1904).

Benson, John, *Poems: Written by Wil. Shake-speare. Gent.* (London, 1640).

Bland, Desmond (ed.), *Gesta Grayorum, or, the history of the high and mighty Prince Henry Prince of Purpoole. Anno Domini 1594* (Liverpool University Press, 1968).

Bearman, Robert, '"Was William Shakespeare William Shakeshafte?" Revisited', *Shakespeare Quarterly*, vol. 53 (2002).

Bloom, Harold, *The Western Cannon: The Books and Schools of the Ages* (New York: Harcourt Brace and Co., 1995).

Boaden, James, *On the sonnets of Shakespeare – identifying the person to whom they were addressed; and elucidating several points in the poet's history* (London:

Thomas Rodd, 1837).

Bond, Edward, *Bingo. Scenes of money and death* (London: Eyre Methuen, 1974).

Boswell, J. (ed.), *The Plays and Poems of William Shakespeare. With a Life of the Poet and an Enlarged History of the Stage. By the late E. Malone* (London: 1821). 21 vols.

Brahms, Caryl, and Simon, S. J., *No Bed for Bacon* (Penguin Books, 1948).

Brandes, Georg, *William Shakespeare* (London: Heinemann, 1898). Translated from the Danish. 2 vols.

Browning, Robert, *Poetical Works* (Oxford University Press, 1905).

Brown, Charles Armitage., *Shakespeare's Autobiographical Poems* (London: J. Bohn, 1838).

Brown, Ivor, and Fearon, George, *The Shakespeare Industry. Amazing Monument* (London: Heinemann, 1939).

Burgess, Anthony, *Nothing like the sun* (London: Heinemann, 1966).

—, *Enderby's Dark Lady ,or, No End to Enderby* (London: Hutchinson, 1984).

—, 'A Meeting in Valladolid' in *The Devil's Mode* (London: Hutchinson, 1989).

—, *A Dead Man in Deptford* (London: Hutchinson, 1993).

—, *Shakespeare* (London: Vintage Books, 1996).

Butler, Robert, 'It's certainly got legs. In fishnets', *The Independent*, 23 November, 1997. (Includes a review of McGuinness's *Mutabilitie*.)

Butler, Samuel, *Shakespeare's Sonnets, Reconsidered and in part re-arranged* (London: A. C. Fifield, 1899).

Capell, Edward, *Notes and Various Readings to Shakespeare* (London, 1779). 3 vols.

Carey, John, and Fowler, Alistair (eds.), *The Poems of John Milton* (London: Longmans, Green and Co, 1968).

Carlyle, Thomas, *On Heroes, Heroes and the Heroic in History* (London: Chapman and Hall, 1901).

Certeau, Michel de, *L'Ecriture de l'Histoire* (Paris: Gallimard, 1975).

Chambers, E. K., *William Shakespeare: A Study of Facts and Problems* (Oxford: Clarendon Press, 1930), 2 vols.

Chettle, Henry, *Kind-Hartes Dreame* (1592) in *The Bodley Head Quartos*, ed. G. B. Harrison (London, 1923).

Clare, Maurice, *A day with Shakespeare* (London: Hodder and Staughton, 1913).

Clark, Andrew (ed.), *'Brief Lives' chiefly of Contemporaries, set down by John Aubrey, between the Years 1669–1696* (Oxford: Clarendon Press, 1898). 2 vols.

Colley, Linda, *Britons: forging the nation. 1707–1837* (London: Yale University Press, 1992).

Collier, J. Payne, *The history of English dramatic poetry to the time of Shakespeare: and Annals of the stage to the Restoration* (London: John Murray, 1831). 3 vols.

—, *New Facts regarding the Life of Shakespeare in a letter to Thomas Amyot esq.*

(London: Rodd, 1835).

Cross, Mary (ed.), *A Century of American Icons* (Westport, CT: Greenwood Press, 2004).

Curling, Henry (ed.), The *Reflections of Rifleman Harris, (Old 95th) with anecdotes of his Officers and Comrades* (London, 1848).

Curling, Henry, *Shakespeare; the poet, the lover, the actor, the man* (London: Richard Bentley, 1848).

——, *The forest youth; or, Shakespeare as he lived* (London: Eli Charles Eginton, 1853).

——, *Merry Wags of Warwickshire* (London: George Wright, 1854).

Deelman, Christian, *The Great Shakespeare Jubilee* (London: Michael Joseph, 1964).

Dennis, John, *The Comical Gallant: or, The Amours of Sir John Falstaffe* (London: A. Baldwin, 1702).

Dictionary of National Biography, ed. Leslie Stephen et al (London: Smith, Elder and Co., 1885–1901).

Dobson, Michael, and Wells, Stanley (eds), *The Oxford Companion to Shakespeare* (Oxford University Press, 2001).

Douglas, Lord Alfred, *The True History of Shakespeare's Sonnets* (London: Secker, 1933).

Dowden, Edward, *Shakespeare: a critical study of his mind and art* (London: H. L. King, 1875). Numerous editions thereafter.

Drake, Nathan, *Shakespeare and his times* (London: T. Cadell and W. Davies, 1817). 2 vols.

——, *Noontide Leisure; or, sketches in summer, Outlines from nature and imagination, and including a tale of the days of Shakespeare* (London: T. Cadell, 1824). 2 vols.

Duncan-Jones, Katherine (ed.), *Shakespeare's Sonnets* (London: Arden Shakespeare, 1997).

——, *Ungentle Shakespeare: Scenes from His Life* (London: Arden, 2002).

Dyce, Alexander (ed.), *The Works of William Shakespeare*, 9 vols., (London: Chapman and Hall, 1864–7)

Eccles, Mark, *Shakespeare* in Warwickshire (Wisconsin University Press, 1963).

Edel, Leon (ed.), *Complete Tales of Henry James* (London; Hart-Davis, 1962–4). 12 vols.

Ellmann, Richard, *Oscar* Wilde (London: Penguin Books, 1988).

Empson, William, *Some Versions of Pastoral* (London: Chatto and Windus, 1935).

Foakes, R. A. (ed.), *Coleridge's Criticism of Shakespeare: a selection* (London: Athlone Press, 1989).

Foulkes, Richard, *The Shakespeare Tercentenary of 1864* (Society for Theatre Research, 1984).

Fox, Levi, *In Honour of Shakespeare: The History and Collections of the Shakespeare Birthday Trust* (Norwich: Jarrold and Sons, 1972).

Franssen, Paul, and Hoenslelaars, Ton (eds), *The Author as Character: Representing Historical Writers in Western Literature* (Madison: Faileigh Dickinson University Press, 1999).

Freud, Sigmund, *The Interpretation of Dreams*, trans. James Strachey (London: George Allen and Unwin, 1954).

Fripp, E. I., *Master Richard Quiney: Bailiff of Stratford-upon-Avon and Friend of William Shakespeare* (Oxford University Press, 1914).

Fuller, Thomas, *The history of the worthies of England, who for parts and learning have been eminent in the several counties* (London: Thomas Williams, 1662).

Furnivall, F. J. (ed.), *A Letter describing a part of the entertainment unto Queen Elizabeth at the castle of Kenilworth in 1575 by Robert Laneham* (London: Chatto and Windus, 1907).

Garnett, Richard, *William Shakespeare: Pedagogue and Poacher* (London: Bodley Head, 1905).

Garrick, David, *Ode upon dedicating a Building and erecting a Statue to Shakespeare, at Stratford-upon-Avon* (Annual Register, 1769).

Gentleman's Magazine, (London: E. Cave, 1736–1850).

Gifford, William (ed.), *The Works of Ben Jonson* (London, 1816). 9 vols.

Gildon, Charles, *Measure for Measure or, Beauty the Best Advocate* (London: D. Brown and R. Parker, 1700).

Gollancz, Israel (ed.), *1916: A Book of Homage to Shakespeare* (Oxford University Press, 1916).

Gordon, Colin (ed.), *Michel Foucault, Power/Knowledge: Selected Interviews and Other Writings 1972–1977* (New York: Pantheon Books, 1980).

Graves, Robert, *They hanged my saintly* Billy (London: Cassell, 1957).

Grazia, Margreta De, *Shakespeare Verbatim: The Representation of Authenticity and the 1790 Apparatus* (Oxford University Press, 1991).

Greenblatt, Stephen, *Will in the World: how Shakespeare became Shakespeare* (London: Jonathan Cape, 2004).

Grosart, Alexander B. (ed.), *Complete Works of John Davies of Hereford* (London: Chertsey worthies' Library, 1878). 2 vols.

——, (ed.), *Life and Complete Works in prose and verse of Robert Greene* (1881–6). 15 vols.

Gross, John (ed.), *After Shakespeare: an anthology* (Oxford University Press, 2002).

Gruner, E. Hamilton, *With Golden Quill* (Stratford-upon-Avon: Shakespeare Press, 1936).

Gurr, Andrew, 'Shakespeare's first poem; Sonnet 145', *Essays in Criticism*, vol. 21 (1971).

Halliday, F. E., *The Cult of Shakespeare* (London: Duckworth, 1957).

Halliwell-Phillipps, J.O., *Outlines of the Life of Shakespeare* (London: Longmans,

Green and Co., 1887: Seventh edition).

Hamer, Douglas, review of Schoenbaum's *Shakespeare's Lives* in the *Review of English Studies*, vol. 85 (1971).

Hamer, E. J., *The Polarisation of Elizabethan Politics. The Political Career of Robert Devereux, 2nd Earl of Essex, 1585–97* (Cambridge University Press, 1999).

Harris, Frank, *Shakespeare and his Love* (London: F. Palmer, 1910).

——, *The Man Shakespeare and His Tragic Life-Story* (London: F. Palmer, 1911: 2nd revised edition).

Harrison, G. B., *Shakespeare under Elizabeth* (New York: H. Holt and Co., 1933).

Hawkes, Terence, *That Shakespeherian Rag* (London: Methuen, 1986).

Herford, C. H., and Simpson, P & E.(eds), *Works of Ben Jonson* (Oxford: Clarendon Press, 1954). 11 vols.

Holden, Anthony, *William Shakespeare: His Life and Work* (London: Little, Brown and Co., 1999).

Holland, Peter (ed.), *A Midsummer Night's Dream* (Oxford: Clarendon Press, 1994).

Honan, Park, *Shakespeare: A Life* (London: Oxford University Press, 1998).

Honigmann, E. A. J., *Shakespeare's impact on his contemporaries* (London: Macmillan, 1982).

——, *Shakespeare: the 'lost years'* (Manchester University Press, 1985).

——, *Myriad-minded Shakespeare* (London: Macmillan, 1998).

——, 'The Shakespeare/Shakeshafte Question, Continued', *Shakespeare Quarterly* vol. 54 (2004).

Hornby, Mary, *The Battle of Waterloo* (Stratford-upon-Avon: W. Barnacle, 1819).

Hosely, R., Kirsch, A. C., and Veltz, J. W. (eds), *Studies in Shakespeare, Bibliography and Theater in honour of James G. Macmanaway* (New York: Shakespeare Association of America, 1969).

Hotson, Leslie, *Mr W. H.* (London: Hart-Davis, 1964).

House, Madeleine, Storey, Graham, and Tillotson, Kathleen (eds), *Letters of Charles Dickens* (Oxford: Clarendon Press, 1974), vol. 3.

Hunt, Leigh, 'Shakespeare's birthday', *The Examiner*, 3 May, 1820.

Ireland, Samuel, *Picturesque views on the upper, or Warwickshire Avon [...] with observations on public buildings, and other works of art in its vicinity* (London: R. Faulder and T. Egerton, 1795).

——, (ed.), *Miscellaneous Papers and Legal Instruments under the Hand and Seal of William Shakespeare* (London, 1796).

Ireland, William Henry, *The Confessions of William-Henry Ireland – containing the particulars of his fabrication of the Shakespeare manuscripts; together with anecdotes and opinions of many distinguished persons in the literary, political, and theatrical world* (London: T. Godard, 1805).

Irving, Washington, *The Sketch Book of Geoffrey Crayon, Gent.* (Paris: L. Baudry, 1825). 2 vols.

Jack, Ian, *English Literature: 1815–1832* (Oxford University Press, 1963).

Jaggard, William, *Shakespeare Bibliography: a dictionary of every known issue of the writings of our national poet* (Stratford-on-Avon, 1911).

James, Henry, *The Better Sort* (London: Methuen, 1903).

Jameson, Anna, *Loves of the Poets* (London: H. Colburn, 1829). 2 vols.

——, *Characteristics of women: moral, political, and historical* (London: Saunders and Otley, 1832). This is the book also published under the titles *Essays on Shakespeare's female characters* or *Shakespeare's heroines.*

Jephson, J. M., *Shakespere: his birthplace, home, and grave: a pilgrimage to Stratford-upon-Avon in the autumn of 1863* (London: Lovell Reeve, 1864). With photographic illustrations by Ernest Edwards.

Jerrold, Douglas, 'Shakespeare in China', *New Monthly Magazine,* vol. 50 (June, 1837).

Johnson, S. (ed.), *Works of William Shakespeare* (1765). 8 vols.

——, and Steevens G. (eds), *Plays of William Shakespeare* (London: C. Bathurst, 1778). 10 vols. Fourth edition in 15 vols. 1793.

Jongh, Nicholas De, 'Muddying the waters and taking liberties with an Irish bard', *Evening Standard,* 21 November, 1997.

Jonson, Ben, *The Workes of Benjamin Jonson* (London: W. Stanley, 1616).

Joyce, James, *Ulysses* (London: Bodley Head, 1960).

Kingsmill, Hugh, *The Return of William Shakespeare* (London: Duckworth, 1929).

Knight, Charles, *William Shakspere: A Biography* (London: C. Knight, 1843). The 1886 edition was published by George Routledge.

Lanier, Douglas, *Shakespeare and Modern Popular Culture* (Oxford University Press, 2002).

Lawrence, D. H., 'Introductory Note' to *Collected Poems* (London: Secker, 1928).

Lee, Sidney (ed.), *The Complete Works of William Shakespeare* (London: John Murray, 1906–9. 40 vols. The Renaissance edition.

Lee, Sidney, *A Life of Shakespeare* (London: Smith, Elder and Co., 1915).

Lewis, R. Roland, *The Shakespeare Documents* (Stanford University Press, 1940).

Lillo, George, *Marina* (London: J. Gray, 1738).

Lodge, David, *Author, Author* (London: Secker and Warburg, 2004).

Looney, J. Thomas, *'Shakespeare' identified in Edward de Vere, the seventeenth earl of Oxford* (London: C. Palmer, 1920).

Luna, B. N., *The Queen declined: an Interpretation of 'Willobie his Avisa',* (Oxford: Clarendon Press, 1970).

Macray, W. D. (ed.), *Pilgrimage to Parnassus, with the two parts of the Return from Parnassus* (Oxford: Clarendon Press, 1886).

Madden, Dodgson Hamilton, *The diary of Master William Silence. A study of Shakespeare and of Elizabethan sport* (London: Longmans, Green, 1897).

Malone, Edmond, *Supplement to the edition of Shakespeare's plays published in 1778 by George Steevens and Samuel Johnson* (London, 1780). 2 vols.

——, (ed.), *Plays and Poems of William Shakespeare* (London: J. Rivington and Sons, 1790). 10 vols.

——, *An Inquiry into the Authenticity of Certain Miscellaneous Papers published by S.W. H. Ireland and attributed to Shakespeare, Queen Elizabeth, and Henry Earl of Southampton* (London: T. Cadell, 1796).

Marquis, Dom, *archy and mehitabel* (New York: Doubleday, 1927).

Martin, Robert Bernard, *Tennyson: The Unquiet Heart* (Oxford: Clarendon Press, 1980).

Masson, David, (ed.), *The Collected Writings of Thomas De Quincey* (London: Black, 1896–7). 14 vols.

McCrimmon, Barbara M., *Richard Garnett. The Scholar as Librarian* (American Library Association, 1989).

McGuinness, Frank, *Mutabilitie* (London: Faber, 1997).

McMillin, Scott and Maclean, Sally-Beth, *The Queen's Men and Their Plays* (Cambridge University Press, 1998).

Melly, George, in *Flook at 30: A Celebration* (University of Kent: Centre for the Study of Cartoons and Caricature, 1979).

Mortimer, John, *Will Shakespeare* (London: Hodder and Stoughton, 1977).

Moston, Doug (ed.), *Facsimile of the First Folio of 1623* (New York and London: Routledge, 1998).

Nashe, Thomas, *Pierce Penniless: his Supplication to the Divell* , in the Bodley Head Quartos, ed. G. B. Harrison (London, 1924).

Nash, Joseph *Mansions of England in the olden time*, re-edited by J. Corbett Anderson with the original one hundred and four illustrations carefully reduced and executed by lithography by M. & N. Hanhart (London: Henry Southern and Co., 1871).

Nashe, Thomas, *Nashes Lenten Stuffe, containing, the description and first procreation and increase of the towne of Great Yarmouth in Norffolke: with a new play never played before of, The praise of the red herring* (London, 1599).

Newdigate-Newdegate, Lady, *Gossip from the Muniment Room* (London: D. Nutt, 1897: 2nd edition).

Noyes, Alfred, *Tales of the Mermaid Tavern* (Edinburgh: Blackwood, 1914).

Nungezer, Edwin, *A Dictionary of Actors* (Yale University Press, 1929).

Nye, Robert, *Mrs Shakespeare: the complete works* (London: Sinclair-Stevenson, 1993).

——, *The late Mr. Shakespeare* (London: Chatto and Windus, 1998).

O'Sullivan Jnr., Maurice J., *Shakespeare's Other Lives. An Anthology of Fictional Depictions of the Bard* (London: McFarland and Co., 1997).

Pedicord, H. W., and Bergmann, F. L. (eds), *The Plays of David Garrick* (Southern Illinois Press, 1980). 7 vols.

Peter, John, 'There may be troubles ahead', *The Times*, 30 November, 1997. (A review of McGuinness's *Mutabilitie*.)

Pope, Alexander, *Poetical Works*, ed. Herbert Davis (Oxford University Press, 1966).

Quiller-Couch, Arthur ('Q'), `Shakespeare's Christmas' and other stories (London: Smith, Elder, 1905).

Rollins, Hyder Edward, *A new Variorum edition of Shakespeare*. Vols. 1 & 2, *The Sonnets* (London: Lippincott, 1944).

Rowse, A. L. (introduction and notes), *Shakespeare's Sonnets. The problems solved* (London: Macmillan, 1973).

Rowse, A. L., *Shakespeare the Man* (London: Macmillan, 1988).

Ryan, Richard (ed.), *Dramatic Table Talk* (London: John Knight and Henry Lacey, 1825). 3 vols.

Santaniello, A. E., (ed.), *The Boydell Shakespeare Prints* (New York: B. Blom, 1968).

Schoenbaum, S., *A Documentary Life* (Oxford: Clarendon Press, 1975).

—, *Shakespeare, the Globe, and the World* (Oxford University Press: Folger Shakespeare Library, 1979).

—, *William Shakespeare: Records and Images* (London: Scolar Press, 1981).

—, *Shakespeare's Lives* (Oxford: Clarendon Press, 1991: revised ed.).

Scott, Walter, *Kenilworth* (London: Walter Scott, 1883).

Severn, C. (ed.), *The Diary of John Ward* (London: Colburn, 1839).

Shapira, Morris (ed.), *Selected Literary Criticism of Henry James* (London: Heinemann, 1963).

Smith, G. C. Moore, *Gabriel Harvey's Memorabilia* (Stratford-upon-Avon: Shakespeare Head Press, 1913).

Smith, Hallett, '"No Cloudy Stuffe to Puzzell Intellect". A Testimonial Misapplied to Shakespeare', *Shakespeare Quarterly*, vol. 1 (1950).

Somerset, Charles A., *Shakespeare's Early Days* (London: John Dicks, 1880).

Sorlien, Robert Parker (ed.), *The Diary of John Manningham of the Middle Temple. 1602–1603* (University Press of New England, 1976).

Spence, Joseph, *Observations, Anecdotes and Characters of Books and Men*, ed. Edmond Malone (London; John Murray, 1820).

Spurgeon, Caroline F. E., *Shakespeare's imagery and what it tells us* (Cambridge University Press, 1935).

Steevens, George (ed.), *Plays of William Shakespeare* (London, 1793). 15 vols.

Stewart, Randall (ed.), *The English Notebooks of Nathaniel Hawthorne* (London: Russell and Rusell, 1962).

Summers, Montague (ed.), *Dryden: the Dramatic Works* (London: Nonesuch Press, 1931–2). 6 vols.

Taylor, Gary, *Reinventing Shakespeare: a cultural history, from the Restoration to the present* (London:Hogarth, 1989).

—, 'Forms of Opposition: Shakespeare and Middleton', *English Literary Renaissance*, vol. 24, no. 2 (Spring, 1994).

Trevelyan, G. O. *Life and Letters of Lord Macauley* (London: Longmans, Green and Co., 1908).

Tyler, Thomas, *Shakespere's sonnets; the first quarto of 1609* (London: Charles Praetorius, 1886).

Vaughan, Virginia Mason and Alden T. (eds), *The Tempest* (Arden, 1999).

Viereck, G. S. and Eldridge, Paul, *My first two thousand years: the autobiography of the Wandering Jew* (London: Duckworth, 1929).

Wallace, W., 'New Shakespeare Discoveries: Shakespeare as a Man among Men', *Harper's Monthly Magazine*, vol. 120 (March, 1910).

Webb, Francis (*Philalethes*), *Shakespeare's manuscripts, in the possession of Mr. Ireland, examined: respecting the internal and external evidences of their authenticity* (London: J. Johnson, 1796).

Welby, T. Earle (ed.), *The Complete Works of Walter Savage Landor*, (London: Chapman Hall, 1927–36). 16 vols.

Wells, Stanley, *Shakespeare for All Time* (Oxford University Press, 2003).

West, William, *The first part of the syboleography: which may be termed the art, or description, of instruments and presidents* (London: 1598).

Whelan, Peter, *The School of Night* (London: Warner Chapell, 1992).

—, *The Herbal Bed* (London: Warner Chapell, 1996).

Wheler, R. B., *An Historical Account of the Birthplace of Shakespeare*, ed. J. O. Halliwell (Stratford upon Avon: Chiswick Press, 1863).

White, Hayden V., *The content of form: narrative discourse and historical representation* (Baltimore: Johns Hopkins University Press, 1987).

Wilde, Oscar, *Complete Works*, with an introduction by Vyvyan Hollond (London: Collins, 1948).

Wilkes, Thomas, *General View of the Stage* (London, 1759).

Williams, Robert Folkestone, *Shakespeare and His Friends* (Paris: Galignani, 1838).

Williams, Robert Folkestone, *The youth of Shakespeare* (Paris: Galignani, 1839).

Wilson, J. Dover, *The Essential Shakespeare: A Biographical Adventure* (Cambridge University Press, 1932).

Wood, Michael, *In Search of Shakespeare* (London: BBC Worldwide Ltd., 2003).

Woodward, George Moutard, *Familiar Verses from the ghost of Willy Shakespeare to Sammy Ireland* (London: R. White, 1796).

Wordsworth, William, *Poetical Works* (Oxford University Press, 1904).

Index

Figures in **bold** type refer to pages containing illustrations